Sustainable Development Goals Series

The Sustainable Development Goals Series is Springer Nature's inaugural cross-imprint book series that addresses and supports the United Nations' seventeen Sustainable Development Goals. The series fosters comprehensive research focused on these global targets and endeavors to address some of society's grand challenges. The SDGs are inherently multidisciplinary, and they bring people working across different fields together toward a common goal. In this spirit, the Sustainable Development Goals series is the first at Springer Nature to publish books under both the Springer and Palgrave Macmillan imprints, bringing the strengths of our imprints together.

The Sustainable Development Goals Series is organized into eighteen subseries: one subseries based around each of the seventeen respective Sustainable Development Goals, and an eighteenth subseries, "Connecting the Goals," which serves as a home for volumes addressing multiple goals or studying the SDGs as a whole. Each subseries is guided by an expert Subseries Advisor with years or decades of experience studying and addressing core components of their respective SDG.

The SDG Series has a remit as broad as the SDGs themselves, and contributions are welcome from scientists, academics, policymakers, and researchers working in fields related to any of the seventeen goals. If you are interested in contributing a monograph or curated volume to the series, please contact the Publishers: Zachary Romano [Springer; zachary.romano@springer.com] and Rachael Ballard [Palgrave Macmillan; rachael.ballard@palgrave.com].

More information about this series at
http://www.palgrave.com/gp/series/15486

Eric Kwame Adae
John Paul Basewe Kosiba
Robert Ebo Hinson
Kojo Kakra Twum
Nathaniel Newman
Francis Fonyee Nutsugah
Editors

Responsible Management in Emerging Markets

A Multisectoral Focus

palgrave
macmillan

Editors
Eric Kwame Adae
Drake University School of Journalism and Mass Communication
Des Moines, IA, USA

Robert Ebo Hinson
University of Ghana Business School
Accra, Ghana

Nathaniel Newman
University of Ghana Business School
Accra, Ghana

John Paul Basewe Kosiba
University of Professional Studies, Accra
Accra, Ghana

Kojo Kakra Twum
Presbyterian University College
Abetifi, Ghana

Francis Fonyee Nutsugah
Ho Technical University
Ho, Ghana

ISSN 2523-3084 ISSN 2523-3092 (electronic)
ISBN 978-3-030-76562-0 ISBN 978-3-030-76563-7 (eBook)
https://doi.org/10.1007/978-3-030-76563-7

Cover Image Credit: Reed Kaestner / getty images

This Palgrave Macmillan imprint is published by the registered company Springer Nature Switzerland AG.
The registered company address is: Gewerbestrasse 11, 6330 Cham, Switzerland

Preface

The social and environmental ills the world over are partially attributable to the activities and operations of businesses in their quest to meet the needs and demands of their customers and, of course, for their strategic motives. The consequences are dire. Resources are being depleted at an alarming rate, threatening the survival of current and future generations, as well as our fragile ecosystem. Wastes, effluents and emissions are on the increase, accelerating the rate of ozone layer depletion, a catalyst for climate change and its attendant consequences.

To address these negative trends of business activities, a call is made on businesses to be responsible and balance the conflicting interests of divergent stakeholders, including the biosphere and future generations. This requires the installation of responsible and sustainable management practices that seek to integrate economic, social and environmental missions into corporate goals and strategies. However, it remains a myth urging businesses to adopt responsible management practices without providing them with a practical guide on how to do so. This book—*Responsible Management in Emerging Markets: A Multisectoral Focus*—is a response to the dearth of literature on responsible management, particularly in emerging markets.

This edited volume is unique in its approach. It discusses various issues, trends and challenges at the crucial intersection of corporate social responsibility (CSR), green business (marketing) and sustainability management, with the view to comprehensively addressing some of the big begging issues of sustainable and responsible management.

CSR enjoins firms to be aware of the impacts of their activities on their stakeholders and to consider the interests of the wider society and the environment in their business pursuits. In this regard, the book describes strategies and tactics aimed at ensuring that organisations undertake activities that are not necessarily required by law but done with the view of protecting the welfare of stakeholders as well as the environment at large, beyond firm financial profit maximisation.

The book's discussion of the green business model provides an environmentally conscious perspective of business operations by incorporating environmental protection and the sustainability logic throughout the entire corporate value chain. This encompasses processes and systems for value creation and delivery, from green resources and sourcing through green processes and operations to green products for green consumers.

Regarding sustainability management, this book focuses on strategies for meeting and maximising the economic, social and environmental needs and values of both the current and future generations.

The book is structured in 14 chapters, with each chapter delineating a unique sectoral dimension of responsible management. The highlights of each chapter are as follows:

Chapter 1 lays the foundation that anchors the entire book. As an introductory chapter, it heightens the needs for the book by indicating that business practice is still replete with environmental and social ills that require urgent responsible management attention. The chapter conceptualises and introduces responsible management as an art and science of designing business systems, processes and activities in a way that balances the economic, social and environmental needs of both present and future generations. The chapter further elaborates on and seeks to integrate sustainability transitions, ethics and social responsibility and green business practices as its main thematic areas of focus. The chapter highlights the overview of each chapter of the book and concludes by summarising the book's theoretical and practical contributions.

Chapter 2 introduces the concept of micro corporate social responsibility (MCSR) into the responsible management literature. The chapter discusses what MCSR entails, expatiates its streams and dimensions and elaborates on some of its positive and negative outcomes.

Chapter 3 assesses the contribution of CSR activities in the educational sector of emerging economies. The evaluation is based on the argument that governments alone cannot provide universal equitable education. Instead, complete access and quality of education is a shared responsibility, which should come from the contributions of private business concerns.

Chapter 4 argues that sustainability is everyone's responsibility, not a preserve of large enterprises. The chapter proposes that green entrepreneurship should be structured to contribute to economic growth and sustainable business practice at the micro, meso and macro levels.

Chapter 5 examines green marketing practice—a tool for achieving sustainable management—by small and medium-sized enterprises (SMEs). This chapter presents some benefits and challenges of green marketing in SMEs and proposes strategies for improving green marketing by SMEs.

Chapter 6 recommends setting new guidelines for sustainability reporting standards in emerging economies. The chapter proposes collaboration between private and public sectors across local and regional jurisdictions for transparency and data quality in sustainability reporting.

Chapter 7 recognises the critical roles played by management and employees in building environmental sustainability culture in organisations through green HR practices such as creating eco-participation opportunities, attracting and selecting green human capital, developing green teams and green jobs, training and transforming green leaders, and managing green performance and compensation.

Chapter 8 explores sustainability in operations and supply chain management. The chapter opines circular economy—a new wave of sustainable operations where waste is used as an input and is transformed into new products and services.

Chapter 9 examines the concept of sustainable enterprise to unearth building of sustainable business models. The chapter reveals that sustainable enterprises integrate social, environmental and economic dimensions into their business models for the attainment of sustainable development missions.

Chapter 10 examines the drivers of source separation and reuse behaviour of food waste in households, the relationship they have with the perceived lack of facilitating conditions and the moderating effects of subjective norms on the relationship.

Chapter 11 explores the goals of plastic waste management among governments, firms and consumers and suggests a triparty approach to sustainably manage plastic wastes.

Chapter 12 assesses the carbon emission of industrialisation and urbanisation, as well as the interactive effect of electricity crises. The chapter concludes that industrialisation and urbanisation increase carbon emission, which is greatly influenced by electricity crises.

Chapter 13 investigates economic, social and environmental sustainability of the dairy sector, with a special focus on sustainable practices, challenges and opportunities.

Chapter 14 evaluates sustainable mining practices—environmental protection, corporate social responsibility and long-term community development—of mining firms in Africa.

This book is positioned differently and is designed to be relevant and uniquely appealing to a wide range of readers. These include students taking courses in corporate social responsibility, sustainability management, responsible management and green business and marketing. It is a must-have for managers and consultants in industry who are concerned about being responsible and sustainable in their business strategies and operations. The academia should find this book relevant for teaching and research purposes. It is a perfect guide for sustainability policy formulators and implementers.

Following its multisectoral treatment and focus, this book is useful to a broad swath of readers from diverse socioeconomic sectors, such as governments; non-governmental organisations; civil society organisations; education; industry; commerce; construction and mining; food; banking and finance; hospitality and leisure; manufacturing; agribusiness; waste management; small-medium enterprises; and energy, logistics and supply chain management. Others include international organisations, green businesses, responsible management practitioners and just about anyone who is keen to gain an interpretive understanding of how corporate and individual pursuits and interests can impact the society, the biosphere and future generations.

Contents

Notes on Contributors

Eric Kwame Adae, Ph.D., APR is Assistant Professor of Public Relations at Drake University School of Journalism and Mass Communication. He holds a doctorate degree in media and communication studies from the University of Oregon School of Journalism and Communication. He is from Ghana in West Africa, where he earned undergraduate and master's degrees from the University of Ghana. He is an accredited public relations practitioner and was a communications consultant for over 15 years in Ghana. His research interests include responsible management, corporate advocacy, corporate social responsibility, sustainability, critical public relations, strategic communications and Afrocentricity.

Kwame Adjei-Mantey worked as a faculty member in the Department of Economics, University of Ghana where he taught principles of economics and public sector economics. He is a doctoral candidate at the Graduate School of Economics, Kobe University, Japan, and a part-time lecturer at the School of Economics and Management, University of Hyogo, Japan. His research interests include environmental economics, energy economics, health economics, household behaviour and programme impact evaluation.

Frank Adusah-Poku is a lecturer in the Department of Economics, KNUST. He is also a fellow at the Africa Research and Impact Network (ARIN), Nairobi, Kenya, and a junior research fellow at the Environment and Natural Resource Initiative-EfD Ghana. He holds a PhD in Economics from Kobe University, Japan. He also holds an MPhil in Economics and a BA in Economics with Statistics, both from the University of Ghana. His research interests are applied microeconometrics, energy economics, environmental economics and development economics.

George Cudjoe Agbemabiase is a senior lecturer at the Faculty of Management Studies and the Head of the Department of Marketing. He holds a PhD from Putra Business School, University Putra Malaysia, and an MPhil from the University of Ghana Business School, University of Ghana. He has accumulated significant years of teaching and research experience having been in academia for over ten years. He has co-authored and published academic papers including book chapters in peer-reviewed journals including Scopus-indexed and high impact factor journals. His areas of interest include customer relationship management, service quality, relationship marketing, customer perceived value, service recovery and customer loyalty. He has contributed towards the growth of the industry by consulting for multinational giants like Melcom Group and Duraplast Ghana Limited.

Andrews Agyekumhene holds a PhD in Integrated Coastal Zone Management, an MPhil in Oceanography and a BSc in Fisheries and Oceanography. He trained in wetland management and multistakeholder processes at the Wageningen UR Center for Innovation and Development, Netherlands. He is a lecturer in the Department of Marine and Fisheries Sciences, University of Ghana. His research interest lies in marine ecology, wetland ecosystems, sea turtles and mammals. He has extensive experience in assessment of anthropogenic impact on biodiversity and natural resources. He is a board member of the International Sea Turtle Society and a co-chair for Africa at the Annual Sea Turtle Symposium. He is part of the editorial team for the peer-reviewed African Sea Turtle Newsletter and has published extensively in different fields of ecological and social sciences.

Atia Alpha Alfa is a lecturer at the University of Professional Studies, Accra (UPSA), Ghana. He holds a Master of Business Administration (Marketing) from the University of Ghana (UG) and a Master of Arts in

Peace and Development Studies from the University of Cape Coast (UCC), Ghana. He is a PhD candidate in the Ghana Institute of Management and Public Administration (GIMPA). His research interests are corporate social responsibility, corporate reputation, customer citizenship behaviour and customer and employee well-being.

Hamdiyah Alhassan, Ph.D. is a senior lecturer in the Department of Applied Economics, University for Development Studies. Her key research areas include environmental and resource economics and financial economics. She is a member of the European Association of Environment and Resource Economics (EAERE) and the African Association of Environment and Resource Economics (AFAERE).

Anthea Amadi-Echendu has 19 years of experience in industry and is employed as a senior lecturer in the Department of Operations Management at the University of South Africa (Unisa). She holds the following academic qualifications: BCom (Unisa), BCom Honours (Unisa), MCom (Unisa), LLB (Unisa) and DPhil (University of Pretoria). She is supervising four masters and five doctoral candidates. She is a founding member of the Society of Operations Management (SOMA) and holds a directorship in the Society that is registered as a non-profit organisation. She has presented papers at local and international conferences and has also published in accredited journals. Her research includes optimisation of processes in conveyancing, business process reengineering, supply chain management, supply network design, process technology and operations improvement. She has contributed chapters to various books and is a co-editor of a book. She has founded and successfully chaired the African Operations Management Conference that was introduced in 2017. She is also a director of Destiny Environmental and Infrastructure Development (Pty) Ltd.

Martin Kwadwo Amaniampong is a lecturer, financial consultant and an Alternative Dispute Resolution practitioner. He holds a BSc in Accounting from Presbyterian University College, Ghana, Bachelor of Law (LLB) from Mountcrest University College, Ghana, and Master's in Business Administration (Accounting) from Wisconsin University College, Ghana. His research interests include finance, taxation and corporate governance. His consulting activities are aimed at improving financial reporting by firms and financial literacy of business owners.

Peter Ansu-Mensah holds a PhD in Marketing from Cyprus International University, Nicosia, Cyprus, an MBA in Marketing from the University of Leicester, UK, an MSC in Procurement Management from the Kwame Nkrumah University of Science and Technology, Ghana, and a Bachelor of Education (Arts) from the University of Cape Coast, Ghana. He is the Head of the Department of Secretaryship and Management, Sunyani Technical University, Ghana. His research interest is in marketing and consumer studies.

Christina Appiah-Nimo is a PhD student at Tomas Bata University in Zlin, Czech Republic. She holds a Master of Commerce in Marketing and Bachelor of Management Studies, both from the University of Cape Coast, Ghana. She is open to research in marketing and innovation, entrepreneurship development and sustainability, and small and medium-sized enterprises development.

James Telari Bonn is a Lecturer at Presbyterian University College, Ghana. He holds a BSc in Accounting and Finance from Presbyterian University College, Ghana, and an MSc in Accounting from GIMPA. The courses he teaches include financial accounting and mathematics for management. His research interests are accounting, corporate governance and sustainability reporting. He is passionate about imparting knowledge on accounting and business sustainability practices to small business owners.

Kerry Brown is Professor of Employment and Industry in the School of Business and Law at Edith Cowan University (ECU). She is the ECU Research Theme Leader for the Natural and Built Environments. Brown is the current Program Leader of Governance and Organisational Planning at the Asset Institute. She is a former Professor of Human Resource Management at the School of Management, Director of Workplace Skills and Training Research Cluster at Curtin University. From 2009 to 2013, she was Mulpha Chair in Tourism Asset Management and Director of the Research Centre for Tourism, Leisure and Work at Southern Cross University. Brown is the former Program Leader of Sustainability and Organisational Performance, CRC Infrastructure and Engineering Asset Management (CIEAM).

Giacomo Ciambotti holds a PhD in Management and Innovation from Università Cattolica del Sacro Cuore, where he is Adjunct Professor of Business Strategy and collaborates at the course of corporate strategy in the Bachelor and Master of Science in Economics. He is also a research fellow at ALTIS (Graduate school of Business & Society, Università Cattolica), where his studies involve management and strategies of social enterprises and hybrid organisations, with a particular focus on the African context. In ALTIS, he is Lecturer in Business Planning in the MBA programmes in "Strategic Management and Global Business, SMGB" and "Master in Sustainable Business Administration, MSBA." He is involved in the activities of E4Impact Foundation, where he is Lecturer in Financial Planning in the MBA programmes in Kenya, Uganda, Rwanda, Ethiopia and Zimbabwe. His research involves managerial dynamics and strategies of hybrid organisations and social enterprises, especially in challenging contexts such as African emerging countries. His research has been published in various academic journals, including the *Journal of Business Ethics* and *Knowledge and Process Management*. He has also served as a guest editor in *Africa Journal of Management*.

Gilbert Dagunga holds an MPhil in Agricultural Economics from the University for Development Studies, Ghana. His research interests include food security, poverty studies and environmental economics.

Jacob Naabong Dapilah is an assistant lecturer in the Department of Marketing and Supply Chain Management, Ghana Communication Technology University. He is a PhD candidate at the University of Cape Coast Business School. His research interests include reverse logistics, waste management and sustainable consumption and production.

Eric Delle holds PhD in Work and Organisational Psychology from Macquarie University, Australia. Delle is a freelance HR and research consultant and a lecturer. His research interests include proactivity, corporate social responsibility, work characteristics, entrepreneurship and employee well-being.

Sakir Erdem is Professor of Marketing at Marmara University, Faculty of Business Administration. His lecture topics are focused on marketing and brand management skills at graduate and postgraduate levels. He is also a marketing and brand consultant focused on FMCG and fashion marketing. His research areas include corporate and consumer brand management, marketing research, marketing communication, digital marketing and e-commerce, and customer relationship management.

Maria Fernanda Figueroa is Professor and Researcher in Business Administration at undergraduate and postgraduate levels, teaching and researching sustainable business models, social enterprises, impact investing, fair trade, among other disciplines relating business to sustainable development. She has a master's degree in Government and Culture of Organisations (Institute of Enterprise and Humanism, University of Navarra) and is a doctoral student in Business Administration at the Universidad de Buenos Aires, with a doctoral fellowship from the National Council of Scientific and Technical Research (CONICET) and Universidad Austral.

Karim Fusheini is a Zonal Programme Administrator of Ghana Agricultural Sector Investment Programme of Ministry of Food and Agriculture, Accra, Ghana. Before this position, he had been a tutor and had taught at both the basic and senior high school levels for 15 years. He holds Master of Research (MRes) in Business Administration Management and BSc Operations and Project Management both from GIMPA, Accra, Ghana. His research interests are corporate social responsibility (CSR), human resources management, education, agriculture, and the environment, project management, and public accountability and corruption. He has a publication in the *International Journal of Educational Management*. Fusheini is also a consultant in business planning and project development.

Robert Ebo Hinson, Ph.D., D.Phil. is a professor and Head of the Department of Marketing and Entrepreneurship at the University of Ghana Business School. He is also the Acting Director of Institutional Advancement at the same institution, a research associate at the University of the Free State Business School and an Extraordinary Professor at the North-West University School of Business and Governance in South Africa. Hinson has authored/edited several books and has over a hundred scientific publications to his credit.

Ruth N. Kiraka (PhD, Victoria University, Melbourne; MSc, Wageningen University, Netherlands; BSc, Egerton University, Kenya) is Associate Professor of Strategy and Entrepreneurship, Strathmore University, Kenya. She has published two books, journal articles, book chapters, conference proceedings, research reports and case studies. She has also won a university teaching excellence award. She has supervised several PhD and master's students. She serves as an external examiner for several local and international universities and as an external reviewer for Kenya's and Namibia's Higher Education Commissions. Kiraka has been a journal reviewer for *Eastern Africa Social Science Research Review*, *International Journal of Knowledge, Culture and Change Management* and *International Academy of African Business and Development*. She is also a member of the International Peer Review College of the UK Research and Innovation (UKRI).

John Paul Basewe Kosiba is a lecturer in the Marketing Department at the University of Professional Studies, Accra (UPSA). He is also a doctoral student at the University of the Free State Business School. His research focuses on branding, consumer behaviour, internet communication, social responsibility and business ethics in sub-Saharan Africa. In the field of academia, he has taught marketing, management and research-based courses.

Anthony Sumnaya Kumasey is a senior lecturer at the University of Professional Studies, Accra (UPSA), Ghana, and an honorary fellow at the Global Development Institute of the University of Manchester. He holds a PhD in Development Policy and Management from the University of Manchester, UK. His general interests are in ethics and leadership, public administration and management, human resources management, organisational behaviour and public policy. His publications have appeared in top-tier journals, including the *International Review of Administrative Sciences* (IRAS), *International Journal of Public Sector Management* (IJPM) and *Development Policy Review* (DPR). He has also served as an ad-hoc reviewer to a number of top-rated journals. Further, Kumasey has had extensive administrative and academic experience in Ghanaian and UK universities.

Paul Adjei Kwakwa, Ph.D. is a senior lecturer at Presbyterian University College, Ghana, where he handles economics and economics-related subjects. He is a member of the African Association of Environment and Resource Economics (AFAERE) and his research interests focus on economic growth, economic development and environmental and resource economics. His recent articles have been published in the *Journal of Energy and Development*, *OPEC Energy Review*, *The International Journal of Energy Economics and Policy*, *The Journal of Rural and Industrial Development*, *Renewable and Sustainable Energy Review* and *Journal of Environmental Management*.

David Littlewood is Senior Lecturer (Associate Professor) in Strategic Management at Sheffield University Management School. He conducts research in the field of business and society and, more specifically, on social entrepreneurship, corporate responsibility and the informal economy. By geography, Littlewood's work focuses particularly on emerging and developing economies. His research has been published in various academic journals, including the *Academy of Management Perspectives*, *Business & Society*, *California Management Review*, and *Journal of Business Ethics*. Littlewood is a Marie Curie Fellow alumnus. He is also a regular speaker at international conferences and collaborates with academics and practitioners in Europe, North America, Asia and Africa.

Gisel Machain is a Professor and Research Assistant in Accounting at the Universidad Católica Argentina. She is finishing her MBA, researching sustainability accounting and sustainable business models.

Albert Martins is Senior Lecturer in Marketing and the Director of Business Development at the University of Professional Studies, Accra (UPSA). Earlier, he was the Vice-President (Academic) at Accra Business School, a leading private university in Ghana. He holds a PhD in Marketing (UK); MSc in Marketing (UK); MBA in Marketing (Ghana); diploma in Marketing and Social Research (UK); postgraduate diploma in Marketing (CIM) and a BA Honours in Social Sciences (Ghana). He has previously lectured in marketing at the School of Administration, University of Ghana; University of Ghana (external division); London Metropolitan University; and the Ghana School of Marketing. Martins further wields considerable experience in corporate marketing practice and marketing consultancy having worked in industry in Ghana and the UK. His research interests are in SMEs, export marketing, green marketing, strategic marketing and consumer behaviour.

Abel Kinoti Meru is an associate professor and Dean, Riara School of Business, Riara University, Kenya, and the founding Chair of the Academy of International Business Sub-Saharan Africa Chapter. He is a seasoned innovation and business incubation consultant. He holds a PhD in Commerce from Nelson Mandela Metropolitan University, South Africa, an MBA (Marketing) and a Bachelor of Commerce (Accounting) degree. He is a fellow of the United Kingdom Higher Education Academy and a member of the African Incubation Network (AIN), a World Bank (INFODEV) Initiative and Marketing Society of Kenya. He also holds a postgraduate certificate in Academic Practice from York St. John University, UK, and International Faculty Programme Certificate from IESE Business School, University of Navarra-Barcelona, Spain, in addition to extensive training in case writing and the use of case teaching methods at Lagos Business School, Pan African University, Nigeria, and Gordon Institute of Business Studies, University of Pretoria, South Africa.

Nathaniel Newman is a doctoral student at the University of Ghana Business School with the Department of Marketing and Entrepreneurship. His research interests include corporate social responsibility, brand positioning and customer service, but lately issues of customer stewardship and green marketing concerns have also gained his attention.

Francis Fonyee Nutsugah, Ph.D. has over 20 years of experience as a lecturer and a researcher. He is a lecturer at Ho Technical University and a Director in charge of Economic, Social and Environmental Sustainability at the Sustainable Impact Research Initiative (SiRi). He holds a PhD (Marketing) from the University of Ghana and is an associate member of the Chartered Institute of Marketing, Ghana (CIMG).

Nicholas Asiedu Nyarko is a practising finance administrator and an entrepreneur. He holds a BCom degree from the University of Cape Coast, Ghana, and a Master's in Finance from the Central University, Ghana. His research interests include finance, cost accounting, financial literacy and corporate governance. He is interested in enhancing sustainability of small businesses.

Daniel Ofori is an assistant lecturer in the Department of Marketing and Supply Chain Management, School of Business, University of Cape Coast. He is a PhD researcher at the University of Cape Coast Business School and a full member of the Chartered Institute of Procurement and Supply (CIPS, UK). He also holds a certificate in Sustainable Consumption and Production (SCP) in Africa from the United Nations Institute for Training and Research. He has considerable experience in working with informal sector in electronic and plastic waste value chain. His research interests include green consumerism, waste management in the supply chain, and sustainable consumption and production.

Subhadarsini Parida is an experienced multidisciplinary researcher in the areas of sustainability, green HRM, social leadership, asset management, green buildings, autonomous vehicles, information warfare, disinformation and social licence to operate. She has been awarded a scholarship from Cooperative Research Centre Low Carbon Living for undertaking her PhD. She was recently awarded Chancellor's commendation for an outstanding PhD.

Hussein Salia is a Partner at Massim Consult and senior lecturer at the Heritage Christian University, Ghana. He holds a PhD in Accounting from Capella University in the USA. He is a member of the ICA (Ghana), Chartered Institute of Public Finance and Accountancy (UK), South Africa Institute of Tax Practitioners, Chartered Institute of Taxation (Ghana), CPA (Liberia) and the Institute of Internal Auditors (Ghana). His research interests span the spectrum of accounting, auditing, taxation, corporate governance, CSR, and project and public financial management. Salia's works have appeared in top-tier journals and books. He is an ad-hoc reviewer for six top-tier journals. He has consulted for the World Bank, the African Development Bank and IFAD.

Cristina Santhià is a PhD candidate in Innovation for the Circular Economy at the University of Turin (Italy). Among her research interests are corporate environmental strategy and responsibility, sustainability accounting and accountability, and circular business models and metrics.

Andrea Sottini is a PhD student in Management and Innovation at the Università Cattolica del Sacro Cuore (UCSC) in Milan and a research fellow at ALTIS. He is a professor in Winter and Summer Schools of Management at UCSC, teaching entrepreneurship. He is also Marketing Stream Tutor in the Global MBA of E4Impact Foundation with a proven experience in Africa, where he did consultancy and research projects. His main research interests are institutional intermediaries, entrepreneurial ecosystem and informal economy in Africa.

Ceyda Aysuna Turkyılmaz has graduated from Istanbul University Business Administration Programme in English in 2004. In 2006, she graduated from Production Management and Marketing Master Programme of Marmara University and started as a research assistant in the same department. In the same year, she began a PhD programme in the Production Management and Marketing Department and finished her dissertation in 2011. She works as Associate Professor of Marketing at Marmara University, Faculty of Business Administration. She also works as a part-time lecturer at Bahcesehir University. Ceyda Aysuna Turkyilmaz studies consumer behaviour, marketing, sales, entrepreneurship, distribution channels and logistics and social media. She has several national and international papers published in journals and presented at conferences.

Kojo Kakra Twum is a lecturer at Presbyterian University College, Ghana. He is also a tutor at the University of Ghana, College of Distance Education. The courses he teaches include marketing research, service marketing, corporate social responsibility and sales management. He holds a Bachelor of Science in Marketing from the University of Cape Coast, Ghana, a Master of Philosophy (MPhil) in Marketing. He is a PhD student at the University of Cape Coast, Ghana. He is interested in researching service marketing, marketing communication, marketing of higher education and public sector, and social responsibility and sustainability.

List of Figures

List of Tables

1

An Introduction to Responsible Management: A Corporate Social Responsibility, Green Marketing, and Sustainability Management Perspective

Eric Kwame Adae, John Paul Basewe Kosiba, Robert Ebo Hinson, Kojo Kakra Twum, Nathaniel Newman, and Francis Fonyee Nutsugah

1.1 Introduction

There is a deepening consciousness that responsible management objectives deserve as much attention as poverty-reduction targets (Sachs, 2012). Unlike the relative success stories surrounding the Millennium Development Goals (MDGs) that seek to reduce global poverty, hunger, and disease, the world is still caught up in the throes of significant

E. K. Adae (✉)
Drake University School of Journalism and Mass Communication, Des Moines, IA, USA
e-mail: eric.adae@drake.edu

J. P. B. Kosiba
University of Professional Studies, Accra, Accra, Ghana
e-mail: johnpaul.kosiba@upsamail.edu.gh

E. K. Adae et al. (eds.), *Responsible Management in Emerging Markets*, Sustainable Development Goals Series, https://doi.org/10.1007/978-3-030-76563-7_1

environmental ills, calling for the introduction of the Sustainable Development Goals (SDGs) (Sachs, 2012). The United Nations (UN) envisioned the SDGs as a clarion call for a more responsible and sustainable management of the world's resources and the environment. Responsible management seeks to integrate ethics, sustainability, and social responsibility, as well as green practices, to achieve a combination of economic development, environmental sustainability, and social development. These objectives of sustainability have promoted the use of a common term 'triple bottom line'. Responsible management can be described as seeking to balance the interests of the entire world (profit, people, and planet) for the benefit of both current and future generations.

The 2007 United Nations-supported initiative, the Principles for Responsible Management Education (PRME), focuses on raising the profile of sustainability in schools around the world and equipping today's business students with the understanding and ability to deliver change tomorrow (Guenola & Kerul, 2016). The PRME stresses on the skills needed to balance economic and sustainability goals, while drawing attention to the SDGs and aligning academic institutions with the work of the UN Global Compact. This is because the environment does not exist in isolation from human activities, ambitions, and needs. Ergo, efforts to protect the biosphere without concerns for human activities will not be effective (Robert et al., 2005). Hence, development involves ways to improve human lives, while the environment simply denotes where we live, and that these two realms exist in symbiosis (Robert et al., 2005). Given this intricate relationship, responsible management is conceptualised as "the deliberate management of a corporation's impact on

R. E. Hinson • N. Newman
University of Ghana Business School, Accra, Ghana
e-mail: rhinson@ug.edu.gh

K. K. Twum
Presbyterian University College, Abetifi, Ghana

F. F. Nutsugah
Ho Technical University, Ho, Ghana

society" (De Novellis, 2016). De Novellis (2016) therefore considers responsible management as the designing of business processes and activities in a way that meet certain social and environmental minimum standards, without compromising the ability of future generations to actualise their own needs.

The SDGs represent a roadmap for realising "a better and more sustainable future for all" (UN, 2017). The SDGs target people (the determination to end poverty and hunger and ensure dignity and equality of people), planet (protecting the planet from degradation and managing natural resources sustainably), and prosperity (ensuring that all humans enjoy fulfilling and prosperous lives, and that economic and technological development is kept in harmony with nature). It can be seen as a manifesto that ensures economic, social, and environmental sustainability.

The UN's 2030 Agenda for Sustainable Development aims to achieve important targets relating to humanity and the planet. The SDGs are made up of 17 goals framed around three main pillars of sustainability which are economic, environmental, and social issues (Elmqvist et al., 2019), including such goals as poverty reduction, provision of clean water and sanitation, affordable and clean energy, sustainable cities and communities, as well as responsible consumption and production and climate action.

Underpinning responsible management is the concept of needs in particularly poor parts of the world that require urgent attention, and the limitations imposed on the environment's ability to meet present and future needs. Consequently, there have been strident calls for embedding responsible management thinking in virtually every sector, including promoting sustainability in the tourism sector (Goffi et al., 2019), responsible supply chain management (Baz & Laguir, 2017; Mani et al., 2016), project management (Banihashemi et al., 2017), social and environmental accounting (Deegan, 2017), and energy conservation (Nathaniel & Adeleye, 2021) in developing countries. The current literature is focused on understanding ways to enhance responsible management of the various sectors of production. There is a need for more research and policy discussions on how to make context-specific sustainable production and responsible management effective.

A central goal of most developed and emerging economies is to attain economic growth and sustainable development (Asongu et al., 2020). However, there are impediments to this noble dream including environmental degradation, which hinders firms' capacities to attain their sustainable development targets. Seeking to achieve economic growth and maintaining a high level of environmental sustainability is compounded and aggravated because of the nature of interactions between economic growth and environmental degradation (Jamel & Derbali, 2016). Climate change and global warming have assumed increased salience in such discussions due to high carbon emissions and several other causes of environmental degradation.

Contribution to sustainability and responsible management practice from developing countries is parsimonious and often limited to the numerous international treaties signed by its leaders. Advocacy for sustainable management practices among small and medium-sized enterprises (SMEs) in developing economies emanates from the need to reduce the impact of environmental pollution as a result of increased production, minimising the impact of product development on the environment and creating a better environmental performance to gain competitiveness. From a developing country perspective, including small and medium-sized enterprises in discussions about sustainable and responsible business practices can be a catalyst for competitiveness and internationalisation.

Many developing economies are at the precipice of industrialisation and with increases in industries come high greenhouse gas emissions (Alam et al., 2012), which are often associated with environmental, air and water pollution, and numerous health complications, including increased mother and child mortality rates and reduced life expectancy in most developing countries. The journey to achieving sustainability and responsible management within most emerging economies is a long and arduous one, and although it is attainable, the statistics are sometimes startling. The UN's Intergovernmental Panel on Climate Change (IPCC) in its 2014 report projected a 20% decline in agricultural production, and a 30% lag in access to water supply, if current climate change rates are not stymied.

It is noteworthy that some developing economies have started taking some action to safeguard water resources. For instance, some African countries have enacted laws to ensure better management of water resources. These efforts include South Africa's National Water Act (Act 36 of 1998), working in tandem with a government White Paper on National Water Policy that also outlines 28 principles for water management and distribution (Pollard & Du Toit, 2008). The West African country of Ghana enacted its National Water Policy in 2007, which illustrates that although the nation is blessed with water resources, there is a deficit in coverage, with projected consumptive water demand for 2020 pegged at 5 billion m^3, equivalent to just 12% of the total surface water (www.gwcl.com.gh).

Evidence suggests that in many developing countries, efforts to attain sustainability and responsible management transcends multiple sectors, including the agricultural, mining, and energy sectors. Adenugba et al. (2019) explain that in most emerging economies, agriculture is tied to sustainable development and poverty reduction. Ethiopia, for instance, illustrates some pathways through which sustainable agricultural practices can lead to poverty eradication (Bachewe et al., 2018), including farm mechanisation and irrigation to deliver food security. Some countries have also started employing renewable energy sources such as solar energy to power their irrigation systems, leading to some significant reductions in harmful gas emissions (Meah et al., 2008; IPCC, 2014; Trilles et al., 2020).

Despite such success stories, the picture is not always so rosy. A bothersome sector in most emerging economies is mining. Although huge revenues are generated annually from the extractive industry, mining is frequently cited for environmental degradation (Nzimande & Chauke, 2012). Thus, emerging markets face many sustainable development dilemmas, as many economic activities that can reduce poverty also come with the risk of threats and damage to the biosphere.

1.2 Corporate Social Responsibility as a Responsible Management Tool

Social responsibility describes strategies and tactics aimed at ensuring that an organisation prioritises its relationships with multiple stakeholders on whom its successes and/or failure depend. The notion of social responsibility enjoins companies to become aware of the impacts of their activities on their stakeholders, including current and future generations, and to duly consider the interests of the wider society and the environment (Pompper, 2015).

Corporate social responsibility (CSR) includes activities undertaken by organisations that are not necessarily required by law, but done with the view of protecting the welfare of stakeholders as well as the environment at large (Falck & Heblich, 2007). CSR concerns an organisation "incurring responsibilities to society beyond profit maximisation" (Pava & Krausz, 1995, p. 1), including "the voluntary actions that a corporation implements as it pursues its mission and fulfills its perceived obligations to stakeholders, including employees, communities, the environment, and society as a whole" (Coombs & Holladay, 2012, p. 8). CSR, thus, represents a broad concept, as it can logically include all actions of the firm that holds some benefits to society in general.

Nalick et al. (2016) distinguish between market or corporate strategy and nonmarket strategy. While market strategies are game plans for ensuring that companies gain the upper hand in the marketplace, nonmarket strategies govern the creation and management of relationships with nonmarket stakeholders. In the marketing literature, CSR has been positioned as a nonmarket strategic tool (Nalick et al., 2016). However, CSR is also positioned as a competitive tool that is increasingly becoming a salient determinant of brand choice (Magnusson et al., 2015). Again, it has been argued that the lack of CSR can threaten the long-term profit-making goal and, hence, the very survival of a company (Saeidi et al., 2015).

Closely related to the concept of CSR is sustainability. Sustainability practices among corporations have gained the attention of scholars and practitioners globally (Benn et al., 2014; Kumar & Christodoulopoulou, 2014). Sustainability stretches the notion of social responsibility in demanding that companies secure their long-term viability by carefully balancing the need to maximise economic profit for investors, with the need to positively impact employees, society, and the environment (Savitz, 2013).

Sustainability balances the oft-conflicting interests of an organisation's multiple stakeholders, by according balanced significance to the progress and prosperity for the organisation, the biosphere, and the society (Savitz, 2013). The concept of sustainability has produced various frameworks, including the Triple Bottom Line (TBL), by John Elkington who argues that rather than pursuing a single financial bottom line that privileges investors, companies should pursue three bottom lines for people (societal responsibility), planet (environmental sustainability), and profits (firm financial performance) (Elkington, 1999).

Despite gaining glowing tribute in the literature, CSR is not without its critics (Moscato, 2018). Some scholars suggest that CSR has fallen below expectations in positively impacting society and the environment since it has largely become a tool for corporate lack of authenticity (Adae, 2021). Elkington recently expressed some frustration about his TBL concept due largely to mounting evidence that many CSR programmes are a code for seeking corporate self-interests and private profit priorities, without much efforts to sustainably meet the needs of *people* and *the planet* (Elkington, 2018).

CSR is sometimes blamed as a strategy for preserving private firm value (Sarkar, 2018), and some scholars go so far as to contest the assertion that improvements in industrial productivity (even with sustainable methods) can reduce ecological harms and deleterious social impacts (Foster, 2000). Others argue that CSR has tended to serve as a tool for averting mounting pressures for environmental and public scrutiny of companies (Enoch, 2007). CSR has also been blamed for being used for various corporate deceptions and diverse expressions of selfishness by business entities (Pompper, 2015). These genres of corporate inauthenticity include *"wokewashing"* (see Adams, 2019; Sheehan, 2019), *"bluewashing"* (see Pompper, 2015), *"pinkwashing"* (see McVeigh, 2012), and *"greenwashing"* (see Sheehan & Atkinson, 2012).

1.3 Sustainability Transitions: Sustainability as a Responsible Management Tool

Still, businesses are keen to express their resolve for the common good (Adae, 2020). Delmas et al. (2019) have described *sustainability transitions* in terms of various movements by businesses, brands, and corporate executives to drive sustainability thought and action. For instance, in a move that runs counter to conventional wisdom, the Business Roundtable, a group of leaders of some of the biggest companies in America, recently reimagined the purpose of the corporation in seeking to align the interests of multiple stakeholders, not only the owners and managers of private capital (Business Roundtable, 2019). In this salvo that departs markedly from the influential default business position advocated by Milton Friedman (1970, 2007), this group of corporate chieftains now say that corporations should uphold sustainability ideals by being accountable to multiple strategic constituencies, including customers, employees, suppliers, communities, but also shareholders (Business Roundtable, 2019).

Sustainability discussions are as rife in emerging markets as they are in the developed economies. Companies across the globe are realising their role in contributing towards the sustainability of the planet, working towards the common social good, even while seeking to make financial profits (Hambrick & Wowak, 2021). It has been suggested that these transitions are mainly a result of what has been described as man's perpetual desire to dominate nature and the current worldview which challenges organisations globally to achieve environmental balance (Clarke & Clegg, 2000).

A domain in which the role of business contributes to the realisation of the Sustainable Development Goals is the area of sustainable practices and responsible management. For firms, responsible management embraces the governance and supervision of social, public, and stakeholder issues of corporate social responsibility, sustainability, and business ethics (Carroll et al., 2020). Responsible management extends beyond the environment, planet, and sustainability to include micro (individual) ethical values and practices, and firm-level values of social equity, welfare, and ethical business practices (Nonet et al., 2016). This indicates that responsible management does not solely focus on environmental protection, but many aspects of business operations that are aimed at enhancing economic objectives and societal well-being.

From an economic perspective, responsible management entails improving firm performance through ethical business behaviour towards diverse stakeholders, such as customers, employees, and shareholders. From a social perspective, socially responsible management practices are aimed at achieving economic gains, while adhering to ethical values and respecting people and communities.

An important aspect of responsible management is the role of individuals in promoting responsible behaviour in organisations and also in communities. This calls for responsible behaviour in many facets of life, having wide-ranging implications for consumers, business managers, suppliers, distributors, and researchers, among others. An evolving focus of responsible behaviour concerns how consumers can contribute to sustainable development. Consumers' understanding of sustainability is manifested in their purchase decisions (Hanss & Böhm, 2012).

Understanding sustainability and responsible management from the consumer perspective has been investigated in many areas including car-sharing (Hartl et al., 2018), responsible purchase of food and grocery products (Hanss & Böhm, 2012), and consumer recycling (Park & Ha, 2014), including consumers' reliance on sustainability labels (e.g., eco-labels) on food products to make purchase decisions (Hanss & Böhm, 2012). The consumption patterns and advocacy of consumers for ethical and responsible business behaviour is a force shaping responsible behaviour and sustainability. The growing movements of "green consumers" and ethical consumerism are profound examples of putting pressure on firms to act responsibly.

The practice of responsible management by firms has been found to generate positive responses from stakeholders, leading to improved firm performance (Hammann et al., 2009). While large corporations continue to lead the charge, small businesses are also playing increasing roles in performing responsible management, and in growing their positive social and environmental impact (Jenkins, 2006). There is advocacy to have small businesses to lead the campaign of social responsibility to augment the efforts of large enterprises (Jenkins, 2006). It could be argued that there is the need for the involvement of SMEs in sustainable management efforts.

Sustainable development and responsible management should be the concern of all. While countries and businesses aim at economic growth and development, issues of social and environmental concerns must not be left in the background. In the area of business operations, sustainability and responsible management practices have become the yardstick for measuring organisations (Savitz, 2013). Firms are now paying attention to social issues of sustainability (Labuschagne et al., 2005), due largely to stakeholder shifts from environmental to socially driven sustainability concerns (Holliday et al., 2002). Economic, social, and environmental issues form the very foundation on which our entire existence as a people rests upon and must not be left in the hands of an individual or a collective few. Everybody must play their part to ensue sustainability and responsible management among emerging economies.

1.4 Green Business as a Responsible Management Tool

The business landscape in emerging economies the world over is an unmistakable hotbed of business activities. As a case in point, on the expiration of the MDGs, the African continent, which is a blanket of several emerging economies, was recognised as one of the fastest developing continents because of its growing number of businesses. However, this business activity upsurge has also been accompanied by some irresponsible business practices (Nutsugah et al., 2020). Such sub-optimal practices have been cited for extinguishing wildlife and ecosystems, depleting resources and destroying vegetation, degrading and polluting the land, contaminating oceans and other waterbodies, polluting the air, increasing ozone layer depletion, contributing to global warming and climate change, endangering lives, and threatening the survival of societies and the biosphere (GRI, 2016).

While governments the world over have accepted and embraced the SDGs, it is also an undeniable fact that governments alone cannot achieve the SDGs. These have led to urgent calls for restoring social and environmental dignity in business practices by incorporating the SDGs into strategic business goals and practices and collaborating with governments in working towards the realisation of the SDGs (GRI, Global Compact & WBCSD, 2015).

Consequently, many businesses, particularly in developed economies, have resorted to green business as a responsible management tool in achieving economic growth and development, social inclusiveness and security, and environmental protection and sustainability. While the green business movement appears to be gaining a significant foothold in the developed economies, it is lagging in adoption in most emerging economies (Kleiner, 1991). Thus, from emerging economy perspective, this introductory chapter positions the green business concept as a responsible management tool to ensure sustainable development of the world's poorest nations, supported by the claim that "in the long run, the principles of economic growth and environmental quality reinforce each other" (Kleiner, 1991, p. 1).

1.4.1 Green Business

Kleiner (1991) argues that green business is an attempt by companies to prove their faithfulness to the earth, as illustrated by the business community's commitment to three critical issues: (1) Is the product environmentally worthwhile? (2) How much environmental information can be disclosed? (3) Where can environmental pollution be prevented? Agreeing with these core issues, Abuzeinab et al. (2017) define the green business model as green value creation and capture, while also diverging from Kleiner (1991) concerning the scope and central elements of green business.

Osterwalder and Pigneur (2010) posit that green business is anchored on five elements that underpin the green business value creation and capture notion, namely green value proposition, target group, key activities, key resources, and financial logic. Thus, we conceptualise green business as a business model that incorporates environmental protection and sustainability in its value creation and delivery, spanning the entire value chain from resource extraction to products consumption. It follows then that the central traits of green business, within the context of the input-process-output (IPO) framework are: (1) green resources and sourcing, (2) green processes, and (3) green products for green consumers, as elucidated in the following sections.

1.4.2 Green Resources and Sourcing

Companies operate with a bundle of firm resources that represent assets owned, controlled, and accessed by a company (Barney, 1991). Abuzeinab et al. (2017) identified six categories of green resources including green people, green brands, green knowledge, green technology, green physical assets, and green partnership. To be responsible towards the environment, an organisation needs to work with green employees who have experiences, training, relationships, and insights with environmental protection and sustainability. Having thus differentiated themselves as environmental champions, such companies are then able to command and charge premium prices for their green brands and increase customer loyalty (Abuzeinab et al., 2017).

The success of a company in its green business movement rests largely on the green resources it owns and/or controls. An organisation's knowledge of its customers' environmental sustainability preferences and its competitors' environmental footprint are critical resources, especially in competitive positioning (Nutsugah, 2019). Thus, many companies in emerging markets are investing in cutting-edge green technologies that enable them to improve and achieve cleaner production processes. Such investments are further bolstered by other relational market-based assets that include partnerships with other like-minded environmental sustainability industry players (Nutsugah, 2019).

Green sourcing has become a major theme in the responsible management literature and is considered an effective way to address sustainability risks in supply chains. Green sourcing refers to "the management of social, environmental, and/or economic sustainability in the supply chain through production data" (Van Den Brink et al., 2019, p. 1389). Thus, green sourcing is reflective of responsible sourcing practices and has become a generic label for all sourcing designed to be socially responsible, green, or sustainable.

Van Den Brink et al. (2019) further identified two pathways to managing responsible sourcing as (1) supply chain due diligence and (2) sourcing via sustainability schemes. These approaches assume that through a proactive and reactive process, management is able to consistently undertake research and analysis of a company in preparation for business sourcing, done in ways that aim to avoid harm, while identifying, assessing, and mitigating perceived risks in the supply chain.

1.4.3 Green Processes

It is one thing to have green resources that are sourced responsibly and quite a different thing to efficiently deploy such resources. Thus, possession of green resources, while a necessary condition, is not sufficient for green business success (Abuzeinab et al., 2017). Equally vital are the adequate existence of green production and value delivery processes, described in terms of key activities undertaken to create and capture green value, including the procedures, routines, and systems by which a company procures green resources, produces green products and services, and delivers the same to green consumers.

The green processes of a responsible company comprise a comprehensive gamut of green supply chain management (Mafini & Muposhi, 2017; Rao, 2019). Green processes are multifaceted, entailing green production (Tiwari, Ahmed & Sarkar, 2018), green human resource management (Mishra, 2017; Yusliza et al., 2017), green marketing (Amoako et al., 2020; Dangelico & Vocalelli, 2017; Nutsugah et al., 2020), green financing (Dikau & Ryan-Collins, 2017; Ng, 2018), green consumption (Perera et al., 2018), and green reporting (GRI, 2016).

1.4.4 Green Products for Green Consumers

The ultimate aim of any successful green business, as a responsible management practice, is long term and comprehensive, involving the production and delivery of green products and services for green consumers. More consumers are becoming environmentally sensitive and conscious, leading to higher demands for environmentally friendly products (Nutsugah, 2019). Such customers are described as green consumers, and more businesses are catering to the demands of these market segments, by delivering environmentally friendly (green) products. Recently in Ghana, for example, Voltic Ghana Limited, one of the leading producers of mineral water, introduced a new eco-friendly bottle called the *Voltic Twist* to facilitate recycling (Modern Ghana, 2019).

Ensuring that bottles used for packaging are easily recyclable is not only a responsible business practice, but also a green value proposition. In the green business model canvas of Abuzeinab et al. (2017), green value propositions are products and services offered by a firm based on their environmental appeal to customers. Green products and green value propositions, therefore, are offerings that meet the environmental sustainability expectations of consumers in particular and strategic stakeholders in general.

Responsible management is embraced as a modern management practice, particularly in emerging economies. Several tools and approaches of responsible management are available. Pivotal among these approaches is green business, defined as the practice and process of producing and delivering products and services that offer economically viable and environmentally beneficial outcomes for stakeholders. It is a comprehensive framework that captures the entire spectrum of a firm's value chain, covering green resources and sourcing, green production and delivery processes, and green products for green consumers.

Scholarship in CSR, Sustainability, Green Business, and Responsible Management has been colonised by Western philosophical standpoints, dogma, and assumptions. There is a preponderance of Western voices and cases. The field also displays a modernist perspective that markedly privileges the corporate interest (Adae, 2021). There is a woeful dearth of cases, based on studies from emerging markets. Particularly, there is currently no volume that features studies on how CSR, Sustainability, Green Business, and Responsible Management are panning out in various sectors in emerging markets.

This book, *Responsible Management in Emerging Markets: A Multisectoral Focus*, is designed to address all these concerns. The discussion on sustainability practice is heightened by the desire of the United Nations to end poverty, protect the environment, and ensure prosperity for all by the year 2030. This book explores efforts by businesses to make deals with green marketing and sustainability challenges in emerging economy contexts. It offers insights into the opportunities that exist to ensure that companies in emerging economies can overcome the challenges of CSR, Sustainability, Green Business, and Responsible Management.

While CSR, Sustainability, Green Business, and Responsible Management practices have become topical issues in recent times, their application has received diverse interpretations concerning the sustainability of what, for whom, and by whom. These contextual interpretations call for a book from an emerging market perspective.

This book not only provides much-needed glimpses into the confluence of CSR, Sustainability, Green Business, and Responsible Management from an emerging economies perspective, but it also showcases how key themes in these inter-penetrating fields are finding expression in various economic sectors of the developing world. This book has profited from the impressive professional and scholarly expertise and experience of contributors who have all maintained an active research agenda at the confluence of the CSR, Sustainability, Green Business, and Responsible Management realms.

1.5 A Brief Overview of the Chapters

The book is organised into various chapters that discuss diverse CSR, Sustainability, Green Business, and Responsible Management programmes, issues, and themes in key economic sectors, and from different emerging markets.

In Chap. 2 entitled "Benefits of Promoting Micro-Level Corporate Social Responsibility for Emerging Economies", Atia Alpha Alfa, Anthony Sumnaya Kumasey, Eric Delle, and George Cudjoe Agbemabiase argue that although the concept of micro-corporate social responsibility is gaining traction as a legitimate field of scholarly inquiry in other fields, it has received relatively scant attention in mainstream CSR scholarship. Noting that micro-CSR could offer useful insights concerning how CSR programmes likely impact representatives of various stakeholder groups, such as employees and customers, it appears that currently, the scope of the concept has been limited to research that describes employees' positive responses to CSR programmes. After a careful map of the field of micro-CSR in ways that consider micro-level, meso-level, and macro-level issues, and some tonic and toxic organisational outcomes produced, the authors call for a heightened focus on the effective management of micro-level CSR initiatives and relevant policies.

In Chap. 3 on "Assessing the Contributions of CSR Activities to the Educational Sector", Karim Fusheini, Atia Alpha Alfa, Hussein Salia, and Anthony Sumnaya Kumasey note that although companies continue to make significant CSR investments in schools, scholars have yet to adequately assess the impact of such contributions to the growth and development of beneficiary educational institutions. The chapter describes various specific ways in which such corporate investments have transformed some schools in Ghana. This chapter makes a case for the inclusion of perspectives on CSR from some actors in the educational sector, including teachers, students, and school administrators. The authors argue that there is an infrastructure gap between urban and rural schools, which provides opportunities for companies to pivot their CSR programmes for a more significant social impact.

Ruth N. Kiraka in Chap. 4 on "Green Entrepreneurship: The Case Study of the Kenyan Climate Innovation Centre", asserts that sustainability concerns us all, rather than the popular perception that it is the preserve of only big businesses. Based on a thematic analysis of literature and a Kenyan case study, a model of green entrepreneurship is offered that examines green initiatives at three levels—micro, meso, and macro levels—that focuses on the effective structuring of green entrepreneurship at all of these levels. The author argues that micro-level factors comprise entrepreneurs' motivations for green entrepreneurship, and the capacity to innovate and integrate green practices into the business enterprise. Meso-level factors identified include the imperative for all facets of the enterprise value-chain to embed green business philosophies, while structural macro-level factors include the pivotal roles of regulatory institutions and a conducive policy framework. Analysis of the case of the Kenya Climate Innovation Centre illustrates the role of this organisation in supporting SMEs at micro, meso, and macro levels.

In Chap. 5, entitled "SME Green Marketing", Albert Martins investigates some complexities and difficulties faced by small and medium-sized enterprises in emerging markets. The author notes that in emerging markets, numerous forms of resource constraints conspire to make implementing green marketing a hard task for SMEs. Based on a desk research that examined the various benefits and challenges of green marketing practices of SMEs, the author offers some recommendations for how issues of sustainability could be better integrated into SME marketing strategies in ways that would benefit both businesses and the wider society.

A collaboration by Gisel Machain, Cristina Santhià, Giacomo Ciambotti, and Maria Fernanda Figueroa, Chap. 6 is entitled "The Quality of Information of GRI Standards in an Emerging Economy: Evidence from Green Accounting Practices in Argentina". The chapter seeks to address the critical missing gap between the theory and practice of efforts being made to ensure that business performance reports effectively capture, organise, and reveal the contributions of companies to the triple bottom line framework. Arguing that current international circumstances have largely produced qualitative and quantitative information that is essentially incomplete and sometimes misleading, these authors analysed local laws and regulations and studied sustainability reports issued by regional companies under Global Reporting Initiative (GRI) standards. The chapter contributes to new guidelines for the study of sustainability reporting standards in emerging economies, makes a case for increased synergy among various interested parties, urges policymakers to adopt a more proactive posture, and calls for a more vibrant debate on the relevance of green accounting standards.

In Chap. 7, Subhadarsini Parida and Kerry Brown address "Green Human Resource Management and Green Innovation". Green Human Resource Management entails the conceptualisation and rollout of eco-friendly initiatives that reduce costs, effectively engage employees, generate greater efficiency, and spark creativity and innovation, while reducing an organisation's overall carbon footprint. With growing calls for the mainstreaming of Green Human Resource Management (HRM), these authors argue that environmental management practices can be better implemented when approached holistically as part of a general pattern of a green social capital organisational ecosystem. As more organisations adopt green practices across the board, we are seeing evidence of an increased alignment of environmental management with the human resource management function. Parida and Brown position human resource practices and the preservation of knowledge capital as the fulcra of Green HRM. Based on a desk research design, these scholars provide exemplars of green innovations from diverse organisational contexts under the rubric of High Involvement Work System. Specific examples and themes of green innovation are presented, including eco-participation; green teams; transforming leaders; green jobs, attraction and selection; organisational culture management; organisational learning; environmental training; performance management; and compensation systems.

We present the work of Anthea Amadi-Echendu in Chap. 8, entitled "Contemporary Issues in Sustainable Operations Management". The discussion in this chapter is set against the backdrop of a world gripped by atmospheric and ecological changes that have necessitated efforts at environmental regulations to curb global warming and other environmental threats. Amadi-Echendu undertakes a deep dive into the subject of sustainability in operations and supply chain management, green labelling, design for the environment, environmental economics, and humanitarian operations management. Following a thematic literature review of journal articles, books, and conference papers, the author argues that we are seeing the evolution of a circular economy, entailing the utilisation of waste as inputs into new products and services. Several spinoffs of this development are discussed, including opportunities for job creation and employment, sustainable operations management, and responsible resource utilisation.

Chapter 9 is entitled "Business Models for Sustainable Development: The Case of a Kenyan Sustainable Enterprise". Here, the authors, Giacomo Ciambotti, Andrea Sottini, David Littlewood, and Abel Kinoti Meru investigate a sustainable enterprise in the East African nation of Kenya, with the view to arriving at a better understanding of how such enterprises could evolve a business model to contribute to environmental, societal, and economic development. Following a case analysis of the Kenyan sustainable enterprise, Corec, a business that provides avenues for marginalised youths in slums to collect and recycle waste plastic bottles, the authors shed light on the company's triple bottom line mission. The chapter contributes to current discussions in literature on sustainable entrepreneurship and the hybrid organisation scholarship in Africa. It also makes a case for how such firms could innovate business model components to ensure consistent growth while driving positive social and environmental transformation.

Chapter 10 is entitled "'Waste Not, Want Not': Assessing the Determinants of Food Waste Separation and Reuse in Ghana" and is authored by Hamdiyah Alhassan, Paul Adjei Kwakwa, and Gilbert Dagunga. The authors investigate the drivers of the source separation and reuse behaviour of food waste in households, focusing on how subjective norms exert their moderating effects on the relationship between perceived lack of facilitating conditions and the source separation and reuse of food waste. Based on the results of the Conditional Mixed Process approach, the authors argue, inter alia, that income tends to reduce food waste separation and reuse behaviour. They further contend that awareness of source separation increases food waste separation, while attitude increases food waste separation and reuse. They also advocate for a policy focus that conditions positive attitudes, user convenience, and subjective norms as pathways for improving households' food waste separation and reuse behaviour.

Entitled "A Tri-party Approach Towards Sustainable Plastic Waste Management: A Developing Economy Perspective", in Chap. 11, Daniel Ofori, Christina Appiah-Nimo, Jacob Naabong Dapilah, and Andrews Agyekumhene focus on the sustainable plastic waste issue. Exploring some contradictions and strains among the goals of the government, firms, and consumers towards the management of plastic waste, the authors advance some arguments for a tripartite approach for the sustainable management of plastic waste. Drawing on sections of the waste management literature, the authors advance some strategies and tactics to achieve behavioural change and to better coordinate policies for effective plastic waste management.

In Chap. 12, the authors, Paul Adjei Kwakwa, Frank Adusah-Poku, and Kwame Adjei-Mantey, ask: "Towards Sustainable Environment: Does Electricity Crisis Matter for the Effect of Industrialisation and Urbanisation on Carbon Dioxide Emissions?" The authors contribute to current literature that seeks to explicate the effects of increased industrialisation and urbanisation on carbon emissions. In doing so, however, Paul Kwakwa and colleagues address the elision of the moderating role of electricity crisis in most developing economies on the emission effect of urbanisation and industrialisation, focusing on the West African nation of Ghana. Based on yearly time series data, and using the autoregressive distributed lag and Fully Modified Ordinary Least Square estimates for regression analysis, they argue that electricity crisis in the country plays a significant positive role in the nexus between industrialisation/urbanisation and carbon emission. They also make some policy recommendations for enhancing efficiency in Ghana's electricity sector.

Chapter 13 is entitled "Sustainability in the Dairy Sector in Turkey: A Case Study Approach" and is co-authored by Sakir Erdem and Ceyda Aysuna Turkyilmaz. This chapter places the spotlight on sustainability in the Turkish dairy sector, seeking to investigate the practices, challenges, and opportunities therein. The authors examined Sütaş, Turkey's leading milk and dairy brand, concentrating on arriving at an understanding on the brand's economic, environmental, and social dimensions. The chapter offers some illumination of the sustainability practices of a player in the dairy sector and offers some suggestions for improved efficiency and sustainable practices of similar firms within an emerging market context.

Chapter 14 is entitled "Sustainable Mining in Emerging Economies: A Case of Reputable Mining Companies in Africa" and was written in collaboration by Kojo Kakra Twum, Peter Ansu-Mensah, Martin Kwadwo Amaniampong, James Bonn, and Nicholas Asiedu Nyarko. The chapter addresses some issues concerning sustainability in the mining sector, with the view to advancing proposals for a more effective mainstreaming of sustainability in this sector. The authors performed a desk research that involved analysis of the sustainability reports of three major African mining firms, and they also interviewed an executive of a Ghanaian mining firm. Kojo Twum and his colleagues suggest that the major African mining sustainability practices include environmental protection, corporate social responsibility, and long-term community development. This chapter makes some recommendations regarding sustainable mining policies and contributes to the literature on the sustainability practices of mining companies in developing economies.

Presented in three parts, the chapters contained in this book provide an overview of the importance of CSR, green marketing, and sustainability as three major concepts propelling responsible management initiatives across various sectors in emerging economies. This book offers fresh theoretical insights into the complex processes and relationships that mediate the ability of businesses to deliver on their development promise, via their sustainability and green initiatives. More importantly, this book offers some ways in which the emerging economy contexts affects social responsibility and sustainability practices and how these, in turn, shape the progress of emerging market economies. In this respect, the chapters provide some practical insights into sustainability challenges and opportunities, while outlining the implications of the concept for theory development, policy formulation, and managerial decision-making in emerging economies.

1.6 Alignment with the UN's Sustainable Development Goals

The UN's SDGs enjoin all to undertake "heroic and imaginative effort, determination to learn about what works, and agility to adapt to new information and changing trends" (SDGs, n.d.). The SDGs serve as a clarion call and a rallying point for "heroic and imaginative efforts" for driving economic, social, and environmental sustainability for current and future generations through broad goals for people, planet, and economic progress and prosperity for the current and future generations (UN, 2017).

The SDGs cover a potpourri of some of the biggest issues and challenges to human social development. They represent broad goals for the attainment of various states judged desirable: (1) No poverty, (2) Zero hunger, (3) Good health and wellbeing, (4) Quality education, (5) Gender equality, (6) Clean water and sanitation, (7) Affordable and clean energy, (8) Decent work and economic growth, (9) Industry, innovation, and infrastructure, (10) Reduced inequalities, (11) Sustainable cities and communities, (12) Responsible consumption and production, (13) Climate action, (14) Life below water, (15) Life on land, (16) Peace, justice, and strong institutions, and (17) Partnerships for the goals (SDG, n.d.).

All these SDGs are laudable in current efforts to create a sustainable planet that assures peace, progress, harmony, and the wellbeing of current and future generations. While the specialised chapters in this edited volume intersect with many of the SDGs, overall, they all share a common theme that aligns with SDG 12 on responsible production and consumption. Thus, we note SDG 12 as offering a dominant node of alignment for all the multisectoral chapters, since it captures the spirit and essence of this edited volume on responsible management.

Indeed, all the SDGs share a parity of primacy, even as we all put our shoulders to the wheel and work to ensure that we "leave no one behind" as supported by "evidence, practical commitments, and action" (SDG, n.d.). While noting that the SDGs are all lofty goals that must be pursued with equal importance, we are of the view that a specific SDG must be accorded the status of *primus inter pares* and serve as an arrowhead in moves towards a more secure future for all. We believe that all the other SDGs revolve around SDG 12 on responsible production and consumption. This is because of the need to set higher standards of responsibility in various domains of the social structure, including business, governance, and within families, if we are to contribute meaningfully as individuals, corporations, and nations at the sub-regional, regional, continental, and global levels to sustainable development.

Based on this logic, we anchor all the diverse sectoral treatments of issues in this book on SDG 12, which places the need for responsible production and consumption at the core of the sustainability transition. In taking this perspective, we concede that some of the chapters in this book align more closely with some other SDGs. For instance, Chap. 2 aligns with SDG 8 (decent work and economic growth); Chap. 3 speaks to SDG 3 (quality education); Chap. 4 connects to SDGs 13 (climate action), SDG 11 (sustainable cities and communities), SDG 6 (clean water and sanitation), and SDG 7 (affordable and clean energy); Chap. 5 resonates with SDG 9 (industry, innovation and infrastructure); Chap. 6 intersects with SDG 16 (peace, justice, and strong institutions) and SDG 11 (sustainable cities and communities); while Chap. 7 is linked up with SDG 9 (industry, innovation, and infrastructure) and SDG 11 (sustainable cities and communities). Similarly, Chap. 8 speaks to SDG 12 (responsible production and consumption); Chap. 9 aligns with SDG 11 (sustainable cities and communities); Chap. 10 involves diverse SDGs, including SDG 3 (good health and wellbeing); Chap. 11 involves SDG 3 (quality education) among others; Chap. 12 speaks to SDG 13 (climate action) among others; Chap. 13 touches on SDG 9 (industry, innovation, and infrastructure); and Chap. 14 aligns with SDG 13 (climate action) among other goals.

Still, we contend that SDG 12 cuts across all the discussions in this edited volume and serve as a useful organising principle for all the chapters and issues examined herein. Thus, it is our considered view that no matter the goal, responsible production and consumption (SDG 12) is a *sine qua non* for the realisation of all the other SDG, at this present-day point in human history. We recognise and are thus motivated by SDG 12 in the development of this book on responsible management because of our conviction that it is a central ethos and a powerful force for energising any sustainable business, national, or global effort to transform the world's societies on the path of righteousness and push us towards sustainable human development.

1.7 Contribution to Theory

The contribution of this book derives from different viewpoints on theory and reality. The theoretical insights arise from such seminal theories as the Schumpeterian view of entrepreneurial motivation, agency theory, theory of planned behaviour, stakeholder theory, and social theory, which were applied in the various chapter discussions.

A key point of this book is that responsible management should be viewed from a multi-theory perspective. In a given situation, the broad applicability of responsible management differs according to contextual variables, actions, and actors. For instance, the composition of a corporation's responsible management activities varies with the firm size, age, and structure of ownership of the company. Consequently, the application of a theory to explain responsible management could be valid or invalid under certain conditions. Therefore, existing theories may need to be viewed as complementary viewpoints, each of which draws on a portion of the entire scenario.

In addition, theory usage has evolved from using theories with a macro-level focus to using theories with a micro-level focus. This has caused researchers to emphasise micro-level dyadic relationships of sustainable marketing rather than grand theories. Therefore, while conducting empirical research based on a holistic multi-theory perspective can be challenging, it is necessary to return to those findings to understand and extend knowledge among complex and hierarchical value relationships in responsible management.

1.8 Contribution to Managerial Practice and Policy

Policymakers, management, and leaders of organisations in emerging markets are key drivers of responsible management. They must note key decisions that this book proposes to drive responsible management.

First, managers in emerging markets must note that there is a shift from organisational level to managerial level actions that have much in common with the vivid discussion of micro-level CSR in achieving responsible management. Insights into micro-level CSR processes dramatically inform employees and customers of the strategic management of CSR activities to boost organisational performance and produce superior financial proceeds through positive reactions from stakeholders. When organisations benefit economically from well-managed micro-level CSR practices, they are increasingly inspired and willing to extend their CSR practices by investing more. The potential outcome of this cycle is a growing social value and macro-level social effect produced by the CSR activities of the company. In this way, insights into stakeholder micro-level responses that inform how CSR activities can be handled to produce stronger financial returns can indirectly facilitate meso-level and macro-level social effects. Such insight and evaluation thus encapsulate managerial ramifications as it unearths the potential relevance of micro-level CSR in business strategy and preparation for competitive advantages.

Second, practitioners and policymakers need to understand that at the heart of responsible management is the personal motivation of the entrepreneur who desires to set up a green enterprise. Business owners must note that, although there may be multiple interventions and policies to promote and support green entrepreneurship, they remain the focal point. However, isolated and fragmented efforts by individual entrepreneurs are limited in the extent to which they can create a green and sustainable economy.

A critical mass of enterprises and value chains are needed to start building a green entrepreneurship ecosystem. This role is best played at the meso level that allows for the creation of multiple green businesses along the value chain and can lobby for access to resources and influence policy. This leads to macro-level interventions that include policy development, as well as building an entrepreneurship culture, infrastructure, and support for education, which together foster an enabling environment for green entrepreneurship and sustainable economic development.

Third, practitioners, enterprises, and policymakers need to create a foundation of synergetic work among society, and the public and private sectors sustainability reporting and standards. There is the need to promote local and regional actions towards sustainable goals that can push better transparency and quality of sustainability accounting information by corporations. Policymakers in emerging economies need to better adjust the legislative framework of the standard to help companies towards their sustainable development. This way, they can then start to question environmental policies, green products, responsible management, and business practices based on stated standards.

Finally, we know that there are limited resources from which to satisfy unlimited wants. It has therefore become imperative to track resources and products throughout the supply chain. Criteria that align with sustainability may be used to choose suppliers and decide on the supply chain configuration. Organisations do not operate in isolation, but depend on other organisations to deliver their products and services to customers. Within the supply chain, leaders of organisations need to reduce the silos and become more integrated for Internet of Things (IoT) technologies to be implemented and used more successfully. Logistics also need to be mindful of carbon emissions that may arise through transportation. Goods and services that are produced need to be either recycled, reused, or remanufactured to reduce the waste at the end of the product's life cycle, through such mechanisms as reverse logistics and waste management. Managers need to employ various Industry 4.0 technologies in their operations. These include drones, big data analytics, artificial intelligence, blockchain technologies, and sensors, which can help to monitor business processes, predict behaviour, reduce costs, enhance efficiencies, and assist to make products and services more sustainable. Blockchain technologies can also help trace the origin of products from source to the end-user.

1.9 Conclusion

CSR, green marketing, and sustainability management are integral building blocks for the movement towards responsible management. Managers, enterprises, and policymakers must understand that responsible management is critical and essential for building sustainable cities in line with United Nations' SDGs. Responsible management requires a paradigm shift through a tri-party approach, involving the people, firms, and governments in managing the world's crisis. These economic actors must close their ranks and join their collective efforts towards sustainable and responsible management.

Past efforts at sustainable and responsible management have shown that legal backing for the process, by way of policy (government supports) and financial resources for infrastructure development (private sector participation) are major factors that could help achieve effective and sustainable responsible management. The role of governments in achieving sustainable responsible management revolves around empowering institutions mandated for ensuring sustainable management and enforcement, development of infrastructure, providing adequate financing, and ensuring that there is the active participation of the citizenry. The development of national responsible management policies must meet the needs of governing authorities, the production economy, and the consuming public. To successfully implement such actions, there should be a coordination of efforts to ensure that all stakeholders have a clearly defined understanding of the design and implementation of policies that will affect their activities.

The chapters in this book have spoken eloquently to diverse problems, issues, and themes in responsible production and consumption (SDG 12), while also bearing close affinity to specific SDGs, including SDG 3 (good health and well-being), SDG 4 (quality education), SDG 6 (clean water and sanitation), SDG 7 (affordable and clean energy), SDG 8 (decent work and economic growth), SDG 9 (industry, innovation and infrastructure), SDG 11 (sustainable cities and communities), SDG 13 (climate action), and SDG 16 (peace, justice and strong institutions), among others.

However, as we argued from the outset, responsible management, production, and consumption is imperative and plays a pivotal role in mobilising current efforts to manifest all the other SDGs, while creating a more sustainable planet for current and future generations. We note that although all the SDGs matter, they must all be anchored on the bedrock of SDG 12 (responsible production and consumption). Thus, we deliberately decided to develop this book, based on the spirit of SDG 12 (responsible production and consumption), since we believe that while all the multisectoral chapters relate to various SDGs, they ultimately coalesce around SDG 12.

In conclusion, we note that a focus on SDG 12 has proven fortuitous for the development of this book. An approach buoyed by a focus on SDG 12 has enabled us to explore the field of responsible management and helped shed some light on many other current and future-leaning themes that are located at the confluence of business management, the SDGs, and human development. While the discussions offer some spluttering of other SDGs, all the multisectoral chapters fit into the spirit of SDG 12 on responsible production and consumption.

We hope that this innovative and long overdue volume of forward-thinking chapters will shed light on some of the active ways in which various sectors in emerging markets are engaging in Corporate Social Responsibility, Sustainability, Green Business, and cognate strands of Responsible Management. Indeed, the multisectoral focus adopted and the survey provided in this book offer ample testimony that we are witnessing a significant sustainability transition (Delmas et al., 2019), that pushes companies beyond simply seeking financial profits, to also seeking the greater good of society and the environment through sustainable corporate practices.

References

Abuzeinab, A., Arif, M., & Qadri, M. A. (2017). Barriers to MNEs green business models in the UK construction sector: An ISM analysis. *Journal of Cleaner Production, 160*, 27–37.

Adae, E. K. (2020). *Beyond corporate profits: Reminiscing about the future of CEO activism in Ghana*. Doctoral dissertation, School of Journalism and Communication, University of Oregon. https://scholarsbank.uoregon.edu/xmlui/handle/1794/25924

Adae, E. K. (2021). Brewed in the African Pot: Examining the influences of Caritas, Ubuntu, Africapitalism, and postmodern values on CEO activism in Ghana. In D. Pompper (Ed.), *Public relations for social responsibility: Affirming DEI commitment with action*. Emerald Publishing.

Adams, P. (2019, July 8). The year of 'woke-washing': How tone-deaf activism risks eroding brands. Retrieved January 15, 2020, from https://www.marketingdive.com/news/the-year-of-woke-washing-how-tone-deaf-activism-risks-eroding-brands/557606/

Adenugba, F., Misra, S., Maskeliūnas, R., Damaševičius, R., & Kazanavičius, E. (2019). Smart irrigation system for environmental sustainability in Africa: An Internet of Everything (IoE) approach. *Mathematical Biosciences and Engineering, 16*, 5490–5503.

Alam, M. J., Begum, I. A., Buysse, J., & Van Huylenbroeck, G. (2012). Energy consumption, carbon emissions and economic growth nexus in Bangladesh: Cointegration and dynamic causality analysis. *Energy Policy, 45*, 217–225.

Amoako, G. K., Dzogbenuku, R. K., Doe, J., & Adjaison, G. K. (2020). Green marketing and the SDGs: emerging market perspective. *Marketing Intelligence & Planning*.

Asongu, S. A., Agboola, M. O., Alola, A. A., & Bekun, F. V. (2020). The criticality of growth, urbanization, electricity and fossil fuel consumption to environment sustainability in Africa. *Science of the Total Environment, 712*, 136376.

Bachewe, F. N., Berhane, G., Minten, B., & Taffesse, A. S. (2018). Agricultural transformation in Africa? Assessing the evidence in Ethiopia. *World Development, 105*, 286–298.

Banihashemi, S., Hosseini, M. R., Golizadeh, H., & Sankaran, S. (2017). Critical success factors (CSFs) for integration of sustainability into construction project management practices in developing countries. *International Journal of Project Management, 35*(6), 1103–1119.

Barney, J. (1991). Firm resources and sustained competitive advantage. *Journal of Management, 17*(1), 99–120. https://doi.org/10.1177/014920639101700108

Baz, E. L. J., & Laguir, I. (2017). Third-party logistics providers (TPLs) and environmental sustainability practices in developing countries. *International Journal of Operations & Production Management, 37*(10), 1451–1474.

Benn, S., Edwards, M., & Williams, T. (2014). *Organizational change for corporate sustainability*. Routledge.

Business Roundtable. (2019, August 19). Business Roundtable redefines the purpose of a corporation to promote 'An economy that serves all Americans.' Retrieved September 17, 2019, from https://www.businessroundtable.org/business-roundtable-redefines-the-purpose-of-a-corporation-to-promote-an-economy-that-serves-all-americans

Carroll, A. B., Adler, N. J., Mintzberg, H., Cooren, F., Suddaby, R., Freeman, R. E., & Laasch, O. (2020). What 'are' responsible management? A conceptual potluck. In O. Laasch, R. Suddaby, R. E. Freeman, & D. Jamali (Eds.), *The research handbook of responsible management*. Edward Elgar.

Clarke, T., & Clegg, S. (2000). Changing paradigms: The transformation of management knowledge for the 21st century. *Australian Journal of Public Administration, 59*(3), 122–122.

Coombs, W. T., & Holladay, S. J. (2012). *Managing corporate social responsibility: A communication approach*. Wiley-Blackwell.

Dangelico, R. M., & Vocalelli, D. (2017). "Green Marketing": An analysis of definitions, strategy steps, and tools through a systematic review of the literature. *Journal of Cleaner Production, 165*, 1263–1279.

De Novellis, M. (2016). *MBA careers: How responsible management is changing the rules of the game*. https://www.businessbecause.com/news/europe/4317/mba-careers-how-responsible-management-is-changing-the-rules-of-the-game

Deegan, C. (2017). Twenty-five years of social and environmental accounting research within Critical Perspectives of Accounting: Hits, misses and ways forward. *Critical Perspectives on Accounting, 43*, 65–87.

Delmas, M. A., Lyon, T. P., & Maxwell, J. W. (2019). Understanding the role of the corporation in sustainability transitions. *Organization & Environment, 32*, 87–97.

Dikau, S., & Ryan-Collins, J. (2017). *Green central banking in emerging market and developing country economies*. New Economics Foundation.

Elkington, J. B. (1999). *Cannibals with forks: The triple bottom line of the 21st century business*. Capstone.

Elkington, J. B. (2018, June 25). *25 years ago I coined the phrase "Triple Bottom Line." Here's why it's time to rethink it.* https://hbr.org/2018/06/25-years-ago-i-coined-the-phrase-triple-bottom-line-heres-why-im-giving-up-on-it

Elmqvist, T., Andersson, E., Frantzeskaki, N., McPhearson, T., Olsson, P., Gaffney, O., & Folke, C. (2019). Sustainability and resilience for transformation in the urban century. *Nature Sustainability, 2*(4), 267–273.

Enoch, S. (2007). A greener Potemkin village? Corporate social responsibility and the limits of growth. *Capitalism Nature Socialism, 18*(2), 79–90. https://doi.org/10.1080/10455750701366485

Falck, O., & Heblich, S. (2007). Corporate social responsibility: Doing well by doing good. *Business Horizons, 50*(3), 247–254.

Foster, J. B. (2000). *Marx's ecology: Materialism and nature.* New York University Press.

Friedman, M. (1970, September 13). The social responsibility of business is to make a profit. *New York Times Magazine.* https://www.nytimes.com/1970/09/13/archives/a-friedman-doctrine-the-social-responsibility-of-business-is-to.html

Friedman, M. (2007). *The social responsibility of business is to increase its profits.* Springer.

Goffi, G., Cucculelli, M., & Masiero, L. (2019). Fostering tourism destination competitiveness in developing countries: The role of sustainability. *Journal of Cleaner Production, 209*, 101–115.

GRI. (2016). *GRI standards. Global reporting initiative.* GRI. https://www.globalreporting.org/standards/gri-standards-download-center/

Guenola, N., & Kerul, K. (2016). Understanding responsible management. In G. Atinc (Ed.), *Academy of management proceedings.* Academy of Management. https://doi.org/10.5465/ambpp.2016.17729abstract

Hambrick, D. C., & Wowak, A. (2021). CEO sociopolitical activism: A stakeholder alignment model. *Academy of Management Research, 46*(1), 33–59. https://doi.org/10.5465/amr.2018.0084

Hammann, E. M., Habisch, A., & Pechlaner, H. (2009). Values that create value: Socially responsible business practices in SMEs – Empirical evidence from German companies. *Business Ethics: A European Review, 18*(1), 37–51.

Hanss, D., & Böhm, G. (2012). Sustainability seen from the perspective of consumers. *International Journal of Consumer Studies, 36*(6), 678–687.

Hartl, B., Sabitzer, T., Hofmann, E., & Penz, E. (2018). "Sustainability is a nice bonus" the role of sustainability in carsharing from a consumer perspective. *Journal of Cleaner Production, 202*, 88–100.

Holliday, C. O., Schmidheiny, S., & Watts, P. (2002). *Walking the talk: The business case for sustainable development*. Berrett-Koehler Publishers.

Jamel, L., & Derbali, A. (2016). Do energy consumption and economic growth lead to environmental degradation? Evidence from Asian economies. *Cogent Economics & Finance, 4*(1), 1170653.

Jenkins, H. (2006). Small business champions for corporate social responsibility. *Journal of Business Ethics, 67*(3), 241–256.

Kleiner, A. (1991). What does it mean to be green? *Harvard Business School*, (July–August 1991). https://hbr.org/1991/07/what-does-it-mean-to-be-green

Kumar, V., & Christodoulopoulou, A. (2014). Sustainability and branding: An integrated perspective. *Industrial Marketing Management, 43*(1), 6–15.

Labuschagne, C., Brent, A. C., & Van Erck, R. P. (2005). Assessing the sustainability performances of industries. *Journal of Cleaner Production, 13*(4), 373–385.

Mafini, C., & Muposhi, A. (2017). The impact of green supply chain management in small to medium enterprises: Cross-sectional evidence. *Journal of Transport and Supply Chain Management, 11*(1), 1–11.

Magnusson, P., Westjohn, S. A., & Zdravkovic, S. (2015). An examination of the interplay between corporate social responsibility, the brand's home country, and consumer global identification. *International Marketing Review, 32*(6), 663–685.

Mani, V., Gunasekaran, A., Papadopoulos, T., Hazen, B., & Dubey, R. (2016). Supply chain social sustainability for developing nations: Evidence from India. *Resources, Conservation and Recycling, 111*, 42–52.

McVeigh, K. (2012, February 15). Susan, G Komen's "pinkwashing" problem a black mark on charity. *The Guardian*. https://www.theguardian.com/world/2012/feb/15/komen-pinkwashing-problem-planned-parenthood

Meah, K., Ula, S., & Barrett, S. (2008). Solar photovoltaic water pumping – Opportunities and challenges. *Renewable and Sustainable Energy Reviews, 12*(4), 1162–1175.

Mishra, P. (2017). Green human resource management: A framework for sustainable organizational development in an emerging economy. *International Journal of Organizational Analysis, 25*(5), 762–788.

Modern Ghana. (2019, October 4). Voltic launches all-new environmentally friendly Voltic twist water. https://www.modernghana.com/news/959197/voltic-launches-all-new-environmentally-friendly.html

Moscato, D. (2018). Corporate social responsibility committing to social and environmental impact in the global economy. In A. V. Laskin (Ed.), *The handbook of financial communication and investor relations*. John Wiley & Sons, Inc..

Nalick, M., Josefy, M., Zardkoohi, A., & Bierman, L. (2016). Corporate socio-political involvement: A reflection of whose preferences? *Academy of Management Perspectives, 30*(4), 384–403.

Nathaniel, S. P., & Adeleye, N. (2021). Environmental preservation amidst carbon emissions, energy consumption, and urbanization in selected African countries: Implication for sustainability. *Journal of Cleaner Production, 285*, 125409. https://doi.org/10.1016/j.jclepro.2020.125409

Ng, A. W. (2018). From sustainability accounting to a green financing system: Institutional legitimacy and market heterogeneity in a global financial centre. *Journal of Cleaner Production, 195*, 585–592.

Nonet, G., Kassel, K., & Meijs, L. (2016). Understanding responsible management: Emerging themes and variations from European business school programs. *Journal of Business Ethics, 139*(4), 717–736.

Nutsugah, F. F. (2019). *Environmental performance and firm performance: The mediating roles of market-based assets and integrated marketing communication*. Doctoral dissertation, University of Ghana.

Nutsugah, F.F., Anning-Dorson, T., Braimah, S.M. and Tweneboah-Koduah, E.Y. (2020), "Candle under a bushel: communicating environmental performance to improve firm performance", International Journal of Productivity and Performance Management, Vol. ahead-of-print No. ahead-of-print. https://doi.org/10.1108/IJPPM-12-2019-0578

Nzimande, Z., & Chauke, H. (2012). Sustainability through responsible environmental mining. *Journal of the Southern African Institute of Mining and Metallurgy, 112*(2), 135–139.

Osterwalder, A., & Pigneur, Y. (2010). Business model generation: A handbook for visionaries. In *Game changers, and challengers*. Wiley.

Park, J., & Ha, S. (2014). Understanding consumer recycling behavior: Combining the theory of planned behavior and the norm activation model. *Family and Consumer Sciences Research Journal, 42*(3), 278–291.

Pava, M. L., & Krausz, J. (1995). *Corporate responsibility and financial performance: The paradox of social cost*. Quorum.

Perera, C., Auger, P., & Klein, J. (2018). Green consumption practices among young environmentalists: A practice theory perspective. *Journal of Business Ethics, 152*(3), 843–864.

Pollard, S., & Du Toit, D. (2008). Integrated water resource management in complex systems: How the catchment management strategies seek to achieve sustainability and equity in water resources in South Africa. *Water SA, 34*(6), 671–679.

Pompper, D. (2015). *Corporate social responsibility, sustainability, and public relations: Negotiating multiple complex challenges*. Routledge.

Rao, P. H. (2019). Green supply chain management: A study based on SMEs in India. *Journal of Supply Chain Management Systems, 8*(1), 15.

Robert, K. W., Parris, T. M., & Leiserowitz, A. A. (2005). What is sustainable development? Goals, indicators, values, and practice. *Environment: Science and Policy for Sustainable Development, 47*(3), 8–21.

Sachs, J. D. (2012). From millennium development goals to sustainable development goals. *The Lancet, 379*(9832), 2206–2211.

Saeidi, S. P., Sofian, S., Saeidi, P., Saeidi, S. P., & Saaeidi, S. A. (2015). How does corporate social responsibility contribute to firm financial performance? The mediating role of competitive advantage, reputation, and customer satisfaction. *Journal of Business Research, 68*(2), 341–350.

Sarkar, C. (2018, October 25). *"Beyond the Triple Bottom Line" – An Interview with John Elkington.* http://www.marketingjournal.org/beyond-the-triple-bottom-line-interview-with-john-elkington/

Savitz, A. W. (2013). *Talent, transformation, and the triple bottom line: How companies can leverage human resources to achieve sustainable growth.* Jossey-Bass Wiley.

Sheehan, K. (2019, August 9). Companies promoting causes can be accused of 'wokewashing' – Allying Themselves only for good PR. Retrieved January 15, 2020, from https://theconversation.com/companies-promoting-causes-can-be-accused-of-wokewashing-allying-themselves-only-for-good-pr-120962

Sheehan, K., & Atkinson, L. (2012). Special issue on green advertising: Revisiting green advertising and the reluctant consumer. *Journal of Advertising, 41*(4), 5–7. https://doi.org/10.1080/00913367.2012.10672453

Sustainable Development Goals (SDG). (n.d.). United Nations Foundation. Retrieved March 20, 2021, from https://rb.gy/hy1ker

Tiwari, S., Ahmed, W., & Sarkar, B. (2018). Multi-item sustainable green production system under trade-credit and partial backordering. *Journal of Cleaner Production, 204*, 82–95.

Trilles, S., Torres-Sospedra, J., Belmonte, Ó., Zarazaga-Soria, F. J., González-Pérez, A., & Huerta, J. (2020). Development of an open sensorized platform in a smart agriculture context: A vineyard support system for monitoring mildew disease. *Sustainable Computing: Informatics and Systems, 28*, 100309.

United Nations. (2017). Resolution adopted by the General Assembly on 6 July 2017, Work of the Statistical Commission pertaining to the 2030 Agenda for Sustainable Development (A/RES/71/313 Archived 28 November 2020 at the Wayback Machine).

Van Den Brink, S., Kleijn, R., Tukker, A., & Huisman, J. (2019). Approaches to responsible sourcing in mineral supply chains. *Resources, Conservation and Recycling, 145*, 389–398.

Yusliza, M. Y., Othman, N. Z., & Jabbour, C. J. C. (2017). Deciphering the implementation of green human resource management in an emerging economy. *Journal of Management Development, 36*, 1230–1246.

Part I

Corporate Social Responsibility

2

Benefits of Promoting Micro-Level Corporate Social Responsibility for Emerging Economies

Atia Alpha Alfa, Anthony Sumnaya Kumasey, Eric Delle, and George Cudjoe Agbemabiase

2.1 Introduction

Increasingly, global organisations are coming to the realisation that the important role played by Corporate Social Responsibility (CSR) cannot be overemphasised. This is evidenced by the growing number of organisations practising CSR in one form or another or even considering adopting it. CSR is a popular academic term, described as "context-specific organisational actions and policies that take into account the expectations of stakeholders and the triple bottom line of economic, social and environmental performance" (Aguinis, 2011, p. 858). Researchers,

A. A. Alfa (✉) • A. S. Kumasey • G. C. Agbemabiase
University of Professional Studies, Accra, Accra, Ghana
e-mail: atia.alfa@upsamail.edu.gh; anthony.kumasey@upsamail.edu.gh; george.cudjoe@upsamail.edu.gh

E. Delle
Macquarie University, Sydney, NSW, Australia
e-mail: eric.delle@hdr.mq.edu.au

E. K. Adae et al. (eds.), *Responsible Management in Emerging Markets*, Sustainable Development Goals Series, https://doi.org/10.1007/978-3-030-76563-7_2

business leaders, and other stakeholders have shown a growing interest in CSR, which is the discretionary acts and policies of a corporation that seem to advance social well-being beyond its immediate financial interests and legal requirements. CSR goes beyond a task, job, intra-individual, intra-organisational, and profit perspective and provides ideals for individuals to seek and find meaning through work.

Whereas some CSR concerns are environmental sustainability, eco-efficiency, responsible procurement, involvement of stakeholders, labour standards, and working conditions, employee and community relations, knowledge disclosure, customer interests, social justice, gender balance, human rights, good governance, and anti-corruption, one-off events such as awards, charitable contributions, and sponsorship are not qualified as CSR activities. Most of these activities are in response to calls for assistance due to critical situations or emergencies, often reactionary and single. For instance, expenditure incurred by companies for the fulfilment of acts such as labour laws and acquisition are not considered as CSR since responsibility by its very nature is long-term and sustainable. To the extent that actions are reactionary, short-term, or non-targeted, they do not achieve desired long-term sustainability.

Since the introduction of the CRS concept in the early 1950s, most related academic works have been dominated by "macro and meso" focus, which emphasised broad, company-wide policies and overall strategies (Frederick, 2016). The macro and meso-levels both are seen by some authors as CSR at the organisation level and by others at society level and organisational level respectively. This is because their beneficial consequences for organisations' effectiveness and success are enormous. There has, however, been a jump since 2010, as the CSR literature has turned its focus on individual-level CSR, now widely known as micro CSR (Glavas, 2016).

At the micro level, researchers examine the psychological micro-foundations of CSR. Micro-level analyses might include employee-focused CSR or customer-focused CSR. Yet, for most people, CSR is typically seen as a concept involving firms that engage in socially responsible activities to contribute to society, thus the macro/meso-level concept. Nevertheless, it is the micro level that drives the CSR concept; it is the individual that expresses the need to engage in CSR, that ardently implements the activities, and that is affected by it (Crilly et al., 2008). The need to expand the CSR literature by looking at it through a person-centric lens has been stressed by various authors (e.g., Aguinis & Glavas, 2019; Rupp et al., 2006) to broaden the scope of the concept from the macro/meso level to the micro-level.

Moreover, given that the level of poverty and inequality in emerging economies is more intensive than elsewhere in the world, CSR, specifically micro-level CSR, offers a ray of hope as it objectively addresses such inequities and impoverishment (Cheruiyot & Onsando, 2016). Furthermore, given that social advancement is a necessity in emerging marketing, it is important to understand how micro-level CSR offers an avenue by which individuals in need can gain greater assistance than the traditional means offered by macro/meso-level CSR. Therefore, the objective of this chapter is to expatiate micro-level CSR by reviewing CSR literature to extract clear definitions and descriptions of the various CSR levels and identify the positive and negative outcomes of micro-level CSR.

2.2 Macro, Meso, and Micro-Level CSR

The macro-level CSR includes all issues that are relevant to welfare, but goes beyond the legal, economic, and technological concerns of the business (Aguilera et al., 2007). The macro-level studies trace the effects of interactions, such as the transfer of political, economic, social, or other capital to a large population as well as to the global level. The macro-level typically explores social systems and organisations in large-scale models (Jones et al., 2017). While some scholars define the company-level emphasis as a "macro" perspective in CSR research (Frederick, 2016), others view it as a "meso" perspective (Jones et al., 2017).

For clarification, Frynas and Stephens (2015) argue that the meso level includes organisational relationship problems and the macro level includes broader political, economic, and social complexities. Though Frynas and Stephens (2015) attempted to clarify this mix-up, there is the need for more explanation. That apart, the psychological bases between people fall within the micro-level. Therefore, Rupp and Mallory (2015,

p. 216) define micro-level CSR as "the study of the effects and experience of CSR (however it is defined) on individuals (in any stakeholder group) as examined at the individual level of analysis". Consequently, micro level captures CSR by individual institutions, enterprises, and entities to communities, employees, customers, shareholders, and the public. Such entities have unique strategies and policies for undertaking CSR activities (Cheruiyot & Onsando, 2016).

The clarification between the micro, meso, and macro social levels has been one of the most deliberated and problematised dimensions in social theory since the beginnings of the establishment of social sciences till contemporary times. Similarly, clarification of micro, meso, and macro-levels of CSR is also not without problems. In a simpler manner, the macro level refers to an organisation's CSR activities towards society in general. The meso-level refers to CSR activities towards another organisation and the micro level refers to CSR towards individual institutions, enterprises, and entities to communities, employees, customers, shareholders, and the public. Figure 2.1 shows an illustration of the macro, meso, and micro-levels of CSR.

2.2.1 Macro-Level CSR

Macro CSR has deep roots and gone through different stages since the inception of CSR. The formal writings on CSR appeared during the

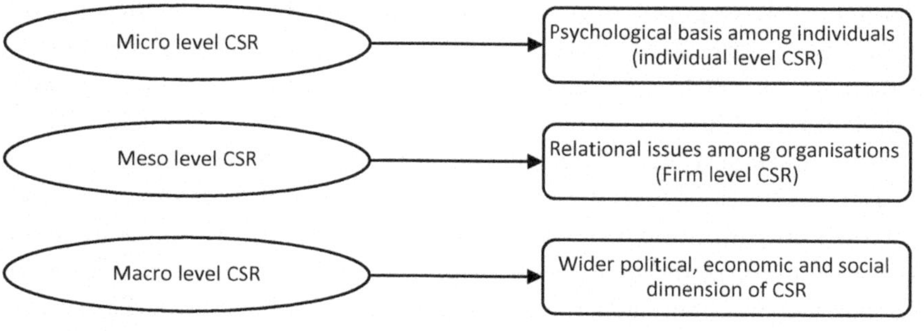

Fig. 2.1 Analysis of micro, meso, and macro-level CSR. (Source: Frynas and Stephens (2015))

period of (Berle, 1931). The formal journey of CSR from 1950 to the 1960s has emphasised the businesses to voluntary and philanthropic actions. The period from 1960 to the 1970s suggested for fulfilment of legal requirement by stakeholders, while the duration from 1970 to the 1980s required to bind with ethical contact with community and a wide range of stake holders (Frederick, 2016). This era that looked at CSR in relation to economic, social, philanthropic and social towards the general society refers to the macro-level CSR (Carroll, 1999).

Macro-level research has also advanced CSR science and practice by stressing how the larger economic, institutional, political, and social contexts are embedded in CSR phenomena (Matten & Moon, 2008; Frynas & Stephens, 2015). In Africa, CSR at the macro-level focuses on regional and global initiatives, paradigms, and relevant theories for mainstreaming social responsibility in the continent. The African peer review mechanism (APRM) introduced more than a decade ago is one of the popular initiatives but seems to have receded. However, there are challenges in implementing CSR at the continental level.

Though sub-Saharan Africa still needs more CSR initiatives (e.g. philanthropic, ethical, legal, and economic), the continent-wide CSR initiatives suffer from such challenges as commitment by political and business leadership, social and political conflicts, weak regulatory frameworks, and corruption, among others (Cheruiyot & Onsando, 2016). Nevertheless, many multinational corporations (MNCs) such as Xerox, Nestle, MTN, and Vodafone among others engage in macro-level CSR. Yin and Jamali (2016) have argued that MNCs localise CSR strategies to address the needs of their communities in their operations. For example, MTN Ghana committed over Ghc100m to complement government's efforts in fighting the deadly Covid-19 pandemic in the country. Further, MTN donated Ghc5million worth of personal protective equipment (PPEs) to frontline health workers and digital equipment worth Ghc42,000 to Noguchi Memorial Institute of Medical Research to help fight the deadly Covid-19 pandemic (Ghanaweb, 7 October 2020). AngloGold Ashanti (AGA) as part of its CSR invests in infrastructural projects such as the construction of schools and roads amongst other things. These macro-level CSR activities are focused on improving the socio-economic conditions of Ghana.

2.2.2 Meso-Level CSR

The meso-level CSR establishes the relationship between the firm-level CSR practices (or corporate social performance) and indicators of firm-level performance, including corporate financial performance. In general, a meso-level analysis indicates population size that falls between the micro and macro levels, such as a community or an organisation (Whittington, 2010). The meso-level simply refers to CSR activities at the firm level. It may also refer to analyses that are specifically designed to reveal the connection between micro and macro levels and is sometimes referred to as mid-range CSR.

Meso-level CSR within each sub-Saharan African country captures cultural antecedents and challenges of implementing CSR at a country level. Many African countries have neither social guidelines nor legal frameworks for mainstreaming social responsibility at the organisational level. While there exist high social expectations of businesses in Africa, it exists on a voluntary basis. Many business organisations in Africa are largely either multinational or small enterprises, both of which have challenges in implementing CSR activities for different reasons. The multinationals engage in some CSR activities due to strong pressure from their western shareholders, while the majority of small enterprises in Africa seldom have enough resources to be deployed to social responsibility. This is exacerbated by lack of systematic and deliberate action to mainstream CSR in African countries and institutions (Cheruiyot & Onsando, 2016).

However, there are some multinational and small organisations that practice meso-level CSR. A good example of meso-level CSR is the donation of a transit shelter project by Vodafone Ghana Foundation to the Ark Foundation, (a non-governmental organisation) that supports and accommodates victims of domestic violence in the country. The project cost GH¢120,000 and was aimed at giving victims of domestic violence temporary accommodation and medical attention before conveying them into the main shelter. That apart, many locally established companies in Ghana also provide meso-level CSR. For instance, the Atwima Kwanwoma Rural Bank (AKRB) Ltd adopted Dominase government hospital and is providing for its upkeep to cater for the basic health needs of the communities around the facility. The bank has also assisted the hospital by constructing a medical block and by providing accommodation for nurses, television sets to the hospital and waiting seats for patients, as well as embarking on routine repair works and the provision of hospital beds to the facility.

2.2.3 Micro-Level CSR

In a more elaborate form, the macro-level and meso-level CSR literature paved the way for research on micro CSR. When CSR issues are connected to the employees and customers as well as individuals' elucidations and discernments, it becomes micro-level issues and affects their outcomes (Islam et al., 2019). Micro-level captures CSR by individual institutions, enterprises, and entities to communities, employees, customers, shareholders, and the public. At the micro level, researchers study the smallest levels of dealings and smallest units of analysis of the individual in their social scenery. Such analyses might include one-on-one interactions between organisations and employees and customers (Jones et al., 2017).

Researchers possibly may be concerned with how an individual's perception of the self is predisposed by their social context such as CSR. In each of these issues, the level of analysis is micro. At the micro level, also referred to as the local level, the population typically consist of individuals in their social setting or a small group of individuals in a particular social context and associated experiences and reactions among the company's own people (Jones et al., 2017). Though the study of micro-level CSR appears to be underdeveloped, its practice may be as old as both macro and meso levels of CSR.

In African countries, most micro-level CSR is undertaken as philanthropic activities, while ensuring maximum media coverage to leverage on marketing and public relations. However, there are some organisations that genuinely perform micro-level CSR without intentions towards marketing or branding. One such example is seen in the case of Newmont Ghana Gold Limited and the Agricultural Improvement and Land Access

Programme (AILAP). The programme, which started in 2006, is one of Newmont Ghana Gold Limited's unique CSR initiatives designed to assist individual farmers who have been directly impacted by the company's mining activities. It is aimed at re-establishing and improving crop productivity. The company also established a land administration office which is responsible for land registration and monitoring of individual farmers. Ghana's Ministry of Food and Agriculture (MOFA) and Opportunities Industrialization Centers International (OICI) are partners under this programme and are responsible for implementation and oversight. MOFA extension officers provide services towards effective distribution of inputs and improved farming techniques. This programme ensures that farmers get an alternative source of livelihood and also helps to maintain the food production capacity of the area.

2.3 Role of HRM in Micro-Level CSR

Micro-level CSR scholars have studied a diversity of individual phenomena and almost all of the micro-level CSR work can be conceptualised within three major domains or streams of research. The three streams have been referred to in management literature as socially responsible human resource management consisting of general CSR facilitation human resource management (HRM), labour law related legal compliance HRM, and employee-oriented human resource management (Shen & Zhu, 2011).

These three components focus on different views of human resource management. The general CSR facilitation HRM is operational HRM functions aimed at facilitating both internal and external CSR programmes. The labour law related legal compliance HRM requires firms to take actions concerning health and safety issues, minimum wage, working hours, equal opportunity, and engaging in child labour or forced labour. Employee-oriented HRM focuses on providing for employees' social needs such as training and professional development, mentoring, and employee participation and involvement (Shen & Zhu, 2011).

The streams were further organised in sub-streams of individual-focused CSR research. The sub-streams refer to conceptually connected studies that are largely nested within the three broader streams. According to Jones et al. (2019), one of the sub-streams comprises research on CSR behaviour such as environmentally friendly behaviours which was categorised as responses to CSR (the third stream). They view this identifiable sub-stream as a meaningful sub-stream because CSR behaviour is presumably driven by employees' CSR engagement (the first stream). But some reactions to CSR may be products of evaluation. For instance, organisational trust and commitment are presumably more influenced by employees' evaluations of CSR (the second stream).

That apart, the second sub-stream involves research in which CSR is conceptualised as part of a company's HRM practices, or vice versa. However, the second sub-stream is not limited to micro research, as a few meso (firms) and multilevel employee-focused CSR studies also exist. A third sub-stream involves studies that integrate CSR with research on ethical leadership and business ethics. Among the broader research streams in which these and other sub-streams are embedded, the majority of existing micro-level CSR studies pertain to the third stream, that is, reactions to CSR (Gond et al., 2017).

2.4 Theoretical Foundation of Micro-Level CSR

Multiple theories are used by researchers in micro-level CSR. Despite theories such as agency theory, attachment theory, attitude formation theory, persuasion theory, attribution theory, and cognitive-affective model which have been used to conceptualise micro-level CSR, Gond et al. (2017) suggest that the social exchange theory, the theory of social identity, and the signal theory provide comprehensive explanations of people's response to CSR. Also, Guzzo et al. (2020) opined that the theory of social exchange and the theory of social identity are the most commonly used theories in the early stages of micro-CSR growth. Therefore, the social exchange theory, the theory of social identity, and the signal theory provide comprehensive explanations of people's response to CSR.

The theory of social identity is the most widely used fundamental theory to describe individual responses to CSR (Gond et al., 2017). According to social identity theory (Tajfel & Turner, 1985), when they believe that it is highly respectable, with a positive and desirable picture, people associate with an organisation. Overwhelmingly, many micro-level CSR studies depend on social identity as an illustrative structure with only a limited number of contributions directly examining whether identification is the underlying mechanism that connects CSR to performance (Farooq et al., 2016). For instance, Jones (2010) shows that organisational identity has an intermediating impact in deciding the responses of employees to voluntary initiatives operated by their businesses. Another fundamental framework used to describe individual responses to CSR is the principle of social exchange. Many articles that specifically draw on the theory of social exchange envisage reciprocity and infer that the responses of individuals can generally be described as mutually dependent, relying on gratification (Gouldner, 1960).

One of the most common theoretical explanations for the effect of CSR on individuals is signal theory (Gond et al., 2017). Market participants, such as job seekers and consumers, rely on measures of possible results to inform their perception of what their work involvement and customer experience would be like according to the signalling principle (Spence, 1974; Rupp & Mallory, 2015). In this example, CSR serves as an acceptable signal that permits potential workers and clients to conclude their probable care. Scholars more regularly consider the outcome of CSR signals on potential workers and consumers than precisely determine if they are predisposed by this fundamental mechanism. Just a few studies have begun to unpack the mechanism of mediation by which signalling functions work (Gully et al., 2013).

2.5 Benefits of Micro CSR to Emerging Economies

Organisational performance increases as organisations participate in more micro-level CSR activities, and as their performance improves, they are better placed and more encouraged to devote other resources to develop their CSR activities. As businesses participate in more tactically treasured CSR activities, it boosts their corporate efficiency and they are motivated over time to sustain and even strengthen their CSR investments. This creates the opportunity to progressively advance their levels of social responsibility. Further, by informing their assumptions about value fit and other issues, micro-level CSR attracts job seekers (Jones et al., 2019). The findings of CSR can be seen as either attitudinal or behavioural at the personal level.

2.5.1 Attitudinal Benefits of Micro CSR to Emerging Economies

Good workplace results have become the dominant subject in terms of attitudinal results. CSR at the micro-level entices clients and job seekers among others (Jones et al., 2017). Micro-level CSR implies that CSR at the individual level will lead to a wide range of results (Glavas, 2016). Although employee micro-CSR research focuses on the effects of worker beliefs and discernments of CSR activities (employee responses to CSR), the CSR initiatives of an organisation are significant foundations of competitive advantage as they improve organisational success in terms of customers and employees (Hsu, 2012).

Many prospective workers are drawn to working with companies known for their engagement in the community's activities that are environmentally friendly. It also builds trust that facilitates favourable responses among job seekers and consumers, and encourages positive attitudes of workers, such as employee involvement, organisational identification, work-related skills, and reduced workplace energy usage (Glavas, 2016). Micro-level CSR activities increase organisational engagement of both employees and customers. Studies have shown positive impacts of CSR on, for example, the affective interaction of employees and customers, the connection of employees and customers, and employee and customer retention (Kundu & Gahlawat, 2015).

- Organisational commitment

Prior studies largely emphasise on the effect of employees' CSR perceptions on affective organisational commitment instead of organisational identification or organisational attraction for prospective employees and customers (Hillenbrand & Money, 2015). Employees' sense of oneness with their organisation (that enables them to make enduring relationships) is developed through organisational identity. Such employees become cognitive and emotionally attached to their organisation, that is, organisational commitment, which further contributes in developing their job-related outcomes including organisational citizenship behaviour (Van Dick et al., 2006).

While much focus remains on dedication, some studies have shown that the positive views of CSR activities by consumers and employees contribute to enhancing the image of the organisation (Hur et al., 2014). Consequently, social output increases CSR's influence, although this effect differs depending on the actors.

- Corporate credibility

Stanaland et al. (2011) discovered that CSR has a positive influence on corporate credibility perceptions. Companies improve their prestige and increase corporate attractiveness by participating in CSR activities, helping them to recruit better workers and attract real customers. As staff play critical roles in the overall success of an organisation, the attraction of 'the right staff' is of vital importance to the continuity of the organisation. The dialogue of the company with future employees is therefore central to its overall success. Garberg and Fombrun (2006) argue that the status earned is significant and noticeable as a result of CSR programmes.

Studies have also identified the positive effects of CSR on specific aspects of organisational engagement including regulatory engagement, and employee attachment or shared organisational engagement. As previously stated, this could be a precedent for commitment at a higher collective level (Chun et al., 2013). Though it appears that there are a number of positive outcomes, an increasing number of studies are also investigating how CSR can improve work satisfaction, employee engagement, and job pursuit intentions (Glavas & Piderit, 2009).

- Organisational identification

  The theory of social identity notes that the CSR operations of a firm have a direct association with the organisational identification of employees. Employee identity may be retained if employees attempt to offer their services among different groups (Ashforth & Mael, 1989). Individuals use their social prestige to gauge their self-worth because they only want to associate with those organisations that have a respectable profile. This employee selection increases their self-worth. Previous studies have found a positive relationship between CSR and organisational identity (OI), based on the same claims (Kim et al., 2010).

  Among other businesses, a company engaged in CSR activities has a lucrative and distinctive role that results in promoting the identity of employees as they feel proud of their companies. Thus, workers' pride in their company's philanthropic or socially conscious initiatives increases their bond or connection with the organisation (Bhattacharya et al., 2009).

  In addition, Van Knippenberg (2000) argued that a clear sense of organisational identity creates a sense of unity. As significant care is instilled in the minds of workers, they consider every job as their own and, subsequently, their workplace output is improved sharply. Rioux and Penner (2001) indicated that OI is the main motivating tool as "it appears to have two interrelated components: a desire to help the organization because one identifies with and takes pride in the organization" (p. 1312). The clear sense of organisational identity motivates employees to build a friendly atmosphere with others such as subordinates, colleagues, supervisors, and superiors (Van Dick et al., 2006).

- Employee and customer engagement

  The attitudinal effect of CSR engagement on the extent to which employees and customers are pleased and employee engagement are closely linked to the findings (Glavas & Piderit, 2009) revealed that CSR (both internal and external) and employee engagement (vigour, absorption, and dedication) have a significant positive relationship with organisational performance. Also, the results revealed that there is a significant positive relationship between corporate social responsibility (internal CSR and external CSR) and employee engagement.

The ability of customers to participate in co-creation of value increases when they consider the business to be socially responsible towards customers (Tuan et al., 2019). Customers demonstrate their loyalty when they believe that the business makes sincere efforts to resolve its social obligations (Aramburu & Pescador, 2019).

Finally, in the set of CSR findings being analysed, many studies exhibit greater diversity. For instance, CSR enhances organisational pride, organisation's perceived external reputation for overall justice, perceived organisational support, perceived quality of work-life, and organisational confidence (Dumont et al., 2017).

2.5.2 Behavioural Outcome of Micro CSR

The practices of CSR affect not only consumer perceptions, but also long-term customer citizenship actions (Hur et al., 2014). The theory of social exchange indicates that clients create the feelings of returning favours when they profit from employees or organisations. Consequently, Grönroos (2011) indicated that any good customer service in an organisation makes the customer want to support the organisation as well as other customers in the organisation. Various behavioural effects have been examined by researchers.

- Organisational citizenship behaviour

Few studies have examined the effect of in-role performance on CSR perceptions (Shen & Benson, 2016). Micro CSR raises the conduct of and improves organisational citizenship (OCB), increases personal effort, decreases the risk of emotional fatigue. Micro-level CSR research is also of an academic and practical interest because workers are key stakeholders who both influence and are affected by the CSR initiatives of their employer (Aguinis & Glavas, 2019).

Evidence has supported the positive effect of employee-focused CSR on employees' OCB at the individual level. OCB is defined as employee voluntary exertions in service beyond formal job descriptions to facilitate customer satisfaction (Özduran & Tanova, 2017). Employees' perceptions of their firm's involvement in CSR-related activities have influenced their OCB, job satisfaction, job performance, organisational commitment, and reduced deviance behaviour. Arguably, OCB is profoundly affected by CSR, possibly due to both concepts being parallel and not applied simultaneously (Islam et al., 2019).

- Employee in-role behaviour

  Another core emphasis has been on in-role behaviour. Whereas, Glavas and Piderit (2009) highlight CSR's positive effect on the innovative behaviours of employees, Farooq et al. (2014) propose benefits for the exchange of information. CSR also leads to employee in-role behaviour. However, there are inadequate research on the determination of how in-role performance is affected by CSR. Furthermore, most research has centred on how CSR promotes positive workplace behavioural results, not the role of CSR relative to negative behaviours (Goodman et al., 2011). Also, CSR has a beneficial impact on employee cohesion, which can increase the efficiency of the employee's mission. The effect on employee social interface is also seen in the degree to which workers share information in companies participating in CSR (Tuan, 2013).

- Customer citizenship behaviour

  In addition, the behavioural effects of clients, such as word of mouth (WoM), loyalty, and citizenship actions to organisations in response to social responsibility, are a comparatively recent line of study. Kim et al. (2017) emphasise the importance of doing more research in this field since CSR has a strong and beneficial effect on client behavioural outcomes such as WoM and consumer loyalty.

  In response to a company's CSR activities and customer citizenship behaviour, Lii and Lee (2012) argue there is a positive correlation between consumer attitudinal assessments, where consumers are likely to reciprocate benefits received from the company participating in CSR. Thus, consumers evaluate the conduct of the business as a "good" citizen and establish the behaviour of citizenship towards it (Tuan, 2018).

When consumers view the CSR of a business as a genuinely altruistic operation, they come to evaluate the company more favourably, encouraging others to participate in reciprocity by extra-role activities that eventually offer benefits to the company (Lii & Lee, 2012). Similarly, as one of their company-favouring reactions, consumer impressions of a company's CSR practices contribute to customer extra-role behaviour.

2.6 Negative Effects on Emerging Economies

The positive benefits of micro-level CSR notwithstanding, there may also be negative implications. When looking at the positive findings on the basis of attitudinal and behavioural outcomes, several studies have found there is insignificant evidence to yield any negative findings (Gond et al., 2017). However, studies in the management literature have supported the conclusion that CSR influences consumers' behaviours and, in that vein, could also negatively influence consumers to boycott companies that behave unethically or that make dubious claims about their CSR (Alhouti et al., 2016). Although these results build confidence that CSR has a range of positive effects on workers, the current debate neglects to consider its possible negative consequences at the micro-level CSR. What is lacking, therefore, is a better understanding of how CSR involvement can adversely affect workers and their attitudes and behaviours.

- Unfairly distributed of resource

Mallory and Rupp (2014) revealed that CSR can lead to negative employee reactions under certain conditions, such as when resources are unfairly distributed towards CSR activities. They also suggested situations in which employees may react negatively towards CSR initiatives, such as when resources dedicated to CSR are seen as misapplied on external stakeholders rather than reinvested towards employees. Rodrigo and Arenas (2008) used grounded theory to identify one type of worker (the dissident employee) that reacts strongly against CSR messages and efforts, seeing them as unjust and unnecessary. This act causes the displeasure of those who have been unfairly treated and undermined.

- Self-righteousness

  Self-righteousness can transpire when employees identify sturdily with their employing organisation. Social identity theory proposes that individuals identify with firms in order to intensify their self-worth and to differentiate themselves from the out-group (Ashforth & Mael, 1989). Accordingly, CSR may not only build bridges by consolidating diversity and cohesion, but may also make walls that isolate individuals from one another, triggering discrimination and other forms of segregation built on moral high ground (thereby determining right from wrong behaviour). Self-righteousness may also lead to the effect that employees are less willing to behave responsibly in non-work contexts if the organisation's CSR engagement results in moral licensing.

- Unethical conduct

  In addition, participating in CSR could lead to 'moral licensing', contributing to less ethical conduct because workers believe they have contributed to society (Ormiston & Wong, 2013). Moral licensing is "the psychological process that leads people to engage in morally questionable behavior after having previously engaged in socially desirable behavior" (Ormiston & Wong, 2013, p. 865).

  Blanken et al.'s 2015 study shows that persons who remembered their own past moral actions afterwards show lower levels of pro-social intentions and behaviours. Accordingly, if employees think they are behaving very morally by working for a responsible business, they might also think they have earned sufficient moral credit to achieve moral balance should they choose to engage in immoral non-work behaviour (Mullen & Monin, 2016).

- Emotional exhaustion

  Recent studies indicate that the awareness of CSR by workers is negatively linked to emotional exhaustion in terms of handling negative results (Watkins et al., 2015) and may avoid scepticism (Goodman et al., 2011). CSR exerts a negative significant effect on emotional exhaustion. The impact of environmental CSR on emotional exhaustion leads to detrimental effects on employees' productivity, job performance, and creativity. For instance, greenwashing perceptions have been negatively connected to purchase intentions and brand credibility.

Several firms use CSR as a greenwashing tool and window dressing interposition to gain legitimacy in order to maintain their licence to operate (Preuss, 2012). In this way, figurative CSR helps firms create a flawless image of a socially responsible organisation, even when irresponsible business practices and power imbalances are established. If CSR activities are used to mask adverse externalities such as low pay, highly inequality in company salary ratios, gender disparity, social class inequality, or work-life imbalances—those activities can have negative impacts on the workforce.

2.7 The Way Forward

CSR is an essential tool in enhancing corporate image which leads to an increase in the sales or revenue base of organisations. It is the conduit by which corporate bodies support both employees and customers and contribute to society. Social responsibility has become a means by which organisations in the contemporary business environment support individuals and society as a whole.

In view of the numerous benefits to organisations, individuals, and society, there is the need for every corporate body to undertake corporate social activities in order to survive in this dynamic environment. These companies need to give maximum attention to CSR, especially micro-level CSR by way of committing more resources to it in order to improve individual-level relationship. For companies to have better relationships with individuals and society in general for growth, the following considerations are observed.

Companies should broaden their social responsibility activities to include micro-level CSR, more especially, individual-level CSR (employees and customers). This will enhance both employee and customer satisfaction, trust, commitment, and loyalty as alluded to in the outcomes. Companies should document their policy on CSR. The policy should spell out the company's intended CSR activities in order to keep efforts focused and relevant.

It will also provide policy direction with respect to micro-level CSR. One example of a micro activity is that companies should establish scholarship schemes to help the needy but brilliant children of employees, customers, and society from basic to tertiary level. This will help in developing the human resource base of the society from which the company will benefit in the future. Also, all CSR activities including micro-CSR activities should be effectively budgeted for. A percentage of profit should be allocated for CSR since its practice enhances enormous positive outcomes. This would guarantee a focus on the CSR activities.

That apart, since the outcomes are enormous, further studies should focus on examining the overall relationship between the individual CSR drivers and their reactions to CSR. Questions like how individual reactions inform individual CSR drivers could be explored. Others include how individuals evaluate CSR as individuals and as a group, how individuals become socially responsible or irresponsible, and what factors lead to these behaviours. These individual factors are vital in determining the extent of CSR reactions by individuals, hence the need for further studies in the arena.

2.8 Conclusion

Insights into micro-level CSR processes dramatically inform employees and customers of the strategic management of CSR activities to boost organisational performance and produce superior financial proceeds through positive reactions from stakeholders. When organisations benefit economically from well-managed micro-level CSR practices, they are increasingly inspired and willing to extend their CSR practices by investing more.

To this end, a 'virtuous cycle' between CSR and corporate success (Orlitzky et al., 2003) leads a business to increase its CSR investments over time. The potential outcome of this cycle is a growing social value and macro-level social effect produced by the CSR activities of the company. In this way, insights into stakeholder micro-level responses that inform how CSR activities can be handled to produce stronger financial returns can indirectly facilitate meso-level and macro-level social effects.

Such insight and evaluation thus encapsulate managerial ramifications as it unearths the potential relevance of micro-level CSR in business strategy and preparation for competitive advantages. The implementation of individual-level CSR, including staff, customers, and investors, would optimise organisational efforts, thereby enhancing organisational efficiency.

References

Aguilera, R. V., Rupp, D. E., Williams, C. A., & Ganapathi, J. (2007). Putting the S back in corporate social responsibility: A multilevel theory of social change in organizations. *Academy of Management Review, 32*(3), 836–863.

Aguinis, H. (2011). Organizational responsibility: Doing good and doing well. In S. Zedeck (Ed.), *APA handbooks in psychology®. APA handbook of industrial and organizational psychology, Vol. 3. Maintaining, expanding, and contracting the organization* (pp. 855–879). American Psychological Association.

Aguinis, H., & Glavas, A. (2019). On corporate social responsibility, sensemaking, and the search for meaningfulness through work. *Journal of Management, 45*(3), 1057–1086.

Alhouti, S., Johnson, C. M., & Holloway, B. B. (2016). Corporate social responsibility authenticity: Investigating its antecedents and outcomes. *Journal of Business Research, 69*(3), 1242–1249.

Aramburu, I. A., & Pescador, I. G. (2019). The effects of corporate social responsibility on customer loyalty: The mediating effect of reputation in cooperative banks versus commercial banks in the Basque country. *Journal of Business Ethics, 154*(3), 701–719.

Ashforth, B. E., & Mael, F. (1989). Social identity theory and the organization. *Academy of Management Review, 14*(1), 20–39.

Berle, A. A., Jr. (1931). Corporate powers as powers in trust. *Harvard Law Review, 44*, 1049–1074.

Bhattacharya, C. B., Korschun, D., & Sen, S. (2009). Strengthening stakeholder–company relationships through mutually beneficial corporate social responsibility initiatives. *Journal of Business Ethics, 85*(2), 257–272.

Blanken, I., van de Ven, N., & Zeelenberg, M. (2015). A meta-analytic review of moral licensing. *Personality and Social Psychology Bulletin, 41*(4), 540–558.

Carroll, A. B. (1999). Corporate social responsibility: Evolution of a definitional construct. *Business & Society, 38*(3), 268–295.

Cheruiyot, T. K., & Onsando, P. (2016). Corporate social responsibility in Africa: Context, paradoxes, stakeholder orientations, contestations and reflections. In *Corporate social performance in the age of irresponsibility-cross national perspective* (pp. 89–110). Information Age Publishing Inc.

Chun, J. S., Shin, Y., Choi, J. N., & Kim, M. S. (2013). How does corporate ethics contribute to firm financial performance? The mediating role of collective organizational commitment and organizational citizenship behavior. *Journal of Management, 39*(4), 853–877.

Crilly, D., Schneider, S. C., & Zollo, M. (2008). Psychological antecedents to socially responsible behavior. *European Management Review, 5*(3), 175–190.

Dumont, J., Shen, J., & Deng, X. (2017). Effects of green HRM practices on employee workplace green behavior: The role of psychological green climate and employee green values. *Human Resource Management, 56*(4), 613–627.

Farooq, O., Payaud, M., Merunka, D., & Valette-Florence, P. (2014). The impact of corporate social responsibility on organizational commitment: Exploring multiple mediation mechanisms. *Journal of Business Ethics, 125*(4), 563–580.

Farooq, O., Rupp, D. E., & Farooq, M. (2016). The multiple pathways through which internal and external identification and multifoci outcomes: The multiple pathways through which internal and external corporate social responsibility influence organizational identification and multifoci outcomes. *The Academy of Management Journal, 60*(3), 954–985.

Frederick, W. C. (2016). Commentary: Corporate social responsibility: Deep roots, flourishing growth, promising future. *Frontiers in Psychology, 7*, 129.

Frynas, J. G., & Stephens, S. (2015). Political corporate social responsibility: Reviewing theories and setting new agendas. *International Journal of Management Reviews, 17*, 483–509.

Garberg, N. A., & Fombrun, C. J. (2006). Corporate citizenship: Creating intangible assets across institutional environment. *Academy of Management Review, 31*, 329–346.

Glavas, A. (2016). Corporate social responsibility and employee engagement: Enabling employees to employ more of their whole selves at work. *Frontiers in Psychology, 7*, 796.

Glavas, A., & Piderit, S. K. (2009). How does doing good matter. *Journal of Corporate Citizenship, 36*(3), 51–70.

Gond, J. P., El Akremi, A., Swaen, V., & Babu, N. (2017). The psychological microfoundations of corporate social responsibility: A person-centric systematic review. *Journal of Organizational Behavior, 38*(2), 225–246.

Goodman, M. B., Johansen, T. S., & Nielsen, A. E. (2011). Strategic stakeholder dialogues: A discursive perspective on relationship building. *Corporate Communications: An International Journal, 16*(3), 204–217.

Gouldner, A. W. (1960). The norm of reciprocity: A preliminary statement. *American Sociological Review, 25*, 161–178.

Grönroos, M. (2011). *Book of vaadin*. Lulu.com.

Gully, S. M., Phillips, J. M., Castellano, W. G., Han, K., & Kim, A. (2013). A mediated moderation model of recruiting socially and environmentally responsible job applicants. *Personnel Psychology, 66*(4), 935–973.

Guzzo, R. F., Abbott, J., & Madera, J. M. (2020). A micro-level view of CSR: A hospitality management systematic literature review. *Cornell Hospitality Quarterly, 61*(3), 332–352.

Hillenbrand, C., & Money, K. G. (2015). Unpacking the mechanism by which psychological ownership manifests at the level of the individual: A dynamic model of identity and self. *Journal of Marketing Theory and Practice, 23*(2), 148–165.

Hsu, K. T. (2012). The advertising effects of corporate social responsibility on corporate reputation and brand equity: Evidence from the life insurance industry in Taiwan. *Journal of Business Ethics, 109*(2), 189–201.

Hur, W. M., Kim, H., & Woo, J. (2014). How CSR leads to corporate brand equity: Mediating mechanisms of corporate brand credibility and reputation. *Journal of Business Ethics, 125*(1), 75–86.

Islam, M. S., Tseng, M. L., & Karia, N. (2019). Assessment of corporate culture in sustainability performance using a hierarchical framework and interdependence relations. *Journal of Cleaner Production, 217*, 676–690.

Jones, D. A. (2010). Does serving the community also serve the company? Using organizational identification and social exchange theories to understand employee responses to a volunteerism programme. *Journal of Occupational and Organizational Psychology, 83*(4), 857–878.

Jones, D. A., Newman, A., Shao, R., & Cooke, F. L. (2019). Advances in employee-focused micro-level research on corporate social responsibility: Situating new contributions within the current state of the literature. *Journal of Business Ethics, 157*(2), 293–302.

Jones, D. A., Willness, C. R., & Glavas, A. (2017). When corporate social responsibility (CSR) meets organizational psychology: New frontiers in micro-CSR research, and fulfilling a quid pro quo through multilevel insights. *Frontiers in Psychology, 8*, 520.

Kim, H. L., Rhou, Y., Uysal, M., & Kwon, N. (2017). An examination of the links between corporate social responsibility (CSR) and its internal consequences. *International Journal of Hospitality Management, 61*, 26–34.

Kim, H. R., Lee, M., Lee, H. T., & Kim, N. M. (2010). Corporate social responsibility and employee–company identification. *Journal of Business Ethics, 95*(4), 557–569.

Kundu, S. C., & Gahlawat, N. (2015). Socially responsible HR practices and employees' intention to quit: The mediating role of job satisfaction. *Human Resource Development International, 18*(4), 387–406.

Lii, Y. S., & Lee, M. (2012). The joint effects of compensation frames and price levels on service recovery of online pricing error. *Managing Service Quality: An International Journal, 22*, 4–20.

Mallory, D. B., & Rupp, D. E. (2014). "Good" leadership: Using corporate social responsibility to enhance leader-member exchange. In T. N. Bauer & B. Erdogan (Eds.), *Oxford library of psychology. The Oxford handbook of leader-member exchange* (pp. 335–350). Oxford University Press.

Matten, D., & Moon, J. (2008). "Implicit" and "explicit" CSR: A conceptual framework for a comparative understanding of corporate social responsibility. *Academy of Management Review, 33*(2), 404–424.

Mullen, E., & Monin, B. (2016). Consistency versus licensing effects of past moral behavior. *Annual Review of Psychology, 67*, 363–385.

Orlitzky, M., Schmidt, F. L., & Rynes, S. L. (2003). Corporate social and financial performance: A meta-analysis. *Organization Studies, 24*(3), 403–441.

Ormiston, M. E., & Wong, E. M. (2013). License to ill: The effects of corporate social responsibility and CEO moral identity on corporate social irresponsibility. *Personnel Psychology, 66*(4), 861–893.

Özduran, A., & Tanova, C. (2017). Coaching and employee organizational citizenship behaviours: The role of procedural justice climate. *International Journal of Hospitality Management, 60*, 58–66.

Preuss, L. (2012). Responsibility in paradise? The adoption of CSR tools by companies domiciled in tax havens. *Journal of Business Ethics, 110*(1), 1–14.

Rioux, S. M., & Penner, L. A. (2001). The causes of organizational citizenship behavior: A motivational analysis. *Journal of Applied Psychology, 86*(6), 1306.

Rodrigo, P., & Arenas, D. (2008). Do employees care about CSR programs? A typology of employees according to their attitudes. *Journal of Business Ethics, 83*(2), 265–283.

Rupp, D. E., Ganapathi, J., Aguilera, R. V., & Williams, C. A. (2006). Employee reactions to corporate social responsibility: An organizational justice framework. *Journal of Organizational Behavior: The International Journal of Industrial, Occupational and Organizational Psychology and Behavior, 27*(4), 537–543.

Rupp, D. E., & Mallory, D. B. (2015). Corporate social responsibility: Psychological, person-centric, and progressing. *Annual Review of Organizational Psychology and Organizational Behavior, 2*(1), 211–236.

Shen, J., & Benson, J. (2016). When CSR is a social norm: How socially responsible human resource management affects employee work behavior. *Journal of Management, 42*(6), 1723–1746.

Shen, J., & Zhu, C. J. (2011). Effects of socially responsible human resource management on employee organizational commitment. *The International Journal of Human Resource Management, 22*(15), 3020–3035.

Spence, M. (1974). Competitive and optimal responses to signals: An analysis of efficiency and distribution. *Journal of Economic Theory, 7*(3), 296–332.

Stanaland, A. J., Lwin, M. O., & Murphy, P. E. (2011). Consumer perceptions of the antecedents and consequences of corporate social responsibility. *Journal of Business Ethics, 102*(1), 47–55.

Tajfel, H., & Turner, J. C. (1985). The social identity theory of intergroup behavior. In S. Worchel & W. G. Austin (Eds.), *Psychology of intergroup relations* (2nd ed., pp. 7–24). Nelson-Hall.

Tuan, L. T. (2013). The role of CSR in clinical governance and its influence on knowledge sharing. *Clinical Governance: An International Journal, 18*(2), 90–113.

Tuan, L. T. (2018). Activating tourists' citizenship behavior for the environment: The roles of CSR and frontline employees' citizenship behavior for the environment. *Journal of Sustainable Tourism, 26*(7), 1178–1203.

Tuan, L. T., Rajendran, D., Rowley, C., & Khai, D. C. (2019). Customer value co-creation in the business-to-business tourism context: The roles of corporate social responsibility and customer empowering behaviors. *Journal of Hospitality and Tourism Management, 39*, 137–149.

Van Dick, R., Ullrich, J., & Tissington, P. A. (2006). Working under a black cloud: How to sustain organizational identification after a merger. *British Journal of Management, 17*(S1), S69–S79.

Van Knippenberg, D. (2000). Work motivation and performance: A social identity perspective. *Applied Psychology, 49*(3), 357–371.

Watkins, M. B., Ren, R., Umphress, E. E., Boswell, W. R., Triana, M. D. C., & Zardkoohi, A. (2015). Compassion organizing: Employees' satisfaction with corporate philanthropic disaster response and reduced job strain. *Journal of Occupational and Organizational Psychology, 88*(2), 436–458.

Whittington, R. (2010). Giddens, structuration theory and strategy as practice. In *Cambridge handbook of strategy as practice* (pp. 109–126). Cambridge University Press.

Yin, J., & Jamali, D. (2016). Strategic corporate social responsibility of multinational companies' subsidiaries in emerging markets: Evidence from China. *Long Range Planning, 49*(5), 541–558.

3

Assessing the Contributions of CSR Activities to the Educational Sector

Karim Fusheini, Atia Alpha Alfa, Hussein Salia, and Anthony Sumnaya Kumasey

3.1 Introduction

Accessibility of education and training is an important benchmark for understanding the social and formative advancement of a country. While it may not be the sole factor involved, education can shape a person's foundation to make progress in other areas, extending from developments in the medical care industry to enhancements in agriculture and entrepreneurship. The rewards of a well-rounded education are generally uncontested, however, obtaining high-calibre and reasonable education is a challenge for a sizeable piece of the populace, particularly in developing

K. Fusheini
GIMPA Business School, Accra, Ghana

A. A. Alfa (✉) • A. S. Kumasey
University of Professional Studies, Accra, Accra, Ghana
e-mail: atia.alfa@upsamail.edu.gh; anthony.kumasey@upsamail.edu.gh

H. Salia
Heritage Christian University, Amasaman, Ghana

E. K. Adae et al. (eds.), *Responsible Management in Emerging Markets*, Sustainable Development Goals Series, https://doi.org/10.1007/978-3-030-76563-7_3

countries where there exists an unmistakable financial gap between various layers of society. Even though attempts are made by the public to connect these variations and give all people similar learning opportunities, the truth is that it is a difficult task. Consequently, private sector corporations are indispensable, and one of the ways by which private associations and organisations have been adding to society is by using corporate social responsibility (CSR).

Globally, CSR issues are currently being fused into each part of business activity including education and training and made known in the goals, missions, and strategies of the organisations (Ofori & Hinson, 2007). CSR in education is aimed at investing a greater amount of resources to the training of future human capital to the advantage of both the businesses and the society as a whole. Organisations get involved in CSR initiatives in the education sector for varied reasons including creating a positive altruistic reputation of the organisation in the eyes of clients, labourers, and different stakeholders; creating brand awareness and customer loyalty; positioning the business as an industry leader; and satisfying the business' mission.

In this day and age, the deficit in the training and education sector cannot be under-assessed and overlooked. According to UNESCO's Global Monitoring Reports on Education (2012, 2014), there are roughly 58 million children across the universe who, under normal circumstances, should be attending basic schools, but unfortunately are denied access. The reports also revealed that around 63 million young people have no access to secondary education. Likewise, around 200 million youth, between the ages of 15 and 24 years, have never gone to elementary school in their entire lives. This widespread illiteracy rate is a worldwide issue that should be fixed; however, a number of countries continue to fail in tackling the issue.

UNESCO also discloses that 250 million young people internationally can neither read nor write even after graduating from school. Additionally, around 130 million cannot read or write even after four years of education (UNESCO, 2014). Dattani et al. (2015) found that 90% of the children in Mali, over half in Uganda, and little over 33% in Honduras are not capable of reading one solitary word contained in the recommended text for the elementary schools. The drill-down of Dattani et al.'s

(2015) report disclosed that close to 774 million grown-ups, predominantly women, could neither read nor write.

In emerging economies, the situation has not witnessed any significant improvement since 2000. While the Africa regional percentage of females that can neither read nor write still stood at its original 66%, the rest of the world has seen a massive decrease to 45% (UNESCO, 2014). The absence of education in numerous areas of the world has become a worldwide issue and, hence, the need to pay attention to it because of its noteworthy impact on illiteracy and joblessness.

The contribution of corporate bodies to education and training worldwide has been very insignificant. Less-developed nations, for instance, received about US$135 million in support from business establishments towards education-related projects every year (UNESCO, 2013). CSR funding support to the health sector is multiple times the amount advanced to the educational sector worldwide. For example, Sanofi and Novartis in the United States of America remain the two biggest donors of health and drugs internationally. Additionally, the information shows that CSR expenditure on medical care alone was 89% in the Republic of Korea between 2007 and 2012, while a paltry 3% was spent on the educational sector (West, 2013). This confirms UNESCO's (2013) assertion that insignificant sums are earmarked by corporate bodies to subsidise education and its related activities annually.

Hence, there is an urgent need for countries to critically reconsider the proportion of corporate support to various sectors of the economy, given that education is a key determinant of a country's level of development. Solid political resolve in addition to adopting varied approaches can be the solitary answers for the difficulties identified. One such approach, for example, can be seen in Ghana as the government has started to offer free senior high school education and vocational training to all persons of school-going age. These measures break down some barriers to education and can strengthen the education sector.

Many research studies have been conducted to examine (Bello et al., 2017; Camilleri, 2016; Ismail et al., 2013; Nehru, 2016) CSR and education. Most of the extant literature focuses on CSR in developed countries and its effect on higher education, which is not necessarily relevant to organisations in a developing country context (Borel et al., 2011;

Naeem & Peach, 2011). In all these studies, the authors did not touch on the assessment of the contributions of CSR in the education sector.

Therefore, the focal point of this chapter is to assess the contributions of CSR initiatives to the education sector. Research in this area is an important contribution to a better understanding of the relationship between organisations and stakeholders, with direct implications for management and the government. The study also serves as a reference point for future research on the importance of CSR interventions in the education sector.

3.2 CSR Patterns in the Education Sector

The education sector recently has been attracting corporate investments worldwide for various reasons. Idemudia (2007) has found many new CSR activities have been designed to boost computer utilisation aptitude in school children; encourage gender balance, especially in the rural schools; promote health and sanitation in school environments; support children suffering from disabilities; provide nutritious foods to students; and train teachers for enhanced instruction of students. The patterns of CSR activities in the education sector are detailed below:

3.2.1 Training Programmes

Corporate establishments can organise training programmes to help train school leavers with marketable skills for the job market. They do this by building up a decent educational plan that contains a rich material on how to survive in the era of high unemployment (Cushla & Hay, 2009). These coaching programmes are highly useful as it is generally seen that academic curricula do not always translate into practical job skills. The young people are given viable work aptitudes and human relations skills, among others. For example, Cisco, a supplier of network equipment, has trained more than 10,000 systems administrators across 165 countries (Camilleri, 2014).

Some 4.75 million people have been mentored to improve their chances of being engaged as future organisational leaders. The training programmes make the recipients effective at their workplaces (Kehoe & Wright, 2013). Simms (2002) related that companies without any clear community development plans have difficulty creating wealth for their shareholders. He concluded that in such instances it becomes increasingly difficult to integrate and harness the social, economic, and environmental success factors in communities to enhance the culture, values, strategy, decision-making, and business operations.

3.2.2 Teacher Professional Development Programmes

Extant literature shows that corporate institutions prefer to implement CSR programmes that are focused on advancing and upgrading teachers' knowledge and competencies. On-the-Job related training programmes are held to enhance teachers' skills in teaching procedures, test assessments, and planning and preparation of teaching and learning materials (Weller & Dillon, 1999). When teachers are well trained, it is expected that will lead to better quality of service delivery in the classrooms, consequently, resulting in improvement in teacher and student interactions.

3.2.3 Supply of Educational Materials

Numerous organisations give instructive resources to support students learning. In Ghana, MTN Ghana Ltd, for example, donated several instructional materials to more than 300 students in the Okere District in the Eastern Region of the country in September 2018. The support consists of reading materials, exercise books, pencils, pens, and school bags (Ghana News Agency, 2018).

3.2.4 Infrastructure Development

A serene atmosphere is an important ingredient for achieving effective teaching and learning. Yet most schools in Ghana, especially in the rural communities, lack access to these important prerequisites. To alleviate these challenges, many corporations have provided science resource centres to aid research work, school blocks to uplift the teaching and learning environment, football pitches to boost recreational activities, fence walls for the protection of lives and properties, dining halls as a convenient place for meals, and vehicles to aid transportation. Consistent with Nelson (2003), infrastructure support is extended to educational institutions free of charge by corporate bodies, especially those in less endowed locations, to enhance effective teaching and learning.

3.2.5 Grants and Scholarships

Corporate bodies also give grants and scholarships to poor but brilliant schoolchildren who are unable to pay for their schooling and who without such support will be out of school. Such assistance takes numerous forms—it could be full or fractional grants. If it is a full grant, then the support will cover all relevant costs incidental to completing the course of study. Students' expenses including tuition fees, living costs, learning materials, and feeding will be fully paid for by the sponsoring organisation.

3.2.6 Provision of Information and Communications Technology Equipment and Skills

Information and Communications Technology (ICT) infrastructure remains another commitment assumed by corporate bodies towards the education sector of many countries, including Ghana. Innovation has contributed to altering the world by expanding the information and related correspondence. For example, on the web, email is instantaneously accessible in all areas of society and every part of the globe. Companies, therefore, have an arduous task to perform in this constantly advancing information and technological age. Some corporate bodies have responded to this call by providing ICT equipment and training support to schools whose products are regarded as the future employees and leaders of those organisations.

Corporations have tried delivering ICT infrastructure to the majority of schools in dire need. ICT facilities can help in the spread of instruction-related data and information to everybody, particularly persons in the developed world. With the aid of ICT equipment, teachers are usually trained in computer use and applications. These teachers will likewise transfer the knowledge and information obtained through training to school children. Nelson (2003) has confirmed the foregoing assertions by noting that ICT training offered to teachers results in knowledge transfer, thus, bridging the computerised literacy gap often witnessed in many countries. Also, through ICT equipment support to educational institutions, corporate bodies are increasingly aiding schools' research foundations, particularly public schools as these represent the major source of research material often employed in planning educational programmes, teaching, and learning.

3.3 Areas of Intervention for Educational CSR Initiatives and Expected Outcomes

Tables 3.1 and 3.2 provide a summary of the areas of intervention for educational CSR initiatives and also the impact of CSR initiatives in the education sector in terms of the immediate and long-term outcomes.

3.4 Issues in CSR Activities in the Education and Training Sector

Financing education in the global south has always been a challenge. For instance, new calculations by UNESCO's Education for All Global Monitoring Report show that the $16 billion annual external funding gap to achieve basic education in poor countries by the 2015 target date has increased to $26 billion over the last few years. The financing gap mainly affects the achievement of universal primary education, the second Millennium Development Goal.

Table 3.1 Areas of intervention for educational CSR initiatives

Area of intervention	Examples of CSR initiatives
Infrastructure development and donation of teaching and learning materials	Fence walls, dining halls, football pitches, sports wears, classroom blocks, library blocks Educational materials such as pens, exercise books, textbooks, library books, sandals, and school bags
Learning methods and capacity building	Teachers and other instructors are given in-service training in modern teaching methodologies, practical ICT lessons, and assessment methods, curriculum development, development of learning material, research
Skill development	Mentoring children, vocational and technical education for young people, extracurricular activities
School-based nutrition and health programmes	Free lunch for students, health education and screening, sex education, provision of sick bays
Cash/in-kind assistance to students	Scholarships and sponsorships for brilliant but needy students, teachers, and educational workers
Remedial classes for senior high school and junior high school graduates who could not pass the exams at the first attempt	Supplementary education for lower-performing students, especially in the core subjects, non-formal education, providing higher education opportunities to deserving employees' children
School administration and management	Public-private partnerships in the construction and management of school blocks, running school management independently, remuneration and incentive for both teaching and non-teaching staff, vehicles to support the running of schools

Source: Authors (2021)

While domestic spending on education has risen by $3 billion annually in low-income countries in recent years, it still amounts to only half the amount needed to achieve basic education for every citizen of school-going age. For example, Ayamdoo and Ayine (2002) suggest that since the start of the education reform programme in 1987, the external donor funding to the education sector has amounted to approximately US$400 million. Similarly, Thompson and Casely-Hayford (2007)

Table 3.2 CSR programmes and their immediate and long-term outcomes

CSR programmes and activities	Short-term indicators	Medium-term indicators	Long-term indicators
Classroom blocks and ancillary facilities	Increase in student enrolment due to increase in classrooms Toilet facilities create and promote good sanitary conditions	Expanded school infrastructure, particularly in rural areas, motivated teachers, and students	Universal education with well-balanced graduates
Information communication technology equipment	ICT is taught for classroom application, helps teachers in the assessment of students and dissemination of test results	ICT graduates with the needed skills to work with industries	Digitalised economy
Research centres and equipment	Help in practical teaching and learning of science-related courses	Improved outcomes in both internal and external science-related courses	Technology-oriented graduates are produced, increased productivity in all sectors of the economy
Financial aid	Increase in the number of brilliant, but needy students attending school	The burden on families and even the government is reduced	Universal education is achieved, illiteracy rate nationally is reduced
Teaching and learning aids	Students get interested in lessons, facilitators also get motivated, students achieve more passes in both internal and external examinations	Increase in the number of passes in both internal and external examinations	Well-educated graduates with the requisite knowledge and skills

(*continued*)

Table 3.2 (continued)

CSR programmes and activities	Short-term indicators	Medium-term indicators	Long-term indicators
In-service training	Educators receive new teaching methodologies to deliver lessons and utilise contact hours well	Teachers' job satisfaction increases, leading to the production of good results	Good academic achievement and a reduced illiteracy rate
Means of transport	Aid the movement of staff, administrators, and students from one place to another	Increase school and student achievement in both indoor and outdoor programmes, promote the good name of the beneficiary schools	Universal education for all. Well-balanced graduates

Source: Authors (2021)

suggested the total value of overall external aid to the education sector from 1986 to 2002 was US$588.3 million. Under the Multi-Donor Budget Support (MDBS) programme, overall international donor support for credit and grants to the education sector from 2003 to 2005 amounted to US$200.9 million (Thompson & Casely-Hayford, 2007; World Bank, 2004). From the analysis above, it is clear that funding in the education sector is inadequate, and so, more private sector support is needed to complement what the government is doing in the sector.

An issue that needs to be looked at is the fact that infrastructure and scholarships top the list of corporate support to the neglect of vocational and skills training, which is very important in this era of high unemployment. More emphasis should be placed on technical education that has the tendency of reducing joblessness in the society, as the graduates from technical institutions are able to establish their own trades after school.

The absence of lucidness in CSR activities by corporate bodies is another issue that needs to be addressed. Duplication of CSR activity happens when there is an absence of eloquence in executing CSR. Corporate bodies apply their CSR activities to the education sector in regions of their choice. Also, numerous organisations consider their CSR interventions as a component of their competitive strategies and are not ready to agree with others (McWilliams et al., 2006; Porter & Kramer, 2006). Another reason behind the absence of coherence or agreement is that organisations are more agreeable in executing CSR activity they think matches the goals they hope to achieve.

Limited corporate bodies involved in CSR to the education sector are also a major issue with regard to CSR and education. Even though companies understand the challenges bedevilling the education and training sector, not many of them are interested in supporting the sector (Sengupta & Mitra, 2020). The number of companies with CSR activities with an aim to support the education sector globally or within a particular country is simply not enough to have a transformative impact in the sector.

The declining support of governments also has an impact on CSR penetration in the education sector. Governments are responsible for coming out with legislation that will force corporations to be ethical and responsible in their operations, but this is not being done. Public-private partnerships could be instituted in executing school infrastructure projects, especially in the rural areas. The state authorities are also required to give incentives like tax holidays to corporate bodies to motivate them to increase CRS support to communities in their respective operating environs. Presently, specific corporate taxes in Ghana are only limited to permitting CSR investment costs to be used as deductible allowances and not in a form of tax holidays to encouraging business establishments to carry out more benevolent activities.

Education and training for adults is another area that needs attention. Saint Honda in Japan, for example, was associated with a CSR-supported adult education crusade. They provide adult education classes as part of their CSR activities with the view to increasing the literacy rate among the uneducated adult population in the country. Essentially, Tata Consultancy Services (TCS) in India had actualised what they had named as an adult proficiency programme. This activity was pointed towards training adults in computer literacy. More attention needed to be given to adult education, particularly in less-developed countries where large portions of the populace are not educated. Agricultural policies and practices, health tips, and nutrition education messages could be designed and used as the curriculum for such adult education.

Girl child education is another issue of concern which calls for CSR initiatives. Past researches have revealed that there is a disparity in gender in all levels of education globally, and especially in developing countries. One of the proposed answers to this issue is improving the education infrastructure for young ladies and women. Several associations have now begun to support the girl child by building model girl schools, providing scholarships, grants, and educational materials. This gesture has brought about increased enrolment in the number of girls attending school. Republic Bank, Fidelity Bank, Stanbic Bank, and some other financial institutions give education sponsorships to female students based on merit.

In the case of telecommunication companies like AirtelTigo, MTN, and Vodafone, their education projects and programmes guarantee that young ladies get additional consideration and support such as sanitary pads, scholarships, feeding grants, uniforms when required—the companies believe these young ladies' study to be the focal point of a significant number of their fellow girls.

Vocational and skill training is also a big problem, especially in developing countries. Studies have shown that students who complete tertiary schools do not have the needed skills that industry needs because they lack practical know-how. Keeping this at the top of the priority list, a few associations have initiated educational courses that help improve the skills and knowledge of the individual to enhance practical skills. Several organisations target computer-based training as they accept that comprehension of ICT tools and skills is fundamental for any undertaking The National Institute of Information Technology (NIIT) which is a multinational education-oriented organisation focused on information and computer technology and Intercom Programming and Manufacturing Co. Ltd which is an information technology training centre, for instance, teach and advance ICT proficiency among students to help improve their job prospects. More support is needed from corporate bodies in this direction to support the government in delivering vocational and skill training to the youth.

The absence of education sector interest in CSR exercises is yet another issue that needs some attention. Schools need an appraisal that is basic in the execution of CSR activities. Without the needed appraisal, CSR exercises may not be successful. Some schools and their stakeholders do not show interest in CSR programmes in their schools and some of them even show resistance to companies coming to support them due to a lack of knowledge about what constitutes CSR Trouble in evaluating the social effect on CSR initiatives by the beneficiaries and the initiators is problematic. The level of impact assessment being done on CSR initiatives, especially in the education sector, is very low because much attention is not given to it (Deshmukh, 2017).

3.5 The Way Forward

Education and training today face a lot of challenges as alluded to before and some of the challenges are inadequate financing, school infrastructure deficit, maintenance of educators, and so on. In their corporate social responsibility activities, organisations have begun to adopt a more focused strategy in line with their own business goals. The contributions of CSR in the education sector are multi-faceted with a lot of trial and error and learning by going along the education value chain. In the long run, all stakeholders stand to benefit from the intention of improving the state of the education system right now.

Globalisation has made it possible for corporations to be aware of their social obligations of adding to the betterment of society. What this means is that because of globalisation, corporations are exposed to every information about their operations and its effects on the society and the environment and sectors of the society that needs support in terms of CSR initiatives. Notwithstanding the worthwhile contribution of many corporations to the education sector, an enormous amount of support is still needed to offset many of the world's social issues, particularly poverty and lack of infrastructure.

Larger or multinational corporations such as Nestle and Pepsi Co. are expected to have a global reach in their CSR activities. This role, however, must always be balanced by two constraints: the confines of permissibility from the governments of the countries in which they operate and the financial needs and expectations of company shareholders. There are shared benefits for organisations and the public, as they develop human resources together. This view is an essential strategy that could bring financial benefits to the corporate bodies (Tang et al., 2012).

To release the shared potential for business and society, organisations ought to take an interest in charitable causes (Porter & Kramer, 2006; Porter & Kramer, 2011). There should be a deliberate public policy with regard to CSR support to the education sector to strengthen the educational foundation at the basic to secondary school levels, increasing access and de-politicising and removing bureaucracy in the education sector. Broader social and economic goals of creating access to education are inconsistent with micromanaging, which creates problems in the supply of education to those that need it. The current educational policy mindset must change to give way to well-functioning education systems.

Governments may assume a position of authority in setting up guidelines and rules in a manner that corporations should support the education sector. Though these legal enactments may not be binding on the corporate bodies with regard to how they do their CSR activities, they could be a guide for operatives. Governments may also provide tax holidays to businesses to motivate them to participate more in CSR activities.

3.6 Conclusions

CSR activities remain a major avenue for social and ecological change by the business sector. Projects and support from the private sector are amazingly valuable to society. Albeit at first flighty in methodology and execution, legislative changes have presented some level of design and are a request to how organisations reward the society in which they operate. Among the different areas, numerous organisations like to give to the education sector. It is clear, however, that even among the educational sector, there are contrasts in the dissemination of support. Most organisations focus on regions that are underserved to bring them up to par.

The discoveries from this research have resulted in some policy suggestions and leave space for recommendations for future exploration and work on related topics. Studies should endeavour to arrive at a superior comprehension of the purposes behind explicit CSR programmes, which would be useful in boosting more organisations to support under-funded areas. Taking everything into account, funding and support from organisations are vital for improving the nature of learning in every country. While a few areas of the education sector have been getting important projects and programmes, others are deficient. Organisations ought to consider these discoveries later on when planning their CSR spending plan to take into consideration a thorough improvement of the education sector.

References

Ayamdoo, C., & Ayine, D. (2002). *Worsening the woes: The Role of Donors in Education. Bank*. www.worldbank.org.oed

Bello, I., Fuad, M., & Shariffuddin, M.D. (2017). Multinational corporations and Nigeria's educational development: An international development perspective. *International Journal of Management Research and Review, 7*(6), 637–647.

Borel, R., Cawagas, V., Jimenez, A., & Salvetti, N. (2011). Education for sustainable development at the University for Peace. *Journal of Education for Sustainable Development, 5*(2), 312.

Camilleri, M. A. (2014). *Re-conceiving corporate sustainability and responsibility for education*. Retrieved November 10, 2019, from www.csrwire.com/blog/posts/1454-re-conceiving-corporate-sustainabilityand-responsibility-for-education

Camilleri, M. A. (2016). Corporate sustainability and responsibility toward education. *Journal of Global Responsibility, 7*(1), 56–71.

Cushla, K., & Hay, S. (2009). Industry school partnerships: Reconstituting spaces of educational governance. *Globalisation, Societies, and Education, 7*(2), 203–216.

Dattani, P., Still, A., & Pota, V. (2015). *Business backs education: Creating a baseline for corporate CSR spend on global education initiatives*. Report of EPG Economic and Strategy Consulting, UNESCO, Paris. http://www.unesco.org/education/BBE-EPGReport2015.pdf

Deshmukh, P. (2017). Corporate social responsibility and education sector: Issues and remedies. *International Journal of Management, 8*(1), 137–144.

Ghana News Agency. (2018). *MTN Ghana Foundation supports 300 pupils with educational materials*. Retrieved September 30, 2020, from www.ghananewsagency.com

Idemudia, U. (2007). Community perceptions and expectations: Reinventing the wheels of corporate social responsibility practices in the Nigerian oil industry. *Business and Society Review, 112*(3), 369–405.

Ismail, M., Amat, R. F., Mohd, R., & Alias, S. N. (2013). School as stakeholder of corporate social responsibility program. *Teacher's Perspective on Outcome in School Development, 23*(2), 321–331.

Kehoe, R. R., & Wright, P. M. (2013). The impact of high-performance human resource practices on employees' attitudes and behaviors. *Journal of Management, 39*(2), 366–391.

McWilliams, A., Siegel, D., & Wright, P. (2006). Corporate social responsibility: Strategic implications. *Journal of Management Studies, 43*(1), 1–18.

Naeem, M. A., & Peach, N. W. (2011). Promotion of sustainability in postgraduate education in the Asia Pacific region. *International Journal of Sustainability in Higher Education, 12*(3), 280–290.

Nehru, R. (2016). Corporate social responsibility & education for sustainable development. *International Research Journal of Engineering, IT & Scientific Research, 2*(3), 72–81.

Nelson, J. (2003). *Economic multipliers: Revisiting the core responsibility and contribution of business to development*. London, Policy Paper (No. 4). International Business Leaders Forum (IBLF).

Ofori, D. F., & Hinson, R. E. (2007). Corporate social responsibility (CSR) perspectives of leading firms in Ghana. *Corporate Governance: The International Journal of Business in Society, 7*(2), 178–193.

Porter, M. E., & Kramer, M. (2006). Strategy and society. The link between competitive advantage and corporate social responsibility. *Harvard Business Review, 84*, 78–92.

Porter, M. E., & Kramer, M. R. (2011). Creating shared value. *Harvard Business Review, 89*(1/2), 62–77.

Sengupta, M., & Mitra, N. (2020). Role of CSR in education: Speciale on India. In *Essential issues in corporate social responsibility* (pp. 73–83). Springer.

Simms, J. (2002). Business: Corporate social responsibility – You know it makes sense. *Accountancy, 130*(1311), 48–48.

Tang, Z., Hull, C. E., & Rothenberg, S. (2012). How corporate social responsibility engagement strategy moderates the CSR financial performance relationship. *Journal of Management Studies, 49*(7), 1274–1303.

Thompson, N. M., & Casely-Hayford, L. (2007). Aid and donor partnerships in Ghana's education sector, 1987–2007: A critical review of the literature and progress.

UNESCO. (2012). *Education for all global monitoring report: Youth and skills – Putting education to work*, 2012.

UNESCO. (2013, February 2013). *Education for all global monitoring report.* Policy Note 06.

UNESCO. (2014). Progress in getting all children to school stalls, but some countries show the way forward. UNESCO Institute for Statistics (UIS), 28(Policy Paper Fact Sheet 14).

Weller, M., & Dillon, P. (1999). Education and business partnerships in the United Kingdom: Initiatives in search of a rationale. *Bulletin of Science, Technology & Society, 19*(1), 60–67.

West, D. M. (2013). Mobile learning: Transforming education, engaging students, and improving outcomes. *Brookings Policy Report, 9*, 1–7.

World Bank. (2004). *Books, buildings, and learning outcomes: An impact evaluation of World Bank support to basic education in Ghana [online]*. World Bank.

Part II

Green Marketing

4

Green Entrepreneurship: The Case Study of the Kenyan Climate Innovation Centre

Ruth N. Kiraka

4.1 Introduction

In response to the impact of climate change, countries around the world are seeking to mitigate its effects and adapt by deploying green business practices. This is especially important in developing countries, where poor populations are likely to be hard hit by climate change and unable to adequately adapt. Green entrepreneurship provides the opportunity for "growing a green economy by providing green products and services, introducing greener production techniques, boosting demand for green products and services, and creating green jobs" (World Bank, 2017, p. 21). The World Bank estimates that between 2017 and 2030, about USD 23 trillion would be accessible to small and medium-sized enterprises (SMEs) for green entrepreneurship investments in emerging markets. This presents an opportunity for developing economies to build local green businesses while ensuring environmental sustainability.

R. N. Kiraka (✉)
Strathmore University, Nairobi, Kenya
e-mail: rkiraka@strathmore.edu

E. K. Adae et al. (eds.), *Responsible Management in Emerging Markets*, Sustainable Development Goals Series, https://doi.org/10.1007/978-3-030-76563-7_4

In this context, strengthening green entrepreneurship at multiple levels seems to be one of the most important priorities to promote its contribution to economic growth and development. Vlados and Chatzinikolaou (2020) argue for the need to focus on three levels of analysis and intervention in discussing both green entrepreneurship and economic growth—the micro, meso, and macro levels. Consistent innovation and change at the individual firm level (micro level) results in practices that build and promote skills development and practices at the sector level (meso level). Sectors develop their own guidelines and practices that become the building blocks for institutional frameworks and policies (macro level) that foster the green business environment. Inevitably, therefore, to promote green entrepreneurship, prudent micro-, meso-, and macro-level policies and practices need to be considered concurrently and in a way that is beneficial for enterprise development. These three levels form the entrepreneurship ecosystem and are a core component for fostering green entrepreneurship and economic development.

4.2 Methodology

The chapter focuses on two questions:

(i) What does green entrepreneurship mean?
(ii) How can green entrepreneurship be developed and promoted at the micro, meso and macro levels?

Based on these questions, the keywords 'green entrepreneurship' and synonyms such as 'sustainable entrepreneurship' and 'eco-entrepreneurship' were used to search for key literature. Additionally, these terms were combined with the terms 'micro-', 'meso-', and 'macro-level' analysis. Thematic analysis was used to identify key debates that combined green entrepreneurship with these three levels of analysis. A thematic analysis grid was used to structure the literature review.

This was followed by an analysis of the Kenya Climate Innovation Centre (KCIC) case study. The Centre was selected for inclusion owing to its focus on green entrepreneurship, and interventions at the three levels relevant for this chapter—the micro, meso, and macro levels. Data for the case study was obtained through interviews with the Chief Executive Officer who has been at the helm since the establishment of the Centre. The thematic semi-structured interview focused on three levels of discussion—the Centre's engagement with individual entrepreneurs (micro level), engagement with various sectors involved in green entrepreneurship (meso level), and how the Centre is influencing policy on green entrepreneurship (macro level). The interview data was transcribed and analysed thematically to identify key findings that were mapped onto the micro, meso, and macro levels of green entrepreneurship.

4.3 Defining Green Entrepreneurship

The Greent Project (2012) defined green entrepreneurship by identifying its five dimensions: (i) conscious activity; (ii) addresses an environmental problem or need; (iii) utilises entrepreneurial ideas; (iv) does not cause harm or damage to the environment; and (v) ensures business sustainability. A green entrepreneur, therefore, starts and runs a venture designed to achieve these outcomes from the time it is set up. Kirkwood and Walton (2010) define green entrepreneurs as those who enter eco-friendly markets because they have strong underlying green values, in addition to making profits. Vatansever and Arun (2016) view green entrepreneurship as the result of the interaction between environmental concerns and personal values. The authors concur that three factors come together to produce the green entrepreneur: first, the need to make money; second, the need to take care of the natural environment motivated by personal values; and third, the need to have innovative solutions that address any business practices that degrade the environment.

The concept of 'green entrepreneurship' is used differently depending on the context of debate (Vatansever & Arun, 2016). The variations include environmental entrepreneurship (enviropreneurship), ecological entrepreneurship (ecopreneurship), sustainable entrepreneurship (focusing on the value chain), and organic entrepreneurship (related to farm production). They further attempted to provide definitions of these four related concepts. The main focus of the environmental entrepreneur (enviropreneur) is ecological within the business approach.

The ecopreneur focuses on protecting and preventing environmental degradation among diverse industries; as well as introducing eco-friendly products and processes into the marketplace. The focus of the sustainable entrepreneur is transforming the society and a desire to change the world; transmitting both environmental and social purpose dimensions into a single enterprise. The organic entrepreneur's concern is on production from the soil—ensuring harmful chemicals are not introduced into the soil and used in agricultural production. The green entrepreneur seeks to protect the environment, and the moral value of the entrepreneur is to change the culture of enterprises. The green entrepreneur in some ways imbues the characteristics of all the other forms. However, these seemingly minor variations are important because they may resonate with different stakeholders in different ways. For example, an entrepreneur in the agribusiness space may relate better to the concept of an organic entrepreneur, while a manufacturing entrepreneur may relate better to the idea of a sustainable entrepreneur as it may resonate with sustainable manufacturing processes. An investor may identify more with the term ecopreneur as it relates to diverse industries and eco-friendly products and processes.

The terms '*green entrepreneurship*', '*eco-entrepreneurship*', and '*sustainable entrepreneurship*' are used interchangeably in this chapter as their definitions tend to overlap, and ultimately, they have the same goal. Although the focus on green entrepreneurship tends to be on the natural environment, it is inconceivable that this can be achieved without the enterprise being socially responsible (creating appropriate workplaces) and economically viable (being able to recover its costs). As such, green entrepreneurship draws upon a holistic understanding of the connectedness of all dimensions, with benefits accruing to the individual, their community, and the society at large.

Based on these arguments, Linnanen (2016) developed a typology of green entrepreneurs to demonstrate the tension between economic imperatives (desire for profit) and the social and environmental imperatives (desire for a better world). Figure 4.1 shows the four categories of

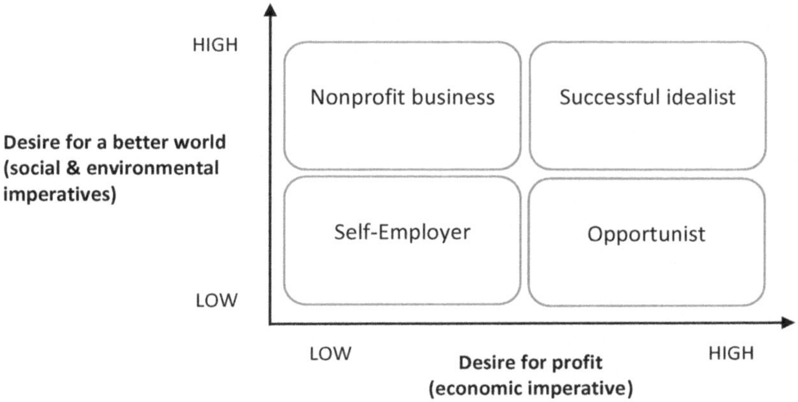

Fig. 4.1 Categories of green entrepreneurs. Source: Adapted from Linnanen (2016, p. 75)

green entrepreneurs: the self-employer, the non-profit business, the opportunist, and the successful idealist.

The economic imperative is driven more by structural extrinsic factors, while the social and environmental imperatives are largely driven by personal values. The relationship between economic, social, and environmental imperatives is key to understanding the drivers and barriers of green entrepreneurship. All successful entrepreneurs are similar with respect to their willingness to take risks, creativity, and innovation. However, it is the psychology of green entrepreneurs that distinguishes them from conventional entrepreneurs. Although the business opportunities may be similar for all businesses, it is the personal values and skills of the green entrepreneurs that translate these opportunities into successful green enterprises.

These types of 'successful idealist' in Linnanen's (2016) framework have been referred to as "green-green" by Kirkwood and Walton (2010). This entrepreneur is deliberate about setting up a green business and seeks to incorporate green practices throughout the value chain from the inception of the business. It is the aspiration of each green entrepreneur to reach the level of a 'successful idealist'.

4.3.1 Three Levels of Analysis for Green Entrepreneurship

Mirzanti et al. (2015) argue that for entrepreneurship policy to be effective and contribute to economic development, three levels of implementation need to be considered simultaneously. At the micro level is the individual business that seeks opportunities and develops appropriate skills to exploit those opportunities. Policies at this level are geared towards supporting the individual entrepreneur to achieve this end. The focus is on the individual's ability to integrate change and innovation into the business endeavour through training, education, mentoring, and consulting services (Vlados & Chatzinikolaou, 2020).

At the meso level are the various enterprises in the value chain that make up the sector. Policies at this level seek to create a competitive sector by enhancing the quality and quantity of exchange along the value chain. For example, when we talk of a competitive tea sector, the assumption is that different players along the value chain—from the farmers to distributors and sellers are all getting value for their role in the chain. Meso-level policies and practices make this possible.

At the macro level, the focus is on creating jobs across multiple sectors, promoting an entrepreneurial culture, developing an entrepreneurship infrastructure, and providing entrepreneurial education. Yousafzai et al. (2016) promote the idea of entrepreneurship as value creation for oneself and others by harmonising the entrepreneurial process at the micro, meso, and macro levels that allows for a bidirectional transfer of value across the three levels. These three levels form the basis for further discussion in this chapter.

4.3.2 Green Entrepreneurship at the Micro Level

At the micro level are the green entrepreneur and the motivations that drive his quest for the green enterprise. To appreciate the motivation driving the green entrepreneur, Schumpeter's theory of entrepreneurship offers some insights. Schumpeter (1934) developed the concepts of "innovative entrepreneur" and "creative destruction". He argued that the entrepreneur causes creative destruction through innovations driven by their value judgments and shaped by their cultural interactions. Specific actions are evaluated according to the value system that constitutes a foundation for individual motives. However, there are individuals who dare to go outside the pattern—the beautifully crafted value system—who Schumpeter referred to as entrepreneurs. The entrepreneur exercises the 'mental freedom' to conceive new ways of doing things and is brave enough to follow through even risking failure or the ridicule of others.

Schumpeter's view of entrepreneurial motivation is useful, in viewing the green entrepreneur as an agent of change who reconfigures the entire value chain—inputs, operations, outputs, marketing, and consumption—and introduces green inputs, processes, products, and services (Greent Project, 2012). This creative destruction and innovative reconstruction, Christensen (1997) referred to as disruptive innovation. Effectively, therefore, green entrepreneurs have been described as innovators that are both 'entrepreneurially virtuous' and 'disruptive'. They are perceived as community-centric, with a heightened sense of accountability for the outcomes (Boluk & Mottiar, 2014). However, green entrepreneurs are still driven by the motivations that drive the conventional entrepreneur. Green entrepreneurs have a need to make money while doing something they are passionate about (Kirkwood & Walton, 2010). They are, however, driven by the primary motivation—their green values.

It is therefore fair to suggest that like all entrepreneurial motivations, the motivations for green entrepreneurs are also multi-faceted. One is a strong ethical reasoning focused on not harming the environment, but improving it (Linnanen, 2016). Green values influence the nature of a new business and inform the operational decisions of management. Second is the motivation to address any market or business practices that may have resulted in degrading or harming the environment (Cohen & Winn, 2007), a motivation that is more important than their educational background or experience (Kirkwood & Walton, 2010). Third, they are also motivated to spread their green values to others. This they do through websites, visiting markets, exhibitions, and word of mouth, and with a focus on younger generations who would take over their businesses (Kirkwood & Walton, 2010). A fourth motivation for 'green values' is passion. Passion for nature and the need to preserve it—a beautiful forest, clean water, clean air—inform the motivation to start and manage a green business—having a 'green cause'. As Kirkwood and Walton (2010) put it, it is difficult to separate 'passion' and 'green values' as motivations of green entrepreneurs.

Although the motivation to make money has been suggested as not central to the green entrepreneur's business start-up decision (DeMartino & Barbato, 2003; Greent Project, 2012; Kirkwood & Walton, 2010), Linnanen's (2016) model suggests that making money and having green business practices are not incompatible with each other. The successful green entrepreneur can have both and balance them well—the 'successful idealist'. However, few entrepreneurs are able to achieve this balance.

In distinguishing the conventional entrepreneur from the green entrepreneur, consider these two scenarios (based on two true stories of Kenyan entrepreneurs).

Scenario 1: A young man is studying at the university. After one of the long trips organised for his class, he notices that many of his classmates are complaining of sore backs and necks, and slightly swollen legs caused by sitting for too long on the bus. He realises that, in Kenya, many people travel on the bus for long hours and that the problem he sees with his classmates may be quite prevalent. He decides to set up a small massage parlour at the shopping mall close to his university. He charges a fee that students and other people can afford. Not too long after setting up the business, he realises he cannot manage the business on a part-time basis—he needs to employ a full-time worker. His massage parlour has become popular with both students and non-students. He opens a second one after a year at a different location. By the time he's graduating from the university, his business is successful in three locations, and potential for further expansion is still there. By this time, his service offerings have grown, and each location has 5 employees (a total of 15 employees).

Scenario 2: A middle-aged man takes early retirement from waged employment. He has always been passionate about environmental conservation. He takes his pension, and with the experience that he has, installs a biogas cooker at his home in the village and starts to train his fellow villagers on the same. As the green energy technology gains popularity, he employs two people to assist with both training and installing biogas cookers at his clients' homes. He also knows how to purify drinking water safely and has set up a water kiosk to sell safe drinking water. The popularity of this solution leads him to set up similar kiosks in five other locations and to increase his water purification capacity. Lastly, he is making char briquettes from recycled agricultural waste. Agricultural waste is readily available in the village where all the people engage in farming activities. He gathers the waste from the community and grows this line of business. The char briquettes are cheaper, environmentally friendly, and last longer than charcoal. He sells these to his neighbours.

The middle-aged man is a green entrepreneur, and the young man is simply an entrepreneur. What is the difference? The young man simply responded to a business opportunity. The middle-aged man was intentional in identifying business opportunities that were consistent with his values of environmental conservation. The key message here is that there are unique characteristics and needs of green entrepreneurs, which as we shall see later in the chapter, need to be addressed at the meso and macro levels.

Relating the motivation for green entrepreneurship to the popular 'push' and 'pull' factors categorisation (Dawson & Henley, 2012), green entrepreneurs appear to be more strongly motivated by pull factors (passion, values, opportunity, care for the environment) as opposed to push factors (need for survival). This is not surprising as green entrepreneurs are unlikely to be pushed to start green enterprises just because of the need to survive. However, there is a concurrence among researchers that there is still room for more studies on motivations for green entrepreneurship.

4.3.3 Green Entrepreneurship at the Meso Level: The Value Chain

For green businesses and indeed a green economy to emerge, all the activities of the value chain need to be 'green'. The Donor Committee for Enterprise Development (DCED) (2012) adopted the concept of Green Value Chain Development. "This is a systematic approach, integrating environmental support functions, environmental rules and regulations, and market players in greening the value chain" (DCED, 2012, p.1). It

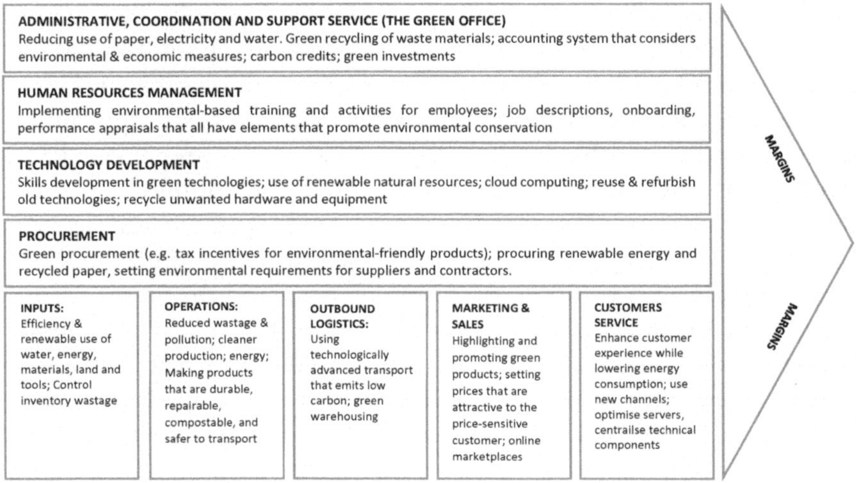

Fig. 4.2 Value chain for green businesses. Adapted from Donor Committee for Enterprise Development (2012) and Hasan et al. (2019)

aims to (i) ensure the sustainable use of natural resources; (ii) increase the share of renewable and recycled inputs; (iii) maximise material and energy efficiency at each stage of the process; and (iv) reduce negative environmental impacts at all points of the chain (Fig. 4.2).

Hasan et al. (2019) used the 3R (reduce, reuse, recycle) concept to argue for the green value chain. This approach is about *reducing* the consumption of natural resources, *reusing* resources where possible, and seeking opportunities to *recycle* waste as much as is feasible. If the 3Rs are considered in every stage of the value chain, a business can really claim to be green. Using Porter's, 1985 value chain analysis model and adapting from DCED (2012) and Hasan et al. (2019), the following value chain model for a green business could be envisaged.

This value chain provides multiple ideas and opportunities for green businesses in multiple industries including green energy, green production, recycling, green transport, green marketing, green financing, green technology, and green human resource practices, all of which promote conservation and responsible use of resources for enterprises at all stages. The idea of the chain is that if a firm needs energy, it gets green energy (from a green enterprise), if it needs production materials, it is able to source for materials that have been produced through green technologies, stationery at the office from recycled paper, and so on.

Green entrepreneurship offers opportunities to make money while taking care of the environment in several ways. First, it offers an opportunity to assess the approaches used in the green value chains. Second, there is an opportunity to create initiatives and programmes that can 'green' the value chains. Third is the opportunity to make environmental concerns the business of every consumer. Fourth is the opportunity to make the world a better place through environmental protection and preservation. As knowledge sharing and transfer continues in this field, green value chains will become more common and can one day be the norm for business.

4.3.4 Green Entrepreneurship at the Macro Level: An Ecosystem for Green Entrepreneurship

At the macro stage, Vatansever and Arun (2016) identified three primary factors that pave the way for green entrepreneurship. Legislation is the first factor. The law plays a key role in environmental economics as businesses try to ensure they avoid penalties, which stimulates green innovations.

A second factor is the social networks in which green entrepreneurs work together with research organisations and universities to grow the market for green goods. The networks developed may differ geographically, technologically, and by sectors. As such, some networks may focus on green energy, while others focus on waste management or green products. The third factor is sustaining competitive advantage by being aware of the market and competitive rivalry. By implementing green practices, firms can minimise their running costs by reducing energy use and recycling materials.

Isenberg's model of an entrepreneurship ecosystem "categorised the **entrepreneurship ecosystem into six domains:** a conducive **culture,** enabling **policies and leadership,** the availability of appropriate **finance,** quality **human capital,** venture-friendly **markets** for products, and a range of institutional and infrastructural **supports**" (Isenberg, 2011, p. 7). The World Bank (2017) added an important domain—technology. These domains are presented in Fig. 4.3. Though generic, the domains represent highly complex and interactive relationships between their components. These interactions are adaptable to different sectors and, therefore, can be analysed in context-specific ways.

The green entrepreneurship ecosystem suggests the need for multiple interventions simultaneously. First is the need for policy support to green entrepreneurs. Second, like most entrepreneurs, green entrepreneurs need financing, not just at the start-up stage, but for scaling up. The 4As of financing—accessible, affordable, appropriate, and adequate—need to be considered. Third, access to markets is critical.

Challenges often associated with marketing green products need to be addressed. These include access to market information, the fact that the market may be perceived as not ready for green products which are considered costlier by the price-sensitive customer and/or the market not being aware of the value of purchasing green products. Fourth, as most green enterprises tend to be sole proprietorships, they tend to lack the diversity of skills and competencies required to develop viable green

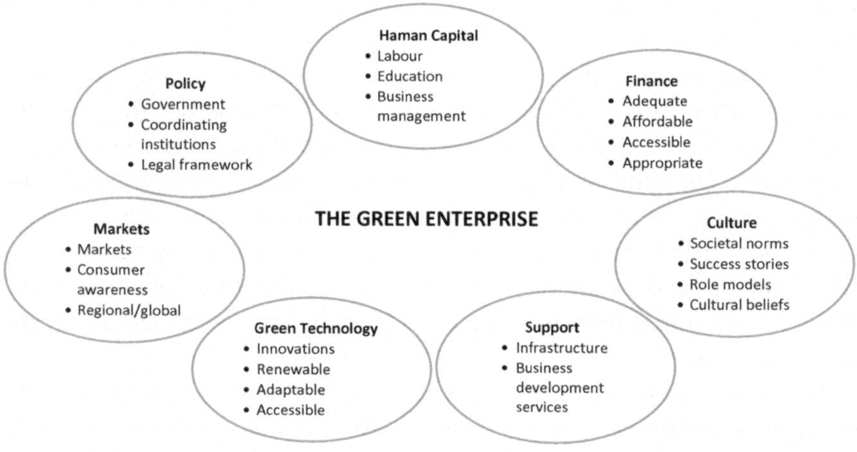

Fig. 4.3 Ecosystem for green entrepreneurship. Adapted from Isenberg's model for an entrepreneurship ecosystem (2011)

businesses. They need access to education and training, mentors, coaches, and business counsellors to enable them to grow, scale up, and even get viable partners.

Additionally, at the national level, it is important to value and embed entrepreneurship education in the curriculum. This builds the critical mass of individuals able and willing to engage in entrepreneurship and positively presents entrepreneurship as a viable career option. Fifth is the need for access to appropriate green technology that is renewable and adaptable, especially at production points.

Sixth is the need for an entrepreneurial mindset and culture that can stimulate business growth. This includes having mentors, role models, success stories, and societal norms that promote trust and a positive attitude towards entrepreneurs and entrepreneurship in general. Finally, is the need for support institutions that include foundations, non-governmental organisations, corporates, business development service providers, and research institutions, all of which collaborate to provide technical support to the enterprises. Overall is the need for coordination of these multiple players. Multi-sectoral agencies set up by governments in relevant trade and industry ministries could play this critical coordination role.

Overall, when the green entrepreneurship ecosystem works in harmony, great successes can be registered. For example, when the entrepreneur is receiving a quality entrepreneurship education; has role models (or experience); and has access to green technology, markets, and support in setting up the enterprise (micro level); and when investors and financial institutions create funding mechanisms to support green businesses (meso level); while the government through policies and regulations provide incentives and an enabling environment for green businesses to thrive (macro level), then the chances of success increase significantly. And because success breeds success, the successful enterprises provide feedback that enhances the seven domains of the green entrepreneurship ecosystem. Figure 4.4 summarises interactions at these three levels.

The arrows A, B, and C in Fig. 4.4 represent interactions between the three levels. The levels reinforce each other through the engagement and learning that happens at each level. This consequently informs and shapes the other levels.

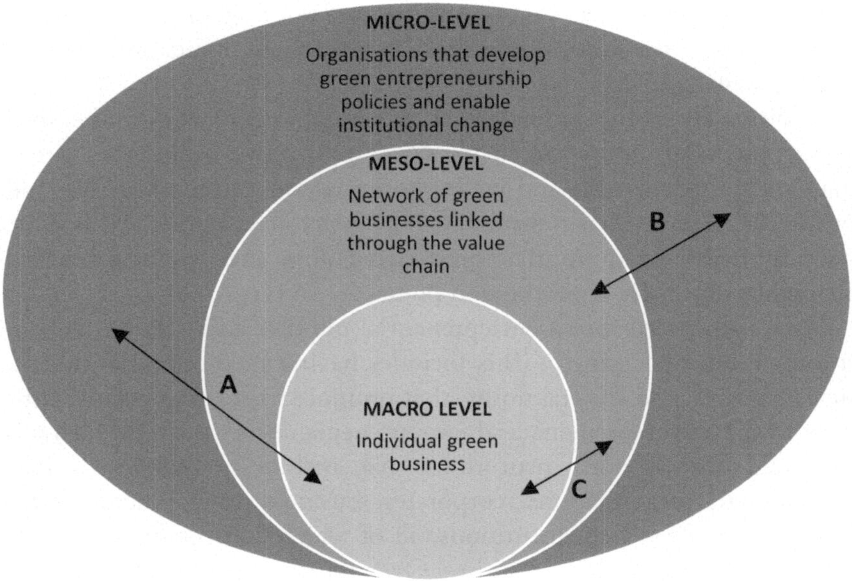

Fig. 4.4 Interactions at the three levels. Source: Author (2021)

4.3.5 Integrating the Three Levels: The Kenya Climate Innovation Centre Case Study

The next section presents a case study of the Kenya Climate Innovation Centre, an initiative of the World Bank that has since taken a life of its own and registered as a Kenyan company. The case study demonstrates how KCIC has been operating in the green entrepreneurship space since its inception eight years ago, and how it is promoting green entrepreneurship at the micro, meso, and macro levels.

At the micro level, capacity building, technical assistance, coaching, and mentorship are provided to small and medium-sized enterprises. They also get start-up financing for enterprises in five focus areas of the Centre (presented in the case study). Later they are provided with individualised services aimed at preparing them for larger investments and growth.

At the meso level are the incubation hub, accelerator hub, the Seed Fund, market development, market intelligence, and the Centre itself (KCIC) that provides business advisory services and is documenting evidence of green entrepreneurship for policy and practical interventions. Additionally, there are investors, commercial banks, and business partners that support ideation, prototyping, and testing of products before commercialisation.

At the macro level are institutions such as the World Bank, the Danish Government, the European Union, and the Kenyan Government and relevant government ministries. These institutions support policy interventions, regulations, and strategies to promote green entrepreneurship at the national and global levels. There are also academic and research institutions involved in policy advice, advocacy, and research. The measurable outcomes and successes of this initiative documented below do point to the value of the ecosystem created by KCIC.

Case Study—Kenya Climate Innovation Centre

History

In 2009, the World Bank conducted an assessment on how enterprises, especially small and medium-sized enterprises, could contribute to addressing the climate change challenge. The idea was to set up incubation and accelerator hubs to promote green enterprises that had a focus on climate change.

They identified seven countries for the assessment, among them Kenya, which was eventually selected as the first county ever to host such a hub. This was in 2012. The World Bank obtained funding to do three things. First was to establish an incubation hub. Second was to set up a Seed Fund to fund the incubated businesses as they started scaling up, after which investors could take over funding them. Third was to fund World Bank's administrative services so they could offer support including capacity building, technical support, setting up the infrastructure for the hub, and monitoring the activities of the hub and the Fund (World Bank, 2016).

After a rigorous Call for Proposals and evaluation exercise to identify firms to implement the project (to manage both the hub and Fund), a consortium of four institutions—PricewaterhouseCoopers, Strathmore

University, Global Village Energy Partnership (GVEP) International, and Kenya Industrial Research and Development Institute (KIRDI) won the tender and were initially awarded USD 4.5 million to run the project for four years (2012–2016). This consortium became the Kenya Climate Innovation Centre (KCIC). The consortium was particularly unique as it brought together a diverse set of skills from a private sector firm (PwC), an international NGO (GVEP), a government institution (KIRDI), and an academic institution (Strathmore University).

During the four-year period that the project was running, it became apparent that the initiatives and activities of the project would need to be sustained beyond the four years; therefore, KCIC was registered as a company in 2015. The benefits of registration as an autonomous entity included its ability to fundraise for its activities beyond the four years, which meant that it could be sustainable after World Bank funding ended. The consortium came to an end in 2016 as the registered company took over the running of the projects. A nine-member board of directors now governs KCIC.

The Areas of Focus

KCIC focuses on green enterprises in five areas:

(a) ***Green energy***: Assists SMEs in realising the opportunities in the renewable energy sector and the development of the industry. KCIC also works with policy makers to establish an enabling regulatory framework.
(b) ***Agribusiness***: Assistance is given to agribusinesses developing innovative agricultural technologies that improve the efficiency of small-scale farms.
(c) ***Water management***: Supports green enterprises that provide innovative water products for safe, clean water and water treatment.
(d) ***Waste management***: The emphasis is on green businesses that innovate recycling and disposal solutions for a variety of waste products.
(e) ***Commercial forestry***: The technologies and green enterprises funded focus on forestry conservation, afforestation, and responsible forestry harvesting.

The Needs of Green Enterprises and KCIC's Response

The World Bank conducted a needs assessment that revealed five key challenge areas that needed to be addressed to promote green entrepreneurship.

First, for entrepreneurs interested in green enterprises, these were largely innovators, and not necessarily businesspeople. As such, there was need to provide them with skills, tools, and insights that would help them translate their innovations to businesses. This need created the function of Business Advisory Services within KCIC. The entrepreneurs receive technical assistance, mentorship in business management, and business training that equips them with the skills required to transform technologies into viable enterprises. KCIC also enables the growth of the market for goods produced by clean tech entrepreneurs.

The second challenge was access to finance. This included assessing the appropriate type of financing for businesses. Three funding mechanisms were identified to address this need. These three mechanisms are currently in place. First is the 'proof of concept'. This has a matching fund structure in which the entrepreneur is expected to contribute 50 per cent of the resources they need. A successful concept is promoted to the second mechanism and receives early-stage financing of up to USD 100,000 to translate the business concept into a viable business. The third stage is financed through a KCIC subsidiary—Kenya Climate Ventures Fund. KCV Fund was established in 2016 and the World Bank awarded it a USD 5 million grant. KCV funds green enterprises to the tune of USD 400,000. In this third stage, KCIC also prepares businesses to be investor-ready and move to commercialisation (e.g., by training them on how to pitch their businesses and clarifying their business models). Businesses that have reached this stage are then able to attract funds from investors or commercial banks.

The third challenge was access to information. This included technological information, access to markets, knowledge and technology transfer mechanisms, and research on various business sectors. KCIC provides this information as well as enhances awareness and adoption of green solutions.

The fourth challenge was enabling a green business environment. Among the key issues were regulations, quality standards, taxation, and an appropriate policy framework to support green businesses. To create visibility for green entrepreneurship, KCIC lobbied government to be included in the Kenya Vision 2030 Economic Blueprint, as one of the key economic pillar projects. In 2017/2018, KCIC was accepted as a Vision 2030 project, which meant it had the support of key government ministries, including the Treasury, the Ministry of Finance, and the Ministry of Planning and National Development to push the agenda for green enterprises. KCIC harnesses the expertise of innovators, and academic and research organisations to advise on government regulations, initiatives, and plans that seek to promote the adoption of profitable green enterprises. Policy support, advocacy, and research continue to be the main areas of intervention.

The fifth challenge was access to facilities. This included space for setting up the business incubation hub. This was made available at the Strathmore University Business School building. Training facilities, meeting venues for coaching and mentorship, networking events, meetings with investors, and other support services to the entrepreneurs were made available through the incubation hub. KCIC also works with partners to provide spaces for idea testing and demonstration, initial production, and manufacturing at negotiated rates. KCIC also recognised that incubation was insufficient to scale up businesses and so created an accelerator hub as well. The accelerator identifies enterprises that meet a particular threshold and have the capacity to scale up to become established businesses.

The Growth of KCIC

As the initial funding by the World Bank came to an end in December 2016, KCIC had developed a relationship with the Danish Government, through which it received USD 15 million for a five-year project (2016–2020). This project ends in December 2020. KCIC has been able to fundraise USD 50 million for its third phase that will commence in January 2021 and run for another five years. The European Union, the Danish Government, and some US-based foundations are funding the third phase.

Currently, KCIC makes a Call for Proposals every six months for green businesses interested in joining either the incubation hub or the accelerator hub. Thirty enterprises are admitted to each hub per cohort. The incubator is a 12-month programme that works with start-ups and early-stage enterprises that have a prototype. The support provided through the incubator programme serves two purposes: validation of the prototype and generation of initial revenues. By the end of the programme, the green enterprises funded are expected to have developed their product, refined the business model, and achieved market entry.

Those that successfully go through the incubator programme graduate to the KCIC Green-Tech Accelerator programme for another 12 months. The accelerator programme supports businesses that are generating revenues and looking to scale. The focus is on measurable growth in customer numbers, revenues, market tractions, and market share. The enterprises are provided with highly individualised services with the aim of setting them up for rapid growth and preparing them for investment. The expected outcomes for enterprises at this stage are funds raised from external sources, team development, process optimisation, and rapid revenue growth. Successful enterprises join the KCIC alumni network and are required to continue to provide data to KCIC about their successes, growth, and other measures of progress. This is documented both for fundraising and for capacity building of other entrepreneurs.

As of August 2020, about 300 green businesses had benefitted from KCIC capacity building initiatives, of which about 250 were successful (registering over 80 per cent success rate). This success has contributed to investor and donor confidence, resulting in raising additional funds for subsequent cycles. Competition to participate in the incubation hub is very high, with an acceptance rate of about 5 per cent. The rigorous selection process has contributed to the high success rate.

Key Successes

Some of the successes registered by KCIC include the following:

Sustainability: KCIC is in its third cycle of funding, having successfully completed two cycles. It has also broadened the funding base and lobbied for Kenya Government support and visibility, all of which have enhanced its credibility.

Successful businesses: Over 250 green businesses have been incubated and continue to grow and expand. They have cumulatively raised over USD 50 million for their businesses.

Job creation: The KCIC initiative has created more than 9000 jobs through 250 businesses. Some of the jobs are for employees of the green businesses, while others are for suppliers in various parts of the value chain.

Environmental impact: The green businesses can identify tangible environmental benefits to which they have contributed. These include clean energy use (especially for lighting and cooking), water management, recycling, and better agricultural inputs for sustainable and organic farming.

Ecosystem support: KCIC has engaged with stakeholders at various levels to support the ecosystem for entrepreneurship. At the policy level, they have lobbied government to ensure inclusion in the Kenya Vision 2030 Economic Blueprint, which unlocks resources and enhances a supportive policy framework for green businesses, especially on taxation matters. At the business level, they have supported the incubated businesses through capacity building, technical assistance, access to financing, access to markets, and raising the standards and quality of products. With regard to human capital, KCIC has continued to partner with Strathmore University Business School to offer training services, research, business coaching, mentoring, and business advisory services. With regard to building a culture of green entrepreneurship, KCIC is documenting the success stories of businesses they have supported to serve as case studies and models for green entrepreneurship.

Key Challenges

The nature of businesses and technical assistance available: The green entrepreneurship space is still in its infancy and there are diverse businesses that entrepreneurs begin. It is not always feasible to get the best match between an entrepreneur and a coach/mentor or to provide them with the technical assistance that precisely meets their individual business needs, especially where they are highly specialised.

Awareness creation to create demand for green products: KCIC has focused largely on the supply side of green enterprises—providing financing and developing skills so that businesses can grow and develop products that are 'green'. However, the market is not always aware, or may not care about 'green products'. It also does not help that 'green products' are perceived to be costlier than the conventional ones. To a price-sensitive customer, there may be little incentive to purchase a 'green product'.

Next Steps

Results-based financing: One shift in the business model is the introduction of results-based financing. This means linking financing to the actual outcomes of the business. Once a business meets a certain level of sales target or revenues or other measures of success, it can unlock a predetermined amount of financing. That will contribute to both raising awareness of products and promoting enterprise growth.

Islamic financing: Plans are underway to introduce Islamic financing in the next cycle of financing enterprises.

Creating awareness of the need for 'green products': Working in partnership with Strathmore University Business School, KCIC is setting up a Centre for Sustainability that will have a think-tank, capacity building, research, and mentors and coaches in green entrepreneurship, as well as documenting best green business practices.

Establishing more incubation hubs: KCIC has introduced eight incubation hubs across Kenya, to enhance outreach and accessibility to green entrepreneurs.

Virtual incubation: As the demand for incubation of green businesses continues to rise, there is a need to move to a virtual incubation programme and platform to reach more entrepreneurs at a lower cost. The virtual platform would be used for training, mentoring, providing 'how-to' tools, and networking, and for the entrepreneurs to provide progress data.

Market access: Working with partners such as supermarkets and other distribution channels, KCIC is helping entrepreneurs to push their products to the market.

Case study documentation: Green enterprises present great opportunities for case writing and documentation on how to develop and grow the green entrepreneurship debate, research, and knowledge base. A green enterprise case bank is planned for the next funding cycle of the Centre. This will also contribute to building more evidence in support of green entrepreneurship as well as tangible examples of green enterprises that others can learn from. Documentation of green value chains will also be beneficial.

Coincidentally, the Strathmore University Business School building in which KCIC is housed is itself a green building. In 2011, the building received the Leadership in Energy and Environmental Design (LEED) Certification, and in 2012, the African Real Estate and Housing Finance (AREHF) Academy Awards recognised it as the Best Green Building Development in Africa.

Acknowledgement: The author wishes to thank the Chief Executive Officer of KCIC for availing time for interviews to write this case study.

4.4 Conclusion

At the heart of green entrepreneurship is the personal motivation of the entrepreneur who desires to set up a green enterprise. Although there may be multiple interventions and policies to promote and support green entrepreneurship, the individual entrepreneur remains the focal point (micro level). However, isolated and fragmented efforts by individual entrepreneurs are limited in the extent to which they can create a green and sustainable economy.

A critical mass of enterprises and value chains are needed to start to build a green entrepreneurship ecosystem. This role is best played at the meso level that allows for the creation of multiple green businesses along the value chain and can lobby for access to resources and influence policy. This leads to macro-level interventions that include policy development, as well as building an entrepreneurship culture, infrastructure, and support for education, which together build the enabling environment for green entrepreneurship and sustainable economic development.

References

Boluk, K. A., & Mottiar, Z. (2014). Motivations of social entrepreneurs: Blurring the social contribution and profits dichotomy. *Social Enterprise Journal, 10*(1), 53–68.

Christensen, C. M. (1997). *The innovator's dilemma: When new technologies cause great firms to fail.* Harvard Business School Press.

Cohen, B., & Winn, M. (2007). Market imperfections, opportunity and sustainable entrepreneurship. *Journal of Business Venturing, 22*(1), 29–49.

Dawson, C., & Henley, A. (2012). Push versus pull entrepreneurship: An ambiguous distinction? *International Journal of Entrepreneurial Behaviour & Research, 18*(6), 697–719.

DeMartino, R., & Barbato, R. (2003). Differences between women and men MBA entrepreneurs: Exploring family flexibility and wealth creation as career motivators. *Journal of Business Venturing, 18*(6), 815–832.

Donor Committee for Enterprise Development. (2012). *Green Value Chains to Promote Green Growth.* Retrieved August 6, 2020, from https://www.enterprise-development.org/wp-content/uploads/Green_Value_Chains_to_Promote_Green_Growth.pdf.

Greent Project. (2012). *An attempt to define green entrepreneurship.* National Centre of Competence in Research Policy Brief No. 6.

Hasan, M., Nekmahmud, M., Yajuana, L., & Patwary, M. A. (2019). Green business value chain: A systematic review. *Sustainable Production and Consumption, 20*, 326–339.

Isenberg, D. (2011). *The entrepreneurship ecosystem strategy as a new paradigm for economy policy: Principles for cultivating entrepreneurship.* Babson Entrepreneurship Ecosystem Project, Babson College.

Kirkwood, J., & Walton, S. (2010). What motivates ecopreneurs to start businesses? *International Journal of Entrepreneurial Behaviour & Research, 16*(3), 204–228.

Linnanen, L. (2016). An insider's experiences with environmental entrepreneurship. In M. Schaper (Ed.), *Making Ecopreneurs: Developing Sustainable Entrepreneurship* (pp. 71–88). Routledge.

Mirzanti, I. R., Simatupang, T. M., & Larso, D. (2015). Entrepreneurship policy implementation model in Indonesia. *International Journal of Entrepreneurship and Small Business, 26*(4), 399–415.

Porter, M. (1985). *Competitive advantage: Creating and sustaining superior performance.* Free Press.

Schumpeter, J. A. (1934). *The theory of economic development: An inquiry into profits, capital, credit, interest and the business cycle.* Harvard Economic Studies.

Vatansever, C., & Arun, K. (2016). What colour is the green entrepreneurship in Turkey? *Journal of Entrepreneurship in Emerging Economies, 8*(1), 25–44.

Vlados, C., & Chatzinikolaou, D. (2020). Macro, meso, and micro policies for strengthening entrepreneurship: Towards an integrated competitiveness policy. *Journal of Business & Economic Policy, 7*(1), 1–12.

World Bank. (2016). *The Kenya Climate Innovation Center: How it operates and lessons for clean technology incubation*. Climate Technology Program (CTP) In Brief Series No.2. Washington, D.C.: World Bank.
World Bank. (2017). *Igniting climate entrepreneurship in Morocco: Findings from the climate entrepreneurship and innovation ecosystem diagnostic*. World Bank.
Yousafzai, M. T., Junaid, M., & Shah, S. (2016). Entrepreneurship and value creation: Curriculum at macro, meso, and micro level. *NICE Research Journal, 1*, 19–35.

5

SME Green Marketing

Albert Martins

5.1 Introduction

Reducing the environmental impact of small and medium-sized enterprises (SMEs) in both manufacturing and services is a key success factor in sustainable management in developing countries. SMEs play a major role in most economies, particularly in emerging economies, where they are the key drivers of development in terms of creating jobs, wealth, improving livelihoods, eradicating absolute poverty, and making a significant contribution to gross domestic product (GDP). For example, SMEs account for over 90% of businesses in Africa and employ about 60% of workers; women and youth significantly included as employees (ITC, 2018).

Large businesses, which are in the minority worldwide, recognise the advantages of cleaner production in terms of reduced costs of resources, environmental compliance, and customer relations. However, most

A. Martins (✉)
University of Professional Studies, Accra, Accra, Ghana
e-mail: albert.martins@upsamail.edu.gh

E. K. Adae et al. (eds.), *Responsible Management in Emerging Markets*, Sustainable Development Goals Series, https://doi.org/10.1007/978-3-030-76563-7_5

SMEs are not concerned with sustainable management when performing their businesses. In spite of their relevance in emerging economies, SMEs face resource constraints and usually lack knowledge, skills, finances, and human resources (Amegbe et al., 2017). Thus, the willingness and capability of SMEs to adopt green marketing (GM) and sustainable practices and to seize green business opportunities generally is hindered by size-related resource constraints, skill deficit, and knowledge limitations.

Sustainable management aims at meeting the needs of the present without compromising the ability of future generations to meet their own needs (World Commission on Environment and Development, 1987). SMEs need to recognise that, as important suppliers of goods and services, improving their green marketing efforts will offer them significant business opportunities. Green marketing practices by SMEs will help develop a long-run environmental vision resulting in the creation of better environmental performance and competitiveness (Kumar, 2015).

The objective of this chapter, therefore, is to examine the concept of GM as operationalised by SMEs and to encourage GM practices by small firms to achieve competitive advantage and improved business performance. The remaining section of the chapter describes the drivers of SME GM practices, SME GM strategies, Green Marketing Mix framework for SMEs, and examples of GM practices by SMEs from emerging economies. Subsequently, GM implementation challenges among small firms and processes of evaluating GM performance are discussed. The chapter concludes by examining the impact of SME GM practices on society and various aspects of business operations.

5.2 Green Marketing

GM refers to the holistic management process responsible for identifying, anticipating, and satisfying the needs of customers and society, profitably and sustainably (Do Paco et al., 2009). It is considered as a company's effort to design, promote, price, and distribute products in a way that promotes environmental protection (Polonsky, 2011). GM is the development and promotion of products and services that yield both economic and environmental benefits by reducing the utilisation of resources and the creation of waste. It involves the marketing strategies used to achieve a firm's financial as well as strategic goals while reducing its negative impact on the environment (Leonidou et al., 2013).

GM-motivated products and services come with a sustainable and lower environmental impact than traditional products or services (Danish Enterprise and Construction Authority, 2010). Other practices include, but are not limited to, the adoption of processes of manufacturing that do not harm the environment (Jabbour et al., 2015). GM has a broader multi-dimensional scope covering several categories such as consumer goods, industrial goods, and services (Polonsky, 1994; Chen, 2009) as well as thematic areas such as biodiversity, clean energy, green technologies, sustainable agriculture, waste management, water, sanitation, and health (SEED, 2020).

5.2.1 Green Marketing and SMEs

SME GM reflects small firms' responsibility towards society, ensuring they conduct their business activities driven by the goal of minimising consequences that threaten the environment. Conservation of the environment, management and reduction of waste, compliance with regulations, recycling, and controlling pollution are some of the practices that characterise sustainable SME GM (Cross, 2019). The importance of SMEs in emerging economies indicates that their environmental impact could be so significant, requiring more research into environmental management practices among smaller firms (Amegbe et al., 2017).

Though many tend to tag GM with larger businesses, it is becoming increasingly clear in emerging economies that it is not the preserve of only large businesses. It has been identified as a systematic tool for SMEs, indicating how competitive they can be (Turyakira et al., 2014). SMEs' decision-making processes, norms, values, access to resources, image, and sensitivity to brand reputation are some of the aspects that researchers suggest may differentiate SMEs from large corporations and thus help to explain differences in their environmental practices. The existence of such differences means that one cannot simply scale down the environmental practices employed by large organisations to fit the SME context.

The improvement of environmental performance by SMEs in both manufacturing and services is a significant business opportunity for SMEs themselves as important suppliers of goods and services (Chahal et al., 2014). Although SMEs' size and limited capacity do not easily accommodate green practices, one feature of SMEs, which predisposes them to succeed through implicit and reactive means to green challenges is their flexibility (Kumar, 2015).

5.2.2 Types of Green SMEs

Three kinds of green SMEs have been identified by the Organisation for Economic Co-operation and Development (OECD) (OECD, 2013). These are described as follows:

(1) Eco-innovators are SMEs engaged in eco-innovation, implementation of a novel or enhanced product or technique, or novel marketing methods or organisational process in business practices, workplace organisation, or external relationships that lessen the environmental effect.

An example of an eco-innovator is *Coliba Ltd.*, a leading plastic waste recycling company in Ghana. As an eco-innovator, its Coliba 2.0 is the first mobile app in Africa that is intended to manage plastic waste within West Africa. This effort represents an innovative approach for addressing the plastic waste pollution via a franchise model that puts Coliba Rangers (Waste pickers) onto a digital platform. This allows households, organisations, and communities to request recycling services at the press of a button.[1]

(2) Eco-entrepreneurs, due to their quest for novel opportunities and commercialisation of these opportunities, are similar to traditional entrepreneurs. That notwithstanding, eco-entrepreneurs differ in how their objectives and motivations are strategic. Also, they consider sustainability as a goal of entrepreneurship (OECD, 2013).

Grameen Shakti is an outfit that typifies eco-entrepreneurs. It is situated in Bangladesh and supplies power to rural communities. Its

[1] https://coliba.com.gh.

product—Solar Home Systems—relies on solar energy, which ensures affordability and improves access to energy (Krämer & Herrndorf, 2012).

(3) **Eco-adopters** include a vast majority of SMEs that believe that green practices are about adopting environmental technologies and sustainable business systems. Unlike eco-innovators and eco-entrepreneurs, eco-adopters do not usually consider sustainability as an aspect of their core business model. Rather, they consider greening practices as compliance with environmental regulations. Thus, it is important to encourage SMEs in this category to move beyond sheer compliance (OECD, 2013, 2018).

5.3 Drivers of SME Green Marketing

5.3.1 Market Opportunities

There are SMEs that pursue GM because of the inherent business opportunities it presents, particularly due to its capacity to improve market share and penetrate new markets from eco-innovation, eco-entrepreneurship, and eco-adoption among SMEs. SMEs can take advantage of increasing market demand for green products, and grow their market share or penetrate new markets, particularly due to their small size and flexibility (UNEP, 2014).

For instance, in 2015, a consumer survey reported that 66% of worldwide respondents stated their readiness to pay premium prices for sustainable goods (Nielsen, 2015). SMEs in emerging economies could leverage this market opportunity by producing sustainable products and charging premium prices. There are many avenues through which SMEs could get commercial benefits from pursuing GM, including acquiring intellectual property rights for green products, thus giving them a competitive edge in the green marketplace (UNEP, 2014).

A number of SMEs are also drawn to GM due to profit opportunities. Besides the benefits which drive SMEs to GM discussed above, trade finance opportunities and other opportunities that characterise the green sector, as well as government and private sector incentives, contribute to attracting SMEs to GM. For example, the Sustainable Energy Fund for Africa, a multi-donor Special Fund managed by the African Development Bank since 2011, provides catalytic finance to unlock private sector investments in renewable energy and energy efficiency (SEFA, 2019).

5.3.1.1 An Example: Green Finance Opportunity

The International Trade Centre (ITC), in partnership with the African Guarantee Fund (AGF) for SMEs through the support of Nordic Development Fund (NDF), has expanded access to climate-focused finance for SMEs in Africa through a memorandum of understanding signed in December 2016. The collaboration introduced a specialised green-guarantee tool developed to unlock funds for SMEs to invest in low-carbon, green growth, and climate-resilient development (ITC, 2017).

5.3.2 Competition and Competitive Advantage

Lee (2008) observed a large sample of Korean SMEs and concluded that they were moving from a command and control method to a market and competition approach. In the current dispensation, SMEs are empowered to respond to the demands of green consumers and to compete with competitors' green offerings (Grant, 2008), while they benchmark their competitors in practising GM and in formulating business strategies. According to Yuningsih and Silaningsih (2019), SMEs capable of implementing environmentally friendly marketing strategies enjoy a competitive advantage.

5.3.3 Government Pressure

Initiatives to reduce green impact include regulatory and government-led programmes. SMEs comply with government regulations, which demand conformity with green practices. Government regulations aim at protecting consumers and society. For instance, Ashurst (2020) reported that 64% of business leaders in Asian G20 countries feel great pressure from the government to invest in low-carbon power. Government pressure was also identified as the largest source of duress for low-carbon investment in the region. Other sources of pressure cited by the research were non-government organisations (NGOs), corporate boards, and institutional investors. Among SMEs in India, current legislation and future legislation were among the top five drivers for the implementation of integrated GM (Gandhi et al., 2018).

5.3.4 Stakeholders

Stakeholders, including buyers, suppliers, workers, and shareholders, hold the greatest influence on a company's strategy development and environmental policies. Raharjo (2019) suggests that stakeholders are the agents who make demands for businesses, including SMEs, to protect and preserve the environment. Employees represent the section of stakeholders who may push businesses to build environmentally friendly work environments.

5.3.5 Social Responsibility

There is a growing realisation among SMEs that they are part of a larger community and are expected to adopt responsible dispositions towards the environment and factor in the well-being of the environment within their business culture. Extreme climate events, such as extended periods of drought or frequent and more intense flooding, can provoke GM practices. In agriculture, for example, farmers may start to consider more sustainable water management solutions in response to prolonged droughts. In spite of all the benefits discussed above as motivators for SMEs to adopt GM, their willingness to implement sustainable practices and take advantage of green opportunities are frustrated by resource constraints as well as a lack of skills and knowledge.

5.4 Selected SME Green Marketing Strategies

5.4.1 Green Approaches

According to Cronin et al. (2011), there are three avenues leading to the adoption of GM to meet the expectations of respective stakeholders. These apply to SMEs.

(1) *Green Innovation*: This is a commonly known strategy in which new green products are developed, thus, positively signalling to stakeholders that the organisation is a green company.
(2) *Greening the Process*: This focuses on the firm's environmental commitments. The initiatives in this regard focus mainly on incorporating greening processes in the production of goods or the delivery of services.
(3) *Green Alliances*: This is where a company opts to utilise partnerships or networks to enhance its green orientation. This suggests that a company is orienting itself towards green practices.

5.4.2 Green Management

The indices that can be used to measure whether a company is applying green management include knowing which green benefits buyers are interested in per its product/service; innovation of products to assist customers to live greener lives; implementation of product life cycle management strategies; and management of products' environmental and social effects (Peng & Lin, 2008). Samsung (2016) conceptualised GM into more specific aspects that are applicable to SMEs:

(1) *Green Product*: Throughout the process of production, the goal should be to develop products or services that are environmentally friendly.
(2) *Green Process*: Using raw materials that are environmentally friendly in the process of production. Alternative technologies must be considered to ensure that energy-efficient resources are used.

(3) *Green Workplace*: The nature of the work environment is important in GM. The workplace must be made 'green' by ensuring there is a clean workplace environment, proper waste disposal, pollution control, and possession of management and recycling facilities.
(4) *Green Community*: By educating the community on the relevance of preserving the environment, the enterprise empowers the community leading to good relationships with loyal suppliers and with the environment.
(5) *Green Workforce*: The company positions itself through policies and procedures to engage workers who possess the training, education, and cultural comprehension of GM.

5.4.3 GM Innovation

Green innovation or 'eco-innovation' involves the development of new products and processes that reduce environmental impacts and improve customer and business values (Oxborrow, 2013). SMEs are not as resourceful as larger firms to carry out marketing innovations. However, they can leverage SME characteristics such as reduced goal conflicts, close customer relations, and quicker and more flexible response to changing market needs than bigger companies. Kumar (2015) conducted a study on small Indian firms and observed that GM innovations were based on six specific factors rather than the marketing mix elements. These are listed in Table 5.1.

5.4.4 Other SME Green Marketing Strategies

SMEs that are focused on financial profit and dedicated to environmental sustainability can achieve both by creating new business models and winning marketing strategies. SME managers can take a more effective approach to GM if they realise that a one-size-fits-all strategy does not work. Based on research, the author has proposed in Table 5.2, various strategies which could be implemented by SMEs for successful GM outcomes.

Table 5.1 SME green marketing innovation factors

Factor	Explanation
Marketing compliance	The ability of SMEs to comply with national and international environmental regulations.
Marketing strategic partnership	Promoting partnerships with other SMEs, focusing on common priorities leading to setting and achieving performance goals collectively.
Marketing environmental commitment	Creating strategic plans that establish SMEs' medium and long-term environmental visions, goals, and targets.
Marketing green team	The availability of a green team, a self-organised cross-functional team of workers of a company or a group of companies that assume responsibility corporately for the creation and implementation of GM policies.
Marketing benchmarking	Comparing the environmental, social, and economic performance of small businesses to that of industry standards and best practices, and quantitatively evaluating and enhancing them.
Marketing (environmental) ethical behaviour	Developing deliberate commitments to establish an ethical environment. It includes information relating to relationships with suppliers and buyers for environment-related privacy and confidentiality.

Source: Kumar (2015)

5.5 SME Green Marketing Mix

It has been established that for firms to be successful in GM, they must leverage the 8Ps of the GM Mix adapted from Liu et al. (2012), namely Product, Promotion and Branding, Planning, Process, People, Place, Positioning, and Project Management. In this section, the 8Ps have been extended to 9Ps to include price, which is considered very crucial to SMEs given their cost constraints. In the implementation of the GM strategy via marketing mix elements, Polonsky and Rosenberger (2001) argue for a holistic and integrated approach.

Table 5.2 Suggested SME green marketing strategies

Strategy	Remarks
Clear definition of eco-friendly brand	This ensures a full buy-in of environmental responsibility.
Creation of eco-friendly selling points	Some examples of eco-friendly selling points include • Low-energy solution • Recycled materials • Healthy living • Buy Fresh, Buy local • Non-toxic ingredients • Low waste (or emissions) • Chemical-free
Branding with green logos or signs	Some examples include a website, advertising, signage, business cards, packaging, vehicle graphics.
Investing in online marketing	To achieve cost-effectiveness.
Promoting local vendors	To minimise travel, gas consumption, and the impact of carbon emissions on the environment.
Seeking approvals and certifications	They act as major selling points for SMEs and provide a sense of authenticity.
Integrating technology	This can help SMEs reduce energy spending and resources needed, ultimately reducing their carbon footprint.

Source: Author (2020)

5.5.1 Product

A green product is a sustainable product intended to lessen its environmental impact in its entire life cycle and even after it is discarded. Green products are developed without utilising toxic chemicals and within a clean environment, have reduced or zero carbon footprint, are eco-efficient, utilise the least resources, have low or zero plastic footprint, come with eco-friendly packing, are capable of being recycled or reused, and are biodegradable in nature. Green products are judged by the entire process that goes into their production, and how they are perceived, as well as the effects they have on the environment.

5.5.2 Price

In going green, there is a perception that price is the major problem due to the inherently high cost and financial limitations that confront SMEs. Small firms may, therefore, adopt premium pricing in striving to meet customers' expectations, knowing customers will pay the premium price for what they perceive to be eco-friendly. Prices of green products may, therefore, be much higher than non-green products because the green ingredient may cost more than the conventional product, which creates a price gap referred to as the green pricing gap. As prices influence customers' purchase decisions, it is very significant that SMEs get their green pricing right.

5.5.3 Promotion and Branding

SME green promotion and branding is about communicating messages on green issues and sustainability. Social media is an inexpensive yet powerful media resource for SMEs to promote their products. Conventional SME environmental advertising usually comes in three forms: a statement of the SME's concern for the environment and a presentation of a corporate image of environmental responsibility, a portrayal of the manner the SME has altered its processes to show its commitment to improving the environment, and a description of specific environmental actions that it is engaged in and outcomes for which it assumes credit (Cross, 2019).

5.5.4 Planning

This aspect involves blending green targets into operational strategy as well as planning resources to achieve them. SMEs' planning goals should be designed to reduce waste, maximise resource efficiency, and use toxic-free ingredients and environmentally friendly procedures. Marketers should grow their GM plan by considering how they can create new opportunities for selling their products and deal with the challenges of competition. SMEs should assure its customers that its products or services are safe and that it is environmentally conscious from the production stage to sales stage.

5.5.5 Process

The process factor is about creating routines and systems to improve resource efficiency and lessen waste in SMEs operations. It could extend to empowering others in the supply chain, for example, suppliers, stakeholders, and buyers, to work in a green manner. The purpose is to ensure the sustainability of the supply chain's effort in the reduction of adverse environmental and social impact.

5.5.6 People

Green people are the staff or employees of green SMEs who are very important in driving the green agenda. They are responsible for developing and implementing green strategies. They can directly affect businesses and can directly influence customer satisfaction. SMEs' competitiveness and reputation depend on the green people strategy. Green staff should, therefore, be carefully recruited, trained, and equipped to ensure they have the awareness, passion, and skills for GM.

5.5.7 Place

Place is about developing alternative green scenarios for service delivery and ensuring the greenness of the physical evidence of the servicescape. SME GM practitioners must ensure that customers experience environmentally friendly service delivery platforms. It means they must encourage channel intermediaries to imbibe green practices. SMEs have to select operational locations that best serve them and their target market.

5.5.8 Positioning

A positioning strategy is about finding the right place for an organisation or a brand in the marketplace as well as in the mind of the buyer. Green SMEs may adopt positioning strategies that distinguish their brands from competitors due to the use of environmentally related attributes. Key green positioning strategies for SMEs to pursue may include 'green business', 'service reliability', 'social responsibility', 'healthy living', 'top-of-the-range', 'value for money', 'attractiveness', 'eco-friendliness', and 'safety', which can increase their long-term competitive advantage.

5.5.9 Project Management

The scope of green project management includes basic green buying and procurement, integration of clean production processes, complete quality environmental management, and green supply chain (Chou et al., 2017). Integrating sustainability into project management enables SMEs to adapt to the complexity of projects, lessen project crises, project terminations and disruptions, and mitigate the instability of project personnel. Additionally, it produces competitive advantage and economic benefits and encourages sustainable project outcomes (Gareis et al., 2010).

5.6 SME Green Marketing Practices

In emerging economies, SMEs are experimenting with strategies of production, development, and marketing green products that sustain the natural environment, care for the environment, meet their clients' expectations as well as generate profit for their businesses (Cross, 2019). Sector-specific GM practice examples are profiled in this section. The examples have been selected from SEED (https://seed.uno/enterprises), a global partner with the United Nations Environment and UNDP for action on sustainable development and green economy.

5.6.1 Biodiversity

Biodiverse SMEs conserve species, habitats, and ecosystems while integrating local, indigenous, and rural communities into their value chains.

Pro-Sofala Verde (PSV) *(Beira, Mozambique)* generates income and restores biodiversity through an innovative and inclusive value chain of eco-friendly high-grade honey production. Hives produced locally from sustainable forestry off-cuts are distributed to families who receive extensive training. Advanced bee-keepers receive additional training and incentive to mentor families in hive and bee maintenance and to ensure hygienic cropping. PSV buys community honey above market rates. After cropping and processing, affordable high-grade honey is marketed in one-portion honey sticks to urban areas, where most Mozambicans do not have access to nutritionally valuable honey. This creates jobs and improves natural resource management through reforestation and sustainable honey production practices that support biodiversity conservation.

5.6.2 Clean Energy

Clean energy SMEs promote resource-efficient and renewable energy solutions that equip energy-deprived communities with off-grid and low-carbon technologies.

Kencoco Enterprise (Mombasa, Kenya) improves cooking in rural Kenya. In addition to selling clean cookstoves, the enterprise produces charcoal briquettes made from coconut shells and husks. The coconut shell briquettes serve the community as a source of clean energy and help reduce deforestation. They are a practical, low-cost substitute for environmentally destructive fuels like firewood, kerosene, and wood charcoal. Kencoco's briquettes are more affordable than most existing fuel alternatives and are user-friendly, clean, and smokeless. The enterprise's products are sold directly to households and to retailers. Along the value chain, mainly women gain opportunities as suppliers of raw materials and sellers of charcoal briquettes in kiosks and markets.

5.6.3 Green Technologies

Green technologies SMEs use information and communication technologies to share agronomic practices and extend access to financing, develop e-commerce markets for sustainable consumption and transport, and process agricultural waste into energy sources for heating and cooking.

Dichung.vn (Hà Nội, Vietnam) is a platform which runs on the blend between social network and e-commerce marketplace. Dichung.vn, as an enterprise interested in reducing traffic jams and environmental pollution in Vietnam, works on an online platform and acts as a middleman connecting users to overcome barriers to vehicle-sharing. This platform provides people who are ready to share or sell their seats in vehicles with the opportunity to find others who need these seats. The main objective of this enterprise is to introduce a novel transport culture in Vietnam in the form of ride-sharing. Consequently, it will minimise traffic jams and tackle the huge problem of city smog. It likewise works with a transport company to offer standardised ride-sharing services (taxi-sharing and vanpools) via a B2C platform.

5.6.4 Sustainable Agriculture

Sustainable agricultural SMEs deliver entrepreneurial solutions to improve the agricultural sector's resource efficiency and crop yields while ensuring that communities are able to adapt to climate change.

Aikya Organics (Kanpur, India) is an alternative organic produce value chain managed by female farmers. Its mission is to create an alternative agricultural value-chain among women-led farmer groups. It promotes an alternative eco-inclusive agro value-chain. Their activities include training female farmers on cheap inputs, natural farming techniques, and setting up of seed and tool banks as well as solar-powered processing and packaging facilities. They ensure the availability and affordability of organic products, shortening the value chain. The produce is sold through B2B and B2C channels, with personally branded organic stores.

5.6.5 Waste Management

Waste management SMEs provide products and services that minimise environmental pollution and health risks associated with waste accumulation and mismanagement.

Intelligent Waste Management Solutions (InteWaste), situated in Lilongwe, Malawi, provides recycled briquettes as a reliable and sustainable energy source. By involving women and youth groups, InteWaste spreads knowledge about the possibilities of briquettes to even further segments of the population and offers them income, education, and employment. Other products offered are compost manure to promote smart agricultural practices among smallholder farmers. The company recruits production, packaging, and sales persons from local youth and women, thereby providing them with formal income and education.

5.6.6 Water, Sanitation, and Health

SMEs in the water, sanitation, and health sector design products and services that support healthy and sustainable livelihoods through improved water security and greater access to adequate sanitation facilities.

WASHKing (Accra, Ghana) is a manufacturer, supplier, and installer of environmentally friendly bio-digester toilets. The toilets are made locally by artisans utilising locally accessible materials. The WashKing innovation uses a biodegradable powder manufactured in India for digestion. Furthermore, the treatment system separates sewage and transforms it into safe water for agriculture or landscaping. The key target groups are low-income urban families and organisations with low or no access to toilets. WashKing offers flexible payment terms, training on hygiene, and after-sales services to facilitate customer loyalty.

5.6.7 Ecotourism

SME Tourist sites ensure environmental responsibility by safeguarding, preserving, and improving nature and the physical environment to facilitate long-term health and life-sustaining ecosystems. They use inexpensive social media sites for promotion.

Niko Green Travels (Kenya) provides integrated green travel solutions that align with international leisure and business travel by empowering communities and improving the environment. The enterprise promotes local, sustainable tourism that creates jobs, promotes local cultures, and preserves the environment and natural resources. Ultimately, they aim to generate adequate carbon finance to invest in carbon offsetting projects, namely clean energy, water filters, biodiversity restoration, and plastic waste management.

5.7 SME Green Marketing Implementation Challenges

Challenges that plague SMEs in addressing environmental issues and implementing green practices as well as proposed remedies are discussed in this section.

GM Is an Emerging Concept: GM is still a relatively new concept in most emerging economies. Usually, SMEs are oblivious of the numerous and financially attractive opportunities for environmental improvement. Some SMEs based in rural areas are still unaware of and cannot reap the full benefits of GM. There is a misconception that protecting the environment comes with technical and cost problems. Governments and Green Movements should intensify and extend green advocacy.

Access to Funding: Green SMEs face challenges when trying to access commercial financing at market rates, given their high-risk profile, low liquidity, and uncertain profitability. Access to funds can be problematic because of how young the eco-innovation market is and the challenges with correctly pricing the risk of investment. Government and private sector financial institutions should assist SMEs in this regard.

Implementation Costs: Green products require a great deal of investment and innovation, making them more expensive than the available alternatives on the market. For instance, installing a solar energy system, recycling, and water treatment technology can be costly. Cost reduction in green-related practices is mainly achieved based on the efficiency of the enterprise, as fewer inputs are needed to produce the same output (OECD, 2018). Listed in Table 5.3 are some of the avenues for cost reduction.

Lack of Appropriate Skills: SMEs usually lack the know-how, expertise, skills, funds, and human resources to create the desired changes towards the wholesale implementation of GM practices (Lee, 2008). The willingness and capability of SMEs to adopt sustainable practices are often inhibited by size-related resource constraints. SMEs would need to leverage membership of trade associations for sponsored skills development and training programmes.

Customer Attitude: In some emerging economies such as Ghana, some customers are reluctant to pay a premium for green products, as they remain uninformed of the benefits of going green and would rather pay less for non-green items (Amegbe et al., 2017). Customers need to be educated on sustainability and environmental values. This calls for

Table 5.3 Cost savings from environmental improvements by SMEs

Process efficiency: When processes are efficient, the performance of existing processes and even new ones that may be introduced is optimised. This leads to minimising the utilisation of raw materials, energy, water, and the generation of waste.
Product design: Products could be redesigned to reduce the resources that go into their production without compromising the level of service it provides.
Waste disposal: When process efficiency is ensured, waste production is minimised. Thus, even when waste is generated, it could be reused or passed on to other firms that can utilise it, therefore, lowering disposal costs.
Source of raw materials: There is cost-reduction when the source of raw materials is changed to recycled materials in a particular process.
Infrastructure: Infrastructural changes such as the installation of energy-efficient lighting, insulation of buildings, and improvement in the efficiency of heating systems could generate savings.
Packaging and transport: Reduction of packaging volume and sourcing local suppliers and customers to reduce transportation costs.

Source: OECD (2018)

extensive campaigns by Governments and Civil Society Organisations, especially in rural areas.

Narrow Focus: Amegbe et al. (2017) discovered that SME approaches to GM narrowly focus on specific aspects of the production process or the product, excluding other aspects of GM practice. They concluded that SMEs usually have a partial view of the course of future innovation and tackle green problems ad hoc. It is important for SMEs to plan for the long term. SMEs should not sacrifice ethics for short-term profits.

Standardisation: In some emerging economies, there is the issue of a lack of standardisation to validate green assertions. It is challenging to certify a product as green or organic as there is no standardisation. Moreover, there are only a few regulatory bodies involved in regulating green practices in emerging economies. There is an urgent need for standard quality control outfits for regulation, labelling, and licensing.

Investment: Lack of resources by SME owners often renders them risk-averse and less ready to invest in new technologies. For some SME investors, the waiting period between investing in green technology and receiving investment proceeds is too long. SME investors need to view the greening process as a major long-term investment opportunity with huge prospects in view.

SME Characteristics: The following SME characteristics listed in Table 5.4 present corresponding limitations to SMEs' successful implementation of GM.

5.8 Evaluating SME Green Marketing Performance

Whilst adopting and implementing GM by SMEs, it is important to evaluate performance by measuring the extent and dimension of 'greenness' being practised. Chahal et al. (2014) identified the following five GM factors listed in Table 5.5 to assess SMEs' performance in India.

The success of GM application is mainly dependent on its effect on consumers. As stated by Grant (2007), there are five major points (5 'I's')

Table 5.4 SME characteristics limiting the implementation of green marketing practices

SME characteristic	Limitations
Ownership and management	Ownership and management are concentrated in one person's hands. Decisions on investments and business strategies are usually determined by the entrepreneur's personal preferences.
Non-strategic focus	The entrepreneur has little time to purposefully reflect on future activities beyond the core business. Investments unrelated to the core business are regarded as unnecessary.
Capacity problems	SMEs have limited capacities such as insufficient resources and expertise for environmental opportunities and compliance.
Lack of information	The entrepreneur is not usually well-informed about green opportunities, their costs, and benefits. They usually rely on suppliers, clients, and so on, who may also lack information.
Risk-averse	SMEs are risk-averse because of their small economic size. They lack knowledge on incorporating GM into core business strategy.
Difficulty in accessing finance	SMEs have difficulties in accessing finance to implement green projects. They are considered high-risk entities, as they lack the required security to back their requests for financial support.

Source: OECD (2018)

that aid the development of efficient GM. These could be employed to evaluate SMEs and are listed in Table 5.6.

5.9 The Impact of SME Green Marketing Practices

GM practices among SMEs have consequential impact in several ways including the following.

Table 5.5 Assessment criteria for successful SME green marketing practices

GM factor	Assessment standards
Green promotion	• Enhancing and designing environmentally friendly packaging • Recycling, reusing, and remanufacturing the material • Publicising the green characteristics of the product
Green process	• Urging customers to take environmental actions • Implementing government-subsidised natural environmental programmes • Using ecological materials for primary packaging • Selecting cleaner transportation methods • Holding awareness creation events for customers or suppliers • Using cleaner technology to ensure savings and lessen pollution
Green strategic policies	• Using environmentally friendly materials • Redesigning products to obtain new environmental criteria • Having insurance plans to cover environmental risks
Green supply chain management	• Using ISO certification on quality and environmental factors • Redefining operation and production procedures to facilitate internal efficiency • Using recyclable or reusable items in logistics • Having environmental management systems
Proactive energy conservation	• Using low energy consumption, for instance, water, electricity, gas, and petrol for production/disposal • Using raw material that can be reused or are harmless • Requiring suppliers to provide certification of testing for green products conformance

Source: Chahal et al. (2014)

Table 5.6 Customer-based evaluative criteria for efficient development of green marketing

Intuitive	Green products and services ought to be seen as normal.
Integrative	Association of trade, technology, social and environmental impact
Innovative	Attainment of new creative products and lifestyles
Inviting	Organisations must incorporate the strategic objectives of creating an organisational culture that promotes a 'green' lifestyle
Informed	The lack of information has an impact on buyers' behaviour

Source: Grant (2007)

5.9.1 Impact on Society

GM protects the environment. Green products are produced with organic and biodegradable materials and are designed to utilise very little non-renewable resources and toxic chemicals to generate energy. This decreases the production of greenhouse gases and prevents pollution of the climate. Furthermore, green products encourage the production of energy utilising natural resources. The adoption of GM practices is a major incentive for business expansion and job creation in emerging economies.

5.9.2 Impact on Labour Market

UNEP (2014) suggests five avenues through which labour markets are adjusting to the green transition: firstly, GM is creating additional jobs; secondly, the greening process has led to the substitution of employment where jobs are shifting from environmentally damaging industries (fossil fuels) to cleaner industries (renewable energy); thirdly, GM has led to the elimination of certain jobs, for example, jobs involving the production of packaging material relying on inorganic and non-biodegradable materials; fourthly, there has been the transformation of jobs; and finally, job migration is occurring where labour is migrating from countries with strict environmental policies to those with more relaxed policies.

5.9.3 Impact on SMEs' Business Strategy

GM has implications for SMEs' business strategy (Nadaf & Nadaf, 2014). In the contemporary business environment, it would be disastrous for SME businesses not to think green. SME firms in emerging markets wishing to outperform competitors have to utilise different green strategies to maximise profit and meet customer demand. SMEs should be able to prove that their products would help in customer's health, lifestyle, and in several other ways to get customer loyalty.

Going green offers a great competitive advantage, and aligning a firm with green practices is a great selling point for SMEs. Mu et al. (2007)

posit that businesses, while implementing GM, can enhance their market position and strengthen their brand and organisational performance. Developing green products provides access to new markets and green consumers who purchase solely green products and even pay premium prices for them. Going green further motivates employees, as they feel honoured and responsible to work for an organisation that protects the environment.

5.9.4 Impact on Customers

Although some eco-products or services may be priced higher, GM has appreciably resulted in profitable products. Green products last longer than regular products and utilise less energy, therefore, reducing the energy bills of customers; for example, solar speakers can last for ten hours when they are charged with solar energy. In some instances, customers can enjoy low costs. When utilised correctly and maintained properly, some green products lead to low maintenance costs. For example, green buildings are not only marketed as environmentally friendly, but likewise require less maintenance or lower operational costs.

5.9.5 Impact on SME Internationalisation

Another important implication is the internationalisation of SME through the 'green movement'. To be competitive, SMEs that export in emerging economies have to improve their skills (Tesfom & Lutz, 2006). SMEs must comply with international green export standards and procedures with respect to sustainable production processes, quality, content, labelling, packaging, and so on. They must also comply with child labour laws and standards for green advertising. To assist emerging economies build their capacities to attain sustainable and inclusive growth through export trade, the United Nations Conference on Trade and Development (UNCTAD) has assessed ways to encourage green exports through Voluntary Sustainability Standards (VSS). These are standards to ensure products are produced, processed, or shipped in line with set sustainability metrics, such as environmental impact, basic human rights, labour standards, and gender equality (UNCTAD Sustainable Trade, 2020). SME exporters should familiarise themselves with VSS protocols to leverage green export opportunities.

5.9.6 Implications of Green Marketing Practices for SMEs in Emerging Economies

To translate green marketing strategy into practice, some options available to small firms in emerging economies include biodiversity, clean energy, green technologies, sustainable agriculture, waste management, water sanitation, and ecotourism.

The marketing mix elements such as product, price, place, and promotion can serve as an opportunity for SMEs in emerging economies to adopt green marketing by offering green products and services and green pricing. SMEs can adopt green scenarios for service delivery and ensure the greenness of the physical evidence of the servicescape. SMEs can further adopt green promotion and branding by communicating messages on green issues and sustainability.

The implementation of successful green marketing by SMEs can be limited by characteristics such as access to funding, implementation costs, risk aversion, lack of skills and information, non-strategic focus, and capacity problems. Policy makers in developing economies must provide support for SMEs such as training, green advocacy, financial incentives, and skills development for standardisation.

Additionally, there is the need to ensure there is monitoring of SME green marketing performance using benchmarks such as green promotions, green process, green policies, green innovation, green workplace, green workforce, and green supply-chain.

Implementation of green marketing practices by SMEs in emerging economies will lead to a number of positive outcomes on society and the business community, the labour market, customers, SME business strategy, and SME Internationalisation.

5.10 Conclusion

GM is a strategic tool for SMEs on how competitive they can be in the marketplace. SMEs in emerging economies are therefore applying GM practices to achieve competitive advantage and improved business performance. Going green definitely poses several challenges. However, it is a cause worth pursuing as it can reduce operational costs in the long-term; increase customer size, market share, and profit; and improve public image. Though resource-constrained, SMEs should endeavour to practice GM in order to be competitive and to reap its benefits.

References

Amegbe, H., Owino, J., & Nuwasiima, A. (2017). Green Marketing Orientation (GMO) and performance of SMEs in Ghana. *American Journal of Management, 11*(1).

Ashurst. (2020). *Major new global energy transition research report*. Retrieved August 14, 2020, from https://www.oilandgas360.com/major-new-global-energy-transition-research-report-launched-by-law-firm-ashurst/

Chahal, H., Dangwal, R., & Raina, S. (2014). Conceptualisation, development and validation of Green Marketing orientation (GMO) of SMEs in India: A case of electric sector. *Journal of Global Responsibility, 5*(2), 312–337.

Chen, M. (2009). Attitude toward organic foods among Taiwanese as related to health consciousness, environmental attitudes, and the mediating effects of a healthy lifestyle. *British Food Journal, 3*(2), 165–178.

Chou, Y. C., Yang, C. H., & Lu, C. H. (2017). Building criteria for evaluating green project management: An integrated approach of DEMATEL and ANP. *Sustainability, 9*(5).

Cronin, J., Smith, J., & Gleim, M. (2011). Green marketing strategies: An examination of stakeholders and the opportunities they present. *Journal of the Academy of Marketing Science, 39*(1), 158–174.

Cross, O. D. (2019). Assessing the role of green marketing in small and medium enterprises. *International Journal of Scientific and Research Publications, 9*(1).

Danish Enterprise and Construction Authority (FORA). (2010). *Green business models in the Nordic Region: A key to promote sustainable growth.* Copenhagen, Denmark.

Do Paco, A. M. F., Raposo, M. L. B., & Leal, F. W. (2009). Identifying the green consumer: A segmentation study. *Journal of Targeting, Measurement and Analysis for Marketing, 17*(1), 17–25.

Gandhi, N. S., Thanki, S. J., & Thakkar, J. J. (2018). Ranking of drivers for integrated lean-green manufacturing for Indian manufacturing SMEs. *Journal of Cleaner Production, 17*(1), 675–689.

Gareis, R., Heumann, M., & Martinuzzi, A. (2010). *Relating sustainable development and project management.* IRNOP IX.

Grant, J. (2007). *The green marketing manifesto.* John Wiley & Sons.

Grant, J. (2008). Green marketing. *Strategic Direction, 24*(6), 25–27.

International Trade Centre. (2017). *SME competitiveness in Ghana: Alliances for action.* ITC.

International Trade Centre. (2018). *Promoting SME competitiveness in Africa: Data for de-risking investment.* ITC.

Jabbour, C., Jugend, D., & Jabbour, A. (2015). Green product development and performance of Brazilian firms: Measuring the role of human and technical aspects. *Journal of Cleaner Production, 87*(15), 442–451.

Krämer, A., & Herrndorf, M. (2012). Policy measures to support inclusive and green business models.

Kumar, P. (2015). Green marketing innovations in small Indian firms. *World Journal of Entrepreneurship, Management and Sustainable Development, 2*(3), 1–16.

Lee, S. (2008). Drivers for the participation of small and medium-sized suppliers in green supply chain initiatives. *Supply Chain Management, 13*(3), 185–198.

Leonidou, C. N., Katsikeas, C. S., & Morgan, N. A. (2013). Greening the marketing mix: Do firms do it and does it pay off? *Journal of the Academy of Marketing Science, 41*(2), 151–170.

Liu, S., Kasturiratne, D., & Moizer, J. (2012). A hub-and-spoke model for multi-dimensional integration of green marketing and sustainable supply chain management. *Industrial Marketing Management, 41*(4), 581–588.

Mu, J., Peng, G., & Tan, Y. (2007). New product development in Chinese SMEs: Key success factors from a managerial perspective. *International Journal of Emerging Markets, 2*(2), 123–143.

Nadaf, Y. B., & Nadaf, S. M. (2014). Green marketing: Challenges and strategies for Indian companies in 21st century. *International Journal of Research in Business Management, 2*(5), 91–104.

Nielsen. (2015). Global survey of corporate social responsibility and sustainability. Retrieved September 12, 2020, from https://www.nielsen.com/us/en/press-releases/2015/consumer-goods-brands-that-demonstrate-commitment-to-sustainability-outperform/

OECD. (2013). *Green entrepreneurship, eco-innovation and SMEs*. OECD Publishing.

OECD. (2018). *Environmental policy toolkit for SME greening in EU Eastern Partnership countries, OECD green growth studies*. OECD Publishing.

Oxborrow, B. (2013). Adoption of "eco-advantage" by SMEs: Emerging opportunities and constraints. *European Journal of Innovation Management, 16*(3), 355–375.

Peng, Y. S., & Lin, S. S. (2008). Local responsiveness pressure, subsidiary resources, green management adoption and subsidiary's performance: Evidence from Taiwanese manufactures. *Journal of Business Ethics, 79*(1), 199–212.

Polonsky, M. (1994). An introduction to green marketing. *Electronic Green Journal, 1*(2).

Polonsky, M. (2011). Transformative green marketing: Impediments and opportunities. *Journal of Business Research, 64*(12), 1311–1319.

Polonsky, M., & Rosenberger, P. J. (2001). Re-evaluating green marketing: A strategic approach. *Business Horizons, 44*(5), 21–30.

Raharjo, K. (2019). The role of green management in creating sustainability performance on the small and medium enterprises. *Management of Environmental Quality, 30*(3), 557–577.

Samsung. (2016). Electronics: Green & Eco Management. Retrieved September 12, 2020, from https://digital.hbs.edu/platform-rctom/submission/samsung-electronics-green-eco-management/

SEED. (2020). Innovating business models for socially inclusive and environmentally sustainable products and services. Retrieved October 4, 2020, from https://seed.uno/enterprises

SEFA. (2019). *Sustainable energy fund for Africa (SEFA) annual report*. Abidjan.

Tesfom, G., & Lutz, C. (2006). A classification of export marketing problems of small and medium sized manufacturing firms in developing countries. *International Journal of Emerging Markets, 1*(3), 262–281.

Turyakira, P., Venter, E., & Smith, E. (2014). The impact of corporate social responsibility factors on the competitiveness of small and medium-sized enterprises. *South African Journal of Economic and Management Sciences, 17*(2).

UNCTAD Sustainable Trade. (2020). *What role for voluntary sustainability standards?* Retrieved July 17, 2020, from https://unctad.org/meeting/sustainable-trade-what-role-voluntary-sustainability-standards

UNEP. (2014). The business case for eco-innovation. United Nations Environment Programme.

World Commission on Environment and Development. (1987). Our common future. Annex to General Assembly Document A/42/427. Development and International Co-operation: Environment. Retrieved December 23, 2020, from http://www.un-documents.net/wced-ocf.htm

Yuningsih, E., & Silaningsih, E. (2019). Implementation of environmentally friendly marketing for SMEs featured products to strengthen competitive advantages. *International Journal of Scientific & Technology Research, 8*(12).

6

The Quality of Information of GRI Standards in an Emerging Economy: Evidence from Green Accounting Practices in Argentina

Gisel Machain, Cristina Santhià, Giacomo Ciambotti, and Maria Fernanda Figueroa

6.1 Introduction

Accounting has historically dealt with business aiming at economic profit. It is traditionally defined as a "factual, cultural, applied science that involves explaining and regulating descriptive tasks, principally

G. Machain (✉)
Argentine Catholic University, Rosario, Argentina
e-mail: gmachain@uca.edu.ar

C. Santhià
Università degli Studi di Torino, Turin, Italy

G. Ciambotti
Università Cattolica del Sacro Cuore, Milan, Italy
e-mail: giacomo.ciambotti@unicatt.it

M. F. Figueroa
CONICET-Universidad Austral, Buenos Aires, Argentina
e-mail: mfigueroa@austral.edu.ar

E. K. Adae et al. (eds.), *Responsible Management in Emerging Markets*, Sustainable Development Goals Series, https://doi.org/10.1007/978-3-030-76563-7_6

quantitative, about the existence and circulation of objects, facts, and persons of each part of the entity or social organism and the projection of them in terms of compliance with organisational goals through systems based on basic assumptions and suitable to each situation" (García-Casella, 2002, p. 201).

In order to meet the current needs, without compromising the ones of future generations, economic and financial consequences of climate change—linked to business activities and transactions—must be measured to balance costs and benefits of economic growth (Slawinski & Bansal, 2012; Ansari et al., 2013). Latin American economies are particularly suffering from vegetative growth, price volatility, and uncontrolled usage of natural resources which might be considered as an obstacle to sustainable economic progress considering that environmental degradation is a market flaw and sustainable development is a promoter of economic growth (González et al., 2019; Ciambotti & Pedrini, 2019).

The transformation of the role of business in society requires addressing profit, people, and the planet as main pillars in their own accounting systems. Pahlen Acuña and Fronti de García (2004) broadened the field of this discipline differentiating segments on which accounting models are based. These include financial, management, governmental, economic, and social and environmental accounting. The financial segment framed at the agency theory sets this science at the service of the owners facilitating information for controlling money delivered to administrators (Pereda, 1988).

As reporting is the final product of any accounting system, professional experts have developed complex and integral instruments to measure profit considering this would also result in human welfare. Meanwhile, tools to measure and describe the impact of company activities on people and the planet have not had a long-term development. As a result, reporting was built to satisfy their needs of operating and strategic decision-making and to facilitate equity control and accountability (Schaltegger & Burritt, 2017), keeping business as usual.

If we manage what is measurable and what we measure defines what is relevant for an organisation (Drucker, 2018), it is important to develop appropriate tools to care for better achievement of social and environmental missions. One of these important tools has been referred to as the accounting information (Gray et al., 1996), but the traditional users were equity shareholders mainly oriented to profit goals. Pereda (1988) expanded the agency theory shifting the focus from the owners to the community that demands the company to produce not only economic results, but also results for the social and environmental resources provided to the business to achieve their objectives.

The birth of reporting for multiple goals and missions occurred with the transformation from shareholders' to stakeholders' perspective (Burritt et al., 2002). So, turning to a stakeholder paradigm, accounting reporting must take into account all the elements and individuals identified in that group covering their particular needs for information. Reporting needs a regulatory framework in order to provide useful information to take assertive decisions, and sustainability reporting is framed by several international standards.

International leaders on sustainability reporting frameworks known as Global Reporting Initiative (GRI), International Integrated Reporting Council (IIRC), Sustainability Accounting Standard Board (SASB), Climate Disclosure Standards Board (CDSB), and Carbon Disclosure Project (CDP) are currently under an alignment process aimed at providing a robust social and environmental accounting system leading to proper performance evaluation of a company's social and environmental results.

Sustainable Development Goal 12, target 6 (12.6), encourages companies, especially large and transnational ones, to adopt sustainable practices and to integrate sustainability information into their reporting cycle. That is to say, that green accounting is set as a useful assessment tool to manage tri-dimensional goals. This statement is rooted in a humanist position that reflects the idea of an ecologically sustainable world that considers the needs of human beings while protecting the coexistence of species without linking it to their usefulness for humans. This approach involves protecting nature and pursuing economic and social objectives that are compatible with environmental conservation (Azcárate et al., 2011).

Heeding these arguments, this chapter aims to address the following question: how are companies located in emerging economies contributing to sustainable development by revealing accurate green accounting information? Not providing information of cost internalisation regarding environmental and social issues reveals a data gap of the net income.

In order to address this question, we firstly disclosed standards, laws, and regulations applicable locally. Secondly, we conducted a quantitative data analysis taking a sample of Argentinean companies that release public sustainability reports according to an international standard and evaluated if they showed the information required to achieve compliance with the requirements.

Our findings reveal that most of the companies do not present that kind of information, and among the ones that actually show related information, they do not achieve integral compliance with the requirements. By consequence, our chapter tries to contribute to the recent research on green accounting application in emerging economies such as Argentina, where many economic activities have a high impact on the environment, such as mining and agriculture.

More broadly, this chapter aims to fill the gaps in sustainability literature, recognising that social accounting has been trying to overcome the serious shortcomings of wild capitalism; by prioritising values and the inclusion of more stakeholders as the foundation of accounting systems. By doing so, high-quality accounting information will pertain to not only financial and economic elements, but also social and environmental factors related to the governance of different organisations and society as a whole (Rodríguez De Ramírez, 2020).

The justification of this study lies in the urgent matter of coming clean about environmental and social outcomes of local companies' management and enforcing the social responsibility of ethical accounting to guarantee transparency and empowerment of society (consumers and workers). This study contributes by highlighting the necessity of the involvement of accounting professionals in the matter of green accounting by providing guidelines on how to evaluate quality of sustainability reporting in Argentina, thus, helping to promote emerging economies towards sustainable development.

6.2 Theoretical Background of Sustainability Reporting and the GRI Initiative

Accounting literature states accounting is the business language of excellence. Regarding green accounting in particular, the Institute of Management Accountants in the USA defined environmental accounting as the management of environmental and economic performance through the development and implementation of appropriate environment-related accounting systems and practices (IFAC, 2005). This may include reporting and auditing in some companies, environmental management accounting leading to life-cycle costing, full-cost accounting, benefits assessment, and strategic planning for environmental management.

As a proper language, accounting is dynamic and constantly refreshing according to reality, so a renewed code must be developed in order to get the message through. Internationally and locally, several regulations and standards have been issued to cover this necessity. Even if they are not exactly the same, each set of standards can be used alongside with other sustainability frameworks and are well-aligned among them.

6.2.1 Sustainability Reporting and the GRI Initiative

Accounting reporting originated in the fact that the owners of the business resources are different from the ones that manage them. The agency theory is grounded in this agreement between the owner and the administrator that has to report back for the results of the management during a certain period of time. Broadening the limits of this theory, "the owner" could be conceived as the society as a whole given the diversity of resources implied in business (Pereda, 1988).

In that case, accounting reporting not only must focus on economic metrics, but also is obliged to account for social and environmental aspects of companies. At the moment of revealing environmental information, entities count on several frameworks to follow. Material issues being social or environmental also had economic consequences in the short, medium, or long term, and having multiple disclosure frameworks increases the administrative burden of disclosure efforts. Specifically, the additional time, cost, and effort required to analyse and disclose new climate-related information could penalise those with less capacity to respond. Acknowledging this fact, in the November 2018 CDP, CDSB, GRI, IIRC, and SASB committed to a two-year project focused on driving better alignment of sustainability reporting frameworks (named Better Alignment Project). They officially state as their mission and objective what is described below:

> Through this new project, participants will map their respective sustainability standards and frameworks to identify the commonalities and differences between them, jointly refining and continuously improving overlapping disclosures and data points to achieve better alignment, taking into account the different focuses, audiences, and governance procedures. This is the key forum in the world for bringing together the major players in the corporate reporting field, with all participants committed to driving alignment. The aim of the project is to drive better alignment, but not one framework. It will ensure that the frameworks are brought closer together, countering false perceptions about competition between standard setters and framework developers. This project will give more confidence to businesses to 'start the journey' towards better, more effective reporting, irrespective of which framework they choose initially. The final objective is to make it easier for companies to prepare effective and coherent disclosures that meet the information needs of capital markets and society. (Corporate Reporting Dialogue, 2018)

All of them are applicable to Argentine companies; however, GRI is the most selected among Latin American companies for their sustainability reports (González et al., 2019). That is why we selected the GRI report database to make the analysis. Find briefly described in the Table 6.1 below the main characteristics of them.

It is important to remark that their language recipients are shareholders and not stakeholders given the fact that they are aligned to financial accounting and not to the social and environmental accounting segment. In other words, they are oriented to investors who might be willing to show leadership and accountability taking into account the existence of legal requirements to report on environmental information and given the

Table 6.1 International green accounting standard frameworks apart from GRI

Standard framework	Integrated Reporting (IR)	Sustainability Accounting Standard Board (SASB)	Climate Disclosure Standards Board (CDSB)	Carbon Disclosure Project (CDP)
Organisation	International Integrated Reporting Council (IIRC)	Independent, non-profit, standard-setting organisation	International consortium of nine business and environmental NGOs	International, not-for-profit organisation
Date of origin	Founded in August 2010. Standards released in December 2013.	Formed in 2011. Standards released in October 2018.	Founded in 2007.	Founded in 2000 and based in the UK.
Objective	Develop an internationally accepted integrated reporting framework New reporting model to enable organisations to provide concise communications of how they create value over time supporting integrated thinking and decision-making.	Develops and maintains industry-specific sustainability accounting standards to identify, manage, and communicate financially material issues in 77 industries.	Advance and align the global mainstream corporate reporting model to equate natural capital with financial capital. Offering companies a framework for reporting environmental and climate information with the same rigour as financial information.	Provide a global system for companies and cities to measure, disclose, manage, and share vital environmental information. Provide vital information back to their customers and investors, and to the market through research, insights, and financial products and services.

(*continued*)

Table 6.1 (continued)

Standard framework	Integrated Reporting (IR)	Sustainability Accounting Standard Board (SASB)	Climate Disclosure Standards Board (CDSB)	Carbon Disclosure Project (CDP)
Main characteristics	Six capitals: financial, manufactured, human, social and relationship, intellectual, and natural. Integrated reports look at how the activities and capabilities of organisations transform these six capitals into outcomes.	Focus on industry specificity and financial materiality. Answer to investor concerns about companies' business practices about financially material sustainability. Evidence based, developed with broad market participation, and designed to be cost-effective for companies and decisions—useful for investors. Capture sustainability matters that are materially financial.	Information about natural capital and financial capital is equally essential for an understanding of corporate performance. Build the trust and transparency needed to foster resilient capital markets. Content reporting structure is defined in requirements that involve relevant topics.	Collect information from companies on their greenhouse gas emissions and assessment of climate change and water risk and opportunity. Holds the largest collection globally of primary climate change and water data and puts these insights at the heart of strategic business, investment, and policy decisions. Scoring methodologies through questionnaires.

Source: Author elaboration—data source official websites (2021)

fact that natural capital dependencies and/or environmental impacts present material risks and opportunities for the business and its ability to carry out its objectives.

In June 2017, CDSB and SASB worked together to develop the Task Force on Climate-Related Financial Disclosures (TCFD) recommendations that contribute to a global foundation for effective climate-related disclosures. This document serves as a response to companies needing to have guidelines on how to disclose environmental issues in a practical way. The Managing Director of CDSB, Mardi McBrien, expressed in 2019 that the guide takes the recommendations from principles to practice, increasing the adoption, and enhancing the robustness, consistency, and comparability of such information.

6.2.2 The Rise of GRI

The GRI Sustainability Reporting Standards (GRI Standards) is an international not-for-profit organisation having the first and most widely adopted global standards for sustainability reporting. GRI was founded in the USA in 1997 and currently has a network-based structure. The main objective is to enable all companies and organisations to report their economic, environmental, social, and governance performance through free Sustainability Reporting Guidelines. GRI standards had gone through a large pathway regarding sustainability reporting to be stated as an independent and generally accepted standard known worldwide. It provides values of transparency in accountability concerning all stakeholders and building strategic and operational management tools. The final aim of these standards, as stated by the organisation is as follows:

> GRI Standards supports companies, public and private, large and small, to protect the environment and improve society, at the same time improving governance and stakeholder relations, enhancing reputations, and building trust. GRI Standards stand in the triple bottom line pillars being stakeholder-oriented and structuring disclosures with reporting requirements and recommendations and guidance. (GRI, n.d.)

Among all the GRI indicators we have selected, Indicator 201-2 named *financial implications and other risks and opportunities due to climate change*, belonging to the economic performance area to examine on the sample of sustainability reports. This is because it specifically addresses investors' increasing interests and also merges elements of the well-developed financial accounting segment and recently born green accounting.

GRI states that climate change presents risks and opportunities to organisations, their investors, and their stakeholders. As governments move to regulate activities that contribute to climate change, organisations that are directly or indirectly responsible for emissions face regulatory risks and opportunities. Risks can include increased costs or other factors impacting competitiveness. However, risk detected can also create opportunities for organisations as new technologies and markets are created. This is especially the case for organisations that can use or produce energy and energy-efficient products more effectively. In addition, in December 2019, Argentina stated by Law 27520 that climate change is a state policy assuring that emerging economies can also be proactive in the agenda of mitigating negative effects on the environment.

6.2.3 Emerging Economies and Challenges Towards Sustainability Reporting

Emerging economies are often characterised by complex political structure and unstable economic context, where businesses of all sizes are struggling to survive. In many of these countries, sustainability reporting is not compulsory. However, for developing countries fostering integral human development, reducing social inequalities, raising the standard of living with the limit of a correct usage of resources, and balancing environmental impact are public and urgent matters.

Since the world is interconnected, the economic instability of developing countries also fosters global financial crises. However, if studies show the relevance of such standards for corporations, less attention has been provided to the quality of such information in emerging economies. Considering that Latin America is the most unequal region in the world

(CEPAL, 2018) and the most biodiverse region on the planet (PNUD, 2013), there is an extraordinary amount of work to do in reducing those inequalities and taking care of the natural richness. In addition, Argentina is one of the top countries most negatively affected by climate change taking almost one point of its GDP to recover from the consequences of natural disasters (Banco Mundial, 2017). Compared to other countries, Argentina is behind sustainability reporting advances. However, interest is increasing concerning these matters resulting in legal and professional regulatory issuance and more experience in the practice of releasing social balances.

6.3 Application of Green Accounting in Argentina

6.3.1 Research Setting: Argentine Local Laws and Regulations on Sustainability Reporting

Our study started with a desk analysis of the recent local laws and regulations to become familiar with the Argentinian context, especially regarding sustainability reporting and the environment.

With the aim of creating social awareness in Argentina about corporate social responsibility, April 23rd was established as the National Day of Social Responsibility. Law 27301 and Decree 1153/2016 were published in the Official Journal in November 2016 selecting that date to commemorate the adherence of Argentina to the Global Pact Universal Principles in 2004. In Argentina, sustainability reporting is not mandatory, however, there are several national and regional regulations regarding social and environmental risks that have equity implications. Unfortunately, most of them have not been sent to Congress over time. Among regulations released since 2011, we could mention the following National Bills: N° 3792 –D–2011 (21/07/2011), N° S-922/12 (17/04/2012), N° S-999/12 (24/04/2012) and N° S- 544/15 (18/03/2015). Other Provincial bills are represented in Table 6.2.

Table 6.2 Provincial bills on sustainable reporting in Argentina

Province	Reference number	Date of release
Buenos Aires	D – 300/12-13-0	28/03/2012
Entre Ríos	19421	28/08/2012
Corrientes	S 4401	01/11/2012
Jujuy	328 –DP- 13	10/05/2013
Santa Fe	27043– DBL	19/06/2013
Jujuy	217- DP-15	09/03/2015
Neuquén	8518 - E015/14	30/03/2014
Entre Ríos	E20666	21/11/2014
Misiones	D-42965-14	12/12/2014
Buenos Aires	D 75/16-17-0	10/03/2016

Source: author elaboration. (2021)

In our study, we also considered the professional laws and technical resolutions that include sustainability reporting issues, as indicated in the next table (Table 6.3).

A legal standardised framework about Social Responsibility applicable for all organisations is necessary for globally changing the paradigm towards the assumption of responsible commitment for sustainable growth. This is also highlighted by Vallaeys (2012, p. 2), who stated: "There is no responsibility without moral and legal order prescribed to give certain social trust continuity in general, relying on underlying constraint". This legal order is under construction all over the world and has already started in Argentina with the introduction of numerous law projects, either national or provincial, and decrees already approved about this subject.

6.3.2 Sample and Data Collection

Our source of data collection was the *GRI Sustainability Disclosure Database*, which is a useful lens to analyse examples of environmental disclosures in Argentina, which is an open and free source. As a result, 61 reports were chosen for the analysis. Those companies selected in 2017 were analysed also for their reports submitted to the official database in 2018 and 2019. For clarification, GRI Database admits modifications of registered information by independent companies related to closed

Table 6.3 Professional laws and technical resolutions in Argentina

Name	Main objective
Decree-Law 517/11 Salta Province. Social Responsibility and Social and Environmental Balance Sheet conceptual framework	Promote socially responsible behaviour of companies, private and public entities, and organisations in general. Design, development, and implementation of policies, plans, programmes, projects, and operations in order to accomplish an objective valuation and evaluation of social, environmental, economic, and financial sustainability.
Law 8488 (24/10/2012) Mendoza Province modified by Law 8583 (21/08/2013) and Regulatory Order 2094 (21/11/2014)	Add to what is mentioned before that includes a legal framework to the social and environmental corporate responsibility balance sheet.
Law 8761/15 (19/03/2015) Tucumán province. Social and Environmental Responsibility.	Promote social and environmental behaviour, design, and implementation of policies and actions guaranteeing society information access related to social behaviour results. Legal framework of the social and environmental corporate responsibility balance sheet is included. This regulation is not in force yet.
Technical Resolution N° 36/44 Accounting professional regulation. Social Balance Sheet released by the Argentine Federation of Economic Science Professional Councils (in Spanish, acronym FACPCE); by means of its standards releasing institute named Accounting and Auditing Standard realising Council (in Spanish, acronym CENCyA).	This regulation, which is voluntary, adopts the GRI model as a reference to prepare Sustainability Reports and sets an Economic Value generated and distributed reporting model in particular. The main objective of the resolution is to remark that certain aspects of social and environmental behaviour are not reflected in financial statements and acknowledge that an increasing number of local companies are elaborating Social Balance Sheets with an auditing process and taking information off the accounting system. Then, accounting standards are required to set Social Balance Sheets to uniform practices, clearing concepts, and definition of specific terminology. (FACPCE, 2012, RT36, page 2)
Technical Resolution N° 37, Fifth title. Other assurance engagement standards. Section A. Other assurance engagements in general.	It sets guidelines to the auditing process of a Social Balance Sheet in charge of an accountant. (FACPCE, 2013, RT37, page 31)

(*continued*)

Table 6.3 (continued)

Name	Main objective
Technical Resolution N° 35: International standards of assurance engagements and other related services adoption (IAASB from IFAC). (FACPCE, RT35, 2016, page 5)	It adopts international standards related to assurance engagements and other related services that provide a framework to achieve auditing of sustainability reports.
General Resolution N° 606/12. File N° 1723/11, labelled "Corporate Governance Code - Modified by General Resolution N° 516" (National Securities Commission).	Produce information regarding management of Boards starting a tendency towards transparency for public companies as an instrument to protect investors, creditors, and people in general, restricting the possibility of asymmetric information. In section VI.2, they are required to answer if the Issuer releases a social and environmental corporate responsibility balance sheet annually and if it is audited externally.

Source: Author elaboration. (2021)

periods. If the companies selected in the sample introduced changes or added data to their reports after the sample selection, it is not included in the current analysis. Reports selected are also available on institutional web pages of the companies. From the sample selected, we assessed accurate disclosure of the indicator 201-2 regarding financial implications of climate change, which we now present in the next paragraph.

6.3.3 Indicator 201-2

Among the various indicators included in the standards, the GRI indicator that concerns economic performance and measures materially financial environment aspects is 201-2 titled *"Financial implications and other risks and opportunities due to climate change"*, taking financial aspects as having the potential to generate substantive changes in company's operations, revenues, or expenditures. The content of the indicator includes:

- Description of the risks and opportunities
- Classification of the risk, either as physical, regulatory, or other

- Description of the impact associated (direct or indirect, likelihood, and magnitude)
- Financial implications of the impact before action is taken (increased or decreased capital and operational costs, demand for product and services, capital availability, and investment opportunities)
- Methods used to manage them (if not, reveal plans and timelines to develop the necessary systems)
- Costs incurred to take action in this matter

Using GRI guidelines as a quality information standard, it is possible to analyse the application of green accounting in the field of an emerging economy. In order to understand how companies are struggling to face these challenges in emerging economies, the focus is done on the GRI indicator of employment in Argentina. The overall objective is to highlight the quality of the information regarding the selected indicator and to show possible pitfalls for an emerging economy, as well as lay the basis for further studies in the field of green accounting.

6.3.4 Data Analysis

With the information referring to the three accounting periods (2017–2019), a data matrix was built in for further descriptive analysis process and study. First, we verified if the entity submitted the three consecutive sustainability reports for all the periods studied in the GRI Database. If positive, we identified if the indicator under examination was explicitly reported following GRI guidelines. To see whether the report properly informed on the indicator or not, we tested if it included all the items cited in the previous paragraph.

6.4 Findings

Our results show how local companies in an emerging economy like Argentina reveal or do not reveal financial implications and other risks and opportunities related to climate change. The first result is reported in

Table 6.4 Periodicity of reporting release on annual basis

Period	2017	2018	2019
Number of entities that submitted GRI Reports	61	36	38
% of entities that submitted GRI Reports	100%	59%	62%

Source: Author elaboration. (2021)

Table 6.5 Declaration of revealing the indicator selected

Period	2017	2018	2019
Number of organisations that do not affirm to reveal the indicator	38	22	21
% organisations that do not affirm to reveal the indicator	62%	61%	55%

Source: Author elaboration. (2021)

Table 6.6 Revealing financial implications and other risks and opportunities due to climate change

Period	2017	2018	2019
% organisation that inform on consequences	4%	36%	29%
Number of organisations that inform on consequences	1	5	5
% organisations that do not inform on consequences	96%	64%	71%
Number of organisations that do not inform on consequences	22	9	12

Source: Author elaboration (2021)

Table 6.4. In fact, we found that from the firms selected in the sample in 2017, only 59% of them continued releasing reports in 2018, increasing to 62% the following year. This has a negative effect on comparability of information, which is a principle of quality accounting information.

Moreover, Table 6.5 gives an overview of the sparse compliance with the guidelines established, given the fact that most of the organisations state that they do not show financial implications and other risks and opportunities due to climate change. This is even true of companies linked to transport, energy, or usage of natural resources. From the items selected that submitted their reports in the following years, a slight decreasing tendency is shown indicating that a little more consciousness about this subject is taken into account over the years (Table 6.6).

Developing countries such as Argentina are still in an early stage of sustainability reporting. Overall, our results show that in a local context, there is a rising awareness of environmental protection issues. However, a serious commitment to environmental protection is still low. Certain similarities are shown in a 2020 study carried by the Climate Disclosure Standard Board about Europe's top 50 largest listed companies, in their report Falling Short, stating:

> As little as one third of companies adequately addressed the environmental and climate-related risks and opportunities faced by their business. Over half of business model disclosures were light touch in nature and did not fully articulate the strategic integration or implications of these risks and opportunities into the company's core business. Furthermore, 42% of companies were noted to omit potential material data on environmental or climate-related issues for their sectors such as principal risks that other industrial companies had reported as material. (CDSB, 2020)

6.5 Guidelines for Studying Sustainability Reporting Standards in Emerging Economies

It is necessary to remark that the application of sustainability reporting standards in emerging economies, and in Argentina in particular, is in its beginning stages. Prospective analysis of recent sustainability reports in this region must be done considering this premise. A large path is required to produce reports that achieve accounting mission for stakeholders (users), thus providing robust and good quality of information to make decisions (as consumers, workers, citizens, investors, suppliers, among others).

Secondly, more emphasis must be put on building integral and strong public databases of sustainability reports with a double objective, facilitating accessibility for stakeholders, and enabling future research that raises awareness on the importance of the issues. Therefore, demanding more accuracy and completeness in the information published is necessary. In relation to this aspect, studying sustainability reporting standards in emerging economies requires the external expert verification of the information issued to achieve, in a more reasonable way, the standards set for the submission of these reports.

Finally, a proper environment needs to be created in order to arrive at a more mature stage of sustainability reporting in emerging economies. The relationships between economic conditions and socially responsible corporate behaviour are mediated by several institutional factors: public and private regulation, the presence of non-governmental and other independent organisations that monitor corporate behaviour, institutionalised norms regarding appropriate corporate behaviour, associative behaviour among corporations themselves, and organised dialogue (Campbell, 2007).

6.6 Contributions and Conclusions

In Argentina, a sample of corporate decision-makers in the country were utilised to examine the above aspects. Only a few of them reported their economic performance linked to impacts in climate change and none of them revealed accurately the integral data required by the principles of information quality. However, even if initiatives of sustainability reporting and practices are sometimes not systematic and given the particular context, developing countries have achieved progress in both theory and practice regarding the environment.

This is evidenced by the issuance of a number of environmental laws and a number of firms that disclose environmental practices. Our germinal study makes some contributions which also open the door for further research. In fact, accounting studies are at a turning point to contribute both to practitioners and to theory. This requires a collaborative and multidisciplinary path to transformational change, setting the pillars of green accounting and green management.

Sustainability reporting is stated to be at the heart of achieving SDG Goals as it is set in target 12.6. Thus, exploring growing concerns of environmental issues in Argentina's accounting discipline sets renewed guidelines to study GRI indicators and reporting standards in light of the quality of information disclosed in a local perspective. Each country's peculiar circumstances, in particular those of emerging economies, must be taken into account during the design, development, and application of sustainability reporting standards. This contribution opens a larger debate on the quality of information of green accounting standards in emerging economies, where more studies are required. Interesting future questions pertain to the factors and motivations that drive companies to provide such information.

The debate around mandatory versus voluntary sustainability reports arise in order to achieve better quality information through accounting auditing engagements. If the final aim of accounting is giving useful information to make right decisions, and also serving as a tool to enable equity control, then green accounting, as a segment concerned about the environment, is a crucial instrument for a careful assessment of monetary and non-monetary factors involved in companies value creation. Gray (2012) states that social and environmental accounting offers a way to recover productive and moral accounting setting development of human beings at the centre. Also, accounting professionals need to be prepared to face these challenges of green accounting the general aspects of which are not well known and not included in the core of universities' curricula.

Finally, our results help practitioners, enterprises, and policy-makers by revealing the necessity of a commitment of synergetic work among society, and the public and private sectors. In particular, this chapter exposes the need of promotion in terms of local and regional actions towards sustainable goals that can push better transparency and quality of information. This final contribution lays the basis for policy-makers of emerging countries to better adjust the legislative framework of the standard to finally help companies towards their sustainable development.

Conclusions from our analysis also point out that companies need to be supported to better prepare their reports, acknowledging that valuable information is a fundamental key to make good decisions to achieve triple value creation business objectives. "What the company is not telling, someone will say it out loud somewhere" (Hernández Velasco, 2017, p. 3). Hence, the way ahead for sustainable development also in emerging economies is set, and overall, this contributes as a little building block to open a larger debate around this important aspect of green accounting standards.

References

Ansari, S., Wijen, F., & Gray, B. (2013). Constructing a climate change logic: An institutional perspective on the "tragedy of the commons". *Organization Science, 24*(4), 1014–1040.

Azcárate, F., Carrasco, F., & Fernández, M. (2011). The role of integrated indicators in exhibiting business contribution to sustainable development: A survey of sustainability reporting initiatives. *Revista de contabilidad, 14*, 213–240.

Banco Mundial. (2017). *El cambio climático requiere de un enfoque integral por parte de las ciudades argentinas*. Retrieved December 21, 2020, from http://www.bancomundial.org/es/news/feature/2017/10/19/cambio-climatico-requiere-de-un-enfoque-integral.

Board-SASB, S.A.S. (2018). Sustainability Accounting Standard: Service Sector. Retrieved December 21, 2020, from https://www.sasb.org/standards-overview/download-current-standards/.

Burritt, R. L., Hahn, T., & Schaltegger, S. (2002). Towards a comprehensive framework for environmental management accounting—Links between business actors and environmental management accounting tools. *Australian Accounting Review, 12*(27), 39–50.

Campbell, J. (2007). Why would corporations behave in socially responsible ways? An institutional theory of corporate social responsibility. D.C.School, Ed. *Academy of Management Review, 32*(3), 946–947.

CDP, Carbon Disclosure Project. (2020). *Guidance and questionnaires for companies*. Retrieved December 21, 2020, from https://www.cdp.net/en/guidance/guidance-for-companies.

CDSB. (2019). *Climate Disclosure Standards Board Framework Advancing and aligning disclosure of environmental information in mainstream reports for reporting environmental & climate change information*. Retrieved December 21, 2020, from https://www.cdsb.net/sites/default/files/cdsb_framework_2019_v2.2.pdf.

CDSB. (2020). Falling short. Retrieved December 21, 2020, from https://www.cdsb.net/sites/default/files/falling_short_report_double_page_spread.pdf on 21 Dec 2020.

CEPAL. (2018). *La Economía del cambio climático en América Latina y el Caribe. Síntesis 201: una visión gráfica*. Retrieved December 21, 2020, from https://repositorio.cepal.org/bitstream/handle/11362/42228/4/S1701215A_es.pdf.

Ciambotti, G., & Pedrini, M. (2019). Hybrid harvesting strategies to overcome resource constraints: Evidence from social enterprises in Kenya. *Journal of Business Ethics, 1*, 1–20.

Corporate Reporting Dialogue. (2018). *Better Alignment Project*. Retrieved December 21, 2020, from https://corporatereportingdialogue.com/better-alignment-project/.

Drucker, P. (2018). *The daily Drucker*. Routledge.

Federación Argentina de Consejos Profesionales en Ciencias Económicas. (2017). *Interpretación 13 de Normas de Contabilidad y Auditoría. Encargo de aseguramiento del Balance Social*. Retrieved December 21, 2020, from http://www.facpce.org.ar:8080/normasweb/index_argentina.php?c=1&sc=3.

García-Casella, C. L. (2002). El problema del uso de modelos en la contabilidad. *Revista Legis Internacional de Contabilidad y Auditoría, 12*(1), 199–236.

Global Reporting Initiative (GRI). n.d. *Information about GRI*. Retrieved December 21, 2020, from http://www.globalreporting.org.

Global Sustainability Standard Board (GSSB), Global Reporting Initiative. (2016). Consolidated Set of GRI Sustainability Reporting Standards. Retrieved December 21, 2020, from https://www.globalreporting.org/standards/gri-standards-translations/gri-standards-spanish-translations-download-center/.

González, J. M., Becerra, O. A. D., & Zevallos, E. E. C. (2019). Retos y propuestas de la profesión contable para el desarrollo de economías sustentables en Latinoamérica. *Quipukamayoc, 27*(54), 73–82.

Gray, R. (2012). Acerca del desorden, los sistemas y la sustentabilidad: hacia una contabilidad y unas finanzas más sociales y ambientales. *Contabilidad y auditoría, 17*, 26.

Gray, R., Owen, D., & Adams, C. (1996). *Accounting & accountability: changes and challenges in corporate social and environmental reporting*. Prentice Hall.

GRI. (2016). GRI 201: *Economic performance*. Retrieved from https://www.globalreporting.org/standards/media/1039/gri-201-economic-performance-2016.pdf.

GRI. (2017, 2018, 2019). *GRI Sustainability Disclosure DATABASE*. Retrieved December 21, 2020, from http://database.globalreporting.org/.

Hernández Velasco, J. (2017). *El camino por recorrer en la información no financiera. KPMG Blogs: Institute of Internal Auditors*. Retrieved December 21, 2020, from https://www.tendencias.kpmg.es/2017/10/el-camino-por-recorrer-en-la-informacion-no-financiera/.

International Federation of Accountants (IFAC). (2005). *International guidance document: Environmental management accounting*. New York, NY: IFAC. Retrieved February 5, 2021, from https://www.ifac.org/system/files/publications/files/international-guidance-docu-2.pdf.

International Integrated Reporting Council (IIRC). (2013). *International Integrated Reporting Framework*. Retrieved December 21, 2020, from https://integratedreporting.org/wp-content/uploads/2015/03/13-12-08-THE-INTERNATIONAL-IR-FRAMEWORK-SPANISH-1.pdf.

Ley 27520. (2020). *Ley de Presupuestos Mínimos de Adaptación y Mitigación al Cambio Climático Global*. Retrieved December 21, 2020, from https://www.boletinoficial.gob.ar/detalleAviso/primera/224006/20191220#:~:text=La%20presente%20ley%20establece%20los,41%20de%20la%20Constituci%C3%B3n%20Nacional.

McBrien, M. (2009). *CDSB and SASB release TCFD Implementation Guide*. Retrieved December 21, 2020, from https://www.cdsb.net/task-force/901/cdsb-and-sasb-release-tcfd-implementation-guide.

Pahlen Acuña, R. J., & Fronti de García, L. (2004). Contabilidad social y ambiental (No. 657/P14c).

Pereda, J. T. (1988). Evolución del concepto de contabilidad a través de sus definiciones. *Contaduría Universidad de Antioquia, 13*, 9–74.

PNUD. (2013). América latina y el Caribe. Una Superpotencia de Biodiversidad. Retrieved December 21, 2020, from https://www.undp.org/content/dam/undp/library/EnvironmentandEnergy/biodiversity/Latin-America-and-the-Caribbean%2D%2D-A-Biodiversity-Superpower%2D%2DPolicy_Brief_SPANISH.pdf.

Rodríguez de Ramírez, M. D. C. R. (2020). La Contabilidad en tiempos del COVID-19. *Contabilidad y Auditoría, 51*, 109–154.

Schaltegger, S., & Burritt, R. (2017). *Contemporary environmental accounting: Issues, concepts and practice*. Routledge.

Slawinski, N., & Bansal, P. (2012). A matter of time: The temporal perspectives of organizational responses to climate change. *Organization Studies, 33*(11), 1537–1563.

Task Force on Climate-Related Financial Disclosures (TCDF). (2017). Final Report: Recommendations of the Task Force on Climate-related Financial Disclosures. Retrieved December 21, 2020, from https://www.fsb-tcfd.org/publications/final-recommendations-report/.

Vallaeys, F. (2012). *Definir la responsabilidad social: una urgencia filosófica*. Retrieved December 21, 2020, from http://www.iesalc.unesco.org.ve/index.php.

7

Green Human Resource Management and Green Innovation

Subhadarsini Parida and Kerry Brown

7.1 Introduction

There is a growing need for the application of Green human resource management (HRM) in industry. Green HRM (GHRM) is a new concept that implements sustainability-related policies and practices in organisations. As a part of green social capital availability in an organisation, the adoption of environmental management practices can be fostered to attain sustainability (Jackson et al., 2011; Jabbour et al., 2019). With the growing concern for environmental issues, organisations are obliged to adopt green practices, including aligning environmental management with human resource management, that is, Green HRM practices. Green HRM practices are powerful tools that may provide

S. Parida (✉)
School of Management and Marketing, Curtin University, Perth, WA, Australia
e-mail: subhadarsini.parida@curtin.edu.au

K. Brown
School of Business and Law, Edith Cowan University, Perth, WA, Australia
e-mail: k.brown@ecu.edu.au

E. K. Adae et al. (eds.), *Responsible Management in Emerging Markets*, Sustainable Development Goals Series, https://doi.org/10.1007/978-3-030-76563-7_7

industries and organisations with the opportunities to embrace sustainability. Green HRM is making use of HRM policies to promote sustainable utilisation of resources in organisations. It involves endorsement of sustainable practices by human resources and increases awareness and commitment towards sustainability (Mandip, 2012). These practices can range from green performance management, green culture, and green skills that are domains of human resource management. Iqbal et al. (2018) suggested a definite link between employees' green behaviour and the environmental sustainability of an organisation. Employees who are specialised in environmental management play a critical role in adopting green strategies (Sarkis et al., 2010). Additionally, leadership and sustainability culture play key moderating roles in enhancing environmental management practices and developing resources in the firm (Renwick et al., 2013). The human resource (HR) department is capable of generating and supporting a culture of environmental sustainability within an organisation by coordinating the sustainable objectives and matching them with the capabilities within the organisation.

Given the arguments, this chapter will seek to discuss and analyse Green HRM practices involving environment management (EM). The discussion further emphasises the role of Green HRM to promote green innovation.

7.2 Green HRM

The term 'green HRM' is often used to focus on the contribution of HR policies and practices towards the broader corporate agenda of environmental management. The topic was established for merging environmental management (EM) in an organisation with HRM principles (Jackson & Seo, 2010). Although sustainability is an influential subject, often quoted as a 'hot topic' (Wilkinson et al., 2012) in business research, 'Green HRM' has received a relatively small amount of consideration from scholars (Ehnert, 2009; Inyang et al., 2011; Zoogah, 2011).

The Green HRM concept was largely discussed theoretically in its early conception (Muster & Schrader, 2011, Jackson et al., 2011, Renwick et al., 2013). Green HRM is often exchanged with Sustainable

HRM. Sustainable HRM utilises employees towards achieving the organisation's strategic policies, whereas Green HRM works as a subset of sustainable HRM focussing specifically on the environmental component of sustainability (De Prins, 2011). The integration of HRM and environmental management such as strategies and policies to recycle, reuse, reduce, or renew is argued to be essential for any responsible business to incorporate innovation (Jabbour et al., 2019; Opatha & Arulrajah, 2014).

HR's greatest success in implementing Green HRM can be realised when employees' efforts are altruistic and seamless in their behaviours or attitudes rather than simply an act of compliance (Collier & Esteban, 2007). As a part of responsible business, firms have emphasised environmental management, however, adding a human dimension is still in its embryonic state (Alzgool, 2019). While the HR policies align with an organisation's core green strategies, Green HRM can maximise their strengths by bringing competitive advantage outcomes. Further, employees can be considered strategic partners and a great asset in strategic HRM (Yong et al., 2019).

Green HRM involves traditional HR practices linking to organisational strategic dimensions involving environmental goals. There are two main elements in Green HRM. First is HR practices and second is preservation of knowledge capital. The HR practices are crucial to implement and maintain environmental management in the organisation (Daily & Su-chun, 2001). Green HRM policies focus on developing a green corporate culture by collaborating the green behaviour of individuals and groups. The green environmental behaviour can be incorporated in the consumption patterns of employees in their private lives (Muster & Schrader, 2011).

Green HRM encompasses taking eco-friendly initiatives leading to reduced costs, better engagement of employees, and greater efficiency, which in turn helps the organisations to reduce their carbon footprints. These initiatives require managerial and technical skills (Callenbach et al., 1993); therefore, Green HR initiatives can be implemented through recruitment and selection practices, compensation and benefits, performance-based appraisals, training and development, and health and safety aimed at increasing green awareness among employees. Organisations should take these initiatives as an investment for the long run rather than considering it as a cost. However, other researchers are of the view that the hiring of environmentally oriented staff is very costly and may create an economic burden on companies (Hahn et al., 2014), especially for firms operating in emerging economies where environmental and institutional voids as well as the lack of environmentally conscious personnel are significant challenges.

7.3 Green HRM: Human Resources Critical to Environment Management

Implementing an effective EM system was blurred by unpredictable outcomes until the traditional conception of routine protocols towards reuse, recycle, and renew, or eco-responsibilities was replaced with more conventional strategies to bring environmental sustainability. Human capital is now considered as significant resources (Alvarez & Busenitz, 2001) of any organisational change.

Although sustainability is an influential subject (Wilkinson et al., 2001) in business research, sustainability's nexus with HR is the most pressing theoretical challenge and many researchers (Zoogah, 2011; Aggerholm et al., 2011) agree that this concept has received a limited amount of attention from their counterparts. HR's greatest success to implement Green HRM can be assumed to be through employees' buy-in as seen in their behaviours or attitudes rather than through enforcement (Collier & Esteban, 2007; Saeed et al., 2019). De Prins (2011), in his four approaches to Sustainable HRM, specifically describes Green HRM as the planet component of the triple bottom line that focuses on developing the green competencies inside organisations.

Based on Strategic Human Resource Management (SHRM), a firm's HR department is instrumental in developing the skills, behaviours, and interactions of a firm's workers as fundamental for any strategy formulation and strategy implementation (Colbert, 2004). In an attempt to explain the core driver to bring competitive advantage inside any organisation, Teece et al. (1997) developed the Dynamic Capability View (DCV) of performance routines inside the firm. In what follows, we focus on soft assets such as a behavioural change, which is generally built rather than bought. That is, apart from product development and alliancing at firm level, strategic decision-making is one of the key processes of DCV that creates value for the firms by manipulating resources into creating new strategies (Eisenhardt & Graebner, 2007). Managers have the capability to fully develop, recombine, and generate the pool of employees towards organisational competitive advantage and this finding is well established in the literature.

The existing green strategies and green HR practices can interact with each other. SHRM studies have discussed the need of HR to influence employees' attitudes and behaviours. While the sustainability practices can be based on policies and processes followed by a particular organisation's core green strategies, Green HRM can display a high level of cohesion to bring about behavioural changes. Replication may be difficult as the innovative HR functions are developed by the HR managers to accomplish environmental solutions and this is linked to behavioural change, which might be difficult to copy by other organisations (Schroeder, 2013). The link between HRM and environmental sustainability by integrating the internal resources into unique capabilities drives green innovation in different organisations.

7.4 Green HRM to Create Competitive Advantage

The landmark Brundtland report (World Commission of Environment and Development, 1987) highlights that incorporating environmental sustainability into an organisation's core policies and strategies generate competitive advantage. Strategically switching to an energy-efficient system or using/producing eco-friendly products and services (Gupta & Sharma, 1996) impacts an organisation's productivity, financial benefits, and growth (Jennings & Zandbergen, 1995; Russo & Fouts, 1997).

Almost every business area from marketing, logistics and supply chain, accounting, and retailing are taking a lead to promote a company's eco-responsibilities (Zoogah, 2011). However, the HR department has not been centrally involved in the firm's EM initiatives. According to Teece et al. (1997), what can be unique to firms is not just achieved by price systems. To make organisations more meaningful and understand how competitive advantage is maintained, Teece et al. (1997) acknowledge a need for an expanded paradigm. Based on this requirement, we agree with many scholars (Daily & Su-chun, 2001; Russo & Fouts, 1997; Schroeder, 2013) that there is a need to widen the scope of environmental sustainability from the existing paradigm of creating environmental protocols to more state-of-the-art approaches.

The underlying assumption is such radical and dynamic organisational structures call for behavioural changes. Behavioural changes are strategic assets influenced largely by the HR system (Becker & Huselid, 2006) as they can directly impact an organisation's workforce. Therefore, our measure of environmental sustainability highlights organisations moving beyond existing paradigms and expanding to include HR as a key strategic partner to its EM efforts. Employees possess tacit knowledge that is valuable, rare, and difficult to imitate (Barney & Wright, 1998), and we propose that the choice to focus on an organisation's workforce is a highly effective strategy in creating environmental sustainability.

7.5 Transforming Employee Resources into Unique Capabilities

Given that adopting a 'green and competitive' mantra is an organisational change that demands behavioural changes, we propose that the capacity of Green HRM is realised if the employee resources are subjected to constant development. According to the argument by Bowen and Ostroff (2004), certain HR practices can be linked to a firm's performance and consequently to competitive advantage.

Central here is the focus on firms that have followed a resource-based strategy (Barney, 1991) in 'recognising' and 'choosing' employees as a source for competitive advantage rather than, as explained by Becker and Huselid (2006), 'developing' the employee resources for long-term sustained competitive advantage. DCV, one of the arenas in the strategic management field attempts to incorporate resource development and renewal in rapid societal change. A range of literature discusses DCV as the predominant paradigm to explain superior and long-term competitive advantage in organisations (Ambrosini et al., 2009; Easterby-Smith et al., 2012). To advance this line of argument, Barrales-Molina et al. (2015) also agree that HR contributes to the competitive advantage of a firm.

HR impacts employees' attitudes and behaviours for a particular organisational outcome and during this process of value creation, employee resources are generally rare and non-substitutable (Bowen & Ostroff, 2004). To explain further, most resource-based arguments that are rooted in HRM often are complex and are built over time. Green HRM can be a guiding proposition for building an environmentally responsible reputation and, more specifically, bringing sustained competitive advantage or competitive survival because Green HRM directly influences employees that possess tacit knowledge that is difficult to replicate.

The dynamic capabilities can explain how management can change their existing mental models and paradigms to adapt to and create value by including human dimensions into a reputed environmentally friendly organisation. However, the way in which HRM practices influence employees to show desired environmental behaviours and outcomes at a strategic level can be explained by High Involvement Work System (HIWS).

7.6 High Involvement Work System for Green HRM

Although we have explained the significance of DCV's effectiveness in the area of human resources, there still exists a wide array of questions surrounding the features of an HR system that will engender strong environmental behaviours and attitudes in employees. HRM practices can be used by HR managers to communicate strategic goals and values from the employer to employee. They also add that for any task requirement or task accomplishment, a specific set of HRM practices are necessary to understand and enable the desired and appropriate behaviours.

According to Mendelson et al. (2011), human capital is viewed as resources under a HIWS framework. HIWS designs a set of HR practices known as High Involvement Work Practices (HIWP) to enrich the employees and gain competitive advantage. HIWS is argued to bring a participatory change process as it can be used as strategy by the managers to influence employees' capabilities and attitudes and bring real changes.

Lawler (1992) discussed four aspects as key to HIWP to emphasise employee engagement. These aspects are based on providing employees power, information, knowledge, and rewards (Mendelson, 2005; Konrad, 2006). To explain further, empowering employees is critical for employees to be accountable and authorise them to take important decisions to enhance the overall quality of their lives.

Information is another key element of HIWP to provide transparent and timely data to improve the overall understanding of the process and align the actions with the performance in the organisation. Knowledge aspect of HIWP provides employees with the necessary skills and competencies to make critical workplace decisions. Lastly, the rewards component highlights its influence on employees' discretionary effort. These HIWP components demonstrate higher engagement levels by considering human capital in a firm to be its resources rather than just controlled expenses.

By adopting the principles of DCV under the HIWS framework, it may be possible for companies to begin to change the rules of competition and establish environmental sustainability in a more meaningful way. This aligns with Bowen and Ostroff's (2004) study of four characteristics of HR and links to competitive advantage and developing resources: visibility, understandability, legitimacy of authority, and relevance. Green HR practices determined by HR managers should be readily observable, easily practised without ambiguity, easily adopted and adapted by employees, and create behaviours that are demonstrative of the organisation's priority of environmental sustainability.

7.7 Green Innovation Through Green HRM Practices

Green innovation is related to developing eco-friendly products and processes by adopting key organisational practices (Albort-Morant et al., 2016), such as reducing waste in production or using recycled materials. The organisations that implement green innovations have a competitive advantage over their counterparts as they leverage green resources and capabilities to respond to the environmental concerns of consumers.

Specific HRM practices are capable of promoting a culture of commitment rather than forced compliance that can impact an organisation's effort to incorporate innovation (Verburg et al., 2007). Drawing from the Resource Based View (RBV) (Barney, 1991) and DCV (Teece et al., 1997), the organisation can leverage the human capital through Green HRM practices to create opportunities for green innovation. Specific HR functions such as attraction, training, performance, or rewards are likely to provide green innovation in processes, products, and services (Gerhart, 2005). Based on the HIWS framework (power, information, knowledge, and rewards), the following section explains the role of different HRM functions that organisations are likely to undertake to create green innovation opportunities.

7.8 Power

The underlying idea to empower employees is to give them the authority to make crucial decisions without being micromanaged (Mallak & Kurstedt, 1996). Organisations can target and utilise specific HR processes: *employee participation* (Konrad, 2006), *self-managed teams* (Jabbour & Santos, 2008b), and *management* and *leadership* (Renwick et al., 2013), to enhance the capabilities of the employees to work towards environmental sustainability

7.8.1 Eco-participation Opportunities

Employee engagement can be achieved through participation. Employee participation involves employees having positive attitudes to any change impacting their behaviours towards any environmental activities. When employees are included in the decision-making on environmental projects, they tend to invest more in behaving responsibly towards the environment.

Participating in environmental related innovation is likely to provide employees the opportunities where they are likely to seek self-actualisation beyond just their regular job responsibilities. These meaningful opportunities to be a part of ethics and social responsibility can make them stay committed to the organisations in which they are working. The HR function is important to encourage employees to pursue green commuting habits like taking public transportation through free or discounted transportation passes, carpooling, creating environmental volunteering programmes, and involving employees to reduce waste from the workplaces (Mandip, 2012). Such participative opportunities empower employees to contribute to environmental issues while at work without any extra burden to do so.

The HR of various organisations are providing self-actualised and meaningful opportunities to the workforce, beyond their functional contribution to the jobs, to participate in green practices as a part of ethics and social responsibility. 3M empowers its employees by providing 15% of their job hours to work on their own projects under Pollution Prevention Pays (3M, 2015). Similarly, Bank of America has engaged its employees in various events such as World Water Day and Earth Day (BOA, 2021). It is managing waste through its 'Think Eat Save' Waste Less Lunch programme. Organisations such as Fuji Xerox (Fuji Xerox, 2021), IBM's 'Think Green' (IBM, 2021), American Airlines' 'Fuel Smart' (AA, 2021), BT's 'Carbon Clubs' (BT, 2015), Dow Chemical's Waste Reduction (WRAP) programme contest (Dow, 2021), FedEx (FedEx, 2021), and IBM (IBM, 2021) are involving employees to raise awareness among people as well as involving themselves in green practices such as fuel-saving opportunities, car-sharing, cycle fit initiatives, flexible working hours, and to protect environment. Similar traces of involving employees in environmental management can be seen in HSBC's workers (HSBC, 2021), Airlines flight attendants (AA, 2021), and Kodak's engineers (Kodak, 2021), as they are managing waste. Danone (Danone, 2021), Tata (Tata, 2021), Intel (Intel, 2021), and Panasonic (Panasonic, 2021) are encouraging their employees to participate in various volunteering environmental projects to spread eco-ideas to local communities.

7.8.2 Creating Green Teams

The HR can create participative opportunities through cross-functional teams to empower employees and dissolve status differences (Mendelson, 2005) or hierarchical layers (Pfeffer, 1998) to bring best practices (Jabbour and Santos, 2008) in solving environmental issues while at work.

Self-managed green teams formed to solve environmental problems, allow the freedom to create ideas and draw attention to bring best practices in environment management into the organisations. Further, the elimination of status differences fosters involvement and flexibility, and this creates better involvement in green initiatives that are taking place in an organisation. Examples of such organisations are American Airlines' Waste Minimisation Team; BT's The Grad Green Team of Carbon Club (BT, 2015); and P&G's Global Asset Recovery Purchases (GARP) team (P&G, 2021), while Google's green teams work closely with facility managers to implement innovative strategies (Google, 2021), and Adidas (Adidas, 2021) and Kodak to encourage colleagues to 'think green' (Kodak, 2021). UK teams at FedEx (FedEx, 2021) and Bank of America (BOA, 2021) are involved in various volunteering programmes in the local community.

7.8.3 Transforming Leaders

Senior management plays a significant role in checking the progress and effectiveness of the environmental management in an organisation. The

HR managers identify the training needs to sustain teams' motivation towards green commitment in the firm (Zacharatos et al., 2005). Supportive management provides socio-political support and encourages the employees to voice their opinion in sensitive environmental matters and gives them the freedom to make environmental improvements.

Transformational Leadership has not only the potential to counterbalance the negativity that could hinder teams to achieve their green goals but also help the followers exceed performance. Mandip (2012) also suggests that the trade unions take a leadership role in creating a participative environment in bringing sustainability to workplaces or encouraging employees to take more green jobs. HSBC is training senior managers as a part of its Sustainability Leadership Programme and Dow is also cultivating the next generation of sustainability leaders. IBM's 'Think Green' programme (IBM, 2021) and PepsiCo's Sustainability Task Force (Pepsico India, 2021) are particularly created to engage the leadership group in sustainability efforts.

7.9 Information

The HR function can be the communication path to enable constant and transparent information flow from the higher levels (Daily & Su-chun, 2001), thereby enabling employees to take considerate decisions on their future carbon footprints (Zoogah, 2011). The HR functions that can be highly committed under the information category green jobs, green recruitment and selection, and creating a green culture inside the organisation.

7.9.1 Green Jobs and Attraction and Selection

The new generation workforce is emphasising environmental sensibility as they choose their employers, even taking a lower salary to work with a green employer (Renwick et al., 2016), and hence, firms with green employer brand (Jackson et al., 2011) will be able to attract these knowledge workers. Environmental vision as company's identity could largely influence the workforce through the creation of more green jobs and attracting and selecting sustainability-driven individuals (Fernández et al., 2003). This approach can be applicable where the HR department prefers candidates who are 'green-aware' and commit to the firm's sustainability agenda. With the increase of green business, the HR department creates jobs related to waste management in a firm, thus giving more employment opportunities.

With the onset of technology, the HR can switch into a total paperless recruitment and selection process. This can be done by switching all the processes such as job adverts, application submission, acceptance letters, offers, employee portals, boarding documentation to online. Moreover, a web-based recruitment conveys more information on the firms' ecological performances.

The interview process is a significant part as it can be integrated with the company's sustainable development to evaluate the potential capability of the interviewees with the organisation's green goals. Moreover, job advertisements can ask the candidates to give proof of their environmental consciousness in their resumes. After recruitment, the new recruits can be well informed about the company's environmental targets during the induction.

7.9.2 Organisation Culture Management

HR can be instrumental in recognising, integrating, and spreading long-term sustainability (Jabbour & Santos, 2008; Jackson et al., 2011) by incorporating deep embedded green values into the organisation's corporate culture (Renwick et al., 2016). Employees in a leadership role can be instrumental in recognising, integrating, and spreading the corporate values emphasising ecological dimensions as a part of an organisation's culture. For example, encouraging employees to bring lunch bags or prohibiting plastic bottles or paper cups in the office can encourage recycling or reusing habits.

Many energy-saving options such as fluorescent lights at workstations, switching to public transport or carpooling, using frequent tele and video conferencing to minimise travel can create a company culture that can contribute to the environment on a daily basis. Having such options and informing the employees about these options is a responsibility that HR management should perform.

Setting up an ecological dimension in corporate culture creates a green influence in other HR functional areas such as recruitment, selection, training and development, performance management, and rewards. For example, Google has integrated environmental consciousness by encouraging employees to commute in a shuttle run on bio-diesel and equipped with Wi-Fi to help employees work during their travel time (Google, 2021). Google has a culture of go-green initiatives like solar car parking and 100% recyclable cups and plates (Google Green, 2021). To cut down on carbon emission released during commuting and travel, HSBC is using Conferencing and Tele-presence solutions (HSBC, 2021). IBM also has its human resources creating corporate values aiming to build a 'Smart Planet' brand (IBM, 2021).

7.10 Knowledge

To make employees capable enough to get committed to innovative activities, essential knowledge and skills are required along with information. HR is critical to nurturing the right amount of knowledge and technicalities of specific work processes (Schroeder, 2013) required to demonstrate green behaviours (Renwick et al., 2013). We suggest that organisational learning and training are highly committed HR functions that are essential for securing engagement among the employees.

7.10.1 Organisation Learning

The significance of organisational learning strengthens an organisation's efforts to create ecological balance. Incorporating this aspect could enable employees to learn new techniques and develop green skills. HR departments can use a preventive approach to make the employees aware of how pollution is caused and ways to reduce it.

Organisational learning surrounding environmental management can be achieved by Learning by Doing: as employees can be involved in environmental activities, in which they acquire pertinent knowledge on being green. Also, new concepts related to green contributions can be acquired through Learning by Exploration as posited by Jabbour and Santos (2008a). Organisational learning qualifies employees to absorb, develop, transfer, and reflect on knowledge about the environment. American Airlines and BT have incorporated their Utilities Management council to focus on sharing eco-best practices among the employees and implement them in daily life. Similarly, DuPont through its monthly webinars (DuPont, 2014) and GE (GE, 2021) with its 'ecomagination' and 'healthymagination' initiatives are motivating employees to focus on research for improving the firm's environmental impact and maintaining environmental standards. GE and Google spread the organisational knowledge and their environmentally friendly policies have gained a lot of media exposure.

7.10.2 Environmental Training

Training is a different function from learning, where the latter encompasses the former. Participating in training needs prior learning and brings learning to some extent. As employees in a dynamic capability environment are viewed as resources (Mendelson, 2005), they need constant development. Training is widely seen as a significant intervention to GHRM engagement (Jackson, 2013). Renwick, Redman, and Maguire (2013) explain that training that is provided to all levels in the firm increases the 'eco-literacy' level of the employees and equips them with necessary KSAs (Knowledge, Skills and Abilities) and self-efficacy to deal with environmental issues.

Mandip (2012) mentions a requirement of training need analysis (TNA) to scrutinise the level of environmental knowledge that the employees require. This can extend to re-training staff that have lost jobs in 'polluter' organisations. Imparting effective training is essential to creating experiences of psychological meaningfulness at work, and hence, the HR department must keep the training simple and relevant, involving top management as role models and evaluating the training effects. HR departments can upgrade skills of the workforce with relevant training opportunities. For instance, Fuji Xerox has started Go Green Workshops to train the employees on how to implement eco-practices at offices (Fuji Xerox, 2021). It also offers IT professionals training to become a Singapore Certified Green IT Professional (SCGP). Similarly, HSBC and Toyota's 'TogetherGreen' trains senior managers. IBM trains its employees for environment concerns (IBM, 2021).

7.11 Rewards

HR could utilise its performance management role and compensation practices to motivate employees to promote Environment Management.

7.11.1 Performance Management

The findings suggest that performance management systems in a green company set green targets to be the Key Performance Area (KPA) as performance standards or green behaviour indicators during performance appraisal. This is suggested as a significant yardstick for managers' capability in managing environmental performance desired by the organisation. Environmental HR can be introduced by the HR department to assist staff to measure their own carbon footprints.

HR plays an important role in maintaining disciplinary procedures attached to environmental issues, but they need to be cautious of using negative enforcement such as suspension or criticism in the case of low violation because it might create self-protective behaviours to conceal environment problems (Renwick et al., 2016). Tata's HR department has incorporated Tata Code of Conduct as a Performance Management indicator to monitor employees' environmental behaviours (Tata, 2021). Similarly, Panasonic has green indexes (Panasonic, 2021) that encourage internal whistleblowing as PMS.

7.11.2 Compensation

HIWS emphasises rewards and enhances the motivational level to engage in the desired behaviours. Contingent compensation depends on an employee's performance with respect to company benchmarks and this is critical to HIWS (Pfeffer, 1998), as it adjusts the employees' interests with a firm's environmental targets (Mendelson, 2005). Rewards also empower the staff to make independent decisions about whether to continue with environmental practices.

As a part of green rewards and promoting an environmentally friendly workplace and lifestyle, employers may provide tax exemptions on loaning bicycles to commute to the office and green benefit cards to create more green product sales. The variable pay attribute is linked to compensation on the basis of an employee's eco-performances. To encourage the manager, strong bonuses may be connected to their Environment Management outcomes. Even the CEO and executives' compensation can be linked to the firm's environmental reputation. Non-monetary rewards such as recognition-based programmes or award dinners for staff engaged in EM activities creates intrinsic motivation among the employees who invest more in corporate environmental initiatives.

3M's Pollution Prevention Pays (3P) awards employees who implement creative environmental solutions (3M, 2015). Organisations such as Nordstrom (Nordstrom, 2021), Neste Oil (Nesteoil, 2021), P&G (P&G, 2021), and Shell (Shell, 2011) offer rewards and bonuses to their employees and managers for their environmental behaviour. American Airlines (AA, 2021) and Bank of America (BOA, 2021) offer environmental benefits in terms of discounts and reimbursement for buying eco-friendly products. FedEx tracks monthly performance and reviews the senior management's CSR involvement (FedEx, 2021). Dow's unique WRAP Award programme (Dow, 2021) and DuPont (DuPont, 2014) through its annual Sustainable Growth Excellence Awards recognise key employees involved in bringing sustainable practices to the company.

7.12 Recommendations

This study highlights how Green HRM effectively engages employees in green business that finally creates organisational effectiveness. The organisations studied in this research provide examples of specific HR processes to support in environmental management under HIWS's attributes of power, information, knowledge, and rewards.

HR processes use an HIWS to create a situation in which employees are more willing to contribute to the environment rather than being enforced. The strategy to integrate, develop, and release brings behavioural change by individuals. It is argued throughout the process of HIWS, HR can integrate the green policies of the organisation to develop Green HRM strategies.

The two ways that the potential of these green HR practices is released include effective employee engagement determined by employees' psychological motivation arrangements and competitive survival determined by organisational effectiveness. The main feature of HR's potential in environment management can be observed as how it can create capability and opportunity within the firm.

The intersection of environmental sustainability and HR management is a new area in organisational change and development, and therefore this area is not characterised by a fully developed body of research. All the stakeholders of HRM from employers, employees, practitioners, and academics are key drivers to competitive advantage and it is evident that Green HRM is an emergent concept for competitive advantage and, more specifically, competitive survival. There is a substantial scope for Green HRM research, but there is a lack of practical application especially from a Strategic HRM perspective.

Strategic HRM seeks HR as a strategic partner in green companies. Hence, further research is needed to develop an HR system that achieves both horizontal fit and vertical fit. Horizontal fit refers to achieving internal consistency of Green HR policies and vertical fit refers to Green HR's alignment to firms' environmental goals. Furthermore, this study recommends more academic research is needed around High Involvement

Work concepts to study the impact of these concepts on Green HRM to bring competitive survival outcomes.

7.13 Conclusion

In sum, HR has the potential to identify people-related risks and opportunities for environmental innovation. This aspect can be different from organisation to organisation and thus, will create competitive advantage as discussed in the study by different innovative HR practices. Fundamentally, the role of human resources is to develop employees according to the organisation's strategic objectives.

The concept of Green HRM can enhance the contribution of HRM as a strategic partner in the firm to deliver competitive advantage and employees as the most important stakeholders for implementing innovation in the organisation. HR has the potential to identify people-related risks and opportunities in environmental management through creating innovative practices.

This chapter is a starting point for additional empirical studies that attempt to explain how organisations' HR may initiate and create awareness about implementing green strategies in any firm. We acknowledge that the different HR functions under the HIWS framework can be innovative and unique to create competitive advantage for the organisation.

HR has the capacity to understand how the idiosyncratic attributes of a particular HR strategy play out at a firm level and largely impact the competitive fundamentals of the organisation. Essentially, implementing green innovation can be critical when specific human resource strategies promote employee engagement and offer the prospect of developing and enhancing environmental management.

References

3M. (2015). Corporate Responsibility. 3M. Retrieved March 20, 2021, from http://solutions.3m.com/

AA. (2021). Corporate responsibility. American airlines. Retrieved March 7, 2021, from http://www.aa.com/i18n/aboutUs/corporateResponsibility/environment/progress.jsp

Adidas. (2021). Green Company. Sustainability. Adidas Group. Retrieved March 11, 2021, from http://www.adidas-group.com/en/sustainability/planet/green-company/

Aggerholm, H. K., Andersen, S. E., & Thomsen, C. (2011). Conceptualising employer branding in sustainable organisations. *Corporate Communications: An International Journal, 16*(2), 105–123.

Albort-Morant, G., Leal-Millán, A., & Cepeda-Carrión, G. (2016). The antecedents of green innovation performance: A model of learning and capabilities. *Journal of Business Research, 69*(11), 4912–4917.

Alvarez, S. A., & Busenitz, L. W. (2001). The entrepreneurship of resource-based theory. *Journal of management, 27*(6), 755–775.

Alzgool, M. (2019). Nexus between green HRM and green management towards fostering green values. *Management Science Letters, 9*(12), 2073–2082.

Ambrosini, V., Bowman, C., & Collier, N. (2009). Dynamic Capabilities: An Exploration of How Firms Renew their Resource Base. *British Journal of Management, 20*(1), S9–S24.

Barney, J. (1991). Firm resources and sustained competitive advantage. *Journal of Management, 17*(1), 99–120.

Barney, J. B., & Wright, P. M. (1998). On becoming a strategic partner: The role of human resource in gaining competitive advantage. *Human Resource Management, 37*(1), 31–46.

Barrales-Molina, V., Montes, F. J. L., & Gutierrez-Gutierrez, L. J. (2015). Dynamic capabilities, human resources and operating routines: A new product development approach. *Industrial Management & Data Systems, 115*(8), 1388–1411.

Becker, B. E., & Huselid, M. A. (2006). Strategic human resources management: Where do we go from here? *Journal of Management, 32*(6), 898–925.

BOA. (2021). Environmental Sustainability-Global Impact. Bank of America. Retrieved March 13, 2021, from http://about.bankofamerica.com/en-us/global-impact/environmental-sustainability.html#fbid=aZSAPwqaHtN/hashlink=first_goal

Bowen, D. E., & Ostroff, C. (2004). Understanding HRM-firm performance linkages: The role of the "Strength" of the HRM system. *The Academy of Management Review, 29*(2), 203–221.

BT. (2015). BT's Environmental Policy. Retrieved March 2, 2021, from https://www.btplc.com/Betterfuture/BetterFutureReport/pdf/2013/BT_Environmental_Policy.pdf

Callenbach, E., Capra, F., Lutz, L., Goldman, L., Lutz, R., & Marburg, S. (1993). *EcoManagement: The Elmwood guide to ecological auditing and sustainable business*. Berrett-Koehler Publishers.

Colbert, B. A. (2004). The complex resource-based view: Implications for theory and practice in strategic human resource management. *Academy of Management Review, 29*(3), 341–358.

Collier, J., & Esteban, R. (2007). Corporate social responsibility and employee commitment. *Business Ethics: A European Review, 16*(1), 19–33.

Daily, B. F., & Su-Chun, H. (2001). Achieving sustainability through attention to human resource factors in environmental management. *International Journal of Operations & Production Management, 21*(12), 1539–1552.

Danone. (2021). A sustainable food chain-Danone. Retrieved March 12, 2021, from http://www.danone.com/en/for-all/mission-strategy/our-strategy/a-sustainable-food-chain/

De Prins, P. (2011). Duurzaam HRM: synthetische academische introductie, cited by: Rompa I. *Explorative research on sustainable Human Resource management,* 1.

Dow. (2021). Dedicated to Sustainability. Dow. Retrieved March 4, 2021, from http://www.dow.com/sustainability/

DuPont. (2014). Global Reporting Initiative Report. DuPont. Retrieved March 1, 2021, from http://www.dupont.com/content/dam/assets/corporate-functions/our-approach/sustainability/documents/DuPont2014GRIReport.pdf

Easterby-Smith, M., Thorpe, R., & Jackson, P. R. (2012). *Management research*. Sage Publications.

Ehnert, I. (2009). *Sustainable human resource management: A Conceptual and Exploratory Analysis from a Paradox Perspective*. Physica-Verlag HD.

Eisenhardt, K. M., & Graebner, M. E. (2007). Theory building from cases: Opportunities and challenges. *Academy of Management Journal, 50*(1), 25–32.

Fedex. (2021). Social Responsibility. FedEx. Retrieved March 17, 2021, from http://about.van.fedex.com/social-responsibility/environment-efficiency/

Fernández, E., Junquera, B., & Ordiz, M. (2003). Organizational culture and human resources in the environmental issue: A review of the literature. *International Journal of Human Resource Management, 14*(4), 634–656.

Fuji Xerox. (2021). Fuji Xerox's Ecology and Sustainability. Retrieved March 20, 2021, from http://www.fujixerox.com.sg/company/sustainability

GE. (2021). General Electric. Retrieved March 14, 2021, from http://www.ge.com/

Gerhart, B. (2005). Human resources and business performance: Findings, unanswered questions, and an alternative approach. *Management Revue, 16*(2), 174–185.

Google. (2021). Google's green. Retrieved March 20, 2021, from http://www.google.com.au/green/bigpicture/

Google Green. (2021). Campus operations. Google. Retrieved March 20, 2021, from http://www.google.com.au/green/efficiency/oncampus/

Gupta, M., & Sharma, K. (1996). Environmental operations management: An opportunity for improvement. *Production and Inventory Management Journal, 37*(3), 40–46.

Hahn, J., Reilly, P. M., & Buchanan, T. M. (2014). Development of a hospital reiki training program: training volunteers to provide reiki to patients, families, and staff in the acute care setting. *Dimensions of Critical Care Nursing, 33*(1), 15–21.

HSBC. (2021). Environmental Efficiency- Sustainability-HSBC. Retrieved March 20, 2021, from http://www.hsbc.com/citizenship/sustainability/environmental-efficiency

IBM. (2021). IBM and the Environment. IBM. Retrieved March 20, 2021, from http://www.ibm.com/ibm/environment/

Intel. (2021). Sustainability Initiatives and Policies, Intel. Retrieved March 21, 2021, from http://www.intel.com/content/www/us/en/corporate-responsibility/sustainability-initiatives-and-policies.html

Inyang, B. J., Awa, H. O., & Enuoh, R. O. (2011). CSR-HRM nexus: Defining the role engagement of the human resources professionals. *International Journal of Business and Social Science, 2*(5), 118–126.

Iqbal, Q., Hassan, S. H., Akhtar, S., & Khan, S. (2018). Employee's green behavior for environmental sustainability: A case of banking sector in Pakistan. *World Journal of Science, Technology and Sustainable Development, 15*(2), 118–130.

Jabbour, C. J. C., & Santos, F. C. A. (2008a). The central role of human resource management in the search for sustainable organizations. *The International Journal of Human Resource Management, 19*(2), 2133–2154.
Jabbour, C. J. C., & Santos, F. C. A. (2008b). Relationships between human resource dimensions and environmental management in companies: Proposal of a model. *Journal of Cleaner Production, 16*(1), 51–58.
Jabbour, C. J. C., Sarkis, J., De Sousa Jabbour, A. B. L., Renwick, D. W. S., Singh, S. K., Grebinevych, O., Kruglianskas, I., & Godinho Filho, M. (2019). Who is in charge? A review and a research agenda on the 'human side' of the circular economy. *Journal of Cleaner Production, 222*(1), 793–801.
Jackson, S. E. (2013). Behavioral perspective of strategic human resource management. *Encyclopedia of management theory, 1*(1), 66–72.
Jackson, S. E., & Seo, J. (2010). The greening of strategic HRM scholarship. *Organization Management Journal, 7*(4), 278–290.
Jackson, S. E., Renwick, D. W., Jabbour, C. J., & Muller-camen, M. (2011). State-of-the-art and future directions for green human resource management: Introduction to the special issue. *Zeitschrift für Personalforschung/German Journal of Research in Human Resource Management, 25*(2), 99–116.
Jennings, P. D., & Zandbergen, P. A. (1995). Ecologically sustainable organizations: An institutional approach. *Academy of Management Review, 20*(4), 1015.
Kodak. (2021). Kodak environmental activities. Kodak Australasia. Retrieved March 4, 2021, from http://wwwau.kodak.com/AU/en/corp/environ.shtml
Konrad, A. M. (2006). Engaging employees through high-involvement work practices. *Ivey Business Journal, 70*(4), 11–14.
Lawler, E. E. (1992). *The ultimate advantage: Creating the high-involvement organization*. Jossey-Bass.
Mallak, L., & Kurstedt, H. (1996). Understanding and using empowerment to change organizational culture. *Industrial Management-Chicago then Atlanta, 38*(1), 8–10.
Mandip, G. (2012). Green HRM: People management commitment to environmental sustainability. *Research Journal of Recent Sciences, 1*(ISC-2011), 244–252.
Mendelson, M. B. 2005. *The nature of high-involvement work systems: A test of competing models*. 1(1), 1423-1423.
Mendelson, M. B., Turner, N., & Barling, J. (2011). Perceptions of the presence and effectiveness of high involvement work systems and their relationship to employee attitudes: A test of competing models. *Personnel Review, 40*(1), 45–69.

Muster, V., & Schrader, U. (2011). Green work-life balance: A new perspective for green HRM. *German Journal of Human Resource Management, 25*(2), 140–156.

Nesteoil. (2021). Neste Oil's sustainability. Retrieved March 20, 2021, from http://2012.nesteoil.com/

Nordstrom. (2021). Nordstrom Cares. Nordstrom. Retrieved March 20, 2021, from http://shop.nordstrom.com/c/nordstrom-cares-restaurants

Opatha, H. H. P., & Arulrajah, A. A. (2014). Green human resource management: Simplified general reflections. *International Business Research, 7*(8), 101–112.

P&G. (2021). Environmental sustainability. P&G. Retrieved March 10, 2021, from http://www.pg.com/en_US/sustainability/environmental_sustainability/worth_from_waste.shtml

Panasonic. (2021). Global Citizenship Activities Promoted by Employees. Retrieved March 20, 2021, from http://panasonic.net/citizenship/environment/

Pepsico India. (2021). Performance with Purpose. Pepsico India. Retrieved March 20, 2021, from http://www.pepsicoindia.co.in/purpose/performance-with-purpose.html

Pfeffer, J. (1998). Seven practices of successful organizations. *California Management Review, 40*(2), 96–124.

Renwick, D. W. S., Redman, T., & Maguire, S. (2013). Green human resource management: A review and research agenda*. *International Journal of Management Reviews, 15*(1), 1–14.

Renwick, D. W. S., Jabbour, C. J. C., Muller-camen, M., Redman, T., & Wilkinson, A. (2016). Contemporary developments in Green (environmental) HRM scholarship. *The International Journal of Human Resource Management, 27*(2), 114–128.

Russo, M. V., & Fouts, P. A. (1997). A resource-based perspective on corporate environmental performance and profitability. *Academy of Management Journal, 40*(3), 534–559.

Saeed, B. B., Afsar, B., Hafeez, S., Khan, I., Tahir, M., & Afridi, M. A. (2019). Promoting employee's proenvironmental behavior through green human resource management practices. *Corporate Social Responsibility and Environmental Management, 26*(2), 424–438.

Sarkis, J., Gonzalez-torre, P., & Adenso-diaz, B. (2010). Stakeholder pressure and the adoption of environmental practices: The mediating effect of training. *Journal of operations Management, 28*(2), 163–176.

Schroeder, H. (2013). The importance of human resource management in strategic sustainability: An art and science perspective. *Journal of Environmental Sustainability, 2*(2), 4.
Shell. (2011). Annual Environmental Statement for Shell U.K Upstream Operations. Retrieved March 10, 2021, from http://www.shell.co.uk/content/dam/shell-new/local/country/gbr/downloads/upstream/environmental-statement2011.pdf
Tata. (2021). The climate of change. Tata Group. Retrieved March 5, 2021, from http://www.tata.com/article/inside/f5KCaVEfP8s=/TLYVr3YPkMU=
Teece, D. J., Pisano, G., & Shuen, A. (1997). Dynamic capabilities and strategic management. *Strategic Management Journal, 18*(7), 509–533.
Verburg, R. M., Den Hartog, D. N., & Koopman, P. L. (2007). Configurations of human resource management practices: A model and test of internal fit. *The International Journal of Human Resource Management, 18*(2), 184–208.
Wilkinson, A., Hill, M., & Gollan, P. (2001). The sustainability debate. *International Journal of Operations & Production Management, 21*(2), 1492–1502.
Wilkinson, S., Rashid, M., Spreckelmeyer, K., & Angrisano, N. J. (2012). Green buildings, environmental awareness, and organizational image. *Journal of Corporate Real Estate, 14*(1), 21–49.
World Commission on Environment and Development. (1987). *Our Common Future*. Oxford University Press.
Yong, J. Y., Yusliza, M., Ramayah, T., & Fawehinmi, O. (2019). Nexus between green intellectual capital and green human resource management. *Journal of cleaner production, 215*(1), 364–374.
Zacharatos, A., Barling, J., & Iverson, R. D. (2005). High-performance work systems and occupational safety. *Journal of Applied Psychology, 90*(1), 77–93.
Zoogah, D. B. (2011). The dynamics of Green HRM behaviors: A cognitive social information processing approach. *German Journal of Human Resource Management, 25*(2), 117–139.

Part III

Sustainability Management

8

Contemporary Issues in Sustainable Operations Management

Anthea Amadi-Echendu

8.1 Introduction

Operations management integrate people, technology, processes, and procedures of design, management, and the production of products and services according to customer specification at a lower cost (Jaehn, 2016). Operations management is, therefore, responsible for converting resources from inputs into outputs as goods and services that are exchanged for money by an organisation through a transformation process (Slack et al., 2017). The products and services span across various industries that range in size and price. Inputs may be obtained from various suppliers. Outputs from one organisation may become an input into a different process for another supplier.

When it comes to operations management, efficiency in the design, improvement, management, or administration of business practices to generate value by converting inputs (such as raw materials, technology,

A. Amadi-Echendu (✉)
University of South Africa, Pretoria, South Africa
e-mail: amadiap@unisa.ac.za

E. K. Adae et al. (eds.), *Responsible Management in Emerging Markets*, Sustainable Development Goals Series, https://doi.org/10.1007/978-3-030-76563-7_8

equipment, and workforce) into outputs (such as goods or services) is important because the higher the efficiency, the higher the profit generated by the business. The delivery of goods and services to customers at the right time, in the right quantity, and at the right quality is another major responsibility of operations management. Failure to ensure the right standards and quantities may negatively affect the business' credibility, market share, and profits. In addition, operations managers must deal with the challenges of climate change and the sustainability of the natural environment by controlling environmental pollution and minimising waste.

Many organisations are involved in the end-to-end process of producing goods and services for the end customer which forms a supply chain that needs to work together to enhance efficiencies by reducing turnaround times, coordinating deliveries, managing costs, and ensuring that the correct quantities reach the right end-users at the right time. Warehousing and logistical services may be secured from external organisations to the manufacturer of the products and services.

Operations management is also responsible for ensuring that limited resources are available to meet people's unlimited needs and wants. Hence, operations management, which is responsible for producing the products and services that a business sells, must be able to manage in a way that ensures that manufacturing processes are not harmful to the environment, that materials can be recycled and are not toxic to the environment (Ogunlela, 2018), and scarce resources are well managed to meet the demands of future generations.

Traditional methods of production and operations management practices have been critiqued for contributing to greenhouse gas (GHG) emissions in the form of carbon dioxide, methane, nitrous oxide, and fluorinated gases. These greenhouse gases contribute to global warming and climate change by trapping heat in the atmosphere. Climate change affects the primary sector through rising sea levels that affect the fishing industry, wildfires that may affect wildlife, and droughts that may affect agriculture (Mkansi et al., 2020).

Unsustainable operations also result in negative social and environmental consequences such as pollution and health and safety problems. Consequently, reducing the environmental impact of operations management is a key success factor in the sustainability of the economy. Improving sustainable operations management is also a significant business opportunity for firms as suppliers of goods and services. Operations management practices must, therefore, respond to demands to address sustainability.

The objective of this chapter is to discuss the contemporary trends in operations management with a particular focus on sustainability within operations management to help stakeholders update their business processes to accommodate sustainability aspects and adjust supply chain management principles to enhance the efficiencies and effectiveness of operations. Many different aspects of operations management can be considered from a sustainability perspective.

This chapter focuses on the problem of limited resources, aspects that relate to green operations management principles, and sustainability in operations and the supply chain. These aspects include environmental design, green labelling, migrating from a linear economy into a circular economy, incorporating technology into operations, humanitarian operations management, and improvement strategies.

8.2 Sustainable Operations and Green Supply Chain Management

Sustainable operations encompass product design, choice of technology, logistics, supply chain network design, and supply chain management (Jaehn, 2016). It also requires recyclability and ease of disassembly for economic value with biodegradable products (Mkansi et al., 2020) and sustainable energy consumption.

A sustainable operations system provides optimum value to the marketplace through value creation processes with minimum waste in the manufacturing and operational phases of the product life-cycle. Green supply chain management (GSM) is defined as "integrating environmental thinking into supply chain management, including product design, material sourcing and selection, manufacturing process, delivery of the final product to the consumers as well as end-of-life management of the product after its useful life" (Srivastava, 2007).

8.2.1 Current Trends in Operations Management

Operations management traditionally has been concerned with the production aspect only. In recent times, it starts with design so that waste can be minimised, scarce resources can be used appropriately, and products can be more environmentally friendly. Design has to do with the design of products and services as well as the design of processes.

Design is, therefore, integral to operations management as it is more than determining how the product will look, but includes the configuration of resources (people, equipment, raw materials, physical shape, nature of processes, etc.) and activities. Resources that are not environmentally friendly could harm the environment and incur financial losses for the business through fines, penalties, recalls, and redesign activities.

8.2.1.1 Design for the Environment

Greenhouse gases are measured and verified in publications by the International Organisation for Standardisation (ISO), namely, the ISO 14064 standard for the quantification, reporting, review, and verification of greenhouse gases at organisational and project level; the ISO 14065 for certification bodies; and the ISO 14067 that deals with product carbon footprint requirements (Zhu et al., 2016). ISO 14064 and ISO 14062 focus on the integration of environmental aspects into product design and development.

Designing for a greener environment requires attention to energy usage and consumption, the selection of materials, and the designing of manufacturing processes. Design for the environment (DfE) is a design approach that emanates from the suppliers of raw materials, through the manufacturing stages of the production process, to the end consumer of the product or service. Products and services follow a life-cycle as illustrated in Fig 8.1.

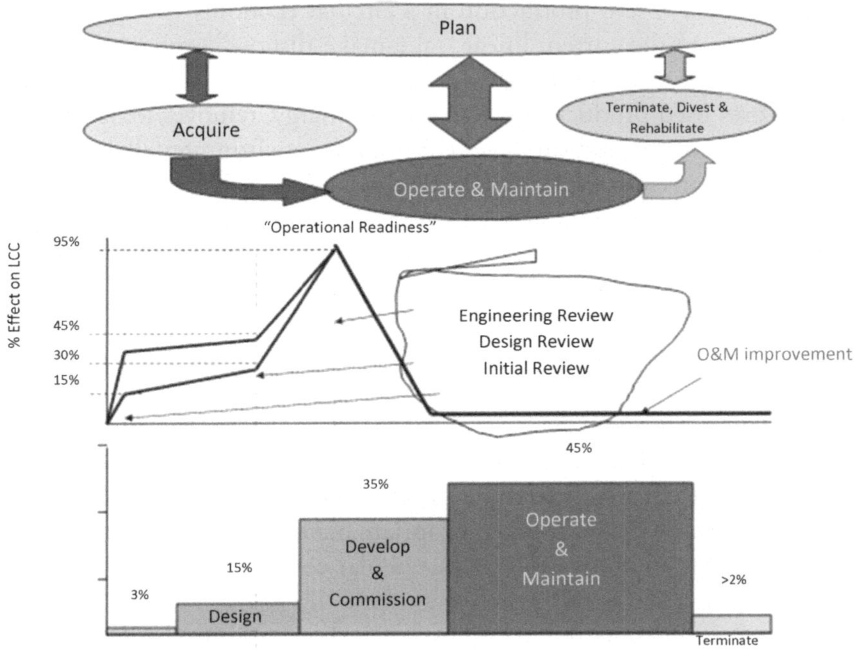

Fig. 8.1 Engineering asset management life-cycle phases and stages. (Source: Amadi-Echendu and Amadi-Echendu (2015))

The management of an asset involves several phases (i.e., acquire, operate and maintain, and divest) and life-cycle stages (i.e., concept, design, develop and commission, and terminate). Typically, 95% of the total life cost is calculated when the asset is acquired (Amadi-Echendu & Amadi-Echendu, 2015).

Different role players are involved in different life-cycle stages of the product or service. Traditionally, a linear life-cycle was observed, as illustrated in Fig. 8.1, whereby a product was either terminated, divested, or rehabilitated at the end of its life-cycle. In recent times, the circular economy (CE) has replaced the linear economy. CE entails the end-of-life management of a product whereby a product's functional life is extended through reintroduction into the supply chain as non-waste (Govindan &

Soleimani, 2017). No production in a circular economy is wasted, thus advancing from the current linear "take-make-dispose" economy.

A CE is planned and designed to be a regenerative industrial system and restores used products, uses renewable energy, removes toxic chemicals, and aims to eradicate waste by using environmentally friendly designs, resource systems, and business models. CE promotes reuse, remanufacturing, rebuilding, recovery, restoration, and recycling.

The circular economy is based on three basic principles (Tóth Szita, 2017), namely:

- regulating how resources are used to protect and develop environmental capital;
- circulating products, parts, and materials in the economy to extend their life through remanufacturing, refurbishing, and maintenance; and
- minimising negative externalities, eliminating toxic substances, and reducing waste by choosing appropriate materials in the design phase. Figure 8.2 is an illustration of the circular economy.

Figure 8.2 illustrates that recycling was introduced into the reuse economy whereby parts or products may be reused and not necessarily destroyed, resulting in lower manufacturing needs. Remanufacturing is incorporated into product design processes due to increased environmental and resource governance. Environmentally friendly products are easier to remanufacture (Zheng et al., 2019). When designing products and

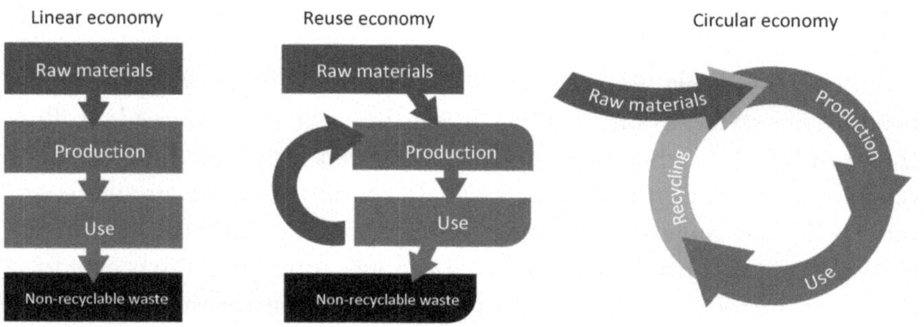

Fig. 8.2 The circular economy. (Source: de Estarrona et al. (2019))

services, recyclable materials should be used to promote reuse and remanufacturing processes. Materials should not be hazardous and should be safe to handle to minimise health and safety risks.

Products may be returned to an organisation because of defects, damage, dissatisfaction, or another reason. These products form waste through a process known as reverse logistics. Some of the parts may be disassembled, sorted, and cleaned for use in subsequent life-cycles. Certain worn assets may be reprocessed to restore them to their original state through remanufacturing. Remanufacturing may realise additional incomes for organisations and adhere to environmental and regulatory requirements and sustainability goals. Both recycling and reuse methods are dependent on the structure of the reverse channel and the product differentiation strategy (Agrawal & Singh, 2019). Systems need to be redesigned to consume less energy and use resources more efficiently. The CE promotes greater land productivity, reduces waste in the food value chain, improves soil nutrients to increase the value of land, and endorse soil as assets. Sustainability promotes good governance throughout products' life-cycles.

Environmentally friendly or eco-friendly products are organic, energy-efficient, recyclable, non-toxic, and not dangerous to consumers. DfE is involved throughout the entire process and all life-cycle stages of a product. It ensures that all environmental specifications are integrated into how products are designed and manufactured, which may affect supply network configuration. Policies, procedures, strategies, and objectives should reflect environmental considerations that should be mirrored in operational activities like process layouts and processes. The product design activity passes through various stages (Slack et al., 2017).

First, the **concept-generation** stage is where innovative ideas are gathered from customers, competitors, staff, research, and innovation initiatives. Environmental considerations are encouraged from this stage.

Second, **concept screening** occurs when the ideas are evaluated and assessed against predetermined design criteria. The feasibility, acceptability, and vulnerability of the design options are screened to reduce the number of available options.

Third, in **preliminary design**, the components and their order of addition are specified. The most elegant designs are typically the simplest where common elements are used. Costs are often offset by standardising products, offering alternative products, and modularisation in line with set environmental standards.

The fourth stage entails **evaluation and improvement** that may occur before the product is tested in the market. The final design must meet customer needs and environmental requirements. Costs must support value and performance imperatives by applying innovative and creative thinking to reduce the number of components, use less expensive input materials, and/or simplify the process.

In the fifth stage, the **prototyping and final design** stage, a prototype is created for testing. All potential effects and impacts on the environment and natural resources must be evaluated from the production phase to disposal, that is, from cradle to grave (Deniz, 2017).

Products and services follow similar steps. In the manufacturing of products, the following environmental requirements should be considered:

- pollution during manufacturing should be avoided;
- fewer materials should be used;
- waste needs to be discarded responsibly;
- the variety of materials should be less; and
- environmentally safer materials and processes should be used.

Carbon footprint refers to calculating CO_2 of the organisational or an individual's output of greenhouse gases to determine the effect it has on climate change. The product carbon footprint refers to the carbon emission produced through the exploitation of raw materials, production, transportation, manufacturing, consumption, and eventual disposal (Zhu et al., 2016). Governments have implemented taxes to curb high emissions and pollution.

Pollution is introduced by humans in the form of pollutants of gas, liquids, and solids or waste material that deteriorates the quality of the air, water, or land. Pollution may result in infections, diseases, premature deaths, and premature births by pregnant women. Clean water for drinking and cooking is essential for good health and life. A lack of access to clean water may increase the risk of bacterial diseases that may lead to urinary tract infections, cholera, diarrhoea, typhoid, and death. Sources of water pollution include factories, wastewater treatment facilities, septic systems, fertilisers, chemicals, construction sites, mines, and animal wastes from farms and fields. Damage can cause loss of ecosystems, biodiversity, and fishery resources. To clean contaminated water is costly (treatment costs, health costs from illnesses, and costs to the economy).

Energy efficiency refers to methods to reduce energy consumption and usage and is used to assess manufacturers' competitiveness and drives economic development (Benedetti et al., 2015). Enhanced energy efficiency can be realised by finding alternatives that reduce total energy consumption. The environmental requirements are reduced energy demand during use, flexible energy use, and designs for:

- use with renewable energy
- zero emissions
- carbon neutrality
- zero toxins

The use of smart grids is also increasing. A smart grid allows for large-scale integration of renewable energy sources to distribute power to deliver more cost-effective and environmentally friendly electricity through the active involvement of customers on a digital platform (Benedetti et al., 2015).

8.2.1.2 Green Labelling

Ecolabelling identifies overall environmental preferences for products and allows consumers to practice environmental considerations in their purchasing decisions (Deniz, 2017). There are numerous green labelling programmes that follow different rating systems and qualifying characteristics that include focusing on only the end results, focusing more on economic issues and energy savings, looking at the distance a material travels, or analysing toxin emissions in the air (Beatson et al., 2020).

Green marketing may essentially communicate the environmental benefits of products to potential consumers. Ecolabels encourage the demand for and supply of environmentally friendly products.

Ecolabelling has educated consumers about reducing negative environmental effects (Gossling & Buckley, 2016). Agricultural producers are focusing on organic farming (avoiding chemical fertilisers and pesticides) for their products to become labelled as environmentally friendly. The International Organisation for Standardisation provides general definitions and principles for the creation of voluntary ecolabels (Minkov et al., 2020). The standards apply to all businesses of any size as a generic framework (Mkansi et al., 2020). According to Minkov et al. (2020), there are three broad types of voluntary ecolabels to consider:

1. ISO 14024 (ISO 2018) type I ecolabels;
2. ISO 14021 (ISO 2016) type II ecolabels; and
3. ISO 14025 (ISO 2006a) type III environmental declarations, ISO 14040 (ISO 2006b) and product category rules for product groups.

8.2.1.3 Supply Chain Management

Supply chains (made up of producers and suppliers, distributors, retailers, and consumers) focus on various factors that include customer demand, resource availability, consumer behaviour, and regulatory policies. Sustainable supply chain management (SCM) aims to strike a balance among all these factors while managing environmental concerns, different demands, cultures, and contexts on a global scale. The success of trade and commerce depends on a seamless flow of goods, services, money, and information among different supply chain stakeholders (Amadi-Echendu, 2017), as well as coordination of stakeholders, relationships, value, efficiency, and performance (Ahi & Searcy, 2013).

The objective of supply chain sustainability is to create, protect, and grow long-term environmental, social (related to human beings, and includes poverty, violence, injustice, education, public health, labour, and human rights), and economic value for all stakeholders involved in the supply chain so that products and services that are supplied to the market meet customer and environmental requirements. Economic value includes economic activities for people (securing food, water, and shelter, as well as creating prospects on the value of life) and for businesses, growth prospects, and generating profit within the compliance and stewardship parameters of the King IV Report (Institute of Directors in South Africa, 2016).

It is also important that products and services are traced back from the source to the consumer to assist with the recall of products where necessary through reverse logistics. Between 2017 and 2018 there was a listeriosis outbreak in South Africa that killed hundreds of people and resulted in food recalls of ready-to-eat processed meat (Grobler, 2018) that took more than a year to trace. In 2018, *Salmonella* bacteria-contaminated eggs resulted in the hospitalisation of 30 people in South Africa (Knowler, 2018, p. 1) and traceability again was a major problem (Thomas et al., 2020).

8.2.1.4 Logistics

Logistics traditionally dealt with the movement of raw materials and finished products, as well as the protection, storage (warehousing), inventory, and transportation of finished products to their destination (Slack et al., 2017). It is imperative in the traceability of products and services. Supply chain logistics integrates social and environmental aspects which include reverse logistics, waste management, and transportation. Air, land (rail, road, and pipeline) and water (shipping) freight traffic transport significantly contribute to CO_2 emissions (Rodrigues et al., 2017). Maritime transportation has been the most cost-effective way to move large quantities of cargo over long distances.

Highly individualised products and services are increasingly being demanded, and logistics need to adapt to this volatile environment. Industry 4.0 technologies like blockchain were introduced into the logistics space (Tijan et al., 2019), a phenomenon known as Logistics 4.0, to enhance better traceability, accurate information, and faster processes through real-time information-sharing (Barreto et al., 2017). Errors are reduced through intelligent automation of repetitive functions (Zhou et al., 2017).

Procurement is an essential part of supply chains and ensures that required goods and services are sourced and obtained. This function entails the planning of purchases and purchasing strategy development, setting up specific processes with specific suppliers, contract formation and administration, outsource planning, and acquisition planning (Mkansi et al., 2020). Proper supply chain management systems may minimise expenses by allowing a just-in-time approach, whereby materials and other resources are secured as they are needed, instead of carrying huge inventories.

The use of electronic systems in procurement (e-procurement) may reduce costs, enhance efficiencies, and save time due to a shorter purchasing process, higher price transparency, lower administrative costs, improved collaboration with suppliers, being able to access historic data for better forecasting capabilities, improved information flow for better communication, and consolidated supplier information. Green purchasing decisions may be enforced in the procurement process that may lead to a specific supplier selection.

8.2.1.5 Environmental Economics

Environmental and social accounting aims at balancing a company's financial health with its broader obligations by incorporating environmental management principles and conservation into reporting practices and cost/benefit analyses. The impact of ecologically sustainable practices in the supply chain is measured and reported so that decision-making can include meeting environmental regulations and not just financial profit. Environmental costs must be quantified in relation to how natural resources are treated to reduce pollution and environmental damage (degradation), and to develop strategies that can address these environmental issues. In a circular economy, waste production is managed through repair and recycling strategies where waste is used as a resource.

Environmental assets are under threat of depletion and degradation (deterioration of the quality of the environment) from economic activity, thus affecting the welfare of society negatively. Environmental assets comprise soil, land, and surface water, as well as terrestrial (tropical rainforests, deserts, grasslands, deciduous forests, tundra, and taiga) and aquatic (lakes, rivers, ponds, wetlands, oceans, and seas) ecosystems. Environmental degradation causes social and financial costs to society such as poor health, loss of income, and increased poverty and vulnerability.

The degradation of land affects the output of food production, which leads to food insecurity. It is imperative to establish the contributing factors to determine prevention and control measures. Forest degradation and deforestation affect wildlife and the land. The cost imposed by degradation differs from one country to another, depending on the contributing factors and remedial options required to address or renew the resource(s) as well as the maintenance cost.

The degradation of natural resources such as sea, forest, land, and water are of major concern to all economies because it has a direct impact on economic growth, and can have repercussions for employment, attracting foreign investors, and living standards. Natural resource degradation includes agricultural damage from soil salinity and soil erosion, deterioration of grazing areas, deforestation and damage from natural disasters such as cyclones, severe droughts, and floods. The degradation of soil increases soil salinity, soil erosion, and degradation of grazing areas that in turn reduces agricultural productivity and the availability of livestock feed (Mkansi et al., 2020).

The ecological footprint (EF) measures ecological assets by calculating what would be required for a given population to produce the natural resources that it consumes and how waste is managed. It tracks the used cropland, grazing land, fishing areas, urbanised land, forest areas, and the carbon demand on land (Global Footprint Network, 2019). An ecological risk profile is developed for each country. Most countries are recording ecological deficits which means that they demand more from nature than what their ecosystems can restore. Other countries import resources from elsewhere, which burdens the countries of origin. Figure 8.3 depicts the ecological footprint according to Global Footprint Network (2019).

A community has an ecological deficit if its EF exceeds its biocapacity (the capacity of its productive land area to continually generate the required renewable resources and to absorb the wastes it produces). An ecological deficit is an indication of not being sustainable. An ecological

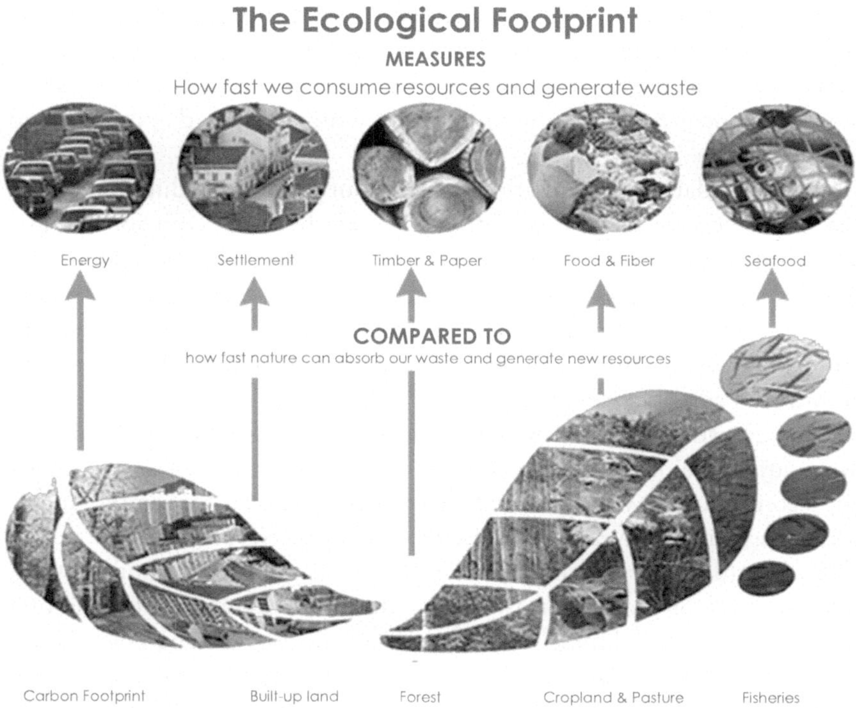

Fig. 8.3 The ecological footprint. (Source: Global Footprint Network (2019))

reserve occurs when the community's EF is less than its biocapacity which indicates sustainability.

The size of a community's EF is directly related to the amount of natural resources consumed and the amount of carbon waste produced by the community. EF is closely related to lifestyle. More luxurious lifestyles that use large amounts of energy have a greater EF than simpler lifestyles.

EF provides useful information to aid governments in the development of policies and decision-making to promote sustainable resource utilisation through maximising resource efficiency. One of the limitations of EF is that it accounts for renewable resources in the biosphere, but not for non-renewable resources and their depletion.

Human activities affect environmental quality the most, which leads to threats to biodiversity that can harm nature. EF also does not consider other greenhouse gases apart from carbon dioxide. As it continues to be improved, EF will become a more widely accepted indicator of sustainability.

8.2.1.6 Economic Valuation

People are generally willing to exchange money for value. Economists use certain methods to calculate (or estimate) the economic value of market and non-market goods and assign a monetary or non-monetary value to the natural resources and ecosystem services. The process of estimating such value is known as environmental valuation. An ecosystem can have concurrent objective and subjective (individual and social perceptions), inherent (non-substitutional), and instrumental (specific) use as well as fluctuating exchange values (exchanged ratio of scarce and useful goods based on subjective preferences) (Spangenberg & Settele, 2016).

Different people can place different values on the same product or service based on factors such as the purpose for which the resource is required, the price, or the quantity of the resource. When deciding on an economic value for a resource or service, one needs to have the following in mind:

- The number of alternative goods and services a person is willing to trade (or sacrifice) to have a natural resource or ecosystem service/product.
- The benefits that people would receive if a policy or management plan was implemented so that the quantity or quality of a resource can improve (e.g., cleaner water or air).

The methods of assigning a value to an ecological resource still produce errors because ecosystems have complex functions and usages. When resources are scarce, choices about how society will use what is available must be made based on complex trade-offs. Decisions about how individuals and society collectively choose to allocate these resources help to reveal value. Linking a price to resources helps to facilitate the production and exchange of environmental goods and services in a market system.

The price is decided through the influence of the consumers' willingness to pay. Economics regards all resources (such as land, water, labour, and plants) as scarce.

8.2.1.7 Resource Scarcity and Utilisation (Supply and Demand)

Resources are inputs that can be combined to produce goods and services. These include land, water, labour, and capital (plants, equipment, and inventories). If the amount of a product or resource supplied is less than what users demand, resource scarcity arises. Some goods or natural resources (e.g., atmospheric oxygen and sunshine) are available in abundance. These are referred to as free or non-scarce goods. A condition of scarcity forces households, businesses, and governments (known as economic agents) to make economic choices regarding scarce resources.

Society has evolved to use disposable goods rather than goods that can be reused and recycled which contributes to waste that is detrimental to the environment. Using wastes as resources must be done with care to avoid the transmission of contaminants into the ecosystem that ultimately affects the food chain. Overexploitation of natural resources and releasing waste into the environment are also contributing to the degradation of ecosystems (Velenturf & Purnell, 2017).

Resource management includes how changing climates affect the environment, economic globalisation, and growing populations so that we can adapt supply chain configurations. Valuation methods that deal with how resources recover from waste must be created. Water scarcity may affect lifestyles and businesses. For example, a Coca-Cola plant in Southern India was shut down due to water shortages (Kalaitzi et al., 2018).

A growing population means that fewer per-capita exhaustible resources are available. Additional wastes and pollution may also hamper sustainability, negatively affect pricing, and impact food security. In India, overconsumption of certain resources has led to hunger, food insecurity, and malnutrition (Tyagi et al., 2014). In Nigeria, floods and soil erosion, the overutilisation of natural resources, and the exploitation of oil has negatively affected forestry, biodiversity, and air that negatively impacted agricultural growth and economic growth (Dalil et al., 2016). UN organisations forecast population growth to be between 8.3 and 10.9 billion people by 2050. Such growth rates will require a 50–75% increase in the food supply. At the same time, the needs of developing countries will double, including a 60% growth of rice-consuming countries and sub-Saharan African growth by 250% (Prosekov & Ivanova, 2018).

According to the UN data, agricultural production will have to grow by 75% by 2050 (Godfray et al., 2010). Modern technologies may assist to increase food production through enhanced fertility of land, using organic ocean resources, switching to renewable energy sources, advances in genetics, and breeding more productive breeds of animals (Prosekov & Ivanova, 2018). Technological innovations and advancements may also assist with renewable energy issues.

8.2.1.8 Operations and Technology

Traditionally, organisations have worked in their own technological systems and shared only certain types of information with competitors and suppliers. Manual follow-ups and tracking of goods/services were conducted via telephone and email, while records were largely maintained by using spreadsheets. Many operations have adopted modern manufacturing equipment to increase their economies of scale, which has also affected the exploitation of natural, human, and economic resources. Now businesses need to integrate sustainability aspects into their operations which necessitates tracking the origin of resources and products. Thus, boundaries and silos need to be removed through the digitalisation of the supply network.

Enabled by the Internet of Things (IoT), digitalisation is associated with organisation-wide and inter-organisational modernisation efforts (Valenduc & Vendramin, 2017). A digitally networked economy will augment value for the supply network through increased collaboration among supply chain partners. All customer interactions, every transaction, and all product and process development should be completely visible throughout the supply chain in the digital economy.

Technological innovations like 3D printing, the Internet of Things, machine learning (ML), and blockchain are transforming operations and creating new value to advance productivity, profitability, and sustainability. Value, therefore, extends beyond simply closing the deal. In the manufacturing process, blockchain can be used to eliminate counterfeits that enter a supply chain because the products would be scanned at every point of the supply chain.

Blockchains can also help to verify the origin of the product and provide information about its path from origin to the final consumer (Dujak & Sajter, 2019). For example, Walmart's blockchain pilot of mangoes and pigs identified which data was important to record and made a list of important features such as tagging the pigs at the farm, types of fertilisers used in the pre-seedling stage of mangoes, the quality of trees, the lot number of where the pigs are stored, the date in which the pork and mangoes were packed, temperatures at the storage facilities and during distribution, the quantity that was shipped, and purchase order numbers (Kamath, 2018).

Many customers demand sustainable products and services, and the origin of these products and services must be traceable to prove that they were sustainably produced and delivered. Blockchain may be used to enhance the traceability of goods in a supply chain (Kshetri, 2018) and may also assist to minimise the distribution of fraudulent and counterfeit products. Automation in factories and machines can be enabled through blockchain connections. Organisations no longer compete on an individual basis, but must globally compete against other networks. Blockchain technology could facilitate trustworthy collaboration by connecting all partners in a peer-to-peer, decentralised production network in real time (Lohmer & Lasch, 2020).

Analysing data to build intelligence is key to gaining insight into customer behaviours, meeting customer needs, building a unique customer experience, helping to cross-sell more products, and growing customer market share while maximising profitability. Information that is needed to achieve a unique customer experience requires more than customer demand, forecasts, and manufacturing data. It requires information about factors that may influence customer behaviour, what the current trends are in the environment and globally, weather patterns, and buying patterns, among other things.

Online platforms allow for customers to place orders within seconds, and the expectation is that goods will be delivered as promised. Organisations must ensure that they have visibility to know what needs to be done, by whom, by when it must be done, and what is required at the push of a button. Interconnectedness among supply chain partners and digitalisation of processes make this possible.

Enterprise resource planning (ERP) integrates information and resources within an organisation as well as across the supply network to streamline operational activities. There is a need to integrate the various ERP systems of different organisations to improve communication between customers, suppliers, and other stakeholders in the supply network. The ERP system enhances visibility across business activities resulting in improved business efficiencies through continuous improvement efforts; it provides accurate and real-time information; and the integration with external sources may advance business performance (Slack et al., 2017).

Digitilisation requires more than sharing of information and the automation of processes. Organisations will also need to adjust their policies and strategies to take advantage of technological advances. Business segments may need to be redesigned as digital technologies are integrated into organisational business processes and operations, thus affecting the composition of distribution channels and hierarchical structures (Plekhanov & Netland, 2019).

Organisations need information to make the right decisions. Smart devices have allowed businesses to gather customer information to understand consumer behaviour which translates to inconceivable amounts of data. It is just data with no real value until it can be converted into a format and perspective that can be used in a business context. The task of making sense of vast amounts of data cannot be managed by humans and has been fulfilled by big data analytics. For example, data can originate from the internet, social media, mobile platforms, sensors, ERP systems, and cloud platforms, and can exist in text, graphics, audio clips, and videos (Choi et al., 2018). Big data analytics helps to make sense of vast amounts of data and provides deeper insights into production processes, quality, and risk management (Lohmer & Lasch, 2020). Big data analytics has been successfully used in forecasting, revenue management, marketing, transportation management, risk analysis, supply chain management, and inventory management (Choi et al., 2018).

Artificial intelligence (AI) aims to programme machines and computers, as well as to perform routine and repetitive tasks that were previously performed by people. Machine learning is a sub-discipline of AI that develops algorithms that can automatically identify and learn associations in large amounts of data in real time (Dogru & Keskin, 2020). AI applications like robotics and automation have enhanced operational productivity, predictive modelling, and marketing predictions of customer demand.

Organisations need to move from responding to customer needs to predicting customer needs. With real-time data, an organisation can move away from responding to machine failures, alerts, and deadlines that have not been met by monitoring all situations continuously in real-time through IoT technologies. Technologies such as machine learning, AI, and advanced analytics can predict and pre-empt future needs through insight into various assets and processes to enable less disruption, fewer costs due to reworks and shortfalls, on-time deliveries, and fewer machine breakdowns. Predicting future trends could enhance an organisation's responsiveness and assist to offer customised products and personalised services at short notice and at reduced lead times (Dogru & Keskin, 2020).

By using AI and IoT to optimise operations, a company can reduce its carbon footprint and the costs of logisticals processes, while improving customer satisfaction. Many companies today are striving for zero waste and zero impact (or even a net positive impact) on the environment, which requires focusing on a circular economy where optimisation of assets, equipment, and inventory is critical and only possible through better use of digital technologies (Mkansi et al., 2020). Organisations, therefore, need to move from linear supply chains to agile ecosystems to meet the needs for constant innovation which requires collaboration and co-innovation with all partners.

Customers are becoming more informed and expect individualised products. As assets and products get "smarter" through IoT, the information transmitted about the state, location, and performance of such products should be used to enhance innovation strategies and business performance (Choi et al., 2018). Organisations are redesigning their manufacturing capabilities to move from continuous production lines to configurable manufacturing capabilities that can produce lower volumes of various configurations.

Organisations are moving away from selling products to delivering outcomes. IoT and the servitisation of assets are enabling new ways of engaging customers and creating value for them. The introduction of servitised business models comprises the selling of the use of a product and not the product itself. For instance, in the transportation sector, providers do not sell cars, but offer rental or lease solutions through a servitised scheme (de Estarrona et al., 2019). Servitisation may include after-sales maintenance and service of the operational assets in the market. Servitisation takes advantage of the digitalisation of assets.

8.2.1.9 Humanitarian Operations Management

It is important to note that the response to acts of God also comprises operations management processes and imperatives, even though humanitarians seek social impact rather than profit. A humanitarian supply chain deals with logistics decisions that need to be made before, during, and after a disaster to provide on-time support and assistance. Disasters could take different forms, including hunger, explosions, infestations, disease outbreaks like COVID-19 and ebola, refugee crises, natural disasters, conflicts, drought and other environmental factors, and manmade disasters. Humanitarian logistics involve various processes of planning and managing efficiencies, managing costs, warehousing, and moving relief supplies to where it is needed. Various role players are involved in this process: governmental and non-governmental bodies, civil society organisations, and humanitarian organisations, all of whom collaborate by integrating relief operations. Supply chains need to be flexible and agile to rapidly respond to unpredictable events.

Technological advancements also play a major role in this area. Drones, big data, and AI technologies are finding application in humanitarian operations (Besiou & Van Wassenhove, 2020). For example, Facebook information assisted to conduct an infrastructure assessment after the Haiti hurricane (Cahill, 2018). Drones transport supplies to affected areas. Satellite images provide real-time information on damage to infrastructure after a disaster. Big data and AI techniques analyse and convert data into intelligence for decision-making. Global positioning system (GPS) equipment can track vehicles and the movement of staff in disaster areas. Social media circulates information faster and accelerates relief distribution after disasters.

Humanitarian operations (HO) centre on all stages of a disaster lifecycle including mitigation, preparedness, and response. When funding is scarce, HO needs to carefully prioritise the core issues and rehabilitation. HO is very different from commercial operations as they operate in volatile environments, face high uncertainty, encounter changing priorities and requirements, have unstable supply chains, and face sudden surges in demand with a limited supply of material and funds (Day et al., 2012). HOs must reach their beneficiaries speedily (effectiveness) and at the lowest possible costs (efficiency) (Besiou & Van Wassenhove, 2020). Regardless, operations management principles remain valid.

8.2.2 Improvement Strategies

Businesses nowadays tend to compete on their ability to continually improve their processes and imply an upgrade of current skills and knowledge of staff on all levels within the organisation and across the entire supply chain (Murray et al., 2016). Therefore, there has been a complete shift towards improving operations performance on a continuous basis.

The scope of operations management has grown from a subject that largely focused on manufacturing to one that embraces all processes across sectors. Emergency services want to reach distressed people faster, customer deliveries need to occur more reliably, manufacturing wants to emit less pollution at lower production costs, while stakeholders require more profits. It is, therefore, clear that improvement strategies will depend on the type of operations, as well as the type of products and services that are being manufactured. Different role players in the supply chain may also attach different types of value and, therefore, different strategies for improvements become necessary.

Improvement strategies can be incremental (also known as continuous improvement) or radical (e.g., a total redesign of systems or installing new machines) and include lean management and Six Sigma principles that identify and eliminate causes of defects and waste in operations. Standards provide the benchmark against which improvements can be measured (Sraun & Singh, 2017). From a green operations perspective, improvement strategies may target the elimination or reduction of waste, remanufacturing strategies, and the reuse of products and resources that have reached the end of their life, enhancing the speed of reverse logistics processes, maintaining the value of soil and other assets, as well as the protection of the environment.

8.3 Conclusion

This chapter examined some contemporary trends in operations management with a particular focus on sustainability within operations management. We saw that there are limited resources from which to satisfy unlimited wants. The resources need to be protected to ensure their use in the future. Sustainability had become a global focus area whereby organisations need to consider the environment, economy, and society in their business dealings. Consumers are more educated and demand sustainable products and services. Green labelling that complies with ISO standards may be used to highlight sustainable products.

It has, therefore, become imperative to track resources and products throughout the supply chain. Criteria that relate to sustainability may be used to choose supply and agree on the supply chain configuration. Organisations do not operate in isolation but depend on other organisations to deliver their products and services to customers. Some of these organisations are suppliers of raw materials or other parts and components, while others may store and deliver the finished products to customers. Within the supply chain, organisations need to reduce the silos and become more integrated for IoT technologies to be implemented and used more successfully. Logistics also need to be mindful of carbon emissions that may arise through transportation.

The concept of the circular economy was explained whereby goods and services that are produced are either recycled, reused, or remanufactured to reduce the waste at the end of the product's life-cycle through reverse logistics and waste management. Essentially, products that have come to the end of their life-cycle may be reused in either the same or a different capacity in order to extend the life of a product and reduce waste in the environment.

Environmental economics is introducing environmental concerns into reporting practices and supply chains are assessed in terms of meeting environmental regulations in addition to financial profits. Environmental depletion and degradation may lead to food insecurity. The ecological footprint measures the human demand for natural capital that is used to assess responsible resource utilisation. Environmental valuation is a process used to assess economic value of products, services, and resources. Economics regard all resources (such as land, water, labour, and plants) as scarce and in need of protection.

Various Industry 4.0 technologies are available to use in operations. These include drones, big data analytics, artificial intelligence, blockchain technologies, sensors, drones, and many more. The technologies can help to monitor business processes, predict behaviour, reduce costs, enhance efficiencies, and assist to make products and services more sustainable. Blockchain technologies can help to trace the origin of products from the source to the end-user.

Humanitarian operations management was introduced as a mechanism to supply needed medical and other supplies in emergency situations and disasters across the world. All elements that pertain to green initiatives in operations management also apply to humanitarian operations management. We have recently experienced the global COVID-19 pandemic where humanitarian operations were at the forefront of delivering masks and other health and safety supplies and equipment during lockdown. The supplies and equipment needed to be sourced, transported, and managed responsibly.

Businesses need to continually improve what they do to enhance efficiencies, decrease cost, improve competitiveness, improve profitability, and remain in business. Various approaches can be linked to improvement strategies that can be radical, incremental, or continuous. Improvement efforts extend to the entire supply chain and not just individual organisations and have become a competitive advantage.

References

Agrawal, S., & Singh, R. K. (2019). Analyzing disposition decisions for sustainable reverse logistics: Triple Bottom Line approach. *Resources, Conservation and Recycling, 150*, 104448.

Ahi, P., & Searcy, C. (2013). A comparative literature analysis of definitions for green and sustainable supply chain management. *Journal of Cleaner Production, 52*, 329–341.

Amadi-Echendu, A. P. (2017). *Towards a framework for the integration of data and data sources in the automation and dematerialisation of land administration systems*. Doctoral dissertation, University of Pretoria.

Amadi-Echendu, J., & Amadi-Echendu, A. (2015). Legal aspects of engineering asset management. In Amadi-Echendu et al. (Eds.), *Engineering asset management-systems, professional practices and certification* (pp. 1797–1805). Springer.

Barreto, L., Amaral, A., & Pereira, T. (2017). Industry 4.0 implications in logistics: An overview. *Procedia Manufacturing, 13*, 1245–1252.

Beatson, A., Gottlieb, U., & Pleming, K. (2020). Green consumption practices for sustainability: An exploration through social practice theory. *Journal of Social Marketing, 10*(2), 197–213. https://doi.org/10.1108/JSOCM-07-2019-0102

Benedetti, M., Cesarotti, V., & Introna, V. (2015). Improving energy efficiency in manufacturing systems: Literature review and analysis of the impact on the energy network of consolidated practices and upcoming opportunities. In *Energy efficiency improvements in smart grid components* (pp. 41–68). Intech.

Besiou, M., & Van Wassenhove, L. N. (2020). Humanitarian operations: A world of opportunity for relevant and impactful research. *Manufacturing and Service Operations Management, 22*(1), 135–145.

Cahill, S. (2018). *Logistics cluster*. Lecture, Coordination, and Partnerships in the ESM Program, December 14. Kuehne Logistics University, Hamburg, Germany.

Choi, T. M., Wallace, S. W., & Wang, Y. (2018). Big data analytics in operations management. *Production and Operations Management, 27*(10), 1868–1883.

Dalil, M., Ilegieuno, A. A., Babangida, M. U., & Husain, A. (2016). Assessment of the impacts of gully erosion on Auchi settlement, Southern Nigeria. *Journal of Geography and Regional Planning, 9*(7), 128–138.

Day, J. M., Melnyk, S. A., Larson, P. D., Davis, E. W., & Whybark, D. C. (2012). Humanitarian and disaster relief supply chains: A matter of life and death. *Journal of Supply Chain Management, 48*(2), 21–36.

de Estarrona, U. M., Seneviratne, D., Villarejo, R., & Galar, D. (2019). The new asset management: Implications of servitization in circular economy. *Journal of Industrial Engineering and Management Science, 2019*(1), 109–120.

Deniz, D. (2017, November 27–29). *Improving environmental awareness through design for sustainable development.* Paper presented at International Multidisciplinary Scientific GeoConference: SGEM 17: 913–920, Vienna, Austria.

Dogru, A. K., & Keskin, B. B. (2020). AI in operations management: Applications, challenges and opportunities. *Journal of Data, Information and Management, 2*, 67–74. https://doi.org/10.1007/s42488-020-00023-1

Dujak, D., & Sajter, D. (2019). Blockchain applications in supply chain. In *SMART supply network* (pp. 21–46). Springer.

Global Footprint Network. (2019). *Ecological footprint: Global Footprint Network*. https://www.footprintnetwork.org/our-work/ecological-footprint

Godfray, H. C. J., Beddington, J. R., Crute, I. R., Haddad, L., Lawrence, D., Muir, J. F., Pretty, J., Robinson, S., Thomas, S. M., & Toulmin, C. (2010). Food security: The challenge of feeding 9 billion people. *Science, 327*(5967), 812–818. https://doi.org/10.1126/science.1185383

Gossling, S., & Buckley, R. (2016). Carbon labels in tourism: Persuasive communications? *Journal of Cleaner Production, 111*(7), 358–369. https://doi.org/10.1016/j.jclepro.2014.08.067

Govindan, K., & Soleimani, H. (2017). A review of reverse logistics and closed-loop supply chains: A Journal of Cleaner Production focus. *Journal of Cleaner Production, 142*, 371–384.

Grobler, R. (2018, September 3). Listeriosis outbreak: How it started, how it was traced, and how it was finally stopped. News24. Retrieved March 12, 2020, from https://www.news24.com/SouthAfrica/News/listeriosis-outbreak-how-it-started-how-it-was-traced-and-how-it-was-finally-stopped-20180903

Institute of Directors in South Africa. (2016). King IV Report on Corporate Governance for South Africa. Retrieved from: https://cdn.ymaws.com/www.iodsa.co.za/resource/collection/684B68A7-B768-465C-8214-E3A007F15A5A/IoDSA_King_IV_Report_-_WebVersion.pdf

Jaehn, F. (2016). Sustainable operations. *European Journal of Operational Research, 253*(2), 243–264.

Kalaitzi, D., Matopoulos, A., Bourlakis, M., & Tate, W. (2018). Supply chain strategies in an era of natural resource scarcity. *International Journal of Operations and Production Management, 38*(2), 784–809.

Kamath, R. (2018). Food traceability on blockchain: Walmart's pork and mango pilots with IBM. *The Journal of the British Blockchain Association, 1*(1), 47–53.

Knowler, W. (2018). Factory fingered as source of listeriosis outbreak to reopen. *TimesLive*. Retrieved October 27, 2020, from https://www.timeslive.co.za/news/south-africa/2018-12-06-factory-fingered-as-source-of-listeriosis-outbreak-to-reopen/

Kshetri, N. (2018). Blockchain's roles in meeting key supply chain management objectives. *International Journal of Information Management, 39*, 80–89. https://doi.org/10.1016/j.ijinfomgt.2017.12.005

Lohmer, J., & Lasch, R. (2020). Blockchain in operations management and manufacturing: Potential and barriers. *Computers and Industrial Engineering, 149*, 106789.

Minkov, N., Lehmann, A., Winter, L., & Finkbeiner, M. (2020). Characterization of environmental labels beyond the criteria of ISO 14020 series. *The International Journal of Life Cycle Assessment, 25*, 840–855. https://doi.org/10.1007/s11367-019-01596-9

Mkansi, M., Amadi-Echendu, A., & de Villiers, G. (Eds.). (2020). *Emerging issues in operations and supply chain management*. Van Schaik.

Murray, A., Papa, A., Cuozzo, B., & Russo, G. (2016). Evaluating the innovation of the internet of things. *Business Process Management Journal, 22*(2), 341–356. https://doi.org/10.1108/BPMJ-05-2015-0077

Ogunlela, G. O. (2018). Green supply chain management as a competitive tool in the fast-moving consumer goods manufacturing industry. *Journal of Business and Retail Management Research, 12*(4), 167–176.

Plekhanov, D., & Netland, T. H. (2019, June 17–19). Digitalisation stages in firms: Towards a framework. In *26th EurOMA Conference*, Helsinki, Finland.

Prosekov, A. Y., & Ivanova, S. A. (2018). Food security: The challenge of the present. *Geoforum, 91*, 73–77.

Rodrigues, J., Slack, B., & Comtois, C. (2017). *The geography of transport systems* (4th ed.). Routledge.

Slack, N., Brandon-Jones, A., Johnston, R., Singh, H., & Phihlela, K. (2017). *Operations management: Global and Southern African perspectives* (3rd ed.). Pearson.

Spangenberg, J. H., & Settele, J. (2016). Value pluralism and economic valuation—Defendable if well done. *Ecosystem Services, 18*, 100–109.

Sraun, J. S., & Singh, H. (2017). Continuous improvement strategies across manufacturing SMEs of Northern India. *International Journal of Lean Six Sigma, 8*(2), 225–243.

Srivastava, S. K. (2007). Green supply-chain management: A state-of-the-art literature review. *International Journal of Management Reviews, 9*(1), 53–80.

Thomas, J., Govender, N., McCarthy, K. M., Erasmus, L. K., Doyle, T. J., Allam, M., Ismail, A., Ramalwa, N., Sekwadi, P., Ntshoe, G., & Shonhiwa, A. (2020). Outbreak of listeriosis in South Africa associated with processed meat. *New England Journal of Medicine, 382*(7), 632–643.

Tijan, E., Aksentijević, S., Ivanić, K., & Jardas, M. (2019). Blockchain technology implementation in logistics. *Sustainability, 11*(4), 1185.

Tóth Szita, K. (2017). The application of life cycle assessment in circular economy. *Hungarian Agricultural Engineering, 31*, 5–9.

Tyagi, S., Garg, N., & Paudel, R. (2014). Environmental degradation: Causes and consequences. *European Researcher, 81*(8-2), 1491.

Valenduc, G., & Vendramin, P. (2017). Digitalisation, between disruption and evolution. *Transfer: European Review of Labour and Research, 23*(2), 121–134.

Velenturf, A. P., & Purnell, P. (2017). Resource recovery from waste: Restoring the balance between resource scarcity and waste overload. *Sustainability, 9*(9), 1603.

Zheng, X., Govindan, K., Deng, Q., & Feng, L. (2019). Effects of design for the environment on firms' production and remanufacturing strategies. *International Journal of Production Economics, 213*, 217–228.

Zhou, W., Piramuthu, S., Chu, F., & Chu, C. (2017). RFID-enabled flexible warehousing. *Decision Support Systems, 98*, 99–112.

Zhu, Y., Wang, L., & Chen, A. (2016, July 24–25). *Carbon footprint calculation and applied research of printing enterprise based on the ISO14064-1 standard.* Presented at 2016 International Conference on Mechatronics, Control and Automation Engineering, Atlantis Press, Bangkok, Thailand.

9

Business Models for Sustainable Development: The Case of a Kenyan Sustainable Enterprise

Giacomo Ciambotti, Andrea Sottini, David Littlewood, and Abel Kinoti Meru

9.1 Introduction

Globally, we continue to see a transition from environmentally destructive business practices to ones that are more sustainable (Bansal et al., 2019; Saebi et al., 2019). This change is being driven by varied factors, including growing recognition of the global climate emergency and the contribution of business to it; increased awareness of the wider ecological impacts of industry and its pollution of the land, air, and oceans; growing

G. Ciambotti (✉) • A. Sottini
Università Cattolica del Sacro Cuore, Milan, Italy
e-mail: giacomo.ciambotti@unicatt.it; andreacarlo.sottini@unicatt.it

D. Littlewood
Sheffield University Management School, Sheffield, UK
e-mail: david.littlewood@sheffield.ac.uk

A. K. Meru
Riara University, Nairobi, Kenya
e-mail: akinoti@riarauniversity.ac.ke

E. K. Adae et al. (eds.), *Responsible Management in Emerging Markets*, Sustainable Development Goals Series, https://doi.org/10.1007/978-3-030-76563-7_9

consumer expectations that firms will reduce their environmental footprints; and increasing acceptance of the existence of a "business case" for going green. Responding to the above, firms are changing how they work, leading to the emergence of new types of business ventures deploying new innovative sustainable business models. This chapter examines one such sustainable venture, operating in East Africa, and how it develops its business model to create, deliver, and capture value whilst contributing to sustainable development.

In recent decades, governments around the world have begun to respond more concertedly to environmental concerns and to encourage business action. Multilateral initiatives have also emerged drawing in business actors. These include, for instance, the establishment of the United Nations Framework Convention on Climate Change in 1992, and more recently, the creation in 2015 of the 17 Sustainable Development Goals (SDGs) aiming to end poverty and tackle environmental challenges (Warnecke & Houndonougbo, 2016; OECD/EU, 2017; Oxfam, 2017). Sustainable development has thus become a crucial concept for scholars and practitioners alike (Hockerts & Wüstenhagen, 2010; Johnson & Schaltegger, 2019).

Sustainable development requires that renewable resources be used wherever possible and that non-renewable resources be husbanded (e.g., reduced and recycled) to extend their viability for future generations. Intergenerational equity is a crucial aspect of sustainable development, as is its confluence and balancing of social, environmental, and economic imperatives (Ciambotti, 2020). Business and sustainable development has been the subject of growing academic study (see, e.g., Johnson & Schaltegger, 2019; Littlewood & Holt, 2018).

Research has examined various facets of their interaction from business and climate change to industry's impacts on biodiversity. Whilst this work generally recognises business' contributions to the serious ecological problems we face, it is also often suggested that it has an important role to play in promoting environmental transformation and wider sustainable development (Bansal et al., 2019).

Within the growing body of scholarship examining business and sustainable development, attention has increasingly turned to so-called hybrid organisations. Hybrid organisations pursue multiple objectives simultaneously (e.g., social, economic, and environmental) and implement divergent processes to achieve their sustainable development-related missions (Holt & Littlewood, 2015; Ciambotti & Pedrini, 2021; Saebi et al., 2019). Hybrid organisations are often identified as ideal vehicles for leading the global transition to sustainability. Social enterprises are an archetypal form of hybrid organisations. They are ventures that aim to address societal and/or environmental issues whilst also maintaining financial sustainability (Santos et al., 2015; Battilana et al., 2017; Hahn et al., 2018).

Addressing environmental concerns may be a central aspect of the mission of social enterprises (Hockerts, 2006; Holt & Littlewood, 2017), often intertwined with meeting an unmet social need. The hybrid social enterprise M-Kopa exemplifies this. It produces and delivers micro-grid solar panels to poor communities in rural areas of East Africa, addressing energy poverty amongst poor people whilst contributing to the transition to renewable energy. Poor people lacking access to clean and affordable energy are often trapped in a repeating cycle of deprivation and poverty (Holt & Littlewood, 2017). They may be forced to use significant amounts of their very limited incomes on expensive and unhealthy forms of energy provision such as dry cell batteries, rudimentary and inefficient kerosene lamps, charcoal, and candles (Boons & Lüdeke-Freund, 2013; Hahn et al., 2018). M-Kopa works towards addressing a "wicked" sustainable development problem, as well as achieving SDG 7 to "ensure access to affordable, reliable, sustainable and modern energy for all" (Ensuring access to affordable, reliable, sustainable, and modern energy for all, n.d.).

Despite increasing recognition of the potential of social enterprises and entrepreneurship for fostering global sustainable development (Warnecke & Houndonougbo, 2016; Johnson & Schaltegger, 2019; Doherty et al., 2020) and growing academic study of them (e.g., Boons & Lüdeke-Freund, 2013; Santos et al., 2015), there remain gaps in our understanding and much scope for further enquiry. Areas in need of further attention include the environmental work of social enterprises, as well as social enterprises where social and environmental dimensions are given equal weighting in their missions, and where they are heavily intertwined in practice. This study describes such ventures as sustainable enterprises and, hereafter, deploys this term throughout the chapter in reference to social enterprise.

This chapter investigates a sustainable enterprise in East Africa and, in particular, how it has developed its business model to create, deliver, and capture value whilst contributing to sustainable development (Schaltegger et al., 2016; Ciambotti & Pedrini, 2021; Bansal et al., 2019). We also shed light on how it overcomes contextual constraints such as resource scarcity and limited formal institutional support (e.g., poor or absent infrastructure, a lack of clear regulations, an inefficient or nonfunctioning legal system), and, in particular, the strategies it deploys to grow its impact and revenues. In so doing, we answer the following research question: *how can a sustainable enterprise build its business model to contribute to environmental, societal, and economic transformation in a developing economy*? In our study, literature on sustainable business models is drawn upon and applied as an analytical lens (Teece, 2010, 2018). The business model concept is useful for our analysis because it allows us to describe the logic and processes of an organisation and how these enable it to create, deliver, and capture value. Business models can also be conceived of as an interrelated set of elements that address customer needs, provide a value proposition, comprise organisational architecture, and include economic dimensions (Fielt, 2013; Boons & Lüdeke-Freund, 2013; Schaltegger et al., 2016; Hahn et al., 2018; Weerawardena et al., 2019).

To answer the research question, we report the findings of in-depth case study research (Eisenhardt, 1989; Gehman et al., 2018) with a sustainable enterprise in Kenya. The case study examined is Corec Ltd. (hereafter Corec), which was founded in 2010 by the entrepreneur Oscar Aghan. Corec is based in Kariobangi (a slum in Nairobi, Kenya) and aims to provide opportunities for marginalised youths through the recycling of waste plastics collected from slums and dumping sites which are then transformed into building materials and sold to developers and construction companies. Corec integrates multiple objectives into its sustainable development mission: (1) to collect plastic waste (environmental); (2) to integrate youths from the street (social); and (3) to sell products in a given market (economic). For this reason, Corec was selected purposively as a sustainable enterprise (Eisenhardt, 1989).

Kenya was selected as the setting for this study because it is a leading country for sustainable entrepreneurship in East Africa (OECD/EU, 2017; African Economic Outlook, 2019). It has many sustainable entrepreneurs and ventures aiming to address grand challenges like poverty alleviation and providing clean energy (British Council, 2017; Holt & Littlewood, 2017). This study is relevant for many entrepreneurs and enterprises. Finally, Kenya is characterised by significant poverty and widespread limited access to energy services and modern conveniences (Holt & Littlewood, 2017; Ciambotti et al., 2020), which further highlights the practical significance of our research.

The results of this research reveal two important phases by which a sustainable enterprise can develop and achieve its triple bottom line mission. First, it builds a business model in which the three mission dimensions (social, environmental, and economic) are closely intertwined. Second, a sustainable enterprise innovates in its business model components to grow and further achieve its sustainable development mission. By providing insights on how sustainable enterprises can effectively build business models to achieve their triple objectives, we contribute to sustainable entrepreneurship and hybrid organisation scholarship broadly and in Africa specifically.

9.2 Theoretical Background

9.2.1 Sustainable Enterprises as Hybrid Organisations

Hybrid organisations have become an increasingly important topic of study (Battilana et al., 2017; Doherty et al., 2020). To date, much attention has been devoted to defining and classifying such organisations (Mair & Marti, 2006; Ciambotti, 2020); however, there is a need for more work to be done going beyond these definitional debates. Nevertheless, a helpful definition of a hybrid organisation is provided by Doherty et al. (2020) who suggest that hybrids are characterised by structures and practices that allow the coexistence of values and artefacts from two or more categories, for example, state, third, and private sectors.

According to Hockerts (2006), social (sustainable) enterprises are a key form of hybrid organisation and can be classified into three main categories. First, work integration social enterprises (WISE) employ people at risk of being excluded from the labour market due to low competences, disabilities, ethnic discrimination, and so on (Battilana et al., 2015). An example of this is the venture Wawoto Kacel (Walking Together in the local language), which was founded in 1997 in the city of Gulu, in northern Uganda. Wawoto Kacel's mission is to rehabilitate and empower vulnerable women with HIV and those displaced by war. It supports them in producing natural textile patterns to be sold in local and overseas markets.

The second category identified by Hockerts (2006) is fair trade hybrid organisations. They aim to create an income for poor and marginalised producers (e.g., farmers), often located in developing economies, by charging a premium price and targeting customers with ethical consciousness and a desire to improve the incomes of vulnerable groups (Doherty et al., 2014). For instance, Meru Herbs is a Kenyan fair trade venture which established a cooperative of tea leaf producers and sells tea bags around the world ensuring a fair profit for growers (Sgrò et al., 2020).

The third category revealed by Hockerts (2006) is base of the pyramid (BoP) ventures which target poor people as consumers to address their unmet needs (e.g., access to clean drinking water, electricity, and healthy food) (Prahalad & Hart, 2002; Yunus et al., 2010; Ciambotti et al., 2020). In such BoP contexts, it has been suggested that to be successful, hybrid organisations need to ensure their products and services possess four main characteristics: affordability, availability, accessibility, and awareness (Anderson & Billou, 2007). An interesting example of this is the Kenyan solar energy company M-Kopa which pioneered a pay-as-you-go energy platform to uplift millions of lives in East Africa.

In summary, hybrid organisations come in various forms. They also pursue multiple objectives through structures and practices derived from the categories of which they are constituted, that is, public and private, private and third, and so on. Sustainable enterprises like the one examined in this study can, therefore, be conceived of as hybrid organisations.

9.2.2 Sustainable Business Models

Sustainable business models require integrated thinking and the reframing of traditional business model aspects such as resources, business networks, stakeholder engagement, and organisational culture (Hahn et al., 2018). Combining such aspects in a way that balances economic, environmental, and social sustainability dimensions is complex and requires a business model capable of creating competitive advantage by fulfilling customer needs, while also ensuring venture sustainability and contributing to sustainable development in society (Lüdeke-Freund, 2010; Evans et al., 2017; Ciambotti et al., 2020).

A business model may be conceived of in terms of three key components: value proposition, value delivery, and value capture (Zott et al., 2011; Teece, 2018). The main pillar of the business model is the value proposition, which reflects the firm's offering that addresses customers' needs or wants. Next, an organisation must create and deliver value through a series of activities, as well as its networks with partners and suppliers (Seelos & Mair, 2005; Zott et al., 2011). This relates particularly to the internal and external value chains of the organisation (Yunus et al., 2010). The third component of the business model concerns the financial equation between value proposition and value delivery. It relates to how value is captured from revenues, and how the costs of value creation are covered through a monetary transaction with customers (Hahn et al., 2018).

While management and entrepreneurship scholars have focused their research mainly on the economic aspects of value, recently, psychologists, sociologists, and ecologists have integrated concepts like "eco-footprint" and "meaningful life" to develop a more holistic conception of value (Schaltegger et al., 2016). From this integration was born the concept of *sustainable value* which includes social, economic, and environmental dimensions.

In a similar vein, recent work by Joyce and Paquin (2016), amongst others (see also Evans et al., 2017; Bocken et al., 2014), asserts that sustainable business models are premised upon the triple bottom line. First, the economic dimension focuses on finding revenue streams that cover costs in order to reach and maintain financial sustainability and thus sustain environmental and social aspects. Second, the environmental dimension builds upon a lifecycle perspective. It stimulates organisations to explore business model innovations that can mitigate environmental impacts as well as create positive ecological value through business actions. Third is the social dimension which adopts a stakeholder orientation. Social value entails the creation of benefits for an organisation's stakeholders and society more broadly (Joyce & Paquin, 2016).

Scholars have argued that business models should evolve over time, including in response to external environmental change. This is especially important in dynamic emerging economy contexts similar to those studied in this research (Dobson, 2007; Hart et al., 2016; Ciambotti, 2020). Creativity and innovativeness are key capabilities for organisations to adapt their business models (Hall & Wagner, 2012; Ciambotti et al., 2020). This includes hybrid sustainable enterprises and wider organisations responding to the global transition towards sustainable development.

9.2.3 Scaling Strategies in Sustainable Enterprises

Innovations in technology and know-how are driving the emergence of new sustainable business models in emerging economies (see, e.g., ventures like M-Kopa Solar, Azuri Group, and Awamu Biomass Energy). Scaling such business models and innovations is crucial for at least two reasons. First, business models for sustainability may not be economically viable, to begin with (e.g., when the first hybrid cars were developed, the low production volumes were a cost obstacle to achieving breakeven) (Ciambotti, 2020).

This fragility may be exacerbated in emerging economies where purchasing capacity is often low. Consequently, given low margins per unit for products/services, sustainable enterprises need to grow to achieve economies of scale and financial sustainability (Bocken et al., 2016). Second, sustainable business scaling can increase social impact by addressing unsatisfied needs (Seelos & Mair, 2005). In so doing, ventures close the gap between real and ideal outcomes in addressing a particular social or environmental need (Dobson, 2007).

To date, work examining sustainable business model scaling has often focused on the role of entrepreneurs. For example, Bloom and Smith (2010) developed their capabilities to scale social impact framework based on the mnemonic SCALERS: staffing, communicating, alliance building, lobbying, earning generation, replication, and stimulating market forces.

Scholars investigating the capabilities necessary for sustainable enterprises to scale in emerging markets have also highlighted the need to develop "social innovation capabilities" to create value for communities, through developing viable solutions, and to penetrate markets (Bocken et al., 2016). In traditional entrepreneurship scholarship, it has been suggested that enterprises can scale through four main strategies: market penetration, market development, product development, and diversification (Ciambotti, 2020). Applying these in a sustainable enterprise context, Bocken et al. (2016) add a further dimension. They highlight that such ventures need to also consider strategies to increase revenue per stream, and revenue streams overall, because of challenges of affordability.

Scaling strategies that entail the expansion of a business into a new context, market, and geographic area may require a change in business model components (Minniti & Bygrave, 2001; Dobson, 2007). For instance, a scaling strategy may necessitate a sustainable enterprise to access new capabilities and resources through new partnerships, particularly when entering new geographic markets (Bocken et al., 2016). The composition of resources in a sustainable enterprise can also change according to the degree of central coordination required by scaling (Dees et al., 2004).

Scholars investigating scaling strategies and their impact on sustainable business models (Ciambotti et al., 2020) have found that scaling of programmes for serving poor people often fails or is very slow (Dees et al., 2002, 2004; Polak, 2009). In emerging economies, the obstacles to scaling business models may be particularly significant and can include fragmented markets, poor infrastructure (Prahalad & Hammond, 2002), limited distribution channels, resource constraints, demand-size adoption problems, illiteracy (Anderson & Billou, 2007), weak legal frameworks, and institutional voids (Holt & Littlewood, 2017). Clear evidence of the challenges of doing and scaling sustainable businesses in emerging economies can be seen in a study of 439 hybrids which scaled within sub-Saharan African markets, where only 13% were found to be operating at scale (Katz et al., 2012).

In summary, despite the existence of literature on how hybrid sustainable enterprises scale, there remain gaps in our understanding of how business models must be configured to achieve such scaling, particularly in developing and emerging markets and even more so in Africa (Bocken et al., 2016). Our chapter addresses this limitation by investigating how hybrid sustainable enterprises can effectively grow their business models to contribute to transformations to sustainability in such settings.

9.3 Research Methodology

This research comprises an in-depth analysis of a sustainable enterprise case study in Kenya (Eisenhardt, 1989; Gehman et al., 2018)—Corec Ltd. This approach was selected to gain rich insights on the case and allows us to answer the research question: *how can a sustainable enterprise build its business model to contribute to environmental, societal, and economic transformation in a developing economy*? Single case designs are widely deployed in entrepreneurship and wider management scholarship, particularly in inductive research where the goal is analytic rather than statistical generalisation.

As explained earlier, Corec was founded in 2010 by Oscar Aghan and is based in the Kariobangi slum in Nairobi, Kenya. Corec aims to integrate marginalised youths by collecting and recycling waste plastics from slums and dumpsites which are transformed into building materials to be sold to developers and construction companies. This case was purposely selected due to its triple bottom line objectives: to collect plastic waste (environmental), to integrate youths from the street (social), and to sell products in a given market (economic). In Table 9.1 we provide some further key information on the case.

Data collection followed several stages and drew upon many sources of information. First, we became familiar with the context in which Corec operates through reviewing reports and institutional data. This first step comprised desk research which allowed the authors to dive deep into

Table 9.1 Case study background

Item	Corec
Founder	Oscar Aghan
Setup year	2010
Industry	Waste management
Firm description	The company employs marginalised people to collect and recycle waste plastics, transforming it into building material, and sell, providing affordable and durable construction products to developers and construction companies
Revenues	Σ 150.000 USD (2019)
Youths integrated	Σ 630 (2019)
Tonnes of plastic	Σ 1.200 Tonnes (2019)
Beneficiaries	– Youth and street boys of slums – Women and disabled people – Parents and wives of youths and disabled people with low incomes
Customers	– Kenyan private citizens – Construction companies – Wholesalers
Products	– Fencing posts – Roofing tiles – Pavement blocks – Walkway slabs – Garden products

Source: Authors (2021)

local specificities concerning waste management practices and regulations. Table 9.2 reports the data sources.

Second, we collected primary data through seven semi-structured interviews, undertaken in multiple phases, for a total of more than four hours of recorded interview data. Interview protocols were developed and refined across the interviews, enabling the collection of more theoretical information (Gehman et al., 2018). Data were collected at different periods to systematically compare the results from interviews with steps in business model component innovation, as well as to validate how the business model affected Corec's multiple mission achievements over time.

To analyse the data, all interviews were transcribed verbatim, and data were consolidated into theoretical constructs through axial coding, by which raw data were systematically linked with theory, which also helped

Table 9.2 Data source

Source	Type of data	Quantity	Use in the analysis
Documents and reports	Report from local and international NGOs, government, corporates, banks	520 pages (.pdf)	Familiarise with the local context and business ecosystem
Primary data	Semi-structured Interviews: – August 2017, Nairobi (2) – March 2018, Nairobi (1) – May 2018, Kariobangi (2) – April 2019, via call (2)	– 4 hours and 35 minutes of interviews (5 in-loco, 1 Skype call) – 1 headquarter visit – 2 production plants visit	Construction of the set of concepts
Secondary data	Business models Business plan Marketing plan Financial model Annual report and social impact report	42 pages (.ppt) 67 pages (.pdf) 43 pages (.pdf) 25 pages (.xls) 36 pages (.pdf)	Support, integrate, and triangulate with evidence from interviews

Source: Authors (2021)

to refine later data collection. This iterative process culminated in the creation of a final data structure. In the next section, we present our findings before proceeding to the discussion and conclusion.

9.4 Findings

Our research question relates to how sustainable enterprises in resource-constrained contexts can grow business models to successfully fulfil their sustainable development missions. Extant literature has documented the challenges of achieving such missions, as well as the balancing of economic aspects associated with financial sustainability (Prahalad & Hammond, 2002) and the achievement of social and environmental goals (Bocken et al., 2016; Davies & Chambers, 2018; Ciambotti, 2020).

As discussed previously, this may also require scaling (Bloom & Smith, 2010; Islam, 2020). Our findings reveal a two-phase process of mission achievement by sustainable enterprises. We found that in order to achieve its triple bottom line mission, Corec first had to build a business model grounded in sustainable value creation. By intertwining economic, social, and environmental value creation, where each element is necessary for and interdependent of the others (Smith & Lewis, 2011), the company was able to create a paradoxical sustainable development frame.

Once relationships between economic, social, and environmental aspects of the mission had settled, Corec started to innovate its business model components to scale. Within this, Corec implemented different strategies purposely for growing revenues or for growing sustainable development impact. The deployment of these strategies led the company to adapt aspects of its business model. This phase brought the company success and allowed it to fulfil its mission, notably through providing opportunities to and integrating more than 600 youths, earning more than US$150,000 per annum, and collecting more than a thousand tonnes of plastic a year.

9.4.1 Intertwining to Build Sustainable Business Models

The first phase entailed the intertwining of economic, social, and environmental mission aspects across different business model components. This interplay is documented in Table 9.3 and is also explored in more detail below.

9.4.1.1 Intertwining in the Value Proposition

To integrate the three mission aspects in the value proposition, Corec first placed social and environmental considerations at the heart of the venture. As alluded to previously, Corec aims to improve the livelihoods of youths—also called *street children* (homeless living in slums)—by providing them with job opportunities, while also contributing to cleaning up an extremely polluted environment. In starting the venture, Corec's founder was impressed by the huge number of youths collecting plastics in landfills throughout Nairobi's suburbs, with these plastics then sold to

Table 9.3 Sustainable value creation

Mission	Value proposition	Value delivery	Value capture
Social dimension	• Integrate groups of street youths to collect raw materials • Human resources that are good for the society	• Training activities for youths in the production line • Youths integration in plastic collection	• Decrease in cost of human resources
Environmental dimension	• Collect plastic from dumping sites and slums • Raw materials that are good for the planet	• Development of partnership/ networking activities to organise the collection of plastics	• Decrease in cost of raw materials (recycled plastic)
Economic dimension	• Produce and sell products and services for the building market	• Create distribution networks for delivery to building companies	• Increase sale of products to building companies

Source: Authors (2021)

"middlemen" for a few Shillings. However, these practices were harmful not only for youths' long-term health but were also a cause of social issues given these youths would often buy illegal substances with the low income earned each day, as discussed in the following quotation:

> *Living closely to the slum, I was able to see the amount of plastic in the Dandora dumpsite and the streets of the slum. Moreover, there was a lot of youth unemployment and criminality.* (Corec)

Corec's founder desired to improve this degraded environment, whilst also helping youths to escape a poverty trap. His idea was to employ them in healthy working conditions, giving them a guaranteed good income, which would also improve their wider lives. To address this social issue, Corec understood that it could also have a positive impact on the environment, as described in the following quotation:

> *The challenge we are addressing is to reduce the amount of waste in landfills, curb deforestation rates, and stem slum proliferation and vandalism.* (Corec)

Corec's founder realised that a large amount of the plastics in landfills can be treated and transformed into workable raw materials. In so doing, Corec could contribute to cleaning landfills and reducing harmful pollutants. To do this, the company required machines to transform plastics into raw materials. It also designed a portfolio of products for internal and external use, as explained in the quotation below:

> *Machineries are critical resources for us.... we needed a lot of machines to get a technological transformation. Our products are based on this transformation from garbage and plastic waste to building products such as roofing tiles.* (Corec)

9.4.1.2 Intertwining in Value Delivery

Once Corec designed its three-dimensional value proposition, the next step was to understand how to deliver it to the market. First, the firm needed to train youths to use proper tools to collect plastic from landfills and to use machines to treat and transform them into raw materials. Corec partnered with NGOs whose missions and activities related to relief programmes for street children and, working with these partners, selected and trained youths who were integrated into the company. These partnerships enabled Corec to access youth groups and programmes, while also supporting the activities of these NGOs and the achievement of their social missions, as illustrated below:

> *Partnership because they help us with the training that is exactly their mission. In this case we are offering them a market for their value proposition. They train street boys and girls to work and use machineries.* (Corec)

Through these partnerships, Corec organised plastic collection activities around landfills. This increased the quantity of plastic collected and enhanced local environments. Furthermore, these network relations and activities increased the notoriety of the company and opened up new connections with distributor firms that were eager to contribute to Corec's mission.

9.4.1.3 Intertwining in Value Capture

Corec's organisation of plastic collection activities and training in the use of machines to transform waste plastic into raw materials allowed it to increase production efficiency and capacity. These two elements enabled Corec to provide good salaries to employees (street youth) as well as decrease the cost of production for internal and external design products, as documented below:

> *We can be cheaper than others because of the social aspect that brings production efficiency.* (Corec)

Moreover, the cost of raw materials itself is only related to the plastic collection activity and recycling activity. This combination allowed Corec to decrease the costs of raw materials compared to purchasing non-recycled plastic from external providers. As a consequence, the reduction of production costs, the integration of street youths in production activity, as well as the positive environmental impact enhanced Corec's reputation in the market, as quoted below:

> *Being social plays an important role. You need to be known! And this is the first aspect, it's important to create strong social ties. … We gained the name and a good reputation in the industry as a green company.* (Corec)

Finally, the low production costs made the company competitive compared to others in the industry. Taken together, these different aspects attracted customers—including local government—to purchase furniture products for houses and offices, as well as materials to build streets and pedestrian areas.

9.4.2 Innovating the Business Model to Scale

Once Corec had designed, developed, and implemented a feasible sustainable business model with intertwining economic, social, and environmental dimensions, the venture was then ready to scale to achieve greater impact and enhance economic viability. This was also documented in Corec's business plan and financial model.

Corec deployed four scaling strategies, focusing on (1) growing the number of beneficiaries; (2) growing impact to beneficiaries; (3) growing the number of commercial customers; and (4) growing products/services to customers. However, the implementation of these strategies required some innovation in its business model components (value proposition, value delivery, and value capture). Table 9.4 details the findings which are further explained in the remainder of this section.

9.4.2.1 Innovating to Grow the Number of Beneficiaries

To grow the number of beneficiaries, Corec aimed to increase the number of marginalised street youths involved in waste collection and production activities (they increased from 30 youths in 2015 to 635 by 2019). To pursue this goal, it also decided to integrate marginalised women and, in so doing, expanded its value proposition. Moreover, they targeted additional dumpsites and slums around Nairobi (as documented in the company's business plan). In this way, Corec began to impact youths from more slums including Korogocho (2010), Dandora, Umoja, Jericho (2013), and Rongai and Huruma (2014).

Pursuing this strategy also required Corec to innovate components in value delivery. As the company expanded plastic collection, it needed to develop additional collection programmes and partnerships with NGOs to expand training to new youths. Finally, in terms of value capture, this strategy brought about an increase in production capacity and transformation of raw materials, as well as an expansion of product offerings leading to further market demand as illustrated below:

> *We were growing the number of our beneficiaries, and we also increased a lot our production capacity! ... For this reason, our missions are very linked, because if you reinforce something, you will impact also the other missions.* (Corec)

Table 9.4 Innovating business models to scale

	Business model innovation		
Scaling strategy	Change in value proposition	Change in value delivery	Change in value capture
Innovating to grow the number of beneficiaries	• Integrate additional beneficiaries (e.g., women, disabled people) • Increase geographic areas (slums and dumping sites)	• Find out new beneficiaries • Increase in training activities • Integration in the production line/plastic collection • Increase plastic collection	• Increase the production capacity for selling more products
Innovating to grow impact for beneficiaries	• Provide additional services to beneficiaries for their needs • Find new problems that are still unaddressed (e.g., insurance for marginalised youths)	• Figure out assistance services in partnership • Develop social programmes for employees	• Increase in the expenses for additional benefits to employees • Reduced cost of training because of partnerships
Innovating to grow the number of commercial customers	• Include private individuals and middle-class citizens in Nairobi • Target construction companies and private individuals who want green building materials	• Invest in market research • Partnership with banks for working capital	• Increase customers • Increase markets (e.g., exterior design market)
Innovating to grow products and services	• Retain attention on quality of products • Develop new products	• Product design • New machineries and product lines	• Sell additional products (e.g., gardening products pavement blocks)

Source: Authors (2021)

9.4.2.2 Innovating to Grow Impact for Beneficiaries

Aligned with its mission to improve the lives of youths, Corec focused on not only the number of youths integrated but also the quality of services and support provided to them, as described in the following quotation:

> *When we train them, we go to a good hotel, we do coaching and many other activities. You have got to be friendly with them, so that they can see someone who loves them, and treats them differently. The need to feel part of the community. … for example, we open them also a bank account, that normally they cannot open.* (Corec)

For this reason, Corec added additional social assistance to its programmes, including insurance policies to protect youths in case of injuries or ill health. While the company delivered this additional assistance through strategic partnerships with local NGOs—in the same way as the training—part of these activities were developed directly by the company, as mentioned below:

> *We decided to partner with some NGOs, like World Vision or Norwegian Refugee Council … they assured free training services to our employees coming from the street. And this is quite important for the quality of our impact! We need to take care, and we cannot do it all by ourselves.* (Corec)

Through these partnerships, Corec was also able to save funds that could rather be devoted to scaling and further growing impact, as outlined below:

> *Also, financial sustainability was affected by those partnerships, as we got this service for free.* (Corec)

9.4.2.3 Innovating to Grow the Number of Commercial Customers

The growing expense of providing additional social services for beneficiaries, as well as the growing demand for Corec's products, motivated the company to offer its products to new customer segments in order to reach and maintain financial sustainability. To do this, Corec expanded its marketing activities to attract the interest of private companies and middle-class citizens in Nairobi who appreciate the social and environmental ethos and activities of the company. Corec partnered with commercial banks to gain the working capital needed to scale the business into new customer segments and to sustain its investment in advertisement and market research, as documented below:

> *I'm still struggling with financial sustainability, because to grow you need to find money! This is also why I'm collaborating with Equity Bank.* (Corec)

Retaining a focus on the social mission allowed Corec to enter new market segments and increase overall sales, as illustrated in the following quotation:

> *Growing the social mission allowed us to grow also financial activity. Sales keep increasing, through the growing demand of such environmental goods! … Beyond the demand, there is the awareness of products and more importantly the social need at the core.* (Corec)

9.4.2.4 Innovating to Grow Products and Services

Corec was aware that its focus on environmental and social concerns would not be enough to achieve success in the market. Therefore, the company decided to enhance the quality of its products and to develop new products. Corec innovated in value creation and delivery by designing new products and deploying new machines brought in from Europe. As a result, Corec was able to not only retain customers through a higher quality of products but also acquire more customers through selling additional products, such as gardening products or paving slabs.

9.5 Discussion

This chapter has explored how a sustainable enterprise has developed its business model, balancing social, environmental, and economic imperatives, and the multiple strategies it has adopted to scale. In so doing, we add to the extant literature on sustainable enterprise as an emerging field of enquiry (Fielt, 2013; Boons & Lüdeke-Freund, 2013; Schaltegger et al., 2016; Hahn et al., 2018; Weerawardena et al., 2019). Consolidating these findings, we introduce the model presented in Fig. 9.1, which documents the process through which sustainable enterprises achieve their missions and grow.

In this model, the first stage entails the integration of multiple mission aspects. This aligns with the work of Weerawardena et al. (2019), documenting how sustainable business models can be constructed leading to sustainable value creation. We shed light on how through processes of interlinking, the achievement of the three dimensions—economic, social, and environmental—can be mutually reinforcing. This finds resonance with paradox thinking, where elements are divergent but also interdependent (Smith & Lewis, 2011), as well as complements the findings of other studies on the business models of sustainable enterprises (see Boons & Lüdeke-Freund, 2013; Schaltegger et al., 2016; Hahn et al., 2018).

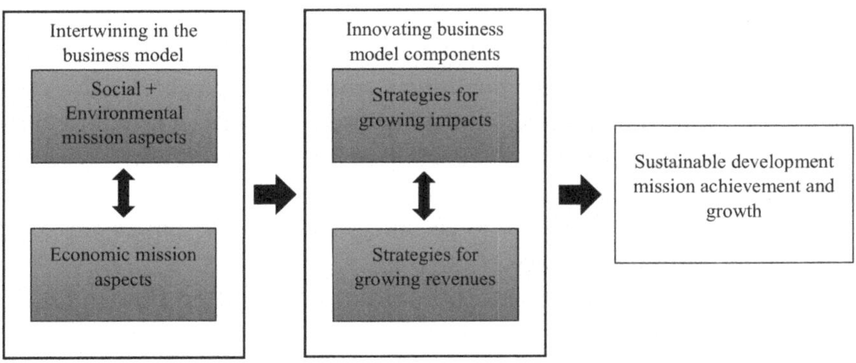

Fig. 9.1 Model of sustainable development mission achievement and growth. (Source: Authors (2021))

Second, our model reveals how after economic, social, and environmental elements have intertwined across business model components in sustainable enterprises (Yunus et al., 2010; Ciambotti et al., 2020), such ventures may need to continue innovating and developing these components to grow and achieve their sustainable development missions. Scaling and growth is a widely discussed topic in sustainable enterprise literature (Doherty et al., 2020; Ciambotti et al., 2020). Our chapter adds to such work providing in-depth insights on the innovation of business model components and their role in sustainable enterprise growth. These insights extend studies like those of Minniti and Bygrave (2001) and Dobson (2007), and open avenues for further research, as documented in conclusions.

9.6 Conclusions: Future Research and Limitations

This chapter addresses an important phenomenon in sustainable enterprise and hybrid organisation scholarship, namely how such ventures can build sustainable business models managing tensions between different dimensions to achieve their missions (Smith & Lewis, 2011; Santos et al., 2015; Battilana et al., 2017; Ciambotti & Pedrini, 2021). Our results provide insights on how multiple mission aspects (social, environmental, and economic) can be intertwined to achieve sustainable development impact. We then showcase how such sustainable ventures can scale through various strategies, the implementation of which may require further innovation in business model components. These findings are summarised and inform the development of a novel conceptual model. This chapter and model contribute to sustainable enterprise scholarship and have implications for practice.

For sustainable entrepreneurs, our work sheds light on how multiple mission dimensions can be successfully managed to achieve positive social and environmental impacts as well as financial sustainability which can be mutually reinforcing. We also show how sustainable enterprises can grow whilst balancing social, economic, and environmental imperatives. Corec provides a successful example that can be learned from, including how it has flourished in a complex and challenging business environment. Finally, we hope that our research can help sustainable entrepreneurs and managers make better decisions when configuring and innovating business model components for the sustainability of their enterprises and for delivering impact across the triple bottom line.

Our research provides avenues for further study of the intersection between sustainable enterprises, hybridity, and business models. The processes and tensions documented in our case might be further explored in other organisations across varied industries and geographies in both developing (Holt & Littlewood, 2017; Saebi et al., 2019; Ciambotti et al., 2020) and developed economy contexts. A further key topic of research in hybridity scholarship is mission drift. Future studies could therefore explore, deploying our framework, when and how mission drift occurs in sustainable enterprises (Yunus et al., 2010).

There has also hitherto been limited consideration of the challenges for sustainable enterprises of growing whilst maintaining a triple bottom line focus, and instances unlike our case where this is not successful. Work might, thus, examine when and why sustainable enterprises lose focus on certain mission dimensions or prioritise some over others, and what the implications of this are for them and their stakeholders.

To conclude, in this chapter we have sought to shed light on how sustainable enterprises can build sustainable development business models and scale to maximise their contributions to global transitions towards sustainability. Although we see significant potential in such ventures and venturing, we think it is also a topic that requires much further academic attention. We hope that this chapter, including the avenues identified above, inspires such future research. We also hope it is practically useful and contributes in some small way to the realisation and achievement of global sustainable development.

References

African Economic Outlook. (2019). African Economic Outlook. Retrieved November 10, 2020, from https://www.africaneconomicoutlook.org/

Anderson, J., & Billou, N. (2007). Serving the world's poor: Innovation at the base of the economic pyramid. *Journal of Business Strategy, 28*(2), 14–21.

Bansal, S., Garg, I., & Sharma, G. D. (2019). Social entrepreneurship as a path for social change and driver of sustainable development: A systematic review and research agenda. *Sustainability, 11*(4), 1091.

Battilana, J., Besharov, M., & Mitzinneck, B. (2017). On hybrids and hybrid organizing: A review and roadmap for future research. In R. Greenwood, C. Oliver, T. B. Lawrence, & R. E. Meyer (Eds.), *The SAGE handbook of organizational institutionalism* (2nd ed., pp. 133–169). SAGE Publications Ltd.

Battilana, J., Sengul, M., Pache, A. C., & Model, J. (2015). Harnessing productive tensions in hybrid organizations: The case of work integration social enterprises. *Academy of Management Journal, 58*(6), 1658–1685.

Bloom, P. N., & Smith, B. R. (2010). Identifying the drivers of social entrepreneurial impact: Theoretical development and an exploratory empirical test of SCALERS. *Journal of Social Entrepreneurship, 1*(1), 126–145.

Bocken, N. M., Fil, A., & Prabhu, J. (2016). Scaling up social businesses in developing markets. *Journal of Cleaner Production, 139*, 295–308.

Bocken, N. S., Short, R. P., & Evans, S. (2014). A literature and practice review to develop sustainable business model archetypes. *Journal of Cleaner Production, 65*, 42–56.

Boons, F., & Lüdeke-Freund, F. (2013). Business models for sustainable innovation: State-of-the-art and steps towards a research agenda. *Journal of Cleaner Production, 45*, 9–19.

British Council. (2017). The state of social enterprise in Kenya. Retrieved November 10, 2020, from https://www.britishcouncil.org/sites/default/files/state_of_social_enterprise_in_kenya_british_council_final.pdf

Ciambotti, G. (2020). Social entrepreneurship and scaling strategies for poverty alleviation. In W. Leal Filho, A. M. Azul, L. Brandli, A. Lange Salvia, P. G. Özuyar, & T. Wall (Eds.), *No poverty. Encyclopedia of the UN Sustainable Development Goals*. Springer.

Ciambotti, G., Littlewood, D., Sottini, A., & M'ithiria, E. N. (2020). Building and scaling social enterprise business models for BOP markets in Kenya. In J. Muthuri, M. Arnold, G. Stefan, & F. Ximena (Eds.), *Base of the Pyramid markets in Africa* (pp. 199–227). Routledge.

Ciambotti, G., & Pedrini, M. (2021). Hybrid harvesting strategies to overcome resource constraints: Evidence from social enterprises in Kenya. *Journal of Business Ethics, 168*(3), 631–650. https://doi.org/10.1007/s10551-019-04256-y

Davies, I. A., & Chambers, L. (2018). Integrating hybridity and business model theory in sustainable entrepreneurship. *Journal of Cleaner Production, 177*, 378–386.

Dees, G. J., Anderson, B. B., & Wei-Skillern, J. (2002). Pathways to social impact: Strategies for scaling out successful social innovations. *Stanford Social Innovation Review*, 1–14.

Dees, G. J., Anderson, B. B., & Wei-Skillern, J. (2004). Scaling Social Impact Strategies for spreading social innovations. *Stanford Social Innovation Review*, 24–32.

Dobson, A. (2007). Environmental citizenship: Towards sustainable development. *Sustainable Development, 15*(5), 276–285.

Doherty, B., Haugh, H., & Lyon, F. (2014). Social enterprises as hybrid organizations: A review and research agenda. *International Journal of Management Reviews, 16*(4), 417–436.

Doherty, B., Haugh, H., Sahan, E., Wills, T., & Croft, S. (2020). *Creating the new economy: Business models that put people and planet first*. Retrieved November 10, 2020, from https://traidcraftexchange.org/policy-resources/2020/1/22/creating-the-new-economy-business-models-that-put-people-and-planet-first

Eisenhardt, K. M. (1989). Building theories from case study research. *Academy of Management Review, 14*(4), 532–550.

Ensuring access to affordable, reliable, sustainable, and modern energy for all. (n.d.). Retrieved from: https://sdgs.un.org/goals/goal7

Evans, S., Vladimirova, D., Holgado, M., Van Fossen, K., Yang, M., Silva, E. A., & Barlow, C. Y. (2017). Business model innovation for sustainability: Towards a unified perspective for creation of sustainable business models. *Business Strategy and the Environment, 26*, 597–608.

Fielt, E. (2013). Conceptualising business models: Definitions, frameworks and classifications. *Journal of Business Models, 1*(1), 85–105.

Gehman, J., Glaser, V. L., Eisenhardt, K. M., Gioia, D., Langley, A., & Corley, K. G. (2018). Finding theory–method fit: A comparison of three qualitative approaches to theory building. *Journal of Management Inquiry, 27*(3), 284–300.

Hahn, R., Spieth, P., & Ince, I. (2018). Business model design in sustainable entrepreneurship: Illuminating the commercial logic of hybrid businesses. *Journal of Cleaner Production, 176*, 439–451.

Hall, J., & Wagner, M. (2012). Integrating sustainability into firms' processes: Performance effects and the moderating role of business models and innovation. *Business Strategy and the Environment, 21*(3), 183–196.

Hart, S., Sharma, S., & Halme, M. (2016). Poverty, business and sustainable development. *Organization and Environment, 29*(4), 401–415.

Hockerts, K. (2006). Introduction to Part IV—Ecopreneurship: Unique research field or Just 'More of the same'? In J. Mair, G. Robinson, &

K. Hockerts (Eds.), *Social entrepreneurship* (pp. 209–213). Palgrave Macmillan.
Hockerts, K., & Wüstenhagen, R. (2010). Greening Goliaths versus emerging Davids. Theorizing about the role of incumbents and new entrants in sustainable entrepreneurship. *Journal of Business Venturing, 25*(5), 481–492.
Holt, D., & Littlewood, D. (2015). Identifying, mapping, and monitoring the impact of hybrid firms. *California Management Review, 57*(3), 107–125.
Holt, D., & Littlewood, D. (2017). Waste livelihoods amongst the poor—Through the lens of bricolage. *Business Strategy and the Environment, 26*(2), 253–264.
Islam, S. M. (2020). Towards an integrative definition of scaling social impact in social enterprises. *Journal of Business Venturing Insights, 13*. https://doi.org/10.1016/j.jbvi.2020.e00164
Johnson, M. P., & Schaltegger, S. (2019). Entrepreneurship for sustainable development: A review and multilevel causal mechanism framework. *Entrepreneurship Theory and Practice, 44*(6). https://doi.org/10.1177/1042258719885368
Joyce, A., & Paquin, R. L. (2016). The triple layered business model canvas: A tool to design more sustainable business models. *Journal of Cleaner Production, 135*, 1474–1486.
Katz, R., Koh, H., & Karamchandani, A. (2012). From blueprint to scale: The case for philanthropy in impact investing. Retrieved November 10, 2020, from https://acumen.org/wp-content/uploads/2017/09/From-Blueprint-to-Scale-Case-for-Philanthropy-in-Impact-Investing_Full-report.pdf
Littlewood, D., & Holt, D. (2018). How social enterprises can contribute to the Sustainable Development Goals (SDGs)—A conceptual framework. In N. Apostolopoulos, H. Al-Dajani, D. Holt, P. Jones, & R. Newbery (Eds.), *Entrepreneurship and the Sustainable Development Goals* (pp. 33–46). Emerald. ISBN 9781787563766.
Lüdeke-Freund, F. (2010). Towards a conceptual framework of 'business models for sustainability'. In R. Wever, J. Quist, A. Tukker, J. Woudstra, F. Boons, & N. Beute (Eds.), *Knowledge collaboration & learning for sustainable innovation* (pp. 25–29). Delft.
Mair, J., & Marti, I. (2006). Social entrepreneurship research: A source of explanation, prediction, and delight. *Journal of World Business, 41*(1), 36–44.
Minniti, M., & Bygrave, W. (2001). A dynamic model of entrepreneurial learning. *Entrepreneurship Theory and Practice, 25*(3), 5–16.
OECD/EU. (2017). *Boosting social enterprise development: Good practice compendium*. OECD Publishing. [Viewed November 10, 2020].

http://www.oecd.org/publications/boosting-social-enterprise-development-9789264268500-en.htm

Oxfam. (2017). *An Economy for the 99%: It's time to build a human economy that benefits everyone, not just the privileged few*. Oxfam GB. Retrieved November 10, 2020, from https://www.oxfam.org/en/research/economy-99

Polak, P. (2009). *Out of poverty*. Berrett-Koehler.

Prahalad, C. K., & Hammond, A. (2002). Serving the world's poor, profitably. *Harvard Business Review, 80*(9), 48–59.

Prahalad, C. K., & Hart, S. L. (2002). The fortune at the bottom of the pyramid. *Strategy + Business*, 26, pp. 2–14.

Saebi, T., Foss, N. J., & Linder, S. (2019). Social entrepreneurship research: Past achievements and future promises. *Journal of Management, 45*(1), 70–95.

Santos, F., Pache, A. C., & Birkholz, C. (2015). Making hybrids work: Aligning business models and organizational design for social enterprises. *California Management Review, 57*(3), 36–58.

Schaltegger, S., Lüdeke-Freund, F., & Hansen, E. G. (2016). Business models for sustainability: A co-evolutionary analysis of sustainable entrepreneurship, innovation, and transformation. *Organization & Environment, 29*(3), 264–289.

Seelos, C., & Mair, J. (2005). Social entrepreneurship: Creating new business models to serve the poor. *Business Horizons, 48*(3), 241–246.

Sgrò, F., Ciambotti, G., Bontis, N., & Ayiku, A. (2020). Intellectual capital in East and West African social enterprises. *Knowledge and Process Management, 27*(4), 332–344.

Smith, W. K., & Lewis, M. W. (2011). Toward a theory of paradox: A dynamic equilibrium model of organizing. *Academy of Management Review, 36*(2), 381–403.

Teece, D. J. (2010). Business models, business strategy and innovation. *Long Range Planning, 43*(2–3), 172–194.

Teece, D. J. (2018). Business models and dynamic capabilities. *Long Range Planning, 51*(1), 40–49.

Warnecke, T., & Houndonougbo, A. N. (2016). Let there be light: Social enterprise, solar power, and sustainable development. *Journal of Economic Issues, 50*(2), 362–372.

Weerawardena, J., Salunke, S., Haigh, N., & Mort, G. S. (2019). Business model innovation in social purpose organizations: Conceptualizing dual social-economic value creation. *Journal of Business Research, 125*. https://doi.org/10.1016/j.jbusres.2019.10.016

Yunus, M., Moingeon, B., & Lehmann-Ortega, L. (2010). Building social business models: Lessons from the Grameen experience. *Long Range Planning, 43*(2–3), 308–325.

Zott, C., Amit, R., & Massa, L. (2011). The business model: Recent developments and future research. *Journal of Management, 37*(4), 1019–1042.

10

"Waste Not, Want Not": Assessing the Determinants of Food Waste Separation and Reuse in Ghana

Hamdiyah Alhassan, Paul Adjei Kwakwa, and Gilbert Dagunga

10.1 Introduction

Food waste is an economic, environmental, and ethical issue that could significantly retard the development of a country. Economically, it results in huge revenue loss to households and countries; environmentally, it pollutes the environment and causes greenhouse gas emissions; and ethically, it violates food rights and reduces the value of food (Pleissner, 2018; FAO, 2018; Alhassan et al., 2020). Approximately one-third of all food produced worldwide ends up being wasted either by rotting in the bins of customers and retailers or by spoiling due to poor transport and

H. Alhassan (✉) • G. Dagunga
University for Development Studies, Tamale, Ghana
e-mail: ahamdiyah@uds.edu.gh

P. A. Kwakwa
Presbyterian University College, Abetefi, Ghana

University of Energy and Natural Resources, Sunyani, Ghana
e-mail: paul.kwakwa@uenr.edu.gh

E. K. Adae et al. (eds.), *Responsible Management in Emerging Markets*, Sustainable Development Goals Series, https://doi.org/10.1007/978-3-030-76563-7_10

harvesting practices that amount to about 1.3 billion tonnes costing close to US$1 trillion (UN, 2019).

This sounds a warning signal to the world's ever-growing population which is expected to exceed 9.7 billion people by 2050 with an expected rise in food demand by 60% during the same period (FAO, IFAD, UNICEF, WFP, & WHO, 2019). The issue of food waste is, therefore, both an international and local policy concern. Government and development partners in every country must be on the alert to find innovative ways to minimise the wastage of food. For example, at the end of the Millennium Development Goals in 2015, the 193 member states of the United Nations found it necessary to address this pattern of wastage in the new Sustainable Development Goals (SDGs).

SDG 12 is focused on ensuring sustainable or responsible consumption and production patterns in which the third target specifically seeks to "halve per capita global food waste at the retail and consumer levels and reduce food losses along production and supply chains, including post-harvest losses, by 2030" (UN, 2015). The realisation of this goal shall be indicative of responsible management on the part of world leaders to promote meeting the needs of the current generation without compromising that of the future generation. The reason is that reducing food waste would imply reducing financial resources spent on food production and distribution. Such funds can then be used for developmental projects that will enhance the well-being of the people. Again, there shall be a reduction in the environmental problems of soil erosion, deforestation, and air pollution that will safeguard the natural resources for future development. Recognising the environmental, social, and financial cost of food waste, scientists and policymakers have identified the 4Rs (i.e., reduce, reuse, recycling, and recovery) as the surest way to overcome these challenges.

In most developing countries including Ghana, efforts are made by both governments and non-governmental organisations (NGOs) to reduce food waste. In Ghana, the average household food waste generation in 2016 was estimated to be about 0.12 kg per person each day (Attipoe & ZaiGui, 2016). In 2018, the Boston Consulting Group (BCG) also announced that food waste will grow to 2.1 billion tonnes per year, a sum worth $1.5 trillion if current trends continue (Ghana Business News, 2018).

The Environmental Protection Agency of Ghana (EPA), the Ministry of Sanitation and Water Resources, and the Ministry of Food and Agriculture (MoFA) among others are operating in Ghana to reduce environmental and food waste. It must be noted that while the impact of food waste is devastating, the cost of control could be very complex. For instance, Oteng-Ababio (2011) reveals that the cost of managing solid waste, which includes food waste in Accra, Ghana's capital town, per month is over US$400,000 which is not enough to curb the situation.

When food waste is minimised, it will go a long way in promoting the country's forest resources which have seen a significant loss in recent years. Protecting the country's forest resources is necessary for the well-being of the present and future generations. As agricultural practices have been identified to contribute to carbon emission, the reduction in food waste shall also be helpful to reduce air pollution in the country. The financial resources to clear the mess associated with food waste and feed the needy can be reserved for other significant projects in the country.

In order to effectively adopt the 4Rs, Ghana's new Environmental Sanitation Policy[1] emphasises the need for source waste separation. However, there are no organised formal structures/facilities in Ghana that ensure that households practice food waste source separation (Alhassan et al., 2018). This, thus, raises the question as to which factors will influence household food waste source separation and reuse behaviour? The factors that drive household source separation and reuse behaviour are vital for development planning aimed at ensuring sustainable production and consumption patterns.

The attention of researchers on the issue of food waste has increased over the past decade. The drivers of food waste-related issues including the 4Rs have been assessed at the household level (Castro et al., 2019; Schanes et al., 2018; Bernstad, 2014; van der Werf et al., 2019), institutional level (Young et al., 2017; Juvan et al., 2018; Dolnicar et al., 2020), and national level (Thyberg & Tonjes, 2016). Among these, household-level studies are dominant possibly because of data availability. Moreover,

[1] https://www.ircwash.org/sites/default/files/MLGRD-2010-Environmental.pdf.

an understanding of what is happening at the household level can give policymakers a fair idea of what may be happening at the national level in case data are not readily available. At the household level, the literature shows that a number of demographic factors including household size, gender, education, age, and income levels drive food waste management (van der Werf et al., 2019; Grasso et al., 2019). As significant as these factors are, recent studies have demonstrated that social, psychological, and contextual factors produce stronger effects on food waste generation and diversion compared to demographic factors (Geislar, 2018).

It is, therefore, not surprising to see an increased number of studies (Russell et al., 2017; Godfrey et al., 2012; Ghani et al., 2013; Stefan et al., 2013) relying on the theory of planned behaviour to assess the effect of social, psychological, and contextual factors on food waste behaviour.

Based on these studies, it has emerged that attitude, subjective norms, and perceived ease of participating, including the availability of required infrastructural and technological facilities, are relevant factors of food waste management (Alhassan et al., 2018). Among these factors, the provision of required infrastructure and technology to reduce food waste requires substantial amounts of money that many developing countries may not be able to raise. In such situations where there is a lack of or inadequate facilities, it is expected that subjective norm which is the social pressure that influences behaviour would be relevant to still drive people to reduce food waste to some extent (Chen & Tung, 2010). This can be very true of societies where subjective norm serves as the unwritten rule to guide behaviour and frowns on deviation. Thus, in the absence of institutionally promoted waste management practices, close community ties and social norms could compel individuals to still observe and exhibit responsible food waste management behaviour. For instance, in many African countries where there are inadequate toilet facilities, societal pressure to shun open defecation compels people to find a more suitable solution.

Based on the above, it can be argued that subjective norms can moderate the relationship between perceived lack of facilitating conditions and household food waste separation and reuse behaviour. Confirmation of such a proposition would go a long way in guiding policymakers to rely on a relatively cheaper means to reduce food waste.

However, this possibility has not been analysed yet in the empirical studies on the subject matter. Consequently, to ensure proper planning and design of appropriate policies to promote source separation and reuse of food waste among households, this study was conducted in the Ghanaian economy, where infrastructural and technological limitations at both the macro and micro levels are major constraints in the management of food waste through source separation and reuse.

This study sought to achieve two main objectives: first, to identify the drivers of food waste source separation and reuse behaviour in Ghana; and second, to examine how subjective norm exerts its moderation effect on the relationship between perceived lack of facilitating conditions and food waste source separation and reuse behaviour in Ghana.

The contribution of this study to the literature is three-fold: first, although studies on waste management issues have been examined empirically in Ghana (Alhassan et al., 2018; Oteng-Ababio, 2011), there is a paucity of empirical studies on food waste separation and reuse. Second, although available literature has prominently revealed subjective norms and situational factors like the effect of perceived lack of facilitating conditions on food waste behaviour, the possibility of subjective norm still pushing individuals to reduce food waste in the event of lack of facilitating conditions has not been explored. Third, the estimation process in this study takes steps to account for the endogeneity problem that could affect the robustness of the results but has been ignored by many of the previous studies. Thus, this study aims to fill in these gaps in the literature on the subject matter.

10.2 Brief Literature Review and Hypothesis Development

FAO (2018) acknowledges that a single concept of food waste for various stakeholders is difficult to define. Food waste refers to raw or cooked food along the value chain that is suitable for human consumption but ultimately ends up unconsumed or discarded, usually at the end of the retail or customer chain or process (Abiad & Meho, 2018).

According to the FAO (2018), food waste is a component of food loss and connotes food suitable for consumption that is either thrown away or left to spoil due to decisions made by actors in the food chain. Food waste is described by Alexander and Gregson (2013) as the failure to use potentially edible products to satisfy human hunger. In all these definitions, potentially edible food is abandoned and not reused. This signals a failure in the food system and food value chain of a country which affects overall food availability, a key component of food security (Marra, 2013).

The literature also classifies the types of food waste into three categories, namely, avoidable food waste, potentially avoidable food waste, and unavoidable food waste (Agyepong, 2015). Agyepong (2015) defines avoidable food waste as the food discarded because it has elapsed its expiry date, which prior to disposal could have been edible. Unavoidable food waste is that which could not be salvaged under any circumstances to make it edible while possible. Potentially avoidable food waste refers to food that is edible or suitable for one group, but not for another group and, hence, instead of being discarded could be used by the other (Agyepong, 2015). Abdul-Rahman et al. (2014) indicated that about 80% of food waste is avoidable or potentially avoidable while unavoidable food waste constitutes the remaining 20%.

This implies that managerial actions could be taken to reduce the waste, as the greater proportion of it could be avoided. This makes the concept of source separation and reuse of food waste extremely relevant due to its ability to reduce or avoid the wastage of food along the value chain. Source separation entails the sorting of food waste into categories at the source based on the characteristics of the food (Yang et al., 2011).

Chen et al. (2017) indicated that source separation for solid waste management is a key reason for cleanliness in many Chinese cities. Alhassan et al. (2020) and Opoko and Oluwatayo (2016) opined that source separation is a useful and cost-efficient strategy to waste management in developing countries. Pleissner (2018) also stated that source separation is the surest way to reduce food waste.

According to Agyepong (2015), food reuse is the collection of food near expiry which cannot be sold at retail markets but is still fit for consumption. Steiner-Asiedu et al. (2017) asserted that the best way of engineering social change is to first examine what drives the behaviour of the people under consideration, and like any other innovative practice, there exist certain predictors of household source separation and reuse behaviour.

The theory of planned behaviour (TPB) (Ajzen, 1991) is widely employed to understand the drivers of household source separation, reuse, and recycling behaviour (Ajzen, 1991; Ghani et al., 2013). Based on this theory, human behaviour towards food waste source separation is driven by three main considerations: attitude, subjective norm, and perceived behavioural control.

Attitude reveals the feeling or thinking of an individual towards an act or a behaviour (Razali et al., 2020). An individual's attitude towards an action or behaviour is about the person's evaluation of the said action as good or bad, favourable or unfavourable, positive or negative. Thus, a person's attitude towards food waste management (separation and reuse) is about whether the person feels or thinks about it as something positive or negative, good or bad, favourable or unfavourable. An individual who thinks food waste separation and reuse is a good, positive, or favourable practice is deemed to have a positive attitude towards the behaviour and can influence them to engage in such behaviour. The opposite also holds.

In their respective studies in Malaysia, Tonglet et al. (2004) and Ghani et al. (2013) concluded that source separation is fostered through a positive attitude of individuals. Alhassan et al. (2018) found that positive attitude encourages source separation behaviour in Ghana. Aschemann-Witzel et al. (2015) and Ghani et al. (2013) found that the attitude of an individual or household crucially influences their decision to source separate food waste.

Subjective norm involves the influence of the environment, friends, and social pressure on the behaviour of individuals. It is the belief in the normative standards of others and the motivation to comply with these expectations. This reveals how people take into consideration the perception of closer relations before they act.

Regarding food waste management, the expectations of significant influential members may determine whether a person would engage in such a practice. In situations where societal pressure is in support of food waste management, an individual is likely to separate and reuse food waste (Kwakwa & Adu, 2017). Evidence from the study of Wan et al. (2017) in Hong Kong revealed that subjective norm influences source separation and reuse behaviours. They also found that subjective norm can increase the probability of recycling for people with a positive attitude to experience and to inspire people with limited awareness of the recycling benefits. Razali et al. (2020) also found that subjective norms significantly influence food waste source separation and reuse behaviours in Malaysia.

Perceived behavioural control is the belief in the existence of facilities/factors that may promote or hinder behavioural performance. Referred to as facilitating condition in this chapter, it also demonstrates how easy it is for an individual to engage in a behaviour or not. Concerning food waste management, it is a situational factor that reveals the perception of an individual about the availability of facilities or otherwise for food waste source separation and reuse behaviour. Thus, the presence of the needed facilities for pro-environmental behaviour usually promotes food waste source separation and reuse (Razali et al., 2020).

Tonglet et al. (2004) found that perceived behavioural control like lack of recycling facilities influences waste separation and reuse behaviour. Bernstad (2014) also studied the behaviour of household food waste separation and the importance of convenience in Sweden and concluded that convenience and infrastructure were necessary for source separation of waste and reuse.

As already argued in the introduction of this chapter, the provision of required infrastructure and technology to reduce food waste requires a substantial amount of money that many developing countries may not be able to raise. However, in such situations, an example was given to show that subjective norm would be relevant to still drive people to reduce food waste to some extent. Thus, it can be argued that subjective norm can moderate the relationship between perceived lack of facilitating conditions and household food waste separation and reuse behaviour. Confirmation of such a proposition would go a long way in guiding policymakers to rely on a relatively cheaper means to reduce food waste. However, this possibility has not been analysed yet in the empirical studies on the subject matter.

Apart from the above factors, demographic indicators have also been identified to influence pro-environmentalism (Alhassan et al., 2020). Thus, to avoid omission bias in the estimation process, many of the empirical studies on food waste behaviour have included demographic factors to assess their impact on food waste behaviour. The dominant ones noted to play significant effects are age, education, household size, and gender (van der Werf et al., 2019; Grasso et al., 2019).

The gap identified in the literature is that although many of the empirical studies have found subjective norm and availability of facilities as crucial to manage food waste, the moderating role of subjective norm on the relationship between perceived lack of facilitating conditions and food waste management has not been explored yet. Again, there are few empirical studies in the context of Ghana which makes this study novel.

Consequently, guided by economic theory, the theory of planned behaviour, and previous empirical literature on food waste source separation and reuse such as Razali et al. (2020), the study formulates the following hypothesis:

Hypothesis 1: *Positive attitudes towards food waste management by households have positive effects on food waste source separation and reuse behaviour.*

Hypothesis 2: *Perceived lack of facilities reduces the influence on source separation and reuse behaviours.*

Hypothesis 3: *Subjective norm promotes food waste separation and reuse behaviour.*

Hypothesis 4: *Subjective norm exerts a moderation effect on the relationship between perceived lack of facilities and source separation and reuse behaviour.*

Hypothesis 5: *Demographic background has significant effects on food waste source separation and reuse behaviour.*

10.3 Methodology

10.3.1 The Study Area and Data

The study was carried out in Tamale Metropolis, Ghana. Tamale is the capital of Ghana's northern region and the largest urban city in the north. The northern region is one of the poorest areas in the country, and many suffer from food insecurity as the population continues to grow rapidly. According to the 2010 Population and Housing Census, the population of Tamale has increased significantly from 135,952 in 1984 to 371,351 in 2010 (GSS, 2014).

The substantial growth in population and increased economic activities in the city have implications for waste management and food security. Data on household food waste generation in Tamale are lacking. However, there is a high perception of household food waste in the city. Attempts to promote waste separation at source to achieve the 4Rs would require organised formal structures which currently do not exist.

In this study, 410 households were selected in the Tamale Metropolis using a multistage sampling technique. In the first stage, Tamale Metropolis was stratified based on their income categories into low, middle, and high-income residential areas while one community was randomly selected from each stratum, making three (3) communities. The selected communities were Aboabo (low-income residential area), Zogbeli (middle-income residential area), and Russia Bungalow (high-income residential area). In the second stage, probability sampling by size was employed to select 150, 195, and 65 households in Aboabo, Zogbeli, and Russia Bungalow, respectively. At the household level, the household head and/or the spouse were interviewed.

The sample size was obtained using the Cochran (1977) sample selection formula. Using an estimated population percentage of 70%, a margin of error of 5.2%, at 95% confidence interval, the minimum sample size obtained was 289. The sample size was increased to 410 to increase the reliability and reduce the margin of error (Cohen, 1992). A structured questionnaire was used to collect data on households' socio-economic and demographic characteristics. Other information collected included questions on perceived lack of facilitating conditions, subjective norms, and attitudes towards food waste separation.

10.3.2 Theoretical Framework

Following the theory of planned behaviour (Ajzen, 1991) and utility maximisation theory (Ben-Akiva & Lerman, 1991), a household *i* will decide to engage in source separation of food waste if the expected utility gained from engaging in food waste separation (Z^*_{if}) is greater than the utility of not engaging in it (Z^*_{in}). Given that the latent net benefit (FWsep*) is FWsep* = $Z^*_{if} - Z^*_{in} > 0$, household latent utility level is expressed in terms of actual household food waste separation behaviour and is presented in equation (1):

$$\text{FWsep}_{\text{i}}* = \pi X_{\text{i}} + \Sigma_i \text{ with FWsep}_{\text{i}} = 1 \text{ if FW}* > 0, \text{or } 0 \text{ otherwise} \quad (1)$$

where FWsep_i is a dummy representing a household's food waste separation behaviour; X_i is a vector of household demographic and socio-economic variables, perceived lack of facilitating conditions, and socio-psychological variables (such as attitude towards food waste separation and subjective norm); π refers to parameters to be estimated; and ε_i is the error term. The probability that a household engages in food waste separation is presented as follows:

$$\Pr\left(\text{FWsep}_{\text{i}} = 1\right) = \Pr\left(\Sigma_i > -\pi X_{\text{i}}\right) = 1 - \text{F}\left(-\pi X_{\text{i}}\right) \quad (2)$$

where F is the cumulative distribution function of the random error term.

Another aim of this study was to examine the factors that encourage the reuse of food waste. To do this, the relationship between household decisions to reuse food waste (RUse) is expressed in equation (3):

$$\begin{aligned}\text{RUse}_{\text{i}}* = \delta X_{\text{i}} + \lambda \text{FWsep}_{\text{i}} + \mu_{\text{i}} \text{ with RUsep}_{\text{i}} \\ = 1 \text{ if RUse}* > 0, \text{or } 0 \text{ otherwise}\end{aligned} \quad (3)$$

where $RUse_i$ is a dummy denoting reuse of food waste; and X and FWsep are as previously defined. It is essential to note that sample selection bias could result in inconsistent estimates, as households may self-select themselves in their adoption decisions and must therefore be accounted for.

Failure to account for selectivity bias may lead to inconsistent and biased estimates of food waste separation and reuse behaviour. Further, the theoretical models given by equations (1) and (3) reflect a recursive simultaneous system in which the *ith* household makes a joint decision regarding their food waste separation (FWsep*) and reuse (RUse*) behaviour.

The system is simultaneous because the variables FWsep* and RUse* are jointly determined by the model and is recursive in the sense that RUse* depends on FWsep*, but not vice versa. In addition, the variable food waste separation is potentially endogenous. Thus, while food waste separation explains variation in the reuse of food waste, it is by itself explained by other variables.

Consequently, estimating without addressing the endogeneity problem may lead to biased and inconsistent estimates. While in theory the individual equations (1) and (3) could be estimated by using a discrete model such as probit or logit model, the recursive nature of the system and the endogenous nature of the food waste separation variable lend themselves to adopting the conditional mixed process (CMP) model (Roodman, 2011) due to equations (1) and (3).

10.3.3 Econometric Technique

To address the potential problem of selectivity bias due to both observed and unobserved factors and the endogeneity problem, the CMP model was employed. Given that food waste separation behaviour is denoted by FWsep and reuse behaviour by RUse and following the objective of this chapter, the empirical models for equations (1) and (3) are expressed as equations (4) and (5), respectively:

$$\text{FWsep}_i = \pi_0 + \pi_1 \text{X}_i + \beta_1 (\text{SN}_i * \text{PF}_i) + \Sigma_i \tag{4}$$

$$\text{RUse}_i = \delta_0 + \delta_1 X_i + \lambda \text{FWsep}_i + \beta_2 \left(\text{SN}_i * \text{PF}_i\right) + e_i \tag{5}$$

where $FWsep_i$, $RUse_i$, and X_i, are as previously defined; υ_i and e_i are the respective random error term; and π_1, δ_1, λ, β_1, and β_2 are parameters to be estimated. The parameters λ and β_2, respectively, represent the effect of food waste separation behaviour and the effect of the interaction term subjective norm (SN) and perceived lack of facilitating conditions (PF) on household reuse behaviour. Food waste separation behaviour was included in equation (5) because households can only reuse food waste if it is separated at the source.

The advantages of using the CMP approach are that it allows for joint modelling of two equations, accommodates cross-equation correlation of the error terms, and allows the individual models to vary by observations, which our model exhibits (Roodman, 2011). Consequently, equations (4) and (5) are expressed in the CMP framework as equations (6) and (7):

$$\text{FW}_i * = \varphi_1 + \epsilon_1 \tag{6}$$

$$\text{RU}_i * = \varphi_2 + \epsilon_{2.} \tag{7}$$

where $\varphi_1 = \pi_0 + \pi_1 X_i + \beta_1(SN_i * PF_i)$, $\varphi_2 = \delta_0 + \delta_1 X_i + \lambda FWsep_i + \beta_2 (SN_i * PF_i)$

$g\,(FWsep_i*, RUse_i*) = (1\{ FWsep_i * > 0\}, 1\{ RUse_i * > 0\})'$

$\epsilon = (\epsilon_1, \epsilon_2)' \sim N(0, \Sigma)$ and

$$\Sigma = \begin{bmatrix} 1 & \rho_{12} \\ \rho_{12} & 1 \end{bmatrix}$$

ρ_{12} represents the correlation between the error terms of food waste source separation and reuse behaviour.

Prior to the CMP estimations, confirmatory factor analysis was used to summarise the large dataset and test the relationship of the constructs with indicators based on the theory of planned behaviour. Then, the Cronbach's alpha test was employed to test the reliability of the five-point Likert-type scale questions (Nunnally, 1978). Based on previous studies on pro-environmental behaviour, the variables used in the estimation are presented in Table 10.1.

Table 10.1 Description and measurement of variables adopted

Variable	Description	Measurement
Ruse	Food waste reuse behaviour	Dummy (1 = the household reuses food waste)
FWsep	Food waste source separation behaviour	Dummy (1 = the household practices food waste source separation)
Gender	Gender of the household head	Dummy (1 = Male-headed household)
Age	Age of the household head	Age in years
Education	Education level of the household head	Years of formal education
HHincome	Total household income	Monthly household expenditure in Ghana cedis
HHsize	Household size	Number of people living in the household
HHten	Tenancy type	Dummy (1 = the house is owned by the head of the household)
HHformal	Formal sector employee	Dummy (1 = the head of the household is a formal sector employee)
Wprivate	Formal private waste service	Dummy (1 = the household employed the services of private waste contractor)
Aware	Awareness of source separation	Dummy (1 = the head of the household is aware of source separation)
Attitude	Household attitude towards food waste separation (Tonglet et al., 2004; Knussen et al., 2004)	The average of the following five-point Likert scale questions [strongly disagree (1), disagree (2), neutral (3), agree (4), and strongly agree (5)]
		Food waste separation is a good task.
		Sorting food waste at home is an interesting activity
		Source separation of food waste is important
		Formalisation of food waste separation in Tamale is important
		Promotion of food waste separation in Tamale should be encouraged

(*continued*)

Table 10.1 (continued)

Variable	Description	Measurement
SN	Subjective norm (perceived role of social pressure) (Tonglet et al., 2004; Knussen et al., 2004)	The average of the following five-point Likert scale questions [strongly disagree (1), disagree (2), neutral (3), agree (4), and strongly agree (5)] My family expects me to sort food waste at the source My neighbours want me to adopt source separation of food waste My friends expect me to sort food waste at the source I will sort food waste at the source if my neighbours sort their food waste too If my community engages in food waste sorting, I will too
PF	Perceived lack of facilitating conditions (Tonglet et al., 2004; Knussen et al., 2004)	The mean of the following five-point Likert scale questions [strongly disagree (1), disagree (2), neutral (3), agree (4), and strongly agree (5)] Inadequate space at home would serve as a barrier to engage in food waste separation at the source Inadequate time would discourage me to engage in food waste sorting at home Inadequate knowledge on food waste separation would be a barrier to participate in source separation Lack of access to collection centres will discourage me from adopting source separation of food waste If the service provider does not collect separated food waste, I would be discouraged from adopting source separation

Source: Tonglet et al. (2004); Knussen et al. (2004); Alhassan et al. (2020)

10.4 Results and Discussions

10.4.1 Socio-economic Characteristics of Respondents

The study first presents the results of the variables used in the model. Results from Table 10.2 provide the mean and standard deviation (in brackets) for adopters and non-adopters of food waste separation and reuse behaviour. The pooled sample results show that about 68.8% of the respondents engage in the reuse of food waste in the study area.

There is a significant difference between adopters and non-adopters of source separation of food waste with reference to their reuse behaviour. About 99.1% of those who adopted the practice of source separation reuse food waste while 31.9% of those who do not adopt source separation do not reuse waste food. On the other hand, 54.9% of the sample households engage in source separation of food waste.

The results show a statistically significant difference in the source separation behaviour between adopters of food reuse and non-adopters of food waste reuse with about 79.1% of the adopters of food waste reuse also engaging in source separation of their waste while as low as 1.6% of the non-adopters of food waste reuse not engaging in source separation of waste. On average, about 69.3% of the sample household heads are males implying that the remaining 30.7% are female-headed households.

There is a statistically significant difference in the source separation behaviour between male-headed households with about 65.8% adopting food waste separation while 73.5% not adopting food waste source separation. With food reuse behaviour, there is no statistical difference between male-headed households.

The average age of a household head in the study is about 44 years which does not significantly differ between adopters and non-adopters of both food separation and reuse behaviour. The average years of education of a household head in the study is about 8 years, of which there is some statistically significant difference in the years of education by household heads for adopters and non-adopters of food waste separation.

The average monthly household income for the pooled sample is about GH¢941.876. The results show that there is a significant difference

Table 10.2 Descriptive statistics of variables adopted in the food waste analysis

	Food waste separation behaviour				Food reuse behaviour			
	Adopters N=225	Non-adopters N=185	Pooled data N=410	t-values	Adopters N=282	Non-adopters N=128	Pooled data N=410	t-values
Variables	Mean[a] (Std. Dev.)	Mean[a] (Std. Dev.)	Mean[a] (Std. Dev.)		Mean[a] (Std. Dev)	Mean[a] (Std. Dev)	Mean[a] (Std. Dev.)	
Food waste reuse behaviour	0.991 (0.094)	0.319 (0.034)	0.688*** (0.464)	-21.068				
Food waste source separation behaviour	–	–	–	–	0.791 (0.407)	0.016 (0.125)	0.549*** (0.498)	-21. 068
Gender	0.658 (0.476)	0.735 (0.442)	0.693* (0.462)	1.691	0.681 (0.467)	0.719 (0.451)	0.693 (0.462)	0.769
Age	44.129 (9.994)	44.600 (9.947)	44.341 (9.994)	0.476	44.731 (9.686)	43.484 (10.537)	44.341 (9.964)	-1.174
Education	7.987 (6.023)	9.097 (6.829)	8.488* (6.416)	1.749	8.301 (6.358)	8.898 (6.549)	8.488 (6.416)	0.873
Household income	772.338 (343.555)	1148.070 (663.887)	94k1.876*** (545.555)	7.374	873.309 (487.813)	1092.938 (632.173)	941.876*** (545.863)	3.838
Household size	5.911 (2.742)	5.962 (2.735)	5.934 (2.736)	0.188	5.965 (2.676)	5.867 (2.874)	5.934 (2.736)	-0.334
House ownership	0.511 (0.501)	0.562 (0.497)	0.534 (0.499)	1.030	0.553 (0.498)	0.492 (0.502)	0.534 (0.499)	-1.147
Formal sector employee	0.364 (0.482)	0.492 (0.501)	0.422*** (0.494)	2.616	0.397 (0.490)	0.477 (0.501)	0.422 (0.494)	0.132
Formal private waste service	0.044 (0.207)	0.357 (0.480)	0.185*** (0.389)	8.814	0.145 (0.353)	0.273 (0.447)	0.185*** (0.389)	3.121

(continued)

Table 10.2 (continued)

	Food waste separation behaviour				Food reuse behaviour			
	Adopters N=225	Non-adopters N=185	Pooled data N=410	t-values	Adopters N=282	Non-adopters N=128	Pooled data N=410	t-values
Variables	Mean[a] (Std. Dev.)	Mean[a] (Std. Dev.)	Mean[a] (Std. Dev.)		Mean[a] (Std. Dev)	Mean[a] (Std. Dev)	Mean[a] (Std. Dev.)	
Awareness of source separation	0.436 (0.497)	0.362 (0.482)	0.402 (0.491)	-1.509	0.429 (0.496)	0.344 (0.477)	0.402* (0.491)	-1.634
Attitude	4.231 (0.470)	3.516 (0.967)	3.908*** (0.818)	-9.781	4.213 (0.485)	3.236 (0.985)	3.908*** (0.818)	-13.460
Subjective norm	4.118 (0.354)	3.394 (0.716)	3.791*** (0.655)	-13.331	4.072 (0.391)	3.172 (0.695)	3.791*** (0.655)	-16. 707
Perceived lack of facilitating conditions	4.205 (0.637)	4.093 (0.709)	4.155* (0.672)	-1.688	4.146 (0.674)	4.173 (0.670)	4.154 (0.672)	0.381

***, **, and * imply statistical significance at 1%, 5%, and 10%, respectively. t-test and chi-square tests are used for continuous and categorical variables, respectively

[a]Connotes that for dummy variables, the means represent proportions

between the income for adopters and non-adopters of household food waste separation and reuse behaviour. For example, while the income for adopters of food waste separation practices is about GH₵772.338, that for the non-adopters is about GH₵1148.070. Similarly, the average income of the adopters of food reuse behaviour is about GH₵873.309, while that for non-adopters is as high as GH₵1092.938. The results seem to suggest that households with lower incomes are more likely to adopt food waste separation and reuse behaviour.

The results on the socio-economic characteristics further reveal that the average household size is about six members which does not differ for all categories. About 53.4% of the household heads own the houses they live in or own the houses given out for rent.

This proportion is not significantly different from the adopters and non-adopters of food waste source separation and reuse. About 42.2% of the household heads are employed in the formal sector. There is a statistically significant difference in the percentage of formal sector employees who adopt food waste separation (36.4%) and non-adopters (49.2%).

The proportion of formal sector employees for adopters and non-adopters of food reuse are about 39.7% and 47.7%, respectively. The results show that there is a significant difference in the proportion of households that access private waste services for both food waste separation and reuse behaviours.

The proportion of households that access private waste services that adopt food waste separation and reuse appears to be low compared to the non-adopters. The reason could be that these private services may be concerned with general waste management such as solid waste with little emphasis on food waste. Moreover, the adopters of food waste separation and reuse may be significantly driven by factors other than accessibility to private waste services.

Moreover, the descriptive statistics reveal that about 40.2% of the sampled households are aware of the process and relevance of source separation, with 43.6% of the adopters being aware while 36.2% of the non-adopters being unaware. There is statistically significant difference between the adopters and non-adopters of food waste reuse with respect to their awareness with about 42.9% of the adopters of food waste reuse being aware while 34.4% of the non-adopters being unaware.

The results suggest a relatively high level of awareness among the adopters of both food waste separation and reuse behaviours. The results show an above-average positive score of 3.908 for attitude and a significant variation in the attitudes of adopters and non-adopters of food waste separation and reuse.

Also, the subjective norm has an average score of 3.791 which is above the average. There is a significant difference between adopters and non-adopters of food waste source separation and reuse in terms of subjective norms. Again, adopters are associated with high scores suggesting that high social pressure towards food waste separation and reuse practices in a community influence their probability to adopt the practice. Finally, the perceived lack of facilitating conditions has an average score of about 4.155 which is about the same for both adopters and non-adopters of food waste separation and reuse.

10.4.2 Analysis of Indicators for Attitude, Subjective Norm, and Situational Factor

Table 10.3 presents the results of the mean reliability and validity of constructs indicators for attitude, subjective norm, and situational factors adopted for their study. The overall reliability of these three constructs is acceptable, as the Cronbach's alpha values for all three factors are greater than 0.5 (Chadal & Singh, 2012).

Households that perceive food waste separation at home as useful and interesting accounted for more of the attitudinal factors, as the standardised factor loadings for these are closer to one. Similarly, respondents' perception of friends and neighbours' involvement was very relevant in defining their subjective norms. Finally, time constraint, inadequate proper knowledge on waste separation and reuse, lack of collecting centres, and service providers are relevant indicators in terms of respondents' situational context.

Table 10.3 Mean, reliability, and convergent validity of the constructs

Construct	Indicator	Mean (Std. Dev.)	Standardised factor loadings	Cronbach's alpha values
Attitude	Food waste separation is a good task	4.273 (1.096)	0.471	0.775
	Sorting food waste at home is an interesting activity	3.983 (1.082)	0.897	
	Source separation of food waste is important	3.688 (1.305)	0.891	
	Formalisation of food waste separation in Tamale is important	3.466 (1.097)	0.537	
	Promotion of food waste separation in Tamale should be encouraged	4.131 (1.038)	0.044	
Subjective norms	My family expects me to sort food waste at the source	3.593 (0.866)	0.350	0.705
	My neighbours want me to adopt source separation of food waste	3.417 (0.963)	0.442	
	My friends expect me to sort food waste at the source	3.793 (0.963)	0.866	
	I will sort food waste at the source if my neighbours sort their food waste too	3.578 (0.961)	0.874	
	If my community engages in food waste sorting, I will too	4.576 (1.072)	0.249	
Perceived lack of facilitating conditions	Inadequate space at home would serve as a barrier to engage in food waste separation at the source	4.187 (0.623)	-0.271	0.915
	Inadequate time would discourage me to engage in food waste sorting at home	4.105 (0.997)	0.912	
	Inadequate knowledge on food waste separation would be a barrier to participate in source separation	4.163 (0.848)	0.962	
	Lack of access to collection centres will discourage me from adopting source separation of food waste	4.156 (0.890)	0.955	
	If the service provider does not collect separated food waste I would be discouraged from adopting source separation	4.161 (0.864)	0.972	

Source: Authors (2021)

10.4.3 Determinants of Households' Food Waste Separation and Reuse Behaviour

The parameter results from the estimation of the CMP models are presented in Table 10.4. The significance of the F-statistics implies that the model fits the data well. The *rho* parameter is positive and statistically significant at 5% implying that there is evidence of self-selection which is accounted for in the model. Thus, the joint estimation of these two equations is superior to single estimations. The positive coefficient suggests that source separation and reuse behaviour are complementary; thus, source separation increases the reuse of food waste.

The results reveal food waste separation behaviour positively affects household reuse behaviour. The marginal effect of food waste separation in the reuse model is 0.206, suggesting that food waste separation increases households' reuse behaviour. Specifically, households that engage in food waste separation are about 21% more likely to reuse their food waste compared to their counterparts who do not practise food waste separation. Thus, the findings validate the argument that food waste separation encourages the reuse of food waste and confirms Pleissner's (2018) observation. It could be argued that as far as there is no separation, there might not be room for reuse.

Socio-economic variables have been reported in previous studies (Ekere et al., 2009; Banga, 2013; Alhassan et al., 2020) to influence waste separation and reuse. In this study, age has a positive significant effect on food waste separation only. This implies that the food waste separation effort increases with age. A possible explanation for this could be that older people are more likely to be on retirement and have a lower opportunity cost for time and have more time to sort food waste. The positive significant effect of education on food waste separation behaviour suggests that an additional year increase in education of the household head also increases the probability of engaging in food waste separation behaviour.

This also supports the theory that education increases individuals' awareness of the environmental benefits of engaging in waste separation (Alhassan et al., 2018). It is, therefore, not surprising that awareness of source separation is found to increase the probability of separating food waste. Household income has a negative influence on the reuse of food waste only. Thus, richer households are less likely to reuse food waste.

Table 10.4 Determinants of households' food waste separation and reuse behaviour

Variable	Food waste source separation behaviour		Reuse of food waste	
	Coefficient (Std. error)	Marginal effect (Std. error)	Coefficient (Std. error)	Marginal effect (Std. error)
Food waste source separation	–	–	1.451*** (0.449)	0.171*** (0.041)
Gender	-0.016 (0.250)	-0.003 (0.040)	0.375 (0.262)	0.044 (0.030)
Age	0.038*** (0.014)	0.006*** (0.002)	0.015 (0.016)	0.002 (0.002)
Education	0.081*** (0.029)	0.013*** (0.005)	0.029 (0.039)	0.003 (0.005)
ln (household income)	-1.001*** (0.352)	-0.160*** (0.056)	-1.059*** (0.371)	-0.125*** (0.046)
Household size	0.049 (0.050)	0.008 (0.008)	0.072 (0.077)	0.008 (0.009)
House ownership	0.286 (0.212)	0.046 (0.034)	0.513** (0.221)	0.060** (0.024)
Formal sector employee	0.232 (0.266)	0.037 (0.043)	-0.177 (0.373)	-0.021 (0.043)
Formal private waste service	-3.511*** (0.442)	-0.562*** (0.054)	–	–
Awareness of source separation	0.410** (0.213)	0.066** (0.033)	–	–
Attitude	2.305*** (0.294)	0.369*** (0.035)	1.678*** (0.258)	0.198*** (0.030)
Subjective norm	-1.590 (1.434)	-0.254 (0.231)	1.511 (1.206)	0.178 (0.139)
Perceived lack of facilitating conditions	-2.210* (1.301)	-0.354* (0.209)	0.805 (1.082)	0.095 (0.126)
Subjective norms* Perceived lack of facilitating conditions	0.609* (0.330)	0.098* (0.053)	-0.146 (0.265)	-0.017 (0.033)
Const.	0.893 (5.776)	–	-7.776 (5.139)	–
Observation	410			
Wald chi-squared test (25)	259.04***			
Log pseudolikelihood	-197.213			
Athrho_12	0.477** (0.218)			
Rho_12	0.444** (0.175)			

Source: Authors (2021)

This can be explained by the fact that their ability to buy food sometimes makes them inefficient.

House ownership has a positive and significant influence on the reuse of food waste suggesting that households living in their own house will reuse more food waste. Also, using the services of a private waste contractor has a negative impact on waste separation, implying that households that have their waste collected in the house by a private contractor are less likely to engage in food waste separation.

Expectedly, a positive attitude towards food waste separation encourages households' food waste separation and reuse. This reflects the fact that the knowledge on the implications of food waste is valuable to promote food waste separation in the study area. This is in line with the findings by Alhassan et al. (2018, 2020).

Perceived lack of facilitating conditions also has an implication for food waste separation. As presented in Table 10.4, inadequate waste separation facilities decrease the probability of households engaging in food waste separation, reflecting the role of adequate skills, resources, and opportunities to source separate waste on food waste separation behaviour (Tonglet et al., 2004). This is not surprising as waste separation facilities are not readily available, and there are no formal local collection centres for collecting separated waste in the study area.

Subjective norm is seen not to directly influence food waste management behaviour in this study which is contrary to previous pro-environmental behaviour studies (Kwakwa & Adu, 2017). The estimated coefficient of the interaction term (i.e subjective norms*perceived lack of facilitating conditions) is positive and significantly influences food waste separation behaviour, reflecting the moderating effect exerted by subjective norm on the perceived lack of facilitating conditions. This suggests that high subjective norm encourages source separation of food waste even though they may not have access to a well-structured and formal programme that makes food waste separation easy and convenient. Thus, indirectly, subjective norm promotes food waste management behaviour.

The result may be counterintuitive but is not a strange occurrence in the context of the study area. This may be attributed to the high level of ethnic homogeneity and the predominance of compound houses with shared facilities such as a courtyard and bathroom, which promote strong interaction among the population and enhance community cohesion and bonding (Alhassan et al., 2018).

10.5 Conclusion and Policy Implications

As part of the efforts geared towards achieving sustainable consumption, it is necessary to promote food waste separation and reuse. Such practices are essential to reduce the amount of wasted food. Accordingly, in this study, the drivers of food waste separation and reuse were examined.

Using household data from the Tamale Metropolis, Ghana, the chapter analysed the effect of factors such as attitude, awareness, subjective norms, perceived lack of facilitating conditions, and the interaction effect between perceived lack of facilitating conditions on food waste separation and reuse. The conditional mixed process model revealed that food waste separation and reuse behaviour are positively influenced by awareness, attitude, age, and education while income, formal private waste service, and perceived lack of facilitating conditions exert negative effects.

Moreover, subjective norm is found to interact with the perceived lack of facilitating conditions to positively affect food waste separation and reuse behaviour. Many policy implications can be derived from these findings. Education and awareness exert a positive effect on food waste separation and reuse; thus, an enhancement in households' food literacy is essential. This calls for an intensification of public education on the need and how to engage in food conservation practices, especially food waste separation and reuse so that individuals will be equipped with the "soft" skills to engage in such practices.

The outcome of the study also reveals that encouraging a positive attitude towards food waste separation and reuse would reduce food waste. In this light, local authorities need to strategically engage in regular well-packaged campaigns against food waste. Such an action is likely to shape the behaviour of those who may have no regard for food waste separation and reuse. As perceived lack of facilitating conditions does not promote food separation, interventions should focus on the provision of needed facilities. Government officials need to invest in the building of structures and/or provision of containers at vantage points to facilitate the separation of food waste. This will make it more convenient for households to segregate food waste. Pressure from close relations can help promote food waste separation and reuse even when facilities may not be readily available. The Tamale Metropolitan Assembly should take advantage of the influence of the expectation of close ties by involving social associations, and respected religious and community leaders to educate and promote source separation and reuse of food waste.

References

Abdul-Rahman, E., Hariri, S., Eng, P., & Mohammed, I. (2014). *Food waste: Reduce, reuse, recycle, re-think*. Paper presented at the international conference of engineering, information technology, and science, 5 June 2013. https://doi.org/10.13140/RG.2.1.1448.2404

Abiad, M. G., & Meho, L. I. (2018). Food loss and food waste research in the Arab world: A systematic review. *Food Security, 10*(2), 311–322. https://doi.org/10.1007/s12571-018-0782-7

Agyepong, V. (2015). *Food wastage in cassava sector of Ghana*. Retrieved October 19, 2020, from https://stud.epsilon.slu.se/8558/

Ajzen, I. (1991). The theory of planned behaviour. *Organizational Behavior and Human Decision Processes, 50*(1), 170–211.

Alexander, C., & Gregson, N. (2013). Food waste. In A. Murcott, W. Belasco, & P. Jackson (Eds.), *The handbook of food research* (pp. 471–484). Bloomsbury Academic Press. https://doi.org/10.13140/2.1.2239.2964

Alhassan, H., Asante, F. A., Oteng-Ababio, M., & Bawakyillenuo, S. (2018). Application of theory of planned behaviour to households' source separation behaviour in Ghana. *Management of Environmental Quality Journal, 29*(4), 704–721.

Alhassan, H., Kwakwa, P. A., & Owusu-Sekyere, E. (2020). Households' source separation behaviour and solid waste disposal options in Ghana's Millennium City. *Journal of Environmental Management, 259*, 110055.

Aschemann-Witzel, J., De Hooge, I., Amani, P., Bech-Larsen, T., & Oostindjer, M. (2015). Consumer-related food waste: Causes and potential for action. *Sustainability, 7*(6), 6457–6477.

Attipoe, S. G., & ZaiGui, L. (2016). Assessing the impact of household food waste on the Ghanaian economy from selected communities in Accra Metropolitan Area. *Research Journal of Agricultural, 3*(11), 1–12.

Banga, M. (2013). Household knowledge attitudes and practices in solid waste segregation and recycling: the case of urban Kampala. *Zambia Social Science Journal, 2*, 27–39.

Ben-Akiva, M., & Lerman, S. R. (1991). *Discrete choice analysis: Theory and application to travel demand.* The MIT Press.

Bernstad, A. (2014). Household food waste separation behavior and the importance of convenience. *Waste Management, 34*(7), 1317–1323.

Castro, C., Chitikova, E., Magnani, G., & Merkle, J. (2019). Less is more: Preventing household food waste through mobile applications. https://www.lse.ac.uk/PBS/assets/documents/Less-is-more-Preventing-Household-Food-Waste.pdf

Chadal, R., & Singh, N. (2012). A factor analysis approach to assess the students' perceptions towards most important factors leading to satisfaction towards B-Schools: A study limited to the management students of Jalandhar region of Punja. *Elixir International Journal, 45*(1), 7993–7998.

Chen, H., Yang, Y., Jiang, W., Song, M., Wang, Y., & Xiang, T. (2017). Source separation of municipal solid waste: The effects of different separation methods and citizens' inclination—case study of Changsha, China. *Journal of the Air & Waste Management Association, 67*(2), 182–195.

Chen, M. F., & Tung, P. J. (2010). The moderating effect of perceived lack of facilities on consumers' recycling intentions. *Environment and Behavior, 42*(6), 824–844.

Cochran, W. G. (1977). *Sampling techniques* (3rd ed.). Wiley.

Cohen, J. (1992). Quantitative methods in psychology: A power primer. *Psychological Bulletin, 112*(1), 155–159.

Dolnicar, S., Juvan, E., & Grün, B. (2020). Reducing the plate waste of families at hotel buffets—A quasi-experimental field study. *Tourism Management, 80*, 104103.

Ekere, W., Mugisha, J., & Drake, L. (2009). Factors influencing waste separation and utilization among households in the Lake Victoria Crescent, Uganda. *Waste Management, 29*(1), 3047–3051.

FAO. (2018). *Food loss and waste and the right to adequate food: Making the connection.* FAO.

FAO, IFAD, UNICEF, WFP, & WHO. (2019). *The state of food security and nutrition in the world. Safeguarding against economic slowdowns.* FAO, IFAD, UNICEF, WFP and WHO.

Geislar, S. (2018). In P. Ferranti, E. Berry, & A. Jock (Eds.), *The determinants of household food waste reduction, recovery, and reuse: Toward a household metabolism*. https://doi.org/10.1016/B978-0-08-100596-5.22448-7

Ghana Business News. (2018). Waste food could be worth $1.5 trillion by 2030. Retrieved October 14, 2020, from https://www.ghanabusinessnews.com/2018/10/02/waste-food-could-be-worth-1-5-trillion-by-2030/

Ghana Statistical Service (GSS). (2014). *2010 population and housing census. District analytical report, Tamale Metropolis*. GSS.

Ghani, K. W. A., Rusli, I. F., Biak, D. R., & Idris, A. (2013). An application of the theory of planned behaviour to study the influencing factors of participation in source separation of food waste. *Waste Management, 33*(1), 1276–1281.

Godfrey, L., Scott, D., Difford, M., & Trois, C. (2012). Part II–The effect of data on waste behaviour: The South African waste information system. *Waste Management, 32*(11), 2163–2176.

Grasso, A. C., Olthof, M. R., Boevé, A. J., van Dooren, C., Lähteenmäki, L., & Brouwer, I. A. (2019). Socio-demographic predictors of food waste behavior in Denmark and Spain. *Sustainability, 11*(12), 3244.

Juvan, E., Grün, B., & Dolnicar, S. (2018). Biting off more than they can chew: Food waste at hotel breakfast buffets. *Journal of Travel Research, 57*(2), 232–242.

Knussen, C., Yule, F., MacKenzie, J., & Wells, M. (2004). An analysis of intentions to recycle household waste: The roles of past behaviour, perceived habit, and perceived lack of facilities. *Journal of Environmental Psychology, 24*(2), 237–246.

Kwakwa, P. A., & Adu, G. (2017). Electricity conservation behavior in Ghana: Evidence from rural and urban households in the Ashanti Region. *Journal of Energy and Development, 42*(2), 90–122.

Marra, F. (2013). *Fighting food loss and food waste in Japan*. Leiden University. http://www.academia.edu/download/35191433/Federica_Marra_-_Fighting_Food_Loss_and_Food_Waste_in_Japan.pdf

Nunnally, J. C. (1978). An overview of psychological measurement. In *Clinical Diagnosis of Mental Disorders* (pp. 97–146). Springer.

Opoko, A. P., & Oluwatayo, A. A. (2016). Private sector participation in domestic waste management in informal settlements in Lagos, Nigeria. *Waste Management and Research, 34*(12), 1217–1223.

Oteng-Ababio, M. (2011). Missing links in solid waste management in the Greater Accra Metropolitan Area in Ghana. *GeoJournal, 76*(5), 551–560.

Pleissner, D. (2018). Recycling and reuse of food waste. *Current Opinion in Green and Sustainable Chemistry, 13*, 39–43. https://doi.org/10.1016/j.cogsc.2018.03.014

Razali, F., Daud, D., Weng-Wai, C., & Jiram, W. R. A. (2020). Waste separation at source behaviour among Malaysian households: The Theory of Planned Behaviour with moral norm. *Journal of Cleaner Production, 271*(2), 122025.

Roodman, D. (2011). Fitting fully observed recursive mixed-process models with cmp. *The Stata Journal, 11*(2), 159–206.

Russell, S. V., Young, C. W., Unsworth, K. L., & Robinson, C. (2017). Bringing habits and emotions into food waste behaviour. *Resources, Conservation and Recycling, 125*(1), 107–114.

Schanes, K., Dobernig, K., & Gözet, B. (2018). Food waste matters-A systematic review of household food waste practices and their policy implications. *Journal of Cleaner Production, 182*, 978–991.

Stefan, V., van Herpen, E., Tudoran, A. A., & Lähteenmäki, L. (2013). Avoiding food waste by Romanian consumers: The importance of planning and shopping routines. *Food Quality and Preference, 28*(1), 375–381.

Steiner-Asiedu, M., Dittoh, S., Newton, S. K., & Akotia, C. (2017). *Addressing sustainable development goal 2: Ghana zero hunger strategic review*. Ghana.

Thyberg, K. L., & Tonjes, D. J. (2016). Drivers of food waste and their implications for sustainable policy development. *Resources, Conservation and Recycling, 106*, 110–123.

Tonglet, M., Philips, P. S., & Read, A. D. (2004). Using the theory of planned behaviour to investigate the determinants of recycling behaviour: A case study from Brixworth, UK. *Resources, Conservation and Recycling, 41*, 191–214.

UN. (2015). *Transforming our world: The 2030 Agenda for Sustainable Development*. Division for Sustainable Development Goals.

United Nations, Department of Economic and Social Affairs, Population Division. (2019). World population prospects 2019: Highlights (ST/ESA/SER.A/423). https://www.un.org/sustainabledevelopment/sustainable-consumption-production

van der Werf, P., Seabrook, J. A., & Gilliland, J. A. (2019). Reduce food waste, save money: Testing a novel intervention to reduce household food waste. *Environment and Behavior, 53*(2), 0013916519875180.

Wan, C., Shen, G. Q., & Choi, S. (2017). Experiential and instrumental attitudes: Interaction effect of attitude and subjective norm on recycling intention. *Journal of Environmental Psychology, 50*(1), 69–79.

Yang, L., Li, Z. S., & Fu, H. Z. (2011). Model of municipal solid waste source separation activity: A case study of Beijing. *Journal of the Air & Waste Management Association, 61*(2), 157–163.

Young, W., Russell, S. V., Robinson, C. A., & Barkemeyer, R. (2017). Can social media be a tool for reducing consumers' food waste? A behaviour change experiment by a UK retailer. *Resources, Conservation and Recycling, 117*, 195–203.

11

A Tri-party Approach Towards Sustainable Plastic Waste Management: A Developing Economy Perspective

Daniel Ofori, Christina Appiah-Nimo, Jacob Naabong Dapilah, and Andrews Agyekumhene

11.1 Introduction

Contribution of plastics to societal progress covers all facets of human endeavour, meeting everyday packaging and storage needs. While the production and use of plastics make packaging and storage easier, more versatile, and convenient to society, its safe and responsible disposal has

D. Ofori (✉)
University of Cape Coast, Cape Coast, Ghana
e-mail: dofori@ucc.edu.gh

C. Appiah-Nimo
Tomas Bata University in Zlin, Zlin, Czech Republic
e-mail: appiah_nimo@utb.cz

J. N. Dapilah
Ghana Communication Technology University, Accra, Ghana

A. Agyekumhene
Department of Marine and Fisheries Sciences, University of Ghana, Accra, Ghana

E. K. Adae et al. (eds.), *Responsible Management in Emerging Markets*, Sustainable Development Goals Series, https://doi.org/10.1007/978-3-030-76563-7_11

become a major issue confronting global economies (O'Brien & Thondhlana, 2019). The rapidly increasing production of single-use and disposable plastic products has overwhelmed the world's capacity to deal with them (Godfrey, 2019). Globally, waste generation rates are on the rise. In 2016, 2.01 billion tonnes of solid waste were generated, mostly in the cities, of which about 25% were single-use plastics (World Bank, 2018). Meanwhile, studies have shown that plastic products take about an average of 400 years to decompose (Litchfield et al., 2020). With rapid population growth and urbanisation, especially in developing economies, annual waste generation is expected to increase by 70% in 2050 from 3.40 billion tonnes in 2016 (World Bank, 2018).

Compared to developed economies, residents in developing countries are severely affected by unsustainable ways of managing solid waste. In low-income countries, over 90% of waste is often disposed of in unregulated landfill sites or openly burned (Ferronato & Torretta, 2019). This has been a source of serious health risk for residents, who often lack access to basic health facilities. Sustainable management of plastic waste is thus critical and essential for building sustainable cities in line with United Nations' SDG 11. Indeed, effective waste management is expensive, often comprising 20–50% of municipal budgets (World Bank, 2019). Nevertheless, it is an essential municipal service that requires integrated systems that are efficient, sustainable, and socially supported by consumers, firms, and government.

The stakeholder theory (Freeman, 1994) proposes a range of actors who influence the value creation process. According to the theory, actors who influence economic decisions are grouped into external and internal stakeholders. Building on Freeman's argument, Fassin (2009) provides three categories of stakeholders: real stakeholders, pressure groups (stakewatchers), and regulators (stakekeepers). In line with this categorisation, three main groups are assumed to be at the centre of sustainable management of plastic waste: consumers, firms, and government. Barriers to the inability to fight plastic pollution relate to conflicting expectations between these stakeholders, and hence ensuring the congruence of interests and power can help combat the plastic waste "pandemic".

Against this background, the objective of the chapter is to discuss the conflicting interest and propose a paradigm of transformation through a tri-party approach. The study was conducted using content analysis of related literature in sustainable plastic waste management. A desk-based review of relevant literature was undertaken to explore the conflicting expectations of these economic agents in current waste management practices, as well as the challenges and implications for sustainable plastic waste management. The chapter begins with an overview of plastic use and management of waste in sub-Saharan Africa. It also examines plastic waste management initiatives in Ghana. Conflicting expectations of consumers, firms, and government are discussed; a proposal for transformation through tri-party collaboration is presented; and a conclusion section summarises and draws implications for theory and practice.

11.2 An Overview of Plastic Use and Waste Management in Sub-Saharan Africa

The use of plastics in packaging has become one of the most critical constituents for both food and non-food products (Orzan et al., 2018). Before the widespread use of plastic in everyday packaging and storage, it was a common phenomenon among food vendors to use traditional packaging methods such as plant leaves for packaging. The katemfe plant, also known as the miracle plant or sweet prayer plant, for example, was widely used to package cooked food by food vendors in Ghana and other parts of sub-Saharan Africa because it is believed to have medicinal properties and adds natural flavour to food. Popular delicacies such as "waakye" and "red red" were usually packaged in these leaves. However, concerns of unhygienic practices characteristic of traditional packaging were identified by health authorities. It became apparent that these modes of packaging could easily spread food and water-borne diseases such as cholera, typhoid, and dysentery (Fobil & Hogarh, 2006). The increasing health concerns necessitated the replacement of most traditional packaging methods with plastic packaging. Since then, plastic packaging has undergone a revolution and has widespread application in various industries for packing, storage, and transportation. They are seen as versatile and convenient, especially in the areas of packaging, transportation, and storage.

Meanwhile, the increased use of plastic for packaging has not witnessed a corresponding plastic waste management policy (Awortwi, 2004), and this has left a lot of cities on the African continent bathed in plastic waste. Ghana, for example, generates over one million tonnes of plastic waste each year, and only between 2% and 5% of this plastic waste gets properly recycled (Keesman, 2019). Many places within the country lack the infrastructure to safely dispose of plastic waste. Most often, containers for collection placed at designated points get overfilled. Also, a common scene across landfill sites in some major African cities is informal sector players who scavenge the waste for plastics with reusable and recyclable properties. The severity of the problem is evidenced in Ghana's ranking among the top 10 most polluted countries in the world. The United Nations Development Programme (UNDP) has emphasised the urgent need to improve the current system for waste management on the African continent.

The cost of solid waste collection and disposal within pro-poor urban enclaves in most developing countries is paid by the government (Alhassan et al., 2017). Meanwhile, these low-income areas make up about 70% of the urban population and generate over 60% of urban total solid waste (Oteng-Ababio, 2007). This places a huge financial burden on local authorities such that they are unable to provide adequate facilities to meet the ever-increasing quantities of solid waste generated. The success and financial sustainability of waste management companies, therefore, rely to some extent on their ability to collect revenue as well as clients' willingness to pay for solid waste management services. African governments have adopted public-private partnership approaches to complement existing collection efforts (Saadeh et al., 2019). Besides, the informal collection and recycling sector forms an important, but often unrecognised, part of the solid waste and resources management system.

In developing economies, this sector employs a lot of economically active men and women, who engage in street and landfill collections as a source of livelihood. It is estimated that about 20–30% of recycling is achieved by way of informal recycling systems, reducing collection and disposal costs (Velis et al., 2012). They play a vital role in the value chain by reprocessing waste into secondary raw materials. Currently, some African governments have adopted diverse approaches in tackling their rising waste. For instance, in 2008, Rwanda took the bold step of banning plastic bags. In 2017, the Kenyan government enacted strict regulations banning the manufacture and use of plastic carrier bags almost entirely, and similar actions were subsequently followed by other Eastern African Union member states (Horvath et al., 2018).

11.3 Early Plastic Waste Management Initiatives in Ghana

Ghana has witnessed a lot of interventions in its effort of curbing the worsening state of waste management and sanitation, especially in urban areas. A discussion of some initiatives and the way in which consumers, firms, and government in the pursuit of their incongruent goals have diminished the successes from these interventions is presented in this section.

11.3.1 Plastic Waste Management Initiatives in Ghana

Ghana has had its fair share of challenges with the current waste management system. Perennial flooding and cholera outbreak in the capital city has been partly attributed to the poor plastic waste management system (Alhassan et al., 2018). The occasional loss of lives and properties to flooding called for great concern among waste managers, urban planners, politicians, public health workers, and the general public, with several unsuccessful efforts, including a gradual ban, to arrest the trend in the past decade. In an attempt to help fight the increasing plastic waste problem, discussions have been renewed in the past six years with a series of interventions designed and developed at various levels in the country. The sector has witnessed the formation of associations to integrate various efforts towards the sustainable management of plastic waste.

Other interventions include the monthly National Sanitation Day aimed at bringing together consumers to undertake communal cleaning while sensitising the citizenry about health-related risks associated with poor waste management practices (Tweneboah-Koduah et al., 2020). Furthermore, the country has mainly relied on a public-private partnership to manage the rising waste. This has been made possible through the integration of private waste collectors into an association called the Environmental Service Providers Association (ESPA). Integration of informal plastic waste collectors into the formal recycling value chain has been scaled up. Some informal sector players have also enhanced their collection rates through the use of tricycles popularly called "aboboyaa".

The government has set up the Accra Composting and Recycling Plant (ACARP), the Integrated Recycling and Composting Plant (IRECOP), the Ga Mashie Aerobic Composting Plant (GMACP), the JVL Fortifer Compost Plant, and the Safi Sana Biogas Digester (SSBD) to recycle waste in the system (Alhassan et al., 2018; Oduro-appiah et al., 2019). Significant progress towards developing a National Plastic Waste Management Policy to solidify gains in the sector has been made. Nevertheless, conflicting interests and expectations of consumers and firms, infrastructure deficits, and weak enforcement mechanisms by the government can be an albatross to sustainable national plastic waste management.

11.3.2 Conflicting Expectations of Consumers, Firms, and Government in Plastic Waste Management

Globally, governments, firms, and consumers are gradually recognising the need to collaborate to manage waste effectively (Triguero et al., 2016). The dangers and threats of plastic pollution affect everyone on the planet, requiring a united front among various actors in the value chain to identify strategies for management (Schnurr et al., 2018). The introduction of some policies such as tax holidays for firms reusing plastic waste as primary raw materials has garnered favourable responses from policymakers (Heidbreder et al., 2019). However, there are setbacks as these economic actors have different beliefs, aims, and expectations, hence the absence of a common goal to solve the plastic pollution problem. Table 11.1 presents some examples of the areas of conflict.

Table 11.1 Plastic waste management expectations and outcomes

Area of responsibility	Consumer expectation	Firm expectation	Government expectation
Financing	1. The consumer believes that financing should be the main prerogative of producers, who make the profit, and the government that takes the taxes	1. Production pollution levy: firms are willing to pay to the extent of their pollution footprint 2. Public-private partnership should be made more efficient 3. Firms will pass on any additional cost of waste management to consumers	1. Ensure financial resource stability via self-generated funds and grants from development partners 2. Public-private partnership is a means to shift waste management responsibility to the private sector 3. Local government still manages service providers and assumes ultimate responsibility for waste outcomes
Stakeholder inclusivity	1. Seldom involved in planning and decision making 2. No feedback to stimulate the feeling of ownership that leads to compliance and responsible disposal behaviour	1. Moderately involved in planning and decision making 2. Participatory/collaborative research to devise more grounded policy domains for implementation	1. The central government, through its municipalities, works in partnership with waste logistics firms
Recovery/recycling	1. Separation/sorting/reduction in consumption	1. Design for waste policy/alternative material designs	1. Infrastructure provision/awareness creation/public education

(*continued*)

Table 11.1 (continued)

Area of responsibility	Consumer expectation	Firm expectation	Government expectation
Regulation	1. Exhibit responsible disposal behaviour in compliance with rules, standards, and norms when involved	1. Compliance with industry and national environmental and post-consumer waste regulations due to legitimacy	1. The initiator of policies, such as ban, but weak implementation and enforcement due to fear of becoming unpopular
Means of behavioural change	1. Laws and social pressure 2. Incentive and awareness creation	1. Regulatory standards/ corporate image/ legitimisation/ competition 2. Consumer demand or pressure	1. Pressure from international bodies, conditionalities, and global standardisation
Perception of plastic use	1. Plastic offers convenience and flexibility	1. Plastic offers a cheaper way of packaging than secondary recycled and other biodegradable materials	1. A public health crisis that must be controlled 2. Encouraging recycling and reuse
Ascription of responsibility	1. Believes the generators must be held responsible	1. Littering and pollution result from indiscriminate disposal by consumers	1. Business must pay; consumers must comply

Source: Authors (2021)

Table 11.1 shows some policy expectations and outcomes. We believe that the current system of plastic waste management suffers setbacks because there is an absence of a national strategy that brings together the expectations, concerns, beliefs, and behaviours of these stakeholders, hence a tri-party approach.

11.4 Proposals for Sustainable Waste Management: A Tri-party Collaboration Approach

Industry-led initiatives are an important component in the transition to a circular economy. As the world battles with diminishing natural capital (Hawken et al., 2013), emphasis on sustainable actions such as waste minimisation, reuse, and recovery are a major strategy towards plastic waste management. The waste management hierarchy, originally called "Lansink's ladder" (Schall, 1992), epitomises these sustainable actions in an order of preference. The hierarchy recommends landfilling as the last option because of its environmental implications. Thus, consumers, firms, and government have roles to play in ensuring cost-effective and environmentally friendly waste management (Halldórsson et al., 2019). This can be effective if there is a unified and collaborative effort among consumers, governments, and firms to implement solutions that address the three sustainability domains: ecology, economy, and society that are directly linked to 11 and 12 of the UN Sustainable Development Goals (SDGs) (Rodić & Wilson, 2017). Figure 11.1 outlines the relationships existing between the government, firm, and consumers. Furthermore, it also outlines the important roles of these actors in achieving sustainable waste management.

Waste management depends on a close collaboration at all levels between consumers, firms, and government. Therefore, sustainable actions by each of these actors are subsequently discussed.

11.4.1 Role of Consumers

Green consumerism is a lifestyle and conscious effort to alter our fundamental consumption values and practices to conserve natural resources and promote a greener economy. Such shifts have been possible in areas where consumers directly see the benefit on their income or expenditure (e.g., energy savings, water savings, etc.). Where the benefit is not directly observed, such as reducing global warming, it takes consumers who

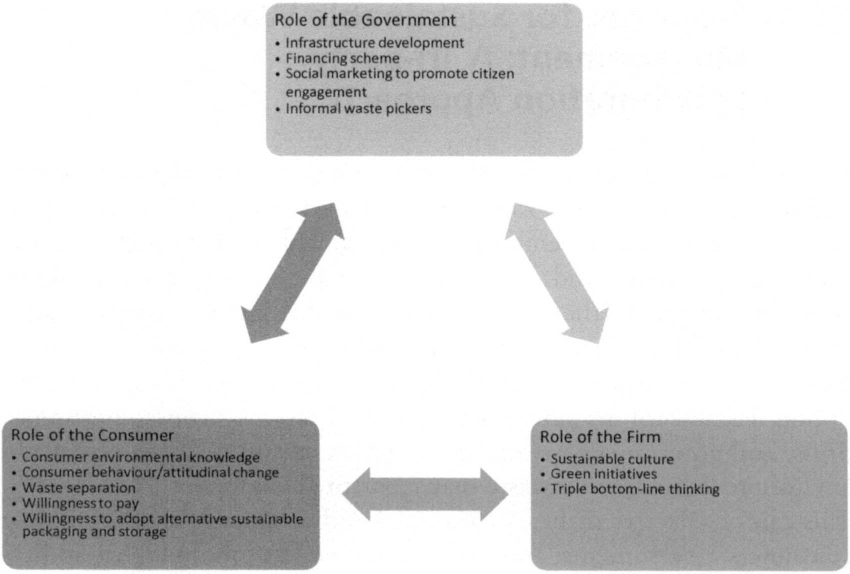

Fig. 11.1 A tri-party collaboration among consumers, firms, and government. (Source: Authors (2021))

possess strong biospheric values to observe pro-environmental behaviours. Translating green intentions into actions has been acknowledged (Elhaffar et al., 2020). Consequently, many studies have investigated the role of consumer behaviour towards sustainable waste management by examining key issues such as consumer environmental knowledge, attitudinal change, availability of environmental services, and facilities that translate intentions into sustainable waste management behaviours among consumers (Li et al., 2015; Zen & Siwar, 2015).

- **Consumer environmental knowledge**

  Environmental knowledge, which reflects peoples' knowledge of the impacts of their behaviours on the environment, is commonly recognised as the first important step in preparing people to contribute to solving environmental problems. This is also backed by Schwartz's (1977) model of altruistic behaviour which is influenced by personal norms, social norms, and awareness of consequences. Barr et al. (2003) find that environmental awareness and behaviours are found to be influenced by values, attitudes, and knowledge. Baker-Brown (2019) asserts that in a recycling programme, deficient task knowledge may lead to alien materials being placed in containers for recyclables, or recyclable materials in containers for garbage. Thus, to achieve environmental protection objectives and mobilise the public to achieve sustainable outcomes, deeper environmental publicity and education is needed. It is important to note that consumers are normally not aware of the true environmental impacts of their consumption. However, their attitude can be influenced by providing them with sufficient information to that effect. For instance, the National Sanitation Day in Ghana offers the opportunity to educate the public. Also, the Ghana Recycling Initiative by Private Enterprises (GRIPE), an industry-led coalition formed under the Association of Ghana Industries (AGI), is championing environmental education through social media campaigns and proposing for the inclusion of environmental education into the basic and secondary school curriculum.

- **Attitudinal change/willingness to pay**

  It is acknowledged that the participation of residents in waste separation is of critical importance for waste management (Jalil et al., 2016; Alhassan et al., 2018). Despite the benefits associated with source separation, little attention has been given to formal source separation in emerging economies (Alhassan et al., 2018). Given that household recycling is a largely voluntary activity, understanding what motivates consumers is essential if recycling practice is ever to attain its full potential and become a part of the everyday household routine (Tonglet et al., 2004; Abbott et al., 2011). The theory of planned behaviour (Ajzen, 1991) explains the motivation underlying certain actions and proposed attitude, subjective norms, and perceived behavioural control as antecedents to people's intention to enact or engage in a particular behaviour. Regular community engagement and promotions to explain and engage them in the discussion towards plastic waste reduction/elimination will also improve commitment and willingness to contribute to the cause. Consumers' behaviour change is examined in light of a positive attitude towards waste separation, willingness to pay, and willingness to adopt alternative packaging and storage methods.

- **Waste separation**

  The proximity principle of the waste management hierarchy proposes that waste is easier to deal with at the point of creation. Therefore, waste separation and recycling is considered the most innovative solution to plastic waste management, and this system demands waste separation, supported with appropriate infrastructure. Consumers will always consider the convenience of separating waste (Khan et al., 2019) compared to the traditional way of disposing waste. Many consumers do not recycle due to the lack of infrastructure for sorting waste and inadequate information on the benefits of recycling (Amoah & Addoah, 2021). Government and businesses must engage consumers on the importance of waste separation and provide more bins for separate waste.

- **Willingness to adopt alternative sustainable packaging and storage**

  A well-packed product is a guarantee of consumer protection by preventing the product from contamination and preserving its freshness (Draskovic et al., 2009). Besides, packaging is described as a powerful communication tool between businesses and the ultimate consumer, and hence, draws the consumer's attention (Simmonds & Spence, 2017). However, due to the current global environment, packaging must meet essential production requirements, marketing objectives, as well as environmental objectives. Technology advancements have made way for other sustainable alternatives such as corn starch, mushroom, and recycled cardboard packaging, as opposed to plastics. Consumers' willingness to change their behaviour can be achieved through education and taxes that affect them directly.

  Marketers can develop a proven approach to modifying behaviour by exploiting the power of nudge. Nudge marketing helps firms to subtly influence the actions of their consumers through advice and gentle encouragement. The role of green nudges in motivating positive consumer lifestyles, education, and willingness to pay is proven in the literature (Wensing et al., 2020). There should be a continuous promotion of environmentally friendly alternatives to help shift preference from single-use plastics to more sustainable ones. Although consumer environmental awareness is increasing, many people do not make a connection between their micro consumption patterns and their contribution to the macro problems in terms of the scale of environmental degradation (Polonsky, 2011). Amoah and Addoah (2021) believe increasing public environmental awareness is a potential way of addressing this.

11.4.2 Role of the Firm

Informed by the institutional theory, corporate bodies work towards a sustainable culture by conforming to social, industry, and regulatory requirements. Stakeholders involved in the plastics value chain have a major role to play in the fight against plastic waste pollution. Ghana Plastic Manufacturers' Association (GPMA), National Association of Sachet and Packaged Water Producers (NASPAWAP), Plastic Waste Collectors Association of Ghana, and Environmental Service Providers Association are major stakeholders in the plastic waste value chain in Ghana. In addition, there are non-governmental organisations that work closely with plastic producers on initiatives to minimise plastic waste pollution. Collectively, these stakeholders are playing a series of roles to harmonise various efforts towards managing plastic waste and implementing innovative technologies to reuse or recycle plastic products (Nielsen et al., 2019). Additionally, green marketing strategies and the promotion of triple-bottom-line thinking are ways of encouraging innovative solutions for improved plastic waste management among firms.

- **Sustainable culture**

  The plastics industry recognises the importance of sustainability, especially regarding the extent of pollution plastics create in the environment. However, there are uncertainties regarding how to position the entire company as sustainable. Organisational culture is a combination of norms, values, attitudes, and behaviours that form the core orientation of a business (Denison, 1984). A sustainable culture values the environment and social setting of the company; hence, it reflects in the working climate, the style of leadership, as well as strategies that inculcate environmental well-being (Song & Yu, 2018). Demirel and Danisman (2019) describe a sustainable culture as one that is characterised by continuous improvement through innovation, green marketing initiatives, and corporate environmental management.

- **Green initiatives**

  Manufacturers and businesses that use plastics in their production have the challenge of bridging the gap between short-term earnings vis-à-vis long-term pollution. Green innovation identifies with the value a business creates for its customers and deliberately reducing the adverse effect its value chain has on the environment (Song & Yu, 2018). This can be achieved through product innovation and process innovation (Xie et al., 2019). Product innovation involves designing new biodegradable plastics with minimal impact on the environment, reducing plastic components of new products, and making new plastic products that have a longer lifespan. Process innovation may include the reuse of plastic products, removal of plastics from the environment by taxing the users, incentives to encourage plastic collection, and recycling to prevent environmental pollution (Xie et al., 2019).

- **Linking corporate social responsibility with triple-bottom-line thinking**

  One of the essential accountability concepts in the sustainability literature is the "triple bottom line" (Elkington, 1997). The concept is made up of three dimensions: an economic aspect which evaluates a firms' financial benefit through its value creation; a social justice aspect concerned with the well-being of internal and external stakeholders; and environmental accountability concerned with the conservation of natural resources, as well as developing and implementing strategies that protect the ecosystem. The private sector, which has embraced corporate social responsibility as a strategic tool, should also encourage waste management awareness and recycling initiatives. For example, MTN Ghana as part of its "21 days of y'ello care" encourages employees to collect plastic waste bottles along some beaches in Accra. Such moves can be scaled up at national levels to serve as an incentive for similar players in the business community.

11.4.3 Role of the Government

Government is an embodiment of leadership, citizen-centred policies, and investment into social infrastructure. Rapid urbanisation, economic growth, and consumers' pursuit of their consumption-oriented lifestyles have intensified the solid waste management problem faced by national governments (Haron et al., 2005). For centuries, waste disposal has been a private and individual responsibility, but the need to protect public health made it a prerogative of government as a public service. Meanwhile, short-term financial and economic performance always takes precedence over the environmental risk that has a long-term negative impact. Past efforts at waste management have shown that legal backing for the process by way of policy (government supports) and financial resources for infrastructure development (private sector participation) are critical success factors to achieve sustainable plastic waste management. The role of governments in achieving sustainable plastic waste management revolves around empowering institutions mandated for waste management and enforcement, the development of infrastructure, providing adequate financing, and encouraging active participation of the citizenry (Ferronato & Torretta, 2019). The government must also ensure that existing systems of plastic waste management such as informal waste collectors are integrated into the waste management system.

- **Infrastructure development**

Two billion people are without access to solid waste collection services, with many cities in low- and lower-middle-income countries having only 30–60% waste collection coverage (UNEP, 2018). Waste management structures are essential for achieving improvement in the environment. Unfortunately, in the developing world, the majority of residents do not have access to proper plastic waste management systems. It is, therefore, imperative that governments invest in waste management infrastructure that will ensure quick and effective removal and processing of plastic waste.

Recycling infrastructure includes accessibility, convenience, awareness creation, and incentive systems. Accessibility to recycle bins means proximity to available recycle bins. The proximity of recycling bins has a great influence on recycling behaviour as it encourages people to participate in recycling and waste separation behaviour (Malakahmad et al., 2010). Household recycling requires people willing to recycle and the supporting infrastructure for them to do so. The nature of household recycling behaviour is affected by accessibility, availability, and convenience, and where these elements diminish, the personal engagement of households in recycling is likely to diminish (Jalil, 2015).

- **Sustainable financing and investment**

  Management of plastic waste involves the collection, transport, storage, and final processing of the waste in different ways. This is an extremely intricate process which, when conducted on a large scale, could consume a large sum of the country's financial resources. This makes plastic waste management a big challenge for developing countries, mainly due to the increasing generation of waste and the financial burden it poses because of the high costs associated with its management (Agyapong, 2017). Though value extraction from waste can be materials, energy, or nutrients, the transition from wastes to resources can only be achieved through investment, which requires a massive financial commitment.

  Agyapong (2017) states that sustainable financing is necessary to ensure sustainable waste management. The establishment of a service fee system has been the most widely used approach to generate revenue for managing waste. In some developed countries, a deposit refund scheme has become a sustainable approach. The development of plastic waste into other useable forms has been a source of revenue in some countries. In Ghana, private enterprises have combined recycled plastic waste and sand in making pavement tiles. With the production process using plastic waste, the method does not only rid the environment of plastics but also reduces environmental degradation by replacing about 50% of the amount of sand used in making original pavement tiles (Collivignarelli et al., 2020). Such business models have the potential to remove plastic waste from the environment and generate the needed finances to sustain it.

- **Social marketing to promote citizen engagement**

  Stakeholders' actions and behaviour play a considerable role in the plastic waste management process. This is particularly important, as the government alone cannot sustain the provision of plastic waste management systems, especially in developing countries (Jalil et al., 2016). In some countries, residents have taken initiatives to assist waste collection in their neighbourhoods.

Martin et al. (2015) demonstrate that community-based social marketing is an effective behaviour change approach. In their study, involving opinion leaders and representatives of groups within communities promotes awareness creation, which is a critical success factor of waste separation. For example, in Ghana, the institution of National Sanitation Day ensured that traditional and opinion leaders, as well as local government officials, through their active participation and enforcement, mobilise the public for cleaning up exercises.

- **Formalising the informal waste collectors**
  Informal waste collectors have been major contributors to the waste management process in many countries for several years (Oteng-Ababio et al., 2017). They play a crucial role in getting wastes from households and areas where formal waste companies do not provide services. In some cases, they remove waste from residential areas (producers) to management facilities (processors) and, therefore, are seen as intermediaries between waste generators and waste processors.

  Though the informal sector plays an important role in the waste management process, the conditions under which they operate leave much to be desired (Ackah, 2017; Oteng-Ababio et al., 2017). Integrating the informal waste collection services with the formal waste management system has been highly recommended because according to Wang et al. (2012), both complement each other and have the potential to empower the informal waste collectors.

11.5 Conclusion and Implications

Sustainable management of plastic waste is critical and essential for building sustainable cities in line with United Nations' SDG 11. Through a review of relevant literature, this chapter aimed at adding to the calls for a sustainable approach towards managing plastic waste by exploring the conflicting interests and expectations of consumers, firms, and governments. It proposes a paradigm of transformation through a tri-party approach because the inability to fight plastic pollution relates to conflicting expectations of consumers, firms, and governments in managing plastic waste. These economic actors must join their collective efforts towards sustainable plastic waste management. Past efforts at waste management have shown that legal backing for the process, by way of policy (government supports), and financial resources for infrastructure development (private sector participation) are major factors that could help achieve effective and sustainable plastic waste management.

The role of governments in achieving sustainable plastic waste management revolves around empowering institutions mandated for waste management and enforcement, development of infrastructure, providing adequate financing, and ensuring that there is the active participation of the citizenry (Ferronato & Torretta, 2019). The development of a national plastic waste management strategy must meet the needs of governing authorities, the production economy, and the consuming public.

To successfully implement such actions, there should be a coordination of efforts to ensure that all stakeholders have a clearly defined understanding of the design and implementation of policies that will affect their activities. The government, as an embodiment of leadership, must be committed towards citizen-centred policies and investment that considers the interests of future generations.

Through green consumerism, consumers contribute by accepting to participate in sanitation events, awareness creation, and efforts to develop sustainable lifestyles. Consumers in developing economies may attach ad-hoc significance to the consumption of green products if they do not see an immediate benefit on living standards. Therefore, understanding consumers' consumption and beliefs about their environment are essential if recycling practice is ever to attain its full potential and become a part of the everyday household routine (Tonglet et al., 2004; Abbott et al., 2011). Through green nudges, consumers could improve their circular economy practices, such as reducing plastic use by reusing and sorting plastic waste for recycling.

Waste management is about social, environmental, and economic development, and it is commonly accepted that public participation is essential for its success. While industry-led initiatives are an important component in the transition to a circular economy, emphasis on consumer sustainable actions such as waste minimisation, reuse, and recovery is a major strategy towards plastic waste management. Stakeholder participation entails the involvement of all groups of actors who influence the value chain. Therefore, governments, businesses, and consumers need to collaborate to manage waste effectively.

Firms must exploit plastic pollution as an opportunity to enhance their visibility through social responsibility while boosting their green marketing and brand positioning. Conventional waste management systems struggle to address the sustainability challenge when waste management is not considered as a tri-party affair. This requires a coordinated tri-party action within the broader society whose interests must be balanced. This chapter also contributes to the scientific literature by using stakeholder theory to explore the collaborative approach towards the management of plastic waste. To the best of our knowledge, the chapter highlights major areas for further exploration by future studies.

References

Abbott, A., Nandeibam, S., & O'Shea, L. (2011). Explaining the variation in household recycling rates across the UK. *Ecological Economics, 70*(11), 2214–2223.

Ackah, M. (2017). Informal E-waste recycling in developing countries: Review of metal(loid)s pollution, environmental impacts and transport pathways. *Environmental Science and Pollution Research, 24*(31), 24092–24101. https://doi.org/10.1007/s11356-017-0273-y

Agyapong, D. (2017). Alternatives for financing waste management: Implications for Ghana's growing electronic and electrical equipment waste. *Asian Journal of Economics, Business and Accounting, 2*(1), 1–14. https://doi.org/10.9734/AJEBA/2017/31409

Ajzen, I. (1991). The theory of planned behaviour. *Organizational Behaviour and Human Decision Processes, 50*(2), 179–211.

Alhassan, H., Asante, F. A., Oteng-Ababio, M., & Bawakyillenuo, S. (2017). Do socio-psychological factors influence households' willingness-to-pay for improved solid waste management services? Evidence from Ghana. *International Journal of Green Economics, 11*(3–4), 183–203.

Alhassan, H., Asante, F. A., Oteng-Ababio, M., & Bawakyillenuo, S. (2018). Application of theory of planned behaviour to households' source separation behaviour in Ghana. *Management of Environmental Quality: An International Journal, 29*(4), 704–721.

Amoah, A., & Addoah, T. (2021). Does environmental knowledge drive pro-environmental behaviour in developing countries? Evidence from households in Ghana. *Environment, Development and Sustainability, 23*(2), 2719–2738.

Awortwi, N. (2004). Getting the fundamentals wrong: Woes of public-private partnerships in solid waste collection in three Ghanaian cities. *Public Administration and Development, 24*(3), 213–224. https://doi.org/10.1002/pad.301

Baker-Brown, D. (2019). *The re-use atlas: A designer's guide towards the circular economy*. Routledge.

Barr, S., Ford, N. J., & Gilg, A. W. (2003). Attitudes towards recycling household waste in Exeter, Devon: Quantitative and qualitative approaches. *Local Environment, 8*(4), 407–421.

Collivignarelli, M. C., Cillari, G., Ricciardi, P., Miino, M. C., Torretta, V., Rada, E. C., & Abbà, A. (2020). The production of sustainable concrete with the use of alternative aggregates: A review. *Sustainability, 12*(19), 7903.

Demirel, P., & Danisman, G. O. (2019). Eco-innovation and firm growth in the circular economy: Evidence from European small- and medium-sized enterprises. *Business Strategy and the Environment, 28*(8), 1608–1618.

Denison, D. R. (1984). Bringing corporate culture to the bottom line. *Organizational Dynamics, 13*(2), 5–22.

Draskovic, N., Temperley, J., & Pavicic, J. (2009). Comparative perception (s) of consumer goods packaging: Croatian consumers perspective (s). *International Journal of Management Cases, 11*(2), 154–163.

Elhaffar, G., Durif, F., & Dubé, L. (2020). Towards closing the attitude-intention-behavior gap in green consumption: A narrative review of the literature and an overview of future research directions. *Journal of Cleaner Production*, 122556. https://doi.org/10.1016/j.jclepro.2020.122556

Elkington, J. (1997). The triple bottom line. In *Environmental management: Readings and cases*, 2. Thousand Oaks, California: SAGE.

Fassin, Y. (2009). The stakeholder model refined. *Journal of Business Ethics, 84*(1), 113–135.

Ferronato, N., & Torretta, V. (2019). Waste mismanagement in developing countries: A review of global issues. *International Journal of Environmental Research and Public Health, 16*(6). https://doi.org/10.3390/ijerph16061060

Fobil, J. N., & Hogarh, J. N. (2006). The dilemmas of plastic wastes in a developing economy: Proposals for a sustainable management approach for Ghana. *West African Journal of Applied Ecology, 10*(1), 221–229.

Freeman, R. E. (1994). The politics of stakeholder theory: Some future directions. *Business Ethics Quarterly, 4*, 409–421.
Godfrey, L. (2019). Waste plastic, the challenge facing developing countries ban it, change it, collect it? *Recycling, 4*(1), 3.
Halldórsson, A., Vural, C. A., & Wehner, J. (2019). Logistics service triad for household waste: Consumers as co-producers of sustainability. *International Journal of Physical Distribution & Logistics Management, 49*(4), 398–415.
Haron, S. A., Paim, L., & Yahaya, N. (2005). Towards sustainable consumption: An examination of environmental knowledge among Malaysians. *International Journal of Consumer Studies, 29*(5), 426–436.
Hawken, P., Lovins, A. B., & Lovins, L. H. (2013). *Natural capitalism: The next industrial revolution*. Routledge.
Heidbreder, L. M., Bablok, I., Drews, S., & Menzel, C. (2019). Tackling the plastic problem: A review on perceptions, behaviors, and interventions. *Science of the Total Environment, 668*, 1077–1093.
Horvath, B., Mallinguh, E., & Fogarassy, C. (2018). Designing business solutions for plastic waste management to enhance circular transitions in Kenya. *Sustainability, 10*(5), 1664.
Jalil, E. E. (2015). *Reverse logistics symbiosis in waste recycling: Investigating municipal systems and household behaviour in England*. Doctoral dissertation, University of Hull.
Jalil, E. E. A., Grant, D. B., Nicholson, J. D., & Deutz, P. (2016). Reverse logistics in household recycling and waste systems: A symbiosis perspective. *Supply Chain Management: An International Journal, 21*(2), 245–258.
Keesman, B. (2019). *Market survey waste and circular economy in Ghana*. The Hague: Netherlands Enterprise Agency.
Khan, F., Ahmed, W., & Najmi, A. (2019). Understanding consumers' behaviour intentions towards dealing with the plastic waste: Perspective of a developing country. *Resources, Conservation and Recycling, 142*, 49–58.
Li, J., Wu, G., & Xu, Z. (2015). Tribo-charging properties of waste plastic granules in process of tribo-electrostatic separation. *Waste Management, 35*, 36–41.
Litchfield, S. G., Schulz, K. G., & Kelaher, B. P. (2020). The influence of plastic pollution and ocean change on detrital decomposition. *Marine Pollution Bulletin, 158*, 111354.
Malakahmad, D., Amirhossein, D., Nasir, C. M., Za'im Zaki, M., Kutty, S. R. M., & Isa, M. H. (2010). Solid waste characterization and recycling potential for university technology petronas academic buildings. *American Journal of Environmental Sciences, 6*(5), 422–427.

Martin, N., Ross, S. R., & Irwin, R. L. (2015). Utilizing community-based social marketing in a recycling intervention with tailgaters. *Journal of Intercollegiate Sport, 8*(1), 57–81. https://doi.org/10.1123/jis.2014-0128

Nielsen, T. D., Holmberg, K., & Stripple, J. (2019). Need a bag? A review of public policies on plastic carrier bags—Where, how and to what effect? *Waste Management, 87*, 428–440.

O'Brien, J., & Thondhlana, G. (2019). Plastic bag use in South Africa: Perceptions, practices and potential intervention strategies. *Waste Management, 84*, 320–328.

Oduro-appiah, K., Scheinberg, A., & Mensah, A. (2019). *Existing realities and sustainable pathways for solid waste management in Ghana*. 115–143. https://doi.org/10.4018/978-1-7998-0198-6.ch005

Orzan, G., Cruceru, A. F., Bălăceanu, C. T., & Chivu, R. G. (2018). Consumers' behavior concerning sustainable packaging: An exploratory study on Romanian consumers. *Sustainability, 10*(6), 1787.

Oteng-Ababio, M. (2007). *Private-public partnership in solid waste management in the Greater Accra Metropolitan Area*. PhD thesis.

Oteng-Ababio, M., Owusu-sekyere, E., & Amoah, S. T. (2017). Thinking globally, acting locally: Formalizing informal solid waste management practices in Ghana. *Journal of Development Societies, 33*(1), 75–98. https://doi.org/10.1177/0169796X17694517

Polonsky, M. J. (2011). Transformative green marketing: Impediments and opportunities. *Journal of Business Research, 64*(12), 1311–1319.

Rodić, L., & Wilson, D. C. (2017). Resolving governance issues to achieve priority sustainable development goals related to solid waste management in developing countries. *Sustainability, 9*(3), 404.

Saadeh, D., Al-Khatib, I. A., & Kontogianni, S. (2019). Public-private partnership in the solid waste management sector in the West Bank of Palestine. *Environmental Monitoring and Assessment, 191*(4), 243.

Schall, J. (1992). *Does the solid waste management hierarchy make sense?: A technical, economic and environmental justification for the priority of source reduction and recycling*. School of Forestry and Environmental Studies, Yale University.

Schnurr, R. E., Alboiu, V., Chaudhary, M., Corbett, R. A., Quanz, M. E., Sankar, K., et al. (2018). Reducing marine pollution from single-use plastics (SUPs): A review. *Marine Pollution Bulletin, 137*, 157–171.

Schwartz, S. H. (1977). Normative influences on altruism. *Advances in Experimental Social Psychology, 10*(1), 221–279.

Simmonds, G., & Spence, C. (2017). Thinking inside the box: How seeing products on, or through, the packaging influences consumer perceptions and purchase behaviour. *Food Quality and Preference, 62*, 340–351.

Song, H. Y., & Yu, R. C. (2018). Optimization of culture conditions for gamma aminobutyric acid production in fermented adzuki bean milk. *Journal of Food and Drug Analysis, 26*(1), 74–81.

Tonglet, M., Phillips, P. S., & Read, A. D. (2004). Using the theory of planned behaviour to investigate the determinants of recycling behaviour: A case study from Brixworth, UK. *Resources, Conservation and Recycling, 41*(3), 191–214.

Triguero, A., Álvarez-Aledo, C., & Cuerva, M. C. (2016). Factors influencing willingness to accept different waste management policies: Empirical evidence from the European Union. *Journal of Cleaner Production, 138*, 38–46. https://doi.org/10.1016/j.jclepro.2016.05.119

Tweneboah-Koduah, E. Y., Adams, M., & Nyarku, K. M. (2020). Using theory in social marketing to predict waste disposal behaviour among households in Ghana. *Journal of African Business, 21*(1), 62–77.

UNEP. (2018). *UN Environment Annual Report*. https://www.unenvironment.org/annualreport/2019/index.php

Velis, C. A., Wilson, D. C., Rocca, O., Smith, S. R., Mavropoulos, A., & Cheeseman, C. R. (2012). An analytical framework and tool ('InteRa') for integrating the informal recycling sector in waste and resource management systems in developing countries. *Waste Management & Research, 30*(9_suppl), 43–66.

Wang, F., Huisman, J., Meskers, C. E. M., Schluep, M., Stevels, A., & Hagelüken, C. (2012). The best of-2-worlds philosophy: Developing local dismantling and global infrastructure network for sustainable e-waste treatment in emerging economies. *Waste Management, 32*(11), 2134–2146. https://doi.org/10.1016/j.wasman.2012.03.029

Wensing, J., Caputo, V., Carraresi, L., & Bröring, S. (2020). The effects of green nudges on consumer valuation of bio-based plastic packaging. *Ecological Economics, 178*(November 2019), 106783. https://doi.org/10.1016/j.ecolecon.2020.106783

World Bank. (2018). Solid waste management. Retrieved October 11, 2018, from http://www.worldbank.org/en/topic/urbandevelopment/brief/solid-waste-management

World Bank. (2019). Solid waste management. Retrieved August 10, 2019, from https://www.worldbank.org/en/topic/urbandevelopment/brief/solid-waste-management.

Xie, X., Huo, J., & Zou, H. (2019). Green process innovation, green product innovation, and corporate financial performance: A content analysis method. *Journal of Business Research, 101*, 697–706.

Zen, I. S., & Siwar, C. (2015). An analysis of household acceptance of curbside recycling scheme in Kuala Lumpur, Malaysia. *Habitat International, 47*, 248–255.

12

Towards Sustainable Environment: Does Electricity Crisis Matter for the Effect of Industrialisation and Urbanisation on Carbon Dioxide Emissions?

Paul Adjei Kwakwa, Frank Adusah-Poku, and Kwame Adjei-Mantey

12.1 Introduction

The aftermath of the financial crisis in 2008 has seen an incredible development pace among emerging countries (a number of medium-sized developing countries that have fairly high incomes) which has gained the attention of the world (Boao Forum for Asia, 2011). As these economies grow, their interaction with the global market also increases. Consequently,

P. A. Kwakwa (✉)
Presbyterian University College, Abetefi, Ghana

University of Energy and Natural Resources, Sunyani, Ghana

F. Adusah-Poku
Kwame Nkrumah University of Science and Technology, Kumasi, Kumasi, Ghana

K. Adjei-Mantey
Graduate School of Economics, Kobe University, Kobe, Japan

E. K. Adae et al. (eds.), *Responsible Management in Emerging Markets*, Sustainable Development Goals Series, https://doi.org/10.1007/978-3-030-76563-7_12

industrialisation and urbanisation have become common features of these economies that have the agenda to achieve rapid economic growth and development.

Rapid industrialisation promotes job creation, increases the value of goods exported in exchange for foreign exchange earnings, and increases tax revenues for the government. Urbanisation also contributes to economic growth as it, among other things, leads to lower production cost for firms through economies of scale. It is commonly observed that industrial firms of many emerging economies are found in urban areas, which can be explained by the fact that factory employment attracts large numbers of job seekers (Kwakwa, 2018). As the population in the said areas increases, other manufacturing firms emerge to meet the needs of this urban population. Moreover, the large population in such areas promotes business development. This stems from the increased demand for commodities of all kinds. Thus, it is clear to a large extent that industrialisation and urbanisation are investable in the economic growth and development agenda of emerging economies.

While industrialisation is a deliberate effort by policymakers and authorities, urbanisation is often unplanned but embraced by policymakers and authorities. However, as urbanisation and industrialisation increase, it is important to be conscious of their environmental effect, including carbon dioxide emissions through production and consumption. Thus, while industrialisation and urbanisation may be helpful in the promotion of economic growth and development, emerging countries need to link them with a sustainable environment.

It is argued that industrialisation increases carbon emissions because it involves a high level of energy consumption (Kwakwa & Adu, 2016). Urbanisation also contributes to carbon emission because of the heavy traffic congestion and clearing of forest resources for construction purposes (Kwakwa & Alhassan, 2018; Adams et al., 2016; Salim et al., 2019). However, an efficient industrial sector and urbanisation that promotes efficiency may reduce carbon emissions.

Accordingly, researchers have paid attention to understanding the direction in which urbanisation and industrialisation affect carbon dioxide emissions. Such attention is warranted, especially now that every country is aiming to achieve Sustainable Development Goals (SDGs) by 2030 which could be influenced by industrialisation and urbanisation because they are associated with high energy consumption and environmental degradation. For instance, SDG 9 aims at ensuring that the process of industrialisation adopts clean and environmentally friendly technologies. SDG 11, which seeks to ensure there is sustainability in the cities and communities, has among its targets to reduce environmental pollution and promote waste management. SDG 12 focuses on responsible consumption and production, seeking to, among others, ensure that natural resources are used in a manner that is sustainable and efficient while at the same time reducing waste (UN, 2015).

However, empirically, the evidence from existing studies on environmental sustainability, especially carbon dioxide emissions' effect of urbanisation and industrialisation, has been conflicting. For instance, Chen et al. (2019), Cetin and Bakirtas (2020), and Ridzuan et al. (2020) recorded in their studies that urbanisation increases carbon emissions, while Kwakwa et al. (2020) found the opposite effect, and others like Tarazkar et al. (2020) recorded no significant relationship between the two. Similarly, Aboagye (2017); Aboagye et al. (2020); and Kwakwa and Adu (2016) found that industrialisation increases carbon emission, but Li and Lin (2015) found both negative and positive emission effects of industrialisation. With such conflicting results, it becomes difficult to generalise the effect of these variables on carbon dioxide emission for policy formulation. There is a need, therefore, to embark on further studies.

Studies have indicated that the dependence of urban towns and industrialisation on electricity cannot be overemphasised (Li et al., 2019; Kwakwa, 2018; Sekantsi & Timuno, 2017). Consequently, in the event of an electricity crisis (inadequate supply of electricity to meet the needs of households and industries, leading to a nationwide and long period of power rationing or load shedding, frequent power outages, and unreliable power supply), industrial firms and urban dwellers in emerging markets economies are compelled to depend on alternative energy sources from fossil fuels. For example, in Africa, a web documentary by Al Jazeera on Ghana's 2016 electricity crisis indicated that during that period, many firms had to acquire generators and buy diesel or gasoline for the generator in order to remain productive (Clerici, Taylor, & Taylor, n.d.).

Further, the frequent power outages in Nigeria have compelled a number of firms and individuals in the country who have the means to acquire at least diesel-fuelled generators to supplement the intermittent supply (Nigerian Energy Supply Crisis, 2014). It is envisaged that such a situation tends to influence the extent to which urbanisation and industrialisation may affect carbon emission. Thus, if the current industrialisation and urbanisation level positively affects carbon emissions, the situation may worsen during an electricity crisis.

Moreover, if the current industrialisation and urbanisation level reduces carbon emission, the situation may change during an electricity crisis where there will be higher dependence on fossil fuels. The extant literature on the subject has not yet analysed the role of the electricity crisis on the industrialisation–urbanisation–carbon emission nexus. This chapter, therefore, investigates the impact of urbanisation and industrialisation on carbon dioxide emissions and ascertains whether an electricity crisis plays any role in the effect that expansion in the industrial sector and urban population has on Ghana's carbon dioxide emissions.

Ghana is an interesting case study for many compelling reasons. Although as a developing country Ghana does not contribute greatly to the global carbon emissions, there has been a rise in the country's carbon emissions from 4954.117 kt in 1994 to 14,466.32 kt in 2014 (World Bank, 2020). Such a trend poses a serious threat to the developing economy in many ways (Tennigkeit et al., 2013). After independence, industrialisation became the country's priority to achieve economic growth and development.

The government's policies over the years have propelled the sector's growth. Its share in the country's GDP is equally high averaging 24% between the years 1994 and 2014 (World Bank, 2020). Since 2010, when Ghana became urbanised, there has been an increasing number of urban towns (Adams et al., 2016), and the urban population growth has been tremendously high (World Bank, 2020). However, the country's energy sector has not been robust enough over the years. "Dumsor," which means "off-on" in the Akan language, has become a household name for the persistent and erratic power outages in Ghana.

The country has experienced multiple power crises since independence: 1984, 1997–1998, 2007–2008, and 2012–2015 (Kumi, 2020). Despite these developments, the environmental effects of industrial and urban growth in Ghana, especially carbon emissions, have received little empirical attention (Kwakwa et al., 2014; Aboagye, 2017; Adom et al., 2018). Moreover, none of the existing studies has ascertained the role the electricity crisis plays in the industrialisation–urbanisation–carbon emissions nexus in Ghana.

The contributions of this study to the literature are threefold. The study contributes to the relatively fewer works on the industrialisation–carbon dioxide emission nexus for a sub-Saharan African country. To the best of our knowledge, this is a novel study analysing the indirect effect of the electricity crisis on carbon emission through industrialisation and urbanisation.

Lastly, both the autoregressive distributed lag (ARDL) and fully modified ordinary least squares (FMOLS) estimation methods are employed in the regression analysis. The remainder of the chapter is structured as follows: in Sect. 12.2, related literature is reviewed; data and methodological issues are presented in Sect. 12.3; in Sect. 12.4, the focus is on the discussion of the study findings; and Sect. 12.5 concludes and offers some recommendations.

12.2 Literature Review

12.2.1 Carbon Emissions and the Economy

Carbon emissions refer to the release of carbon dioxide or other greenhouse gases (GHGs) into the atmosphere as a result of human activities. Energy, agriculture and land use, industry, and residential and commercial activities are often mentioned as the main contributors to carbon emissions. Carbon emissions often focus on the release of carbon dioxide (CO_2).

As a key member of the family of GHGs, rising CO_2 and, by implication, rising carbon emissions have implications for climate change adaptation and mitigation strategies. Thus, excessive carbon emission is dangerous to the sustainability of the environment, as it is a major cause of global warming and eventually climate change which has led to changes in weather and rainfall patterns, the destruction of habitats for animals, and respiratory diseases that affect human lives.

Moreover, rising carbon emissions that cause climate change have been associated with low crop yields. For instance, a review of previous research in the area of climate change and agricultural productivity by Tennigkeit et al. (2013) revealed that owing to climate change, crop yields in Africa and South Asia are likely to suffer an 8% reduction in the 2050s. Specifically in Africa, maize yield is projected to see a 5% reduction at the same time. These and many other detrimental effects of climate change through carbon emission make it necessary for economies to manage the rate of carbon emissions by paying attention to human activities that aggravate carbon emission.

Empirical analysis on environmental quality and its relationship with economic variables began with the work of Grossman and Krueger (1991) who defined the association between economic development and carbon emissions as an inverted U-shaped curve. This curve is widely known in the literature space as the environmental Kuznets curve (EKC) hypothesis. In other words, carbon emissions increase during the early development stages as income increases but tend to decrease beyond a certain threshold of income.

Three main factors have been identified to explain this inverted U-shaped curve, namely the scale effect, composition effect, and technology effect. The scale effect occurs when economic expansion increases production and consumption activities leading to more pollution. The scale effect explains the rising portion of the curve as a result of increasing incomes. On the other hand, the composition and technology effects explain the declining portion of the curve. With regard to the composition effect, increasing incomes tend to cause changes in the composition of goods and services as the economy shifts from the agricultural sector to the manufacturing sector and later to the services sector.

A shift from the agricultural sector to the manufacturing sector increases pollution as there is heavy reliance on energy. On the contrary, less energy is used when the economy moves to the services sector from the manufacturing sector. With regard to the technology effect, increasing incomes induces countries to substitute clean technologies for dirty technologies.

12.2.2 Industrialisation and Carbon Emissions

Over time, researchers have examined the impact of other economic variables including notable ones such as industrialisation. Industrialisation is the transformation of an economy's structure from an agricultural or resource-based economy towards an economy that is based on output from its industries.

The basis for linking industrialisation (and/or urbanisation), on one hand, and the environment, on the other, has been theoretically explored in the literature (Mahmood et al., 2020; Wang & Wang, 2017). Industrialisation has been identified as one of the key factors in the quest to promote the development agenda of most countries. Among other things, industrialisation has been used to produce goods, not only for consumption but also for export, particularly in developed economies.

Most developing countries are following this path of industrialisation in an attempt to get out of underdevelopment and to have an economic advantage (Liu et al., 2018). Although industrialisation has several advantages, the heavy dependence on energy by industrial firms tends to pollute the environment. The exploitation of natural resources, which are often non-renewable, for industrial purpose could also account for degradation in the quality of the environment and could be detrimental to environmental sustainability.

Heavy equipment and machinery employed in industrial operations are also a source of emissions as they are mostly dirty equipment, as clean industrial technology may still be considered too costly for emerging economies now embarking on a development agenda through industrialisation.

Thus, carbon emissions will potentially increase through the supply of energy to meet the industrial demand as well as the operations of the industrial sector. Recent data, for example, show that disaggregated by sector, energy (including electricity generation) was the largest contributor to GHG emissions in Africa, accounting for 36% of emissions in 2016, and was the second largest contributor in sub-Saharan Africa (SSA), accounting for 27.3% of emissions in the same year. Restricting to CO_2, energy accounted for 33.4% of emissions in SSA in 2016, up from 21.7% in 2000.

In Ghana, energy remains the highest contributor to CO_2 emissions with a share of 59.8% in 2017 (Historical GHG Emissions, n.d.) while industry value added stood at 30.4% of GDP in 2017, up from 19.8% in 2006, (World Bank Development Indicators, n.d.) demonstrating the potential association between industrialisation and carbon emissions. As a country becomes more developed, however, citizens demand a cleaner environment and their incomes also reach the levels that allow them to begin to employ clean technology and institute regulations and enforcement for industrial firms to reduce emissions or resort to more sustainable or renewable energy. This could reduce emissions eventually, but the net effect on a country is likely to differ based on different factors (Li & Lin, 2015).

12.2.3 Urbanisation and Carbon Emissions

Urbanisation refers to the movement of people from rural areas to urban areas. There is a close interrelatedness between industrialisation and urbanisation. Industrialisation tends to lead to the creation of industrial cities in a country, mostly in urban areas. As these industries cluster in urban areas, people are attracted to move to these clustered areas, including people from rural areas. Hence, industrialisation enhances the movement of people (urbanisation). The opposite is also true where industries might prefer to set up in urbanised communities to take advantage of the workforce made available by the high population in urban areas.

The congregation of people in these clustered industrial areas increases the demand for energy, particularly the demand for transportation and household energy. Furthermore, urban residents consume more services from durable goods than rural residents, and these goods usually require energy to be functional. For example, in the early 1990s in China, the likelihoods of urban residents owning a TV, refrigerator, and washing machine were 2 times, 25 times, and 8 times more, respectively, than it was for rural residents to own these consumer durables (Torrey, 2004).

This phenomenon is not uncommon in other countries and indicates how urbanisation tends to increase the demand for energy. The increasing demand for energy as a result of increasing urbanisation puts immense pressure on the environment (Kwakwa et al., 2020). Closely associated with the subject of urbanisation is the issue of waste, which also contributes to carbon emissions. Residential and commercial entities generate waste from their usual activities, and increasing urbanisation suggests increasing waste generation in urban areas. Although a minor contributor, the share of waste in GHG emissions in SSA has increased marginally from 2.55% in 2000 to 3.1% in 2016 (Historical GHG Emissions, n.d.).

All of these put development authorities in dilemma as the pursuit of industrialisation and development tends to sometimes erode the benefits of environmental sustainability in the quest to achieve Sustainable Development Goals. Thus, it is imperative for developing countries, in particular, to understand the factors that can aid their development agenda without sacrificing the environment.

12.2.4 Brief Empirical Evidence

Studies have used empirical data to examine the existence of the above relationships within and across countries. The studies by Pata (2018a) in Turkey; Kwakwa and Alhassan (2018) in Ghana; Wang et al. (2011) in China; and Sarkodie et al. (2020) in a global analysis found that both industrialisation and urbanisation contribute to increasing emissions of CO_2. While Kwakwa et al. (2020) found that in Egypt urbanisation harmed the environment by increased CO_2 emissions, Chen et al. (2019) in a study in China found evidence of carbon emissions reducing with increasing urbanisation in the long term.

Another study in China by Zhang and Lin (2012) and Zi et al. (2016) reported that urbanisation positively affects the consumption of energy and the emission of CO_2. Raheem and Ogebe (2017) studied how urbanisation and industrialisation, directly and indirectly, influence CO_2 emissions in a panel study of 20 African countries and found that while these two variables increase emissions directly, they also improve environmental quality indirectly by reducing carbon dioxide emissions through income. The study concluded that industrialisation would ultimately reduce carbon emissions.

This, however, would be possible through the strict enforcement of environmental laws when income increases. Urbanisation, however, will eventually increase carbon emission, as the indirect negative effect on degradation is not strong enough to counter the positive direct effects. Also, Liu et al. (2018) and Wang et al. (2016) found in their study on Asian countries that industrialisation and urbanisation increase carbon emissions. On the contrary, a study of 69 countries over the 1985–2005 period by Sharma (2011) showed that urban growth reduces CO_2 emissions per capita while in sub-group analyses, urbanisation was found to be statistically insignificant in explaining emissions in all income groups.

The works of Li and Lin (2015) and Martinez-Zarzoso and Maruotti (2011) revealed that based on the income level of countries, urbanisation has conflicting effects on carbon emissions. A similar outcome was reported by Li and Lin (2015) regarding the effect of industrialisation on carbon emissions. Among newly industrialised countries, Hossain (2011) found that higher energy consumption over time positively influenced carbon dioxide emissions while urbanisation had no significant effect on emissions in the long run for the entire panel. On the country level, urbanisation over time was found to increase emissions in Turkey, China, India, and Brazil, but reduce emissions in the Philippines, South Africa, and Thailand.

The literature so far reviewed shows mixed results on the urbanisation–industrialisation–carbon emissions nexus but lends credence to the fact that country-specific heterogeneities influence the nature of the total effect. In that regard, additional research, particularly one which introduces new variables to provide further evidence on the direction of impact a country faces, is needed. While Kwakwa and Alhassan (2018) suggest that electricity production could have implications for CO_2 emissions, they stopped short of examining if an electricity crisis influences how industrialisation and urbanisation impact carbon emissions. In this study, we investigate the case for Ghana by examining the role of an electricity crisis in the overall impact of urbanisation and industrialisation on CO_2 emissions.

12.3 Methods

12.3.1 Empirical Modelling

This study adopts the conventional Environmental Kuznets Curve (EKC) framework which specifies the nexus between economic growth and environmental quality, as shown in Eq. (12.1).

$$\mathrm{EQ_t} = \mathrm{Y_t} + \mathrm{Y_t}^2 + \varepsilon_t \tag{12.1}$$

where EQ represents environmental quality (proxied by carbon emissions), and Y and Y^2 represent income and its squared, respectively. Based on the objective of this chapter we subsequently modified Eq. (12.1) to control for our variables of interest (industrialisation, interraction between electricity crisis and indistrialisation, urbanisation and the interraction between electricity cirsis and urbanisation) and also used the natural logarithm of the variables leading to Eqs. (12.2) and (12.3).

$$\begin{aligned} \mathrm{lnCOPC_t} = \alpha + \beta_1 \mathrm{lnYPC_t} + \beta_2 \mathrm{lnYPC_t}^2 + \beta_3 \mathrm{lnIND_t} \\ + \beta_4 \mathrm{CRISIS_t} * \mathrm{lnIND_t} + \varepsilon_t \end{aligned} \tag{12.2}$$

$$\begin{aligned} \mathrm{lnCOPC_t} = \alpha + \beta_1 \mathrm{lnYPC_t} + \beta_2 \mathrm{lnYPC_t}^2 + \beta_3 \mathrm{lnLUB_t} \\ + \beta_4 \mathrm{CRISIS_t} * \mathrm{lnLUB_t} + \varepsilon_t \end{aligned} \tag{12.3}$$

where *COPC*, *YPC*, *YPC*^{2}, *IND*, *LUB*, and *CRISIS* represent carbon dioxide emission, income, square of income industrialisation, urbanisation, and electricity crisis, respectively. From Eq. (12.2), the EKC hypothesis holds if $\ln YPC > 0$ and $\ln YPC^2 < 0$. This would imply that at higher incomes, the negative technological and composition effects outweigh the positive scale effect.

Further, a positive sign for industrialisation and a negative sign for the interaction between electricity crisis and industrialisation (CRISIS*lnIND) imply that industrialisation increases carbon emission while electricity crisis reduces the detrimental effect of industrialisation on carbon emission and vice versa.

However, a positive sign for industrialisation and a positive sign for the interaction between electricity crisis and industrialisation imply that industrialisation increases carbon emission and electricity crisis worsens the detrimental effect of industrialisation on carbon emission and vice versa. The same interpretation holds for Eq. (12.3) especially the interraction between electricity crisis and urbanisation (CRISIS*lnLUB).

12.3.2 Source of Data and Empirical Estimation Techniques

The study relies on yearly time series data from 1971 to 2014 sourced from the World Bank (2020). Data availability influenced the selection of the period at the time of the study. Carbon dioxide emission, which is the dependent variable, is measured as CO_2 emissions in metric tonnes per capita.

Industrialisation is measured by industry value added. Income is measured by per capita income, and urbanisation is the total urban population. All variables are used in their natural logarithmic form and *t* is an indicator for time. *CRISIS* is a binary variable that takes a value of *1* for years in which Ghana experienced electricity crisis, that is, 1984, 1997–1998, 2007–2008, and 2012–2014, and *0* otherwise.

CRISIS interacted with *IND* and *LUB* in the respective equations. As is conventional with analysis involving time series data, we conducted unit root tests to ascertain the stationarity of the data using the Zivot-Andrews unit root test approach. This method is known for robustness in the presence of structural breaks, hence our preference.

Following this, autoregressive distributed lag (ARDL) cointegration tests (Pesaran et al., 1996) was conducted to check for the presence of long-run relationships among the variables. Cointegration tests allow us to identify possible scenarios where two or more explanatory variables (non-stationary) are integrated. In other words, cointegration tests examine the correlations among several non-stationary time series variables in the long run. We reject the null hypothesis if the F-statistic exceeds the upper bound critical values. However, we fail to reject the null hypothesis and conclude that cointegration exists if the F-statistic is smaller than the upper bound critical values.

The ARDL bounds testing approach is very effective in testing cointegration in the presence of time series variables that are integrated of order zero I(0), integrated of order one I (1), or mutually cointegrated. This study followed the ARDL and the Phillips and Hansen (1990) FMOLS method to investigate the long-run association between CO_2 emissions and the independent variables. FMOLS is noted for its ability to deal with potential endogeneities and, hence, was performed along with the ARDL as a means to robustly check the results.

12.4 Empirical Results and Discussion

The results of the study are presented and discussed as follows: summary statistics, unit root results, cointegration results, long- and short-run elasticities result for the model with industrialisation, long- and short-run elasticities result for the model with urbanisation, and diagnostic tests.

12.4.1 Summary Statistics

The summary statistics of all variables used are outlined in Table 12.1. The average per capita income (YPC) over the period is US$990.33 with the lowest being US$693.46 and the highest US$1626.62. For carbon emission (COPC), the average metric tonnes per capita is 0.3157 with 0.2081 and 0.5495 as the minimum and maximum CO_2 emissions (metric tonnes per capita), respectively. The mean values of industrialisation (IND) and urbanisation (UB) are, respectively, US$2.79E+09 and 6,940,017 people.

Table 12.1 Descriptive statistics for variables

Statistics	*YPC*	*UB*	*IND*	*COPC*	*CRISIS*
Mean	990.3383	6940017	2.79E+09	0.315680	0.227273
Median	926.8216	6078848	1.19E+09	0.300209	0.000000
Maximum	1626.623	14543041	2.21E+10	0.549479	1.000000
Minimum	693.4641	2617854	2.52E+08	0.208096	0.000000
Std. Dev.	229.1540	3633414	4.54E+09	0.077766	0.423915
Skewness	1.352171	0.570993	2.975457	1.186389	1.301583
Kurtosis	4.324633	2.067502	11.66759	4.186162	2.694118
Observations	44	44	44	44	44

Source: World Bank (2020)

Table 12.2 Results of Zivot-Andrews unit root test

Series	Level	Breakpoint	At first difference	Breakpoint
lnYPC	-3.2054	2001	-5.4504***	1982
$\ln YPC^2$	-2.7556	2010	-5.3270***	1986
lnIND	-4.6548	1991	-5.6232***	1984
lnCOPC	-4.9998***	1984	-6.4883***	1999
lnLUB	-6.1605***	2008	-7.7590***	1985

Source: Authors' estimation (2021)
Note: ***, denotes 1% level of significance

12.4.2 Unit Root Results

Non-stationary variables included in regression models produce spurious results leading to the failure to detect the real effects of regressors on the dependent variable. Moreover, the mean and covariance of a non-stationary series change over time and, consequently, any shock to the series will have a permanent effect.

To deal with this, it is imperative to conduct a unit root test to ensure that variables are stationary. Table 12.2 presents the Zivot-Andrews unit root test results with structural breaks at levels and first difference. The choice of the Zivot-Andrews unit root test over other conventional unit root tests is based on the fact that our time series variables remain stationary with a structural break. Each variable has different breakpoints.

We find only CO_2 emissions per capita and urban population to be stationary at levels. Subsequently, stationarity tests at first difference were conducted for variables with results in Table 12.2 showing stationarity at a 1% significance level.

12.4.3 Cointegration Results

Having confirmed the stationarity properties of the variables, we proceed to test for cointegration. For this investigation, we use the ARDL bounds testing approach. This approach is used because our series are of different orders of integration, specifically of orders zero I(0) in the cases of CO_2 emissions per capita and urban population and one I(1) for other variables.

Table 12.3 presents the cointegration results of two models—the model with industrialisation and the model with urbanisation. Both models have the same dependent variable, but the model with industrialisation excludes the urbanisation variable, while the model with urbanisation excludes the industrialisation variable. In this test, as already stated, we work with the null hypothesis of no cointegration among the variable, while the alternative hypothesis is the existence of cointegration.

The condition for accepting the null hypothesis is that the F-statistic should be less than the critical values of the upper bound I(1). On the other hand, if the F-statistic exceeds the upper bound critical values, I(1) then the null hypothesis is rejected. The results confirm there is cointegration for both models since the bounds test F-statistics 7.6436 for the model with industrialisation and 9.7099 for the model with urbanisation exceed the upper bound I (1) critical values at a 1% level of significance. Thus, a linear combination among the time series variables is stationary.

Table 12.3 Results of ARDL cointegration test

	Model with industrialisation F-stat = 7.6436		Model with urbanisation F-stat = 9.7099	
Significance (%)	I(0) bound	I(1) bound	I(0) bound	I(1) bound
10	2.45	3.52	2.45	3.52
5	2.86	4.01	2.86	4.01
1	3.74	5.06	3.74	5.06

Source: Authors' estimation (2021)

12.4.4 Discussion of Long-Run and Short-Run Elasticities

12.4.4.1 Long-Run and Short-Run Estimations with Industrialisation

Once cointegration has been established between the variables, the long-run elasticities were estimated. Table 12.4 reports the long and short-run regression results for the industrialisation model. It can be observed that the use of the ARDL and the FMOLS produces very similar results.

It is seen that economic growth significantly increases CO_2 emissions in the long run. Specifically, for every 1% expansion in economic activities, CO_2 emissions in Ghana increase about 13–16%. In order to examine the non-linear impact of economic growth on CO_2 emissions, the square of income per capita is included in the model. The inclusion of both income and its square term aimed at examining the EKC hypothesis in Ghana.

The signs and significance of income and its squared term provide evidence that backs the existence of the EKC hypothesis in the case of Ghana. Higher economic growth implies higher incomes which

Table 12.4 Results of the estimate of CO_2 with industrialisation in the model

	Industrialisation			
	ARDL		FMOLS	
Variable	Coefficient	Std. Error	Coefficient	Std. Error
lnYPC	16.1892***	4.9347	13.0983***	4.6415
$lnYPC^2$	-1.1553***	0.3584	-0.9243***	0.3354
lnIND	0.1222***	0.0289	0.1260***	0.0273
CRISIS*lnIND	0.0117***	0.0027	0.0082***	0.0021
C	-60.4484***	17.0743	-50.1799***	16.1487
D(lnYPC)	-26.2138**	11.8205		
D($lnYPC^2$)	1.9066**	0.8602		
D(lnIND)	0.0044	0.0775		
D(CRISIS*lnIND)	0.0072***	0.0021		
CointEq(-1)	-0.963542***	0.1576		

Source: Authors' estimation (2021)

Note: *** and ** represent 1% and 5% significance level, respectively

stimulate investments and consumption. In Ghana, a significant portion of these investments and consumption go to "second-hand" goods like imported second-hand cars and used electronics and scraps which pollute the environment. This may account for the initial rise in CO_2 emissions with income (in the short run).

However, when there is an expansion in the economy to the point where environmental quality assumes priority and the service sector gains dominance, the effect of income on carbon emission reduces, hence, the quadratic term of income becomes negative, thereby confirming the EKC hypothesis (in the long run). Other studies including Pata (2018b), Solarin et al. (2017), Kwakwa and Alhassan (2018), and Sarkodie and Strezov (2018) have reported similar results.

The results from both ARDL and FMOLS also indicate that industrialisation has a significant and positive CO_2 emissions effect in the long run, an indication that industrialisation exacerbates environmental degradation. We find that a 1% increase in industrialisation leads to about a 0.12–0.13% increase in CO_2 emissions in Ghana. Emerging countries including Ghana tend to have a significant number of polluting industries.

Many of these industries use dirty energy to help meet their energy needs, thereby increasing CO_2 emissions in the long run. It is, therefore, not surprising to see this outcome. The results confirm earlier studies conducted in Ghana by Kwakwa et al. (2014), Aboagye (2017), and Kwakwa and Alhassan (2018). Our key variables in this analysis are the interaction terms between electricity crisis and industrialisation and between electricity crisis and urbanisation. Table 12.4 reports the long and short-run elasticities for the former.

The long-run effect of the interaction term between electricity crisis and industrialisation is statistically positive at 1%. This means that the electricity crisis adversely moderates the detrimental effect of industrialisation on CO_2 emissions in Ghana. This result implies that the effect of industrialisation on CO_2 emissions varies with the electricity crisis in Ghana. Thus, the occurrence of the electricity crisis worsens the overall CO_2 emissions effect of industrialisation. This is because electricity from the national grid serves as the main source of energy for industrial purposes. In the event of electricity crises, industries are forced to resort to unclean energy like diesel and dirty oil for production, hence the positive interactive effect.

The short-run results in Table 12.4 are estimated by employing the ARDL method. First, we find a statistically significant negative elasticity for economic growth and a positive statistically significant elasticity for its squared term. The results suggest that continuous expansion in the economy in the short run results in an increase in CO_2 emissions.

The results also indicate that whereas the EKC hypothesis holds in the long run, it is completely non-existent in the short run. Thus, the EKC hypothesis in Ghana is a long-run phenomenon. An insignificant coefficient for industrialisation in the short run is reported. This reveals that it may take longer for the environmental effect of industrialisation to be realised. With regard to the interaction term between electricity crisis and industrialisation, we find a statistically positive coefficient.

The coefficient of the error correction term, CointEq(-1) has a negative sign and is statistically significant at 1%, confirming the cointegration results for model with industrilaisation in Table 12.3. The coefficient of -0.9635 reveals that any change in carbon emissions towards the long run is adjusted by 96.35% each year.

12.4.4.2 Long-Run and Short-Run Estimations with Urbanisation

The long-run and short-run regression results for the model with urbanisation are reported in Table 12.5. The results from Table 12.5 are explained as follows. First, the EKC hypothesis is confirmed for Ghana, just as it was in Table 12.4. Second, the effect of urbanisation on CO_2 emissions in the long run is positive and statistically significant at a 1% level of significance and is consistent across both estimation techniques.

This is consistent using both the ARDL and FMOLS methods. Specifically, a 1% increase in urbanisation leads to a 0.19–0.20% increase in CO_2 emissions in Ghana. The results lend support to proponents of the modernisation theory pioneered by Kessides (2015). The theory asserts that the rise in energy use and, subsequently, CO_2 emissions could be explained in part by the by-products of urbanisation which include

Table 12.5 Results of the estimate of CO_2 with urbanisation in the model

	Urbanisation			
	ARDL		FMOLS	
Variable	Coefficient	Std. Error	Coefficient	Std. Error
lnYPC	8.3202**	3.8061	6.9838**	3.3133
lnYPC^2	-0.5672**	0.2749	-0.4663**	0.2380
lnUB	0.1917***	0.0359	0.2004***	0.0314
CRISIS*lnUB	0.0121***	0.0026	0.0099***	0.0020
C	-34.5846**	13.0964	-30.2970**	11.5042
D(lnYPC)	-17.5705	11.0788		
D(lnYPC^2)	1.2701	0.8074		
D(lnUB)	0.2094***	0.0502		
D(CRISIS*lnUB)	0.0082***	0.0023		
CointEq(-1)	-1.0921***	0.1578		

Source: Authors' estimation (2021)
Note: *** and ** represent 1% and 5% level of significance, respectively

the concentration of people, production, and consumption. Vehicular traffic congestion, increased demand for high rise buildings to serve commercial purposes, and increased demand for energy-intensive goods are typical features of urban centres in Ghana.

These factors explain why urbanisation positively influences carbon emission in the country and support the findings of Adams et al. (2016), Adusah-Poku (2016), and Kwakwa and Adu (2016).

We find similar results for the interaction term between electricity crisis and urbanisation. The statistically significant positive coefficient is an indication that an electricity crisis reinforces the positive carbon emission effect of urbanisation in Ghana. One can argue this may be so because the bursting economic activities and households that rely on electricity resort to unclean energy, especially diesel and fuelwood for survival during an electricity crisis. In the short run, the results do not validate the EKC hypothesis.

This confirms the earlier results that the EKC hypothesis in Ghana is indeed a long-run phenomenon. We also find a significant and positive coefficient for urbanisation implying that urbanisation contributes to Ghana's CO_2 emissions in the short run. Our interaction term results also show a significant and adverse moderating effect of the electricity crisis on the urbanisation–CO_2 emissions nexus in Ghana in the short run.

Our cointegration results for the model with urbanization is confirmed by the negative and statistically significant error correction term CointEq(-1) shown in Table 12.5.

12.4.5 Diagnostic Tests

Our results in Tables 12.4 and 12.5 are subjected to some diagnostic tests to confirm that the results generated are robust and reliable. Tests of serial correlation, normality, heteroscedasticity, and stability are conducted from the ARDL estimation and tests of normality conducted from the FMOLS estimation. The diagnostic test results for the FMOLS estimation method are reported in Table 12.6, whereas the test results for the ARDL method are reported in Table 12.7.

From Table 12.7, and in particular the model with industrialisation, given the probability values of serial correlation, normality, heteroscedasticity, and stability tests of 0.9468, 0.6777, 0.8310, and 0.1090, respectively, the null hypothesis that the errors are largely free from the problems

Table 12.6 Test of Normality from FMOLS estimation

Diagnostic	Test	Model with industrialisation	Model with urbanisation
Normality	Jarque-Bera	0.3794 (0.8272)	1.6843 (0.4307)

Source: Authors' estimation (2021)
Note: numbers in parenthesis are probabilities

Table 12.7 Diagnostic test from ARDL estimation

Diagnostic	Test	Model with industrialisation	Model with urbanisation
Serial correlation	Breusch-Godfrey (F-stat)	0.0547(0.9468)	0.3151(0.7320)
Normality	Jarque-Bera	0.7777(0.6777)	0.7596(0.6839)
Heteroscedasticity	ARCH (F-stat)	0.0461(0.8310)	0.0061(0.9378)
Stability	Ramsey RESET (F-stat)	1.9480(0.1090)	0.0571(0.9548)

Source: Authors' estimation (2021)
Note: Probability in parenthesis

of serial correlation, nonnormality, heteroscedasticity, and non-stability could not be rejected.

Similarly, for the model with urbanisation and from Table 12.7, the diagnostic results conclude that our results are stable and do not suffer from the problems of serial correlation, nonnormality, and heteroscedasticity. From Table 12.6, our diagnostic test results corroborate with the normality test results in Table 12.7 for the two models.

The coefficients of variance decomposition reported in Tables 12.8 and 12.9 from the FMOLS estimations show that the results are free from multicollinearity, as apart from the income variable, no other variable has its associated eigenvalue to be more than 0.5.

Table 12.8 Coefficient variance of decomposition for model with industrialisation (from FMOLS results)

Eigenvalues	282.4298	0.008679	0.000577	3.19E-06	8.92E-08
Condition	3.16E-10	1.03E-05	0.000155	0.027977	1.000000
Variance decomposition proportions					
	Associated eigenvalue				
Variable	1	2	3	4	5
lnYPC	0.999640	0.000359	3.95E-07	6.45E-11	7.08E-11
$lnYPC^2$	0.998753	0.000347	0.000900	1.97E-07	6.44E-07
lnIND	0.029133	0.345107	0.625735	6.18E-06	1.93E-05
CRISIS*lnIND	0.153714	0.147851	0.000518	0.697745	0.000172
C	0.999998	2.47E-06	4.26E-09	2.19E-13	1.23E-13

Source: Authors' estimation (2021)

Table 12.9 Coefficient variance of decomposition for model with urbanisation (from FMOLS results)

Eigenvalues	143.3706	0.011830	0.000284	3.06E-06	5.34E-08
Condition	3.72E-10	4.51E-06	0.000188	0.017445	1.000000
Variance decomposition proportions					
	Associated eigenvalue				
Variable	1	2	3	4	5
lnYPC	0.999071	0.000928	1.12E-06	1.05E-10	9.00E-11
$lnYPC^2$	0.998742	0.000694	0.000563	2.46E-07	8.28E-07
lnUB	0.000486	0.758769	0.240735	4.00E-06	5.16E-06
CRISIS*lnUB	0.130750	0.111686	0.015056	0.742430	7.81E-05
C	0.999994	6.44E-06	9.60E-09	3.96E-13	1.57E-13

Source: Authors' estimation (2021)

12.5 Conclusion

In an era where emphasis is placed on responsible production and consumption, this chapter has analysed the effect of urbanisation and industrialisation on CO_2 emissions in Ghana. More importantly, this chapter attempted to find answers to the following questions: (1) How do urbanisation and industrialisation affect carbon emissions in Ghana? (2) Does an electricity crisis moderate the effect of urbanisation on carbon emissions in Ghana? (3) Does an electricity crisis moderate the effect of industrialisation on CO_2 emissions in Ghana?

The study reveals that in the long run, urbanisation and industrialisation increase carbon emissions in Ghana. In the short run, however, such a significant relationship between industrialisation and carbon emission was not found. The study also validates the EKC hypothesis in the long run but does not exist in the short run. This result is consistent in both the industrialisation and urbanisation models.

This implies that the EKC hypothesis is a long-run phenomenon in Ghana. Our analysis also provides empirical evidence that an electricity crisis adversely moderates the detrimental effect of industrialisation on CO_2 emissions in Ghana. Similarly, we also find that the impact of urbanisation on carbon emissions also tends to vary with an electricity crisis.

Based on the results, some recommendations are made. In a broad sense, avoiding the occurrence of an electricity crisis in Ghana is even more desirable now considering that such a crisis worsens environmental quality.

Our results show that the moderating effect of an electricity crisis is stronger in the case of urbanisation than industrialisation. We recommend that if the nation is hit with an electricity crisis, load shedding can be planned to slightly favour urban residents to avoid the environment bearing strong negative consequences.

Regarding industrialisation, it is recommended that in the event of an electricity crisis, specific business support is provided to industries to use clean alternatives instead of resorting to cheaper dirty ones. Alternatively, industries that consume a lot of electricity can be given support to invest in energy from renewable sources to free up the load on the national grid.

This will achieve two goals: (a) industries will be incentivised to use clean alternatives and (b) an electricity power crisis will be less likely to occur. In effect, Ghana has to consider developing and implementing the low carbon development strategy contained in the United Nations Framework Convention on Climate Change Conference of Parties 15. This will help Ghana integrate both development and climate mitigation actions to reduce CO_2 emissions.

Emerging market economies including Ghana, Ethiopia, and Nigeria tend to exploit more of their natural resources to propel growth. We recommend that Ghana and in extension other agrarian emerging economies use their comparative advantage in the extractive and agricultural sectors in exchange for modernised technology transfer and innovations on clean energy technologies from industrialised countries to achieve two main purposes of (1) reducing stress and dependency on natural resources; and (2) improving environmental sustainability via CO_2 emissions reduction.

Moreover, our EKC results suggest that economic expansion will eventually reduce CO_2 emissions in Ghana. Hence, there is a need to promote economic growth and development in an environmentally friendly way and address significant growth impediments. Lastly, policymakers in Ghana should pay attention to industrial activities by seeing to it that these are done using low carbon emissions technologies. With regard to urbanisation, programme and policies aimed at rural development are encouraged.

References

Aboagye, S. (2017). Economic expansion and environmental sustainability nexus in Ghana. *African Development Review, 29*(2), 155–168.

Aboagye, S., Appiah-Konadu, P., & Acheampong, V. (2020). Economic expansion and environmental degradation in Ghana: A sector decomposition analysis. *African Journal of Economic Review, 8*(1), 106–124.

Adams, S., Adom, P. K., & Klobodu, E. K. M. (2016). Urbanization, regime type and durability, and environmental degradation in Ghana. *Environmental Science and Pollution Research, 23*(23), 23825–23839.

Adom, P. K., Kwakwa, P. A., & Amankwaa, A. (2018). The long-run effects of economic, demographic, and political indices on actual and potential CO_2 emissions. *Journal of Environmental Management, 218*, 516–526.

Adusah-Poku, F. (2016). Carbon dioxide emissions, urbanization and population: Empirical evidence in Sub-Saharan Africa. *Energy Economics Letters, 3*(1), 1–16.

Boao Forum for Asia. (2011). *The Boao Forum for Asia: The Development of Emerging Economies Annual Report 2011*. http://english.boaoforum.org/u/cms/www2/201109/0714080393sj.pdf

Cetin, M. A., & Bakirtas, I. (2020). The long-run environmental impacts of economic growth, financial development, and energy consumption: Evidence from emerging markets. *Energy & Environment, 31*(4), 634–655.

Chen, S., Jin, H., & Lu, Y. (2019). Impact of urbanization on CO_2 emissions and energy consumption structure: A panel data analysis for Chinese prefecture-level cities. *Structural Change and Economics Dynamics, 49*, 107–119.

Clerici, C., Taylor, S.M., and Taylor, K. (n.d.) Dumsor: The electricity outages leaving Ghana in the dark. Retrieved from: https://interactive.aljazeera.com/aje/2016/ghana-electricity-outage-dumsor/index.html.

Grossman, G. M., & Krueger, A. B. (1991). Environmental impacts of a North American Free Trade Agreement. *NBER Working Papers, 3914*. National Bureau of Economic Research, Inc.

Historical GHG Emissions, (n.d.). Retrieved from: https://www.climatewatchdata.org/ghg-emissions?end_year=2018&start_year=1990

Hossain, M. S. (2011). Panel estimation for CO_2 emissions, energy consumption, economic growth, trade openness and urbanization of newly industrialized countries. *Energy Policy, 39*, 6991–6999.

Kessides, C. (2015). The urban transition in Sub-Saharan Africa: implications for economic growth and poverty reduction. *Working Paper Series No. 97*. World Bank, Washington, DC, Africa region.

Kumi, E.N. (2020, October, 14). Is Ghana's Dumsor Over? Retrieved from: https://www.energyforgrowth.org/memo/is-ghanasdumsor-over/

Kwakwa, P. A. (2018). An analysis of the determinants of electricity consumption in Benin. *Journal of Energy Management and Technology, 2*(3), 42–59.

Kwakwa, P. A., & Adu, G. (2016). Effects of income, energy consumption, and trade openness on carbon emissions in sub-Saharan Africa. *The Journal of Energy and Development, 41*(1/2), 86–117.

Kwakwa, P. A., & Alhassan, H. (2018). The effect of energy and urbanization on carbon dioxide emissions: Evidence from Ghana. *OPEC Energy Review, 42*(4), 301–330.

Kwakwa, P. A., Alhassan, H., & Adzawla, W. (2020). The long-run environmental effect of agriculture and food trade in Egypt. *Review of Agricultural and Applied Economics, 2*, 21–35.

Kwakwa, P. A., Arku, F. S., & Aboagye, S. (2014). Environmental degradation effect of agricultural and industrial growth in Ghana. *Journal of Rural and Industrial Development, 2*(1), 1–8.

Li, K., & Lin, B. (2015). Impacts of urbanization and industrialization on energy consumption/CO_2 emission: Does the level of development matter? *Renewable and Sustainable Energy Reviews, 52*, 1107–1122.

Li, M., Li, L., & Strielkowski, W. (2019). The impact of urbanization and industrialization on energy security: A case study of China. *Energies, 12*(11), 2194.

Liu, J., Yuan, C., Hafeez, M., & Yuan, Q. (2018). The relationship between environment and logistics performance: Evidence from Asian countries. *Journal of Cleaner Production, 204*, 282–291.

Mahmood, H., Alkhateeb, T. T. Y., & Furqan, M. (2020). Industrialization, urbanization and CO_2 emissions in Saudi Arabia: Asymmetry analysis. *Energy Reports, 6*, 1553–1560.

Martinez-Zarzoso, I., & Maruotti, A. (2011). The impact of urbanization on CO_2 emissions: Evidence from developing countries. *Ecological Economics, 70*, 1344–1353.

Nigerian Energy Supply Crisis (2014, March). Retrieved from: https://en.wikipedia.org/wiki/Nigerian_energy_supply_crisis

Pata, K. U. (2018a). Renewable energy consumption, urbanization, financial development, income and CO_2 emissions in Turkey: Testing EKC hypothesis with structural breaks. *Energy, 187*, 770–779.

Pata, U. K. (2018b). The effect of urbanization and industrialization on carbon emissions in Turkey: Evidence from ARDL bounds testing procedure. *Environmental Science and Pollution Research, 25*, 7740–7747.

Pesaran, M. H., Shin, Y., & Smith, R. J. (1996). Testing for the existence of a long run relationship. *Working Paper 9622*. Department of Applied Economics, University of Cambridge.

Phillips, P. C. B., & Hansen, B. E. (1990). Statistical inference in instrumental variables regression with I (1) processes. *Review of Economic Studies, 57*, 99–125.

Raheem, I. D., & Ogebe, J. O. (2017). CO_2 emissions, urbanization and industrialization. Evidence from a direct and indirect heterogeneous panel analysis. *Management of Environmental Quality, 28*(6), 851–867.

Ridzuan, N. H. A. M., Marwan, N. F., Khalid, N., Ali, M. H., & Tseng, M. L. (2020). Effects of agriculture, renewable energy, and economic growth on carbon dioxide emissions: Evidence of the environmental Kuznets curve. *Resources, Conservation and Recycling, 160*, 104879.

Salim, R., Rafiq, S., Shafiei, S., & Yao, Y. (2019). Does urbanization increase pollutant emission and energy intensity? Evidence from some Asian developing economies. *Applied Economics, 51*(36), 4008–4024.

Sarkodie, S. A., Owusu, P. A., & Leirvik, T. (2020). Global effect of urban sprawl, industrialization, trade and economic development on carbon dioxide emissions. *Environmental Research Letters, 15*, 034049.

Sarkodie, S. A., & Strezov, V. (2018). Empirical study of the Environmental Kuznets curve and Environmental Sustainability curve hypothesis for Australia, China, Ghana and USA. *Journal of Cleaner Production, 201*, 98–110.

Sekantsi, L. P., & Timuno, S. (2017). Electricity consumption in Botswana: The role of financial development, industrialisation and urbanization. *Review of Economic and Business Studies, 10*(1), 75–102.

Sharma, S. S. (2011). Determinants of carbon dioxide emissions: Empirical evidence from 69 countries. *Applied Energy, 88*, 376–382.

Solarin, A. S., Al-Mulali, U., Musah, I., & Ozturk, I. (2017). Investigating the pollution haven hypothesis in Ghana: An empirical investigation. *Energy, 124*, 706–719.

Tarazkar, M. H., Dehbidi, N. K., Ozturk, I., & Al-Mulali, U. (2020). The impact of age structure on carbon emission in the Middle East: The panel autoregressive distributed lag approach. *Environmental Science and Pollution Research*, 1–13.

Tennigkeit, T., Wilkes, A., Parker, C., & Kossam, F. (2013). *Climate change and agriculture in LDCs*. LDC Paper Series. https://climatefocus.com/sites/default/files/ldcp13_agriculture.pdf

Torrey, B. B. (2004). Urbanization: An environmental force to be reckoned with. https://www.prb.org/urbanization-an-environmental-force-to-be-reckoned-with/ on 29 December 2020.

UN. (2015). Transforming our world: The 2030 Agenda for Sustainable Development. Division for Sustainable Development Goals, New York, USA.

Wang, C., & Wang, Z.-H. (2017). Projecting population growth as a dynamic measure of regional urban warming. *Sustainable Cities and Society, 32*, 357–365.

Wang, Y., Chen, L., & Kubota, J. (2016). The relationship between urbanization, energy use and carbon emissions: Evidence from a panel of Association of Southeast Asian Nations (ASEAN) countries. *Journal of Cleaner Production, 112*, 1368–1374.

Wang, Z., Shi, C., Li, Q., & Wang, G. (2011). Impact of heavy industrialization on the carbon emissions: An empirical study of China. *Energy Procedia, 5*, 2610–2616.

World Development Indicators. (n.d.). Retrieved from: https://databank.worldbank.org/source/world-development-indicators

World Bank. (2020). World Development Indicators Database. https://databank.worldbank.org/reports.aspx?source=world-development-indicators

Zhang, C., & Lin, Y. (2012). Panel estimation for urbanization, energy consumption and CO_2 emissions: A regional analysis in China. *Energy Policy, 49*, 488–498.

Zi, C., Jie, W., & Hong-Bo, C. (2016). CO_2 emissions and urbanization correlation in China based on threshold analysis. *Ecological Indicators, 61*, 193–201.

13

Sustainability in the Dairy Sector in Turkey: A Case Study Approach

Sakir Erdem and Ceyda Aysuna Turkyilmaz

13.1 Introduction

During the last few decades, the world has encountered several micro and macro changes and improvements. The most important of these are globalisation, the wide-sweeping expansion of information technologies, economic crisis, increased focus on emerging markets, etc. These changes have also increased the global production and consumption rates worldwide. As a result, the world's natural resources are becoming scarce day by day. And this has grabbed the attention of many academicians and practitioners worldwide and has triggered them to focus more on sustainability.

As an emerging economy, Turkey has experienced rapid economic and population growth in recent years. In turn, these pressures have accelerated the destruction of productive, assimilative, and regenerative capacities of the ecosystems, which are essential for the well-being of the society

S. Erdem • C. Aysuna Turkyilmaz (✉)
Marmara University, Istanbul, Turkey
e-mail: caysuna@marmara.edu.tr

E. K. Adae et al. (eds.), *Responsible Management in Emerging Markets*, Sustainable Development Goals Series, https://doi.org/10.1007/978-3-030-76563-7_13

and the economy (Evrendilek & Doygun, 2000). All these issues have increased the importance of sustainability and its practices in Turkey as well as in the world.

The dairy industry accounts for 14% of the worldwide agricultural trade with milk production expected to expand at an average growth rate of 1.8% per annum in the next 10 years (OECD-FAO, 2016). Similarly, dairy production is an important industry of the animal production sector and has an important position in the Turkish economy with its employment rate and values of products (Demircan et al., 2006). On the other hand, milk, the first nutrient of humans, is the most natural, most balanced, and most affordable source of protein, carbohydrates, and vitamins that we need. This is why it is very important for people to consume a sufficient amount of milk and dairy products. Hence, in order to achieve this aim, organisations must work hard while considering the welfare of the society in terms of social, economic, and environmental aspects.

This chapter focuses on these two important issues, sustainability and the dairy sector, and also tries to investigate the practices, challenges, and opportunities in the dairy sector in Turkey. Turkey's leading brand in milk and dairy products that operates with the mission of spreading the goodness and abundance of milk, Sütaş will be examined in terms of sustainability with its economic, environmental, and social aspects. As a framework of the analysis, first, the company's recent corporate social responsibility projects and environmental achievements will be analysed. Then, Sütaş' organisational contributions to the social setting in which it operates will be analysed to reveal the social element of the sustainability practices. Then, the company's contributions to the community will be discussed in detail. especially in terms of ethical performance, social support and contribution, and environmental strategies and applications.

To sum up, by analysing the leading firm in Turkey's dairy sector, this chapter will try to shed light on the sustainability and green marketing practices, applications, strategies, opportunities, threats, and challenges in this sector. And finally, improvement suggestions will be discussed.

13.2 Theoretical Background

13.2.1 The Concept of Sustainability and Its Growing Importance

The concept of sustainability has its roots in the Brundtland Report of 1987 (WCED, 1987). The Brundtland Commission, or the World Commission on Environment and Development (WCED), published a report titled *Our Common Future* in 1987 and proposed the concept of sustainable development as an ideal for the global economy and corporations. In this report, the concept of sustainability was defined as development that meets the needs of the present generation without compromising the ability of future generations to meet their needs (Thomsen, 2013).

In this regard, the role and importance of sustainability increased as a result of the accelerating deterioration of the human environment and natural resources, which have negative consequences on economic and social development. From this point of view, it can be concluded that sustainability has three important dimensions as economic, natural, and social (Purvis et al., 2019).

Economic sustainability can be considered in two ways. One focuses on the sustainable use of natural resources within a defined economic system, meaning that economic sustainability is achieved when the economic activity is not undertaken at the cost of natural resources. This economic concept of external effects is useful in understanding and fully capturing costs associated with production.

The other way of considering economic sustainability focuses on the growth of the economic system. Basically, this implies that in order to achieve economic sustainability, there must be a return on capital invested in the firm (Ayres et al., 2001). To summarise, the economic dimension of sustainability mainly deals with issues such as economic growth, economic development, productivity, trickle-down, and efficiency (Kahn, 1995).

The environmental dimension of sustainability is a natural science-based aspect that includes the total impact human activities may have on the ecosystems. Life-cycle analysis (LCA) is the most commonly used approach for quantification of the environmental impact. It concerns the flows of resources (energy, land, water, etc.) to the production system and emissions from the system and quantifies potential impacts (Segerkvist et al., 2020). Environmental sustainability mainly focuses on ecosystem integrity, carrying capacity, biodiversity, and so on.

Social sustainability can be defined as the development of social structures and processes that meet the needs of the present in a community at the same time as laying a foundation for the community to continue to develop in a sustainable way in the future. The social dimension of sustainability has included aspects such as community development, community resilience, livelihood, social equity, health equity, and labour rights.

Aspects, which have not been directly associated with human societies such as animal health and welfare, have also been included in this dimension (Segerkvist et al., 2020). Also, issues such as equity, empowerment, accessibility, participation, sharing, cultural identity, and institutional stability may be considered in the social dimension of sustainability (Kahn, 1995).

13.2.2 Sustainability in Emerging Markets

Although the World Bank does not have a list of emerging markets, these markets share similar identifying characteristics. They mainly underscore important business opportunities, especially for global firms because they are burgeoning markets with high populations and economic growth.

Emerging markets have high levels of urbanisation, growing middle classes hungry for goods and services, and expanding digital commerce networks. Consumers in these markets usually have rising and rapidly changing expectations. They have large and well-educated, but inexpensive, labour pools with high technological and managerial skills, and a growing entrepreneurial spirit in their younger populations to pursue opportunities for economic prosperity, which is attractive for most of the global companies looking to enter local markets (Yaprak et al., 2018; Khanna & Palepu, 2010; Chattopadhyay et al., 2012). Considering the characteristics of emerging markets mentioned above, Turkey with its population of approximately 84 million people (World Bank, 2019) can be regarded as an emerging market.

Also, Turkey is one of the fastest-growing economies in the world thanks to its youthful demographic profile. About 27% of the Turkish population is younger than 15 years compared with 17% in the UK and 13% in Germany, which makes it an important young emerging market.[1]

As sustainability is a phenomenon that first emerged in developed countries, it gained importance in recent years, especially when global companies started to enter those emerging markets. According to Lacy and Hayward (2011),[2] as emerging market economies continue to grow, so do their incomes, their middle classes, and their consumption. All of these will reinforce the demand towards innovative solutions to long-term trends. For instance, demographic change, urbanisation, and the move towards a low-carbon economy will present new challenges and opportunities.

Some critics argue that when compared with developed market firms, it might be expected that emerging market firms may be less or—not at all—subject to stakeholder pressures from customers, competitors, the public, and so on. Lower income levels, less awareness of and sophistication about social and environmental problems, lower levels of product variety, and greater emphasis on the basic value proposition of products could contribute to less sensitivity by firms to respond to pressures to engage in CSR and sustainable business practices (Doh et al., 2015).

But there is strong evidence that consumers in emerging markets are becoming more and more conscious every day and becoming more sensitive about environmental, social, and economic issues. According to the survey conducted by Lacy and Hayward (2011), emerging market CEOs have a consensus on the belief that sustainability will be critical to the future success of their businesses, even more so than in developed markets. A total of 66% of these executives believe that environmental, social, and governance issues will be "very important", a figure noticeably higher than the global average of 54%. Another important outcome suggested in the report is about the motivations that CEOs in the emerging markets report for taking action on sustainability. In common with CEOs globally, the most commonly cited factor for sustainable business

[1] https://www.treasurers.org/hub/treasurer-magazine/emerging-markets-turkey, 2020.

[2] https://www.treasurers.org/hub/treasurer-magazine/emerging-markets-turkey, 2020.

practices is the impact of sustainability on "brand, trust and reputation", a clear reflection of the importance of sustainability in building trust with stakeholders and in making the case for business in society (Lacy & Hayward, 2011).

13.3 A Qualitative Research on Sustainability in Dairy Sector

Parallel with the evidence suggested above, sustainability has become one of the important actors in today's marketing environment both in emerging and developed markets. This study focuses on one of the most rapidly growing sectors in the Turkish economy—the dairy sector—by investigating the Sütaş brand for its economic, environmental, and social sustainability aspects and impacts.

13.3.1 The Aim of the Study

This study aims to investigate the sustainability practices of a leading brand in the dairy sector in Turkey. By analysing these practices, a framework can be provided showing how efficiently and effectively sustainability marketing can be used in the dairy sector. Also, weaknesses or issues that should be improved will be discussed. In this way, suggestions for improvement will be offered.

As a framework of the analysis, first, the company's corporate social responsibility projects and recent environmental achievements will be analysed. Then, Sütaş' organisational contributions to the social setting, in which it operates, will be analysed to reveal the social elements of the sustainability practices (ethical performance, social support and contribution, and environmental strategies and applications). In this regard, it aims to shed light on the sustainability and green marketing practices, applications, strategies, opportunities, threats, and challenges in this sector.

13.3.2 The Scope of the Study: Overview of the Dairy Sector

Before analysing the case, an overview of the dairy sector in Turkey is presented. Evidence about the importance of the dairy sector will make it easy to justify why this sector was chosen in the study.

The dairy industry is one of the leading industries in the global market. For instance, in 2017, the volume of the dairy market worldwide was estimated to be about 216 metric tonnes, which is projected to grow to 234 metric tonnes by 2021. Perhaps, unsurprisingly, liquid milk takes up the highest share of the global dairy market at 54% as of 2017, followed by yoghurt (Shahbandeh, 2019). According to the report of the Food and Agriculture Organization of United Nations, milk and dairy products account for about 14% of global agricultural trade. World milk production is projected to increase by 177 million tonnes by 2025 at an average growth rate of 1.8% per annum in the next 10 years. Over the same period, per capita consumption of dairy products is projected to increase by 0.8–1.7% per year in developing countries and 0.5–1.1% in developed economies (OECD-FAO, 2016). These statistics prove the rapid growth of the global dairy sector.

According to "The World Dairy Situation" report released by the International Dairy Federation (IDF) in 2018, global milk production has increased by 2.4% and became nearly 864 million tonnes. The same report indicates that in the last decade, the total production of milk is increasing in the emerging markets. By 2018, the average individual milk consumption increased by 1.3% globally and reached 113.7 kg/person. On the other hand, when we look at the statistics of Turkey, it can be noticed that by 2019, milk production increased by 3.8% and became approximately 22,960,379 tonnes (National Milk Council, 2019). The average individual milk consumption reached 276 kg/person.

13.3.3 Brief Description About Sütaş and Justification of Its Selection as a Case

Sütaş was founded in 1975 in the Uluabat village of Karacabey district in Bursa. While it was founded with a daily milk processing capacity of 5 tonnes, today, its daily milk processing capacity has reached 1200 tonnes at the Karacabey facilities, 1500 tonnes at the Aksaray facilities, and 1000 tonnes at the Tire facilities.[3]

From 1975 onward, Sütaş has been operating with a focus on milk and dairy products only. Today, the company processes 900 million litres of milk per year in its four production facilities located in Turkey, Macedonia, and Romania, and offers 78 different products to its consumers. Eight out of every ten households in Turkey have at least one Sütaş package. Sütaş employs 5000 people with a revenue of 3.8 billion TRY. In 2019, Sütaş exported 16.5 million USD to 29 countries, including the USA, Japan, the UAE, Qatar, Libya, Iraq, Kuwait, and Egypt.

According to Brand Finance's report, Sütaş is the 25th most valuable brand in Turkey and the most loved milk and dairy products brand in Turkey. It is the most reputable dairy company and the 57th largest industrial enterprise in Turkey. It has been the leading brand in the dairy sector for 15 years. Sütaş was also granted the corporate governance award for the last five years.[4]

As Sütaş is the leading brand in the milk and dairy products sector in Turkey, this study will take this firm as a case and analyse it to give some insight into sustainability in this sector. In other words, due to the dominance and leadership of Sütaş in this sector, an analysis of this firm's sustainability issues may help us to understand the general sustainability trends in the dairy sector in Turkey.

13.3.4 Research Methodology

Case study methodology has been used in this research. Qualitative case study methodology enables researchers to conduct an in-depth

[3] https://www.sutas.com.tr/en/about-us/sutas-at-a-glance/sutas-in-brief, 2020.

[4] Ibid.

exploration of intricate phenomena within some specific context (Rashid et al., 2019).

Case studies are appropriate and useful when the following situations are valid (Yin, 2009):

- When the research focuses on questions such as "why" and "how";
- When the researcher has less control over the subject that is investigated; and
- If a subject's application in real life is to be analysed.

In a case study approach, Mills et al. (2010) summarised nine stages to collect data. These steps are:

- Place: Investigation of the place;
- Actors: People who are responsible for the subject investigated;
- Activities: Activities held by the people who are responsible for the subject analysed;
- Objects: Physical objects used to continue the process;
- Actions: Activities of the people done at once;
- Events: Sequential activities of the people responsible for the subject investigated;
- Time: The specific time that the data is collected;
- Purpose: The aim of the people who collect data; and
- Emotions: The feelings of the people.

Following the stated steps above, Sütaş is investigated in terms of its sustainable practices by:

- secondary data analysis consisting of reports (Sütaş Sustainability Report, 2019, etc.), magazines, and other secondary data such as documents related to sustainability practices;
- observation of the places and facilities (farms, factories, working areas of the employees, etc.); and
- in-depth interviews with managers and company executives.

13.4 Findings of the Study

Depending on the secondary data analysis, observations, and in-depth interviews, the sustainability practices of Sütaş were identified on the three dimensions of economic, social, and environmental. Thus, in this section, Sütaş' activities and contributions will be analysed in terms of these three dimensions of sustainability.

Contributions to the "Economic Dimension" of Sustainability
The dairy industry is a productive sector that creates high added value, regular employment, and steady income and contributes to social welfare.

Sütaş, Turkey's leading brand in milk and dairy products, operates with the mission of spreading the goodness and abundance of milk. The company details its support to the country's development and welfare of the people by raising awareness of its social responsibility (www.sutas.com.tr). The company doesn't see the dairy business solely as producing milk but applies a ***"From Farm to Table"*** working model, which is the first and only one of its kind in Turkey, to all of its operations from what the cows eat to the milk and dairy products that arrive at the dinner tables.

"From Farm to Table Model", which was developed not just for Sütaş but also to contribute to the development and continuity of Turkey and the dairy sector, includes everything starting from the farm. It includes feed production, feeding animals correctly and nutritionally to supplying its farmers with productive heifers, training farmers, and producing energy in recycling and energy facilities.

With this model, the company creates employment wherever it invests or contributes agricultural production to the formal economy and provides small producers with regular income and membership in the social security network. It provides employment for 7000 people. Considering the increase in unemployment rates in Turkey in recent years, the employment provided by Sütaş is very valuable and important for the Turkish economy. Sütaş processes daily 2.5 million litres of milk and 6.5 million packages of dairy products production capacity. It makes the production of fodder crops on 12,200 decares of a field and has 432,000 tonnes of concentrated feed annually in its feed plants.

In this way, it has important contributions to the Turkish economy. Overall, 99% of its procurements are from local suppliers. This is very important in terms of supporting the local economy and small enterprises. For instance, 1.5 billion Turkish Liras were paid for the milk it procured from 27,000 dairy farmers in 1350 villages of 21 provinces. Also, Sütaş' net turnover has grown by 18% and reached 3.9 billion Turkish Liras, which represents an important success and added value for the Turkish economy.

Contributions to the "Environmental Dimension" of Sustainability
As an environmental investment, Sütaş converts fertiliser and organic waste from its farms to biogas then to electricity and heat in the Aksaray and Karacabey facilities. With nearly 20 million dollars invested in natural energy, Sütaş' electricity production has reached 10.6 MW and heat energy 7.4 tonne/h. In 2015, 300,000 tonnes of fertiliser and waste were used to provide 41% of the total electricity and 10% of the steam needed in the facilities.

Sütaş achieved a 39% reduction in greenhouse gas emission and 26% in water usage for processing raw milk between 2013 and 2015. Sütaş continues to invest in organic fertiliser production, another output of energy production, and plans to produce 150 tonnes of special fertilisers for feed plants. The Sütaş Aksaray Natural Energy Facility is the first biogas facility in Turkey certified by the Gold Standard and the first agricultural solid waste treatment facility certified by the Ministry of the Environment.

Sütaş invested 17 million dollars more in 2016 and 2017 to increase energy production capacity and establish a fertiliser facility. When these investments were completed, Sütaş' facilities achieved 1800 tonnes/day in fertiliser and waste processing capacity; the electricity production will increase to 15 MWh and steam production to 10 tonnes/h. The organic fertiliser production capacity rose to 350 tonnes daily.

As a contribution to the environmental dimension of sustainability, Sütaş returns to nature the natural resources that it uses in its original condition. It perceives the natural resources as entrusted to it, and holds the responsibility of sustainable management and efficient use of natural resources, and of circulating the resources back into the system. Going on with statistical data, in this regard:

- Sütaş has met 80% of the electricity required for the facilities with the renewable energy produced from the animal manure from its farms and its organic wastes.
- Sütaş has achieved 345,000 tonnes of greenhouse gas reduction against 136,000 tonnes of greenhouse gas emission generated by the 2019 production process, equivalent to the amount absorbed by 8 million trees (based on the assumption that one tree absorbs 43 kg of CO_2/year).
- Through its sustainability operations since 2013, Sütaş has achieved greenhouse gas reduction equivalent to the amount absorbed by 28.5 million trees.
- In 2019, 98% of Sütaş' waste was recycled and it used 389 tonnes less in packaging materials.
- Sütaş has travelled 47.3 million km less in the last five years through its logistic optimisation actions, which equals to travelling 1180 times around the Earth.
- Sütaş improved the fertility of 50,000 decares of soil every year.
- It has produced 62,000 tonnes of organic fertiliser from the outputs of its energy production facilities.
- The organomineral fertilisers are produced in its natural energy facilities: restore the physical structure of the soil, ensure soil permeability, increase water retention ability of the soil, hold the chemical nutrients in the soil to improve the effectiveness of use, balance the pH of the soil, act as a nutrition source for the organisms in the soil, and finally serves as an ideal source of nutrients for plants due to the high content of plant nutrients.
- Sütaş engages in practices aimed at achieving water efficiency in line with its goal of reducing water consumption per tonne of raw milk processed in its facilities. Its ongoing R&D projects in this area are:

  - Wastewater recovery: Recovery of the water exiting the treatment facility and reusing it to irrigate the facility grounds.
  - Use of the liquid fermented by-product in agricultural lands: Sanitation and use of the liquid fermented by-product (400 tonnes/day) of biogas in agricultural lands.

- New filtered water production facility: Treatment of the water used in production at a lower cost through physical and chemical methods and getting it ready for use.
- Sütaş also employs an effective wastewater management system. It treats the wastewater resulting from its operations. It has made significant investments to increase the efficiency of the treatment process and turn its waste into value. Since 2008, it has been returning all the wastewater from its production processes to nature after 100% treatment in its "Anaerobic Wastewater Treatment Facilities" using low energy and chemicals.
- The sludge and organic materials generated by this treatment are recycled in its energy production facilities and converted into electricity and thermal energy. For instance, in 2016, the volume of water recycled and reused was 422,500 m^3, but in 2017, this number raised to 465,000 m^3. The volume of water discharged was 2,231,382 m^3 in 2016. This number rose to 3.062.193 m^3 in 2017.

As can be seen from the itemised issues, Sütaş has considerable investments in the environment and adds great value to the environment.

Contributions to the "Social Dimension" of Sustainability
The social dimension of sustainability is related to the welfare of society as a whole. In this regard, Sütaş states that it tries to deliver the goodness of milk to more people.

As mentioned before, milk is the most affordable and easily accessible foodstuff that is useful for the healthy nutrition of society and the mental and physical development of future generations. With the efficiency and effectiveness of production and distribution processes, a Sütaş product is consumed in eight out of ten houses in Turkey. Moreover, Sütaş' contributions to the societal dimension of sustainability are:

- Sütaş' R&D Centre has made 35 utility model and patent applications.
- Its "Cheese Microbiota Development Project" and "Breed Improvement Study", supported by TAGEM (General Directorate of Agricultural Research and Policies), are in progress.

- It has combined the original kefir starter cultures derived from the Caucasus Mountains and the fresh milk from Sütaş Farm and has developed Kaf Kefir, which is one of the healthiest products for the consumers.
- Sütaş promotes good and healthy life. Therefore, without compromising natural taste, it has reduced the sugar content in Sütaş Büyümix, fresh cheese developed for children, by 20%. Considering the harmful effects of sugar (e.g., the World Health Organization recommends daily sugar intake to be reduced to less than 10% of the daily energy intake and daily salt intake to be reduced to less than 5 g), especially for children, this activity adds value for the growth of children and achieving a healthier lifestyle.
- In 2015, it reduced the percentage of salt content in its 23 cheese products to less than the percentage values set in the legislation as part of Turkey's Healthy Nutrition and Active Life Programme and the Reduction of Excessive Salt Consumption programme organised by the Ministry of Health.
- It also increases the nutritional values of certain nutrients inherent in milk to respond to the different needs of the consumers. The products in this category include Büyümix, which is enriched in vitamin D, calcium, and protein; plain yoghurt, which contains 25–28% more protein than the protein values set in the legislation; and strained yoghurt, which contains 36% more protein. These products make up 25.3% of the entire product portfolio.
- With all these efforts, it reduced the amount of salt per product in 2017 by 27% compared to 2015. It reviewed the ingredients of its products containing additional sugar according to the circular on food to be sold in school canteens issued by the Ministry of National Education in 2016 in accordance with the resolution of the School Health Science Board. Although it is not legally required, it has used the specified percentage values in all fruit-flavoured milk, chocolate milk, and fruit-flavoured yoghurt products that it has been marketing since 2017. With all of these efforts, it reduced the amount of sugar per product in 2017 by 13.1% compared to 2015.
- Sütaş applies "The Farm of Happy Cows" principle. In this regard, all of its farms are disease-free and EU-certified Dairy Farms. As the com-

fort and health of the cows are directly related to milk productivity, quality, and food safety, the welfare of its cows is a top priority and it manages its farms, observing "The Five Freedoms" adopted by the World Organization for Animal Health.

- Its total herd of 11,000 is the largest herd in Turkey that is part of a corporate structure. Also, it designs its farms for the comfort of its animals and to prevent accident and injury.
- It carries out medical inspections and treatment on its cows in separate areas it calls infirmary paddocks. Its shelters, which have semi-open systems, have pasture areas that open out from each paddock. There is an open-close curtain system on the side of the shelters for protecting cows from harsh weather. Clean air is circulated constantly with fans, and it uses automatic fertiliser scraping systems to collect the fertiliser on the floors. This is how it maintains hygienic conditions in the shelters and collects fertiliser for electricity production at its biogas facilities.
- Cows at Sütaş are milked in hygienic milking parlours with automatic milking systems. Utilising water treatment systems at its farms, it provides drinking water to its animals at human consumption quality. It gives them natural, healthy, and GMO-free feed that it produces itself.
- Equipped with digital technology, it records the data collected at its farms, analyses it, and develops solutions for the health and welfare of its animals. When its cows are first born, it tags them with an earring, then later at adolescence, it gives them a necklace and installs a pedometer on their feet. The "RIFD" earrings enable it to identify its calves and access all background information. The microphones installed in the rumination collars it puts around the cow's neck enable it to assess rumination and swallowing sounds to monitor the cow's health. With the pedometer it installs in their feet, it can gauge their steps and keep track of their heat cycles.
- Its integrated business model "Farm to Table" guarantees the naturalness and the quality of its products. It has conducted on-site inspections on 5453 milk producers.
- Sütaş has the mentality that milk requires dedication and dairy business requires training. Therefore, Sütaş places great importance on training activities for the future of the sector and invests in increasing the numbers of trained producers. In this scope, the company provides

applied training in the training centre established in the integrated facilities. As of 2015, 17,000 dairy producers have participated in the training to achieve the Ministry of Agriculture and Livestock's approved certificates. Twenty-nine thousand people have visited the Sütaş farms and received consultation services.

- By the year 2019, Sütaş delivered training to 19,177 milk producers and offered training and consultancy to more than 33,000 persons and entrepreneurs at Sütaş Dairy Farming Applied Training Centres, being one of the best examples of Public-University-Industry cooperation initiatives.
- At its dairy farming training centres located in Karacabey and Aksaray, it offers practical and theoretical training to the participants on:
  - Investment requirements in dairy farming;
  - How to grow fodder plants and feed, and manage manure;
  - How to feed animals;
  - Biosafety in dairy farming, herd health, and how to fight against animal diseases;
  - Birth hygiene and metritis;
  - Milking systems and raw milk quality criteria;
  - Farm income-expense accounting, government support for animal husbandry;
  - Protection of the environment, occupational safety; and
  - How to record and evaluate data.

13.5 Conclusion

As issues of environmental degradation continue to be of growing concern globally, sustainability and green marketing practices will continue to gain attention and importance. In this regard, not only individuals but also firms and society as a whole should be more sensitive, especially in terms of the environment. Companies respond to this new necessity by applying green marketing and sustainable marketing practices. In this regard, companies may add value to the world by considering sustainability with its economic, environmental, and social dimensions.

The social dimension is mainly related to labour practices, social justice, laws and regulations, working conditions, community relations, and so on. On the other hand, the economic dimension covers issues such as economic performance, contributions to the economy, financial health and profitability, and policy goals. The last dimension of sustainability that is the environmental dimension deals with subjects such as resource usage (water, air, energy, minerals, etc.), waste management, and emissions.

The Sütaş case showed us how a company may make contributions in each of these dimensions. But of course, there are some important points here that should be taken into account. These issues are summarised into two categories that are contributions to business practices and contributions to academic literature.

13.5.1 Contributions of the Study to Business Practices

The results of the study provide some managerial implications, which are summarised under the contributions to business practices title. These implications or contributions can be summarised as:

- Sustainability is mainly related to the top management's vision and how they perceive it. In other words, if management is sensitive about sustainability, they can make the investments necessary to apply sustainability practices. So, within a systems approach, the mentality of sustainability should be accepted by top management first, and then be extended to the whole organisation. In this way, every single employee working in the company may be aware and sensitive about issues related to sustainability.
- Other important points about applying sustainable practices are the company's or management's attitudes towards sustainability. If management only thinks that releasing sustainability reports help them to increase the company's credibility and reputation, then the mentality of sustainability will fail. And since these activities are not held in the long run, they will bring success for a short period in terms of gaining

a relative advantage. Instead of this, companies should accept that investing in sustainability practices is something necessary for the business and society as a whole. This will increase the role and importance of such actions.

- The case analysis revealed that effectively applying sustainability practices needs long-term orientation, change in the business mentality, applying new business models if necessary (like Sütaş' "farm to table" model), and openness to change and continuous investment. Therefore, instead of considering sustainability and sustainability marketing as a trend that should be applied to gain competitive advantage, these actions should be a part of the business system and mentality.
- As can be seen from the examples stated in the Sütaş case, applying sustainability practices in social, environmental, and economic aspects will provide benefits to both companies and the society. In other words, it will create a win-win situation. On one hand, by the added value provided as the result of such actions, society will win. On the other hand, companies will benefit from the cost savings obtained as a result of applying a sustainability mentality.
- Also, by sharing what they do for the economy, society, and the environment, they can strengthen their brand images and increase credibility which are very important issues for successful brand management policies. This will also affect the other companies in a positive way. In other words, in order to be a part of the competition, the other companies should also practice sustainable actions. As a result, when the number of companies that apply sustainable marketing increase, the society, environment, and economy will win.

13.5.2 Contributions of the Study to Academic Literature

Sustainability has gained the attention of academicians in recent years. But despite this growing importance, there are still limited studies about this concept. Therefore, first, this study with its findings contributes to the academic literature in this aspect.

Another important contribution of this study to the literature is related to some aspects that can be investigated in further research. For instance, the findings stated that the "farm to table" business model increased the efficiency of sustainability practices. According to European Commission, the Farm to Fork Strategy is at the heart of the European Green Deal aiming to make food systems fair, healthy, and environmentally friendly (European Commission, 2019). Therefore, in further research, antecedents and outcomes of such models can be investigated.

Moreover, the relationship between the success of sustainability practices and management's vision or attitudes about sustainability practices on company reputation, brand image, customer loyalty, or willingness to pay more should be investigated in the emerging markets.

References

Ayres, R. U., van den Bergh, J. C. J. M., & Gowdy, J. M. (2001). Strong versus weak sustainability: Economics, natural sciences and 'consilience'. *Environmental Ethics, 23*(1), 155–168.

Chattopadhyay, A., Batra, R., & Ozsomer, A. (2012). *The new emerging market multinationals: Four strategies for disrupting markets and building brands.* McGraw Hill.

Demircan, V., Binici, T., Koknaroglu, H., & Aktas, A. R. (2006). Economic analysis of different dairy farm sizes in Burdur province in Turkey. *Czech Journal of Animal Science, 51*(1), 8–17.

Doh, J. P., Littell, B., & Quigley, N. R. (2015). CSR and sustainability in emerging markets: Societal, institutional and organizational influences. *Organizational Dynamics, 44*(1), 112–120.

European Commission. (2019). *Farm to Fork strategy—For a fair, healthy and environmentally-friendly food system.* https://ec.europa.eu/food/farm2fork_en

Evrendilek, F., & Doygun, H. (2000). Assessing major ecosystem types and the challenge of sustainability in Turkey. *Environmental Management, 26*(1), 479–489.

Kahn, M. (1995). Concepts, definitions, and key issues in sustainable development: The outlook for the future. Proceedings of the 1995 *International Sustainable Development Research Conference*, Manchester, England, Keynote Paper, 2–13.

Khanna, T., & Palepu, K. G. (2010). *Winning in emerging markets: A roadmap for strategy and execution*. Harvard Business Press.

Lacy, P., & Hayward, R. (2011). A new era of sustainability in emerging markets? Insights from a global CEO study by the United Nations global compact and accenture. *Corporate Governance, 11*(4), 348–357.

Mills, A. J., Durepos, G., & Wiebe, E. (Eds.). (2010). *Encyclopedia of case study research*. Sage Publications.

National Milk Council. (2019). Dünya ve Türkiye'de süt sektör istatistikleri. https://ulusalsutkonseyi.org.tr/ulusal-sut-konseyi-sut-raporu-2019-2903/

OECD-FAO. (2016). *OECD-FAO agricultural outlook 2016–2025*. OECD and FAO.

Purvis, B., Mao, Y., & Robinson, D. (2019). Three pillars of sustainability: In search of conceptual origins. *Sustainability Science, 4*(14), 681–695.

Rashid, Y., Rashid, A., Warraich, M. A., Sabir, S. S., & Waseem, A. (2019). Case study method: A step by step guide for business researchers. *International Journal of Qualitative Research, 18*(1), 1–13.

Segerkvist, K. A., Hansson, H., Sonesson, U., & Gunnarsson, S. (2020). Research on environmental, economic, and social sustainability in dairy farming: A systematic mapping of current literature. *Sustainability, 20*(1), 5501–5515.

Shahbandeh, M. (2019). *Global dairy industry*. Statista.com

Sütaş Sustainability Report. (2019). Annual report. https://www.sutas.com.tr/panel/upload/Sutas-annual-report-2019.pdf

Thomsen, C. (2013). Sustainability (World commission on environment and development definition). In S. O. Idowu, N. Capaldi, L. Zu, & A. D. Gupta (Eds.), *Encyclopedia of corporate social responsibility*. Springer.

World Bank. (2019). https://data.worldbank.org/country/tur

World Commission on Environment and Development (WCED). (1987). *Our common future*. Oxford University Press.

Yaprak, A., Yosun, T., & Cetindamar, D. (2018). The influence of firm-specific and country specific advantages in the internationalization of emerging market firms: Evidence from Turkey. *International Business Review, 27*(1), 198–207.

Yin, R. (2009). *Case study research: Design and methods*. Sage Publications Inc.

14

Sustainable Mining in Emerging Economies: A Case of Reputable Mining Companies in Africa

Kojo Kakra Twum, Peter Ansu-Mensah, Martin Kwadwo Amaniampong, James Telari Bonn, and Nicholas Asiedu Nyarko

14.1 Introduction

The mining sector forms an important economic activity in developed and developing economies. Mining activities have contributed immensely to the world's civilisation (Cao, 2007). In developed economies such as Australia, Canada, and the United States, mining has played an important role in economic development (Githiria & Onifade, 2020). In developing economies, the mining sector provides employment and infuses revenue into the local communities and the national economy (Githiria

K. K. Twum (✉) • M. K. Amaniampong • J. T. Bonn
Presbyterian University College, Abetifi, Ghana

P. Ansu-Mensah
Sunyani Technical University, Sunyani, Ghana

N. A. Nyarko
National Security Secretariat, Accra, Ghana

E. K. Adae et al. (eds.), *Responsible Management in Emerging Markets*, Sustainable Development Goals Series, https://doi.org/10.1007/978-3-030-76563-7_14

& Onifade, 2020). The United Nations (2012) acknowledges that the mining sector is very important for all countries with mineral resources, and helps in propelling economic development, reducing poverty, and aiding in the attainment of Millennium Development Goals when the resources are managed sustainably.

However, all these benefits have been offset by considerable negative impacts on the environment and the health and safety of miners and mining communities. Similarly, the impact of mining on the social structure and traditions of Africans in remote areas has a negative influence on the public. For instance, Kenyans living in the mining community like Maasai have shifted from fishing and farming activities to mining, which is now the sole source of survival for the community. Again, children of school-going age are engaged in mining (child labour) instead of going to classrooms (Githiria & Onifade, 2020).

Nonetheless, mining could become sustainable with a minimal impact on the environment if mining companies adopt and incorporate the three dimensions of economic, social, and environmental improvements, thereby reclaiming and restoring the land (Kumar, 2014). Therefore, finding more sustainable answers (regarding methods, clean technologies, and equipment use) should be the concern of mining firms as it will be environmentally and financially advantageous.

The United Nations (2012) recognises the importance of strong policies, practices, and legal and regulatory frameworks in the mining sector that deliver social and economic benefits through effective safeguards and reducing environmental and social impact by implementing conservation activities such as preserving biodiversity and ecosystem. One important sustainability activity identified by the United Nations is mining closure practices.

Sustainability in mining entails ensuring natural resource extraction causes minimal defect to the environment and protecting the health and safety of employees and society. Sustainability in the mining sector will, therefore, entail achieving development that satisfies the needs of the current generation while securing the interest and needs of future generations. This view is supported by Burger (2011) who asserts that sustainability efforts are aimed at maintaining the environment properly for future generations.

In the developed country context, Endl et al. (2019) identified many innovative concepts introduced by mining firms to promote sustainable mining to address the needs of the Sustainable Development Goals (SDGs). In the economic domain, sustainable mining innovations include autonomous mining equipment and operations (the use of trucks, drills, trains, etc., managed using remote controls, robotics, 3D printing, etc.) that lead to cost reductions. An example of this form of mining is Rio Tinto's AutoHaul, which is a technology that enables the mining firm to operate driverless trucks (as cited in Endl et al., 2019).

Further, the use of the internet through big data management and artificial intelligence can help obtain and manage information in real time and sustainably. An example of this technology is Strabag's mat-DOC Software systems, which is part of the "internet and things" systems used by the firm to manage data relating to mining operations (as cited in Endl et al., 2019).

On the societal aspect, mining companies in developed economies are adopting strategies such as sharing mining infrastructure, better land use, enhanced transparency and traceability, low environmental footprint, and renewable energy solutions (Endl et al., 2019). Endl et al. (2019) state that sustainable mining initiatives are aimed at achieving many aspects of the SDGs. Specifically, some aspects of sustainable mining are related to ending poverty through inclusive employment and local procurement (SDG 1), conservation and reuse of water (SDG 6), training and education of workforce (SDG 4), occupational health and safety (SDG 3), improving energy efficiency (SDG7), and local procurement and shared infrastructure (SDG 9).

In European countries such as Sweden and Norway, Kokko et al. (2015) acknowledged that apart from the European Union Directive 2010/75/EU on pollution prevention and control, and other environmental directives, these countries have in place regulations at the national level to promote sustainable mining. The minimum regulation of sustainability of mining activities in Norway, Sweden, and Russia is done using legal rules, which are aimed at seeking a balance between exploration and preservation interest and to ensure the sustainable management of resources (Kokko et al., 2015).

Vintró et al. (2014) mention Royal Decree 975/2009 in Catalonia on waste management in mining transposes the European Directive 200435/EC by the European Commission on waste management. There is, therefore, support from the continental level by the commission to ensure member states adhere to precautions. The sustainability efforts of mining companies in Europe are guided by the standards proposed by the European Commission and national-level policies.

The attention of Amoah et al. (2020) has been drawn to the shortcomings in the implementation of sustainability in the mining industry in developing countries. Generally, mining operations have attracted a negative image among the public due to the negative impact on the environment and the lives of local communities in both developed and developing economies.

However, there is evidence to prove that sustainability practices in developed countries appear to be handled effectively by governments and firms leading to improved environmental performance (Kumah, 2006). Sustainability practices in the mining sector in developing countries are still bedevilled with challenges. The effort by the African Union to regulate mining on the African continent by introducing the African Mining Vision (AMV) in 2009 has been identified as having some shortcomings (Hilson, 2020). One of the tenets of the AMV is "fostering sustainable development principles based on environmental and socially responsible mining, which is safe and includes communities and all other stakeholders" (Hilson, 2020). Some questions have been asked relating to the effectiveness of the AMV. In view of Hilson (2020), these include the AMV seen as a blueprint and whether individual African countries are responding to the recommendation enshrined in the AMV.

Amoah et al. (2020) found that despite the attempts to promote sustainability practices in mining in developing countries, about 75% of mines are closed prematurely leading to negative social and environmental costs on local communities. Hilson and Yakovleva (2007) state that the strained relationship between local communities and large-scale mining companies led to unproductive mining in the Prestea area in Ghana, bringing to the fore crucial issues about community support and engagement.

Another study cited that mining in Konongo has little economic value due to extensive shallow open-pit mines and the upsurge in artisanal mining activities, popularly known in the local parlance as "Galamsey," leading to contamination of soils and river bodies (Brempong et al., 2019). In the Copper Belt of Zambia and DR Congo, Mwitwa et al. (2012) identified that some concerns for community members include forest degradation and the negative impact on the livelihood of forest-dependent communities.

Mhlongo et al. (2019) equally state that all the gold mines in the Sutherland goldfield in South Africa have been abandoned without rehabilitation. There is also a report in South Africa about the discharge of untreated acid mine water into surface streams and wetland in parts of the Witwatersrand and Randfontein area (Ochieng et al., 2010). On the economic sustainability of mines, Akabzaa and Darimani (2001) report that the State Gold Mining Company in Ghana had closed its mines in Bibiani and Konongo, and the Ghana Consolidated Diamonds Limited has been on the divestiture list since 1993 due to the lack of investment and exploration.

Mines that are closed must acquire a closure certificate. Mine closure is part of an attempt to ensure proper procedures are observed when closing mines and to ensure the reclamation and reuse of land for other productive purposes (Watson & Olalde, 2019). Watson and Olalde (2019) examined mining closure certificates from 2011 to 2016 granted in South Africa and concluded that the mine closure system was ineffective.

Despite this, there are reports of effective sustainable mining practices on the African continent. An example is the development of sustainable mining built around the SDGs by a leading mining firm in South Africa (Anglo American, 2019). As a result, Burger (2011) calls for more research into how firms can improve environmental performance and reduce the negative impact of activities on communities.

The use of sustainability reports and an interview from two major mining companies in Ghana provide evidence of the use of sustainable mining practices in developing economies. This chapter presents readers information to understand the mining sustainability practices related to land reclamation. Land reclamation practices findings will be a valuable source of reference for students, industry practitioners, and policymakers on how mining companies reclaim lands they use for mining. Also, the objective of this chapter is to identify the corporate social responsibility (CSR) initiatives that mining companies implement. It also provides some findings on how mining companies enhance societal wellbeing through their long-term social investments. The chapter closes with some recommendations for mining companies and policymakers on what practices can be implemented to enhance sustainable mining.

14.2 Components of Sustainable Mining Practices

The chapter considers three main sustainability practices in the mining industry. These practices form the basis for discussions, data collection, and analysis. They include environmental protection (land and water protection), corporate social responsibility, and long-term sustainable practices (Fig, 14.1) .

14.2.1 Mining Sustainability and Environmental Protection (Land and Water Protection)

It is worth mentioning that land reclamation/rehabilitation certainly plays a starring role among mining communities with regard to their development, both economically and ecologically (Yu et al., 2020). Kumar (2014, 28) defined reclamation as "*the process to bring a site to a condition similar to its pre-mining condition by removing structures, replacing overburden, [and] replanting vegetation where mining operations have completely ceased.*" Reclamation helps to restore the land to a state as close as possible to its original form before the commencement of the mining activity for the resumption of the former land use or new use (Kumar, 2014; Tetteh et al., 2015). Indeed, for a pathway to sustainability, mining and land reclamation call for an all-encompassing environment reclamation procedure (Feng et al., 2019).

Cao (2007), citing Warhurst and Noronha (1999), states that the mining and reclamation effort has the following objectives:

- To ensure all forms of health and safety hazards are eliminated (e.g., removing all structures and facilities that can threaten human health and safety).
- To preserve land and water resources by performing restoration activities such as revegetation and reducing potential acid mine drainage or water contamination.
- To ensure off-site negative environmental impacts are eliminated through activities such as cleaning up sites to improve the environment of the community.
- To put to good use post-mining sites to ensure it provides social and economic benefits for the future. Some initiatives to put post-mining sites to good use include using these lands as recreational sites, for conservation purposes, for historic purposes, or for public amenities and facilities.
- To promote sustainable mining through efficient use of natural resources and energy.

The Environmental Protection Agency (EPA) Act, 1994 (Act 490) provided an amendment and consolidation to the existing laws regulating environmental issues when the Acts of Parliament had frowned on such laws in Ghana. As part of its main functions, the EPA has the mandate to provide directives regarding the standards and guidelines relating to any form of contamination such as air, water, and land pollution coupled with the proper release of toxic substances and waste control. The Act enjoins all agencies, projects, and institutions whose establishment has an influence on the environment to register with the EPA.

In South Africa, Watson and Olalde (2019) state that the granting of mining permits and regulation of operations is managed by the Department of Mining Resources (DMR) using the Mineral and Petroleum Resource Development Act (MPRDA) and the National Environmental Management Act (NEMA). According to Feris and Kotze (2014), a South African legislation currently holds polluters liable for rehabilitation and remediation of water pollution.

However, there are concerns about the ineffective regulation in many African countries such as Zambia (Mwitwa et al., 2012) and Eastern Congo (Stoop & Verpoorten, 2020). In Eastern Congo, for instance, mining companies are reported to have ventured into fragile mining areas leading to artisanal miner's intention to engage in violence (Stoop & Verpoorten, 2020). These instances of ineffective mining regulation can be attributed to the lack of strong regulation at the continental level through the African Union (see Hilson, 2020).

14.2.2 Mining Sustainability and CSR/Social Licence Activities

In order to manage the conflicting interest of various stakeholders, CSR has been adopted by mining companies (Mahmood & Orazalin, 2017). With the introduction of CSR, companies create value for stakeholders and themselves because companies tend to benefit by building reputation and synergy (Prno & Slocombe, 2012). Through CSR, benevolent mining companies have made contributions to development and poverty alleviation (Littlewood, 2014).

While CSR enhances the renewal of former mining areas and the impact of the closure on health and wellbeing (Littlewood, 2014), usually, heavy mining poses serious social problems like poor health, unemployment, poverty, low levels of education, and environmental degradation (Bhatnagar & Sharma, 2015). Hence, mining companies have framed their CSR programmes embedded in sustainability/sustainable development (Bhatnagar & Sharma, 2015; Kumi et al., 2020). Unsurprisingly, it seems as if comprehensive mining sustainability criteria should be adhered to until communities give their consent for projects (Prno & Slocombe, 2012).

For specific CSR projects, a reputable mining company in Ghana designed Livelihood Enhancement and Community Development Program (LECDeP), Agricultural Improvement and Land Access Program (AILAP), "Mmobrowa" (Needy) Scheme, Agricultural Intervention Programme (AIP), Business Intervention Programmes, and more, which are vital to the host communities' development, both economically and socially. This involves training programmes, micro-credit provision, and community infrastructure projects (Ansu-Mensah et al., 2021).

These initiatives are aimed at helping communities to meet their developmental needs. Further, Twum et al. (2020) posit that CSR enables firms to attain a competitive advantage. Another mining company in Ghana states in its sustainability report (AngloGold Ashanti, 2019) that about 16% of the funds spent on social initiatives are as donations to communities.

In view of Raufflet et al. (2014), there are three main sources of CSR practices in the mining sector:

- The first source stems from governments that may enforce complete and specific formal policies regarding an issue and specifically define company requirements. When companies are motivated by governmental policy, CSR projects become similar in different companies because CSR is treated as a coercive practice.
- The second source stems from what has been referred to as "the infrastructure for CSR" which promotes voluntary, that is, non-government-led, CSR initiatives and responses. In the absence of governmental policy, industrial associations, activists, responsible fund managers, and other actors may negotiate CSR frameworks and invite firms to follow them. In the case of developing countries, international financial institutions such as the World Bank and the International Finance Corporation have developed frameworks for CSR.
- The third source of CSR initiatives originates from companies themselves. In the absence of governmental or industrial association policies, companies may decide by themselves which are the best practices and apply these practices according to company interests.

14.2.3 Mining Sustainability as Long-Term Community Development

The involvement of mining companies in long-term sustainability entails operating in a manner that secures the future of the business and the host communities. This sustainability practice is a necessary aspect of sustaining the mining business and the survival of communities. Therefore, mining companies must oversee projects and interventions that enhance community development and standards of living.

The mining communities that benefit from genuine assistance from mining companies tend to support the activities of these companies. A mutual coexistence is, therefore, attained. It is no wonder that the parliament of Ghana passed the Minerals and Mining Act 2006, Act 703, which was later amended in 2015 seeking to expand the frontiers of mining business in Ghana (Hilson et al., 2019). This will also allow mining companies in the country to engage in long-term community development (Amoako, 2017).

Sustainability mining calls for a planned approach to long-term community development that will enhance good relations with communities, other small-scale miners, and eventually be devoid of conflicts in the long term (Kumar, 2014). To achieve cohesion in society, it is crucial to pay heed to the social sustainability of communities so that there will not be subsequent economic activity losses (Bhatnagar & Sharma, 2015). In so doing, communities and mine workers could attain sustainable development through the adoption of the three sustainability dimensions of social, economic, and environmental.

In Newmont Gold Corps, a mining company in Ghana, mining sustainability as long-term community development include health, education, quality of life, and water and sanitation. Communities in the Ahafo region, Kenyasi, and Yamfo have been provided with health amenities such as clinics, maternity blocks, male and female blocks, and doctors/nurses' bungalows. A modern operation theatre has also been built for the Ntotroso Government Hospital. Additionally, many classrooms have been built for communities such as Ntotroso, Kenyasi No. 1, Kenyasi No. 2, Gyedu, Wamahinso, Susuanso, Techire, Yamfo, Afirisipakrom, and Adrobaa (Ansu-Mensah et al., 2021).

AngloGold Ashanti, another reputable mining company in Ghana, reports that the company aims at contributing to resilient and self-sustaining communities (AngloGold Ashanti, 2019). The report states that achieving sustainable community development can be done through building relationships and partnerships, mitigating current and legacy impact, socio-economic development, local procurements, and so on. The company reports that about US$27.69 million have been spent on social infrastructure, education and the youth, health, SME support, arts, culture, and heritage, among others (Fig. 14.1).

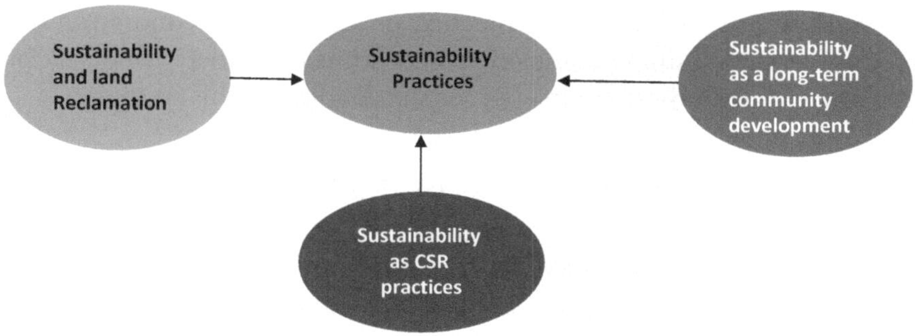

Fig. 14.1 Sustainable mining practices. (Source: Adapted from Essah and Andrews (2016))

14.3 Evidence of Sustainable Mining Practices in Developing Economies

The use of sustainable mining practices in developing economies can be found in academic literature and industry reports. To support the use of sustainable practices identified in the study of Essah and Andrews (2016), secondary data from sustainability reports of four reputable mining firms in Africa were examined.

In addition, an interview with a sustainability manager of a mining company in Ghana was conducted to understand the ways mining firms in developing economies implement sustainable practices. The first company in Ghana is a leading gold mining company in the world and also deals in copper, silver, zinc, and lead.

The company has a strong presence in Africa. Its mining site, which is the focus of this study in Ghana, has been involved in mining for many years. The second company is the third biggest gold producer in the world on the African continent.

The third company included in this study is a leading mining company with a presence in South Africa, Namibia, Zimbabwe, and Botswana. The fourth company is a reputable mining firm with operations in West Africa, Australia, America, and South Africa. These companies have reported on their respective sustainability efforts, which serve as a good example of sustainable mining practices in developing economies. The identity of these mining companies was withheld, as there is no special arrangement with these companies for the conduct of this study.

14.3.1 Sustainable Practices of the Mining Company

Using the mining sustainability framework proposed by Essah and Andrews (2016), the chapter organised the findings under three main themes, namely, environmental protection practices, corporate social responsibility activities, and sustainability as long-term community development activities.

14.3.1.1 Environmental Sustainability

Environmental sustainability practices by mining companies may take the form of land reclamation, efforts to reduce the impact of climate change, water management and conservation, and health and safety of employees and communities. This chapter focuses the discussions of environmental sustainability of mining firms in emerging economies on these practices.

Land Reclamation Sustainability Activities

One of the most important aspects of mining environmental sustainability is land reclamation. Land reclamation refers to the steps and processes that firms adopt to rehabilitate disturbed land. From the Provisional Land Rehabilitation Plan of the first mining company (Akyem Gold Mining Project, 2008a), the land reclamation efforts are aimed at the following objectives:

- To ensure there are no public safety hazards from mining
- To abide by the statutory requirements
- To attain beneficial post-mining land use
- To rehabilitate land disturbed from mining

- To conduct reclamation concurrent with mining
- To ensure sufficient funds are provided to implement reclamation objectives

From the sustainability report of another mining company in Ghana (AngloGold Ashanti, 2019), it is clearly stated that the company's key focus areas of environmental stewardship involve water, air, energy management, biodiversity, and land rehabilitation. An examination of sustainability reports (see Table 14.1) of mining firms in developing countries found some practices aimed at protecting the environment.

Table 14.1 Environmental protection activities

The environmental report (Newmont Corporation, 2021a**)** states the following practices:
Reforestation Offset Programme—The mining company's operations reside in a forest reserve. The land reclamation efforts have led to bringing back over 300 hectares of land.
Biodiversity Offset Programme—The company has secured approval from the Forestry Commission to embark on a biodiversity offset programme. This is aimed at compensating for the residual, unavoidable harm to biodiversity leading to a net gain in biodiversity.
Flora Management—As part of the reforestation and reclamation activities, there is a greenhouse project raising about 70,000 seedlings, with 16,000 indigenous plants, comprising 30 different species and 4000 ornamental plants under controlled conditions.
Wildlife—The study conducted by the Forest Institute of Ghana and the Wildlife Services Division on identifying the wildlife in the mining area did not find any endangered species.
Vetiver Plantation—The company has planted vetiver grass to control erosion. This is important to ensure land is reclaimed by controlling erosion on site.
Community Tree planting and Medicinal Plant Farm—The company has planted about 1600 ornamental plants in one of the resettlement villages. The trees will provide shade and serve as wind brakes. The medicinal plants will also provide for the medicinal needs of the people.
From the sustainability report of a leading company in South Africa, the company has in place a bioremediation facility that treats soil that has been contaminated with hydrocarbons to ensure it can be reused (Anglo American, 2019). The company report claims that the facility can reclaim 250 tonnes of soil per month when operating at full capacity. It reported having reclaimed about 1650 tonnes of contaminated soil in 2019.

Source: Authors (2021)

An interview with a sustainability manager of another mining company led to the identification of the following land reclamation practices:

One important environmentally sustainable practice is related to the protection of plant and animal life. The sustainability manager commented:

> The process includes the recording of tree and animal species within the processed mining site. This is to ensure animals are not harmed during mining. The animals that are captured are sent to zoos or to other forest areas.

Also, to ensure the reclamation of disturbed land, the company engages in stockpiling. The manager stated:

> The stockpiling of soils and rock from mining [is] in three layers. Stockpiling the topsoil (fertile soil) is first collected from the land during the mining. The topsoil is needed to ensure plant growth during reclamation, and is first collected and stored. This is the last type of soil to be brought to cover the land after mining. The second soil layer called the saprolite is also stored. The third layer, which contains rocks are also stored. This waste material is first replaced on the reclaimed land, followed by the saprolite, and the topsoil. The growth of plants is supported [by] manure from the Sewage Treatment Plant (STP).

Also, reforestation is another way to ensure that the mining environment is protected. The manager commented:

> The tree planting exercise is a very extensive activity. The records of the species that will be affected are taken into consideration. The company engages community members to perform seedlings nursing at a fee. This project is [given] out on contract basis.

These land reclamation practices explained by a sustainability manager of the company support the land rehabilitation approach stated in the Rehabilitation Plan of a mining company (see Land Rehabilitation Plan, 2008). The two main approaches used by the company are as follows.

1. Anticipated Pre-construction and Construction Activities

   These involve activities before mining will commence. The period followed by securing mining licence is the pre-construction phase, where the following activities will be performed including the construction of sediment control structures, clearing and grubbing vegetation from the mining sites, putting in place water diversion ditches, stockpiling soil for land reclamation after mining, seeding of soil stockpiles, developing access roads, and providing accommodation for site workers.
2. Anticipated Land Rehabilitation Activities

To reclaim the land, there are a number of activities that will be performed including reshaping, blending, applying soil, and revegetation.

Water Conservation Practices

The next issue of concern about environmental protection is water protection. Effective management of water resources is an important aspect of the physical environment. The environmental impact assessment report provides some insight into water conservation efforts (Akyem Gold Mining Project, 2008b).

The first company has in place steps to ensure water resources are managed sustainably. The company acknowledges that mining projects will undermine the surface and groundwater quality. The modifications of the water drainage systems will lead to overland runoff and peak flow due to the removal of vegetation. Open-pit mining will negatively affect the groundwater quality through the infiltration of water through the tailing storage facility and waste rock disposal.

From the sustainability report of the company (Newmont Corporation, 2021b), the following water conversation practices are identified:

- Watershed baseline—this explains the assessment of watershed conditions, such as water availability and quality prior to mining.
- Characterisation of site hydrology and water balance.
- As part of water stewardship, there is an attempt to reduce freshwater consumption and increase reusing and recycling efficiencies.

From the sustainability reports (see Table 14.2) of mining companies, the effort to conserve and protect water resources was found to be an important aspect of mining firm's sustainability efforts.

The interview with a manager also provides some valuable insight into water management. The managers stated:

> The company before mining in the area connected its water system from a river some kilometres away. A dam was created to store the water used for mining. The connected pipelines from the river to a raw water dam reduced the use of water sources in mining communities. We ensured we do not use vulnerable water sources in nearby communities for our mining purposes.

Another water management practice is the recycling of used water. The manager interviewed stated:

> In order not to waste water, we separate the solid materials from water to get "slurry." This process is handled at the Counter Current Decantation

Table 14.2 Sustainable water management practices

From the sustainability report of AngloGold Ashanti (2019), water is regarded as a scarce resource, hence making its management very crucial to the firm. The company reports that about 57% of its water is sourced from arid and semi-arid sources, 30% from tropical sources, and 13% from dry land (rivers, lakes, and groundwater). Despite the acknowledgement of the use of water in large quantities (301,890 ML) for various purposes, the company has been able to achieve 76% reuse of water.
From the sustainability report of Anglo American (2019), the company states that it seeks to operate waterless mines in water-scarce catchments.
Further, the report provides some highlights on the determination to reduce the abstraction of freshwater by 20% and increase water recycling levels to 75% by 2020. In terms of the provision of potable water, the mining company reports some remarkable investments. The first is the work carried out in the Mogalakwena municipality, where the firm has partnered with Hall Core Water Mapela to provide 3.5 million litres of water daily.
In the report, the company recounts efforts to prevent environmental disaster in its affiliate mine in Brazil when there were two iron-ore slurry leaks from the pipelines. The company quickly provided potable water, an alternative water source for mining, and removed iron-ore sediments from the river.

Source: Authors (2021)

(CCD) and Carbon in Leach (CIL) in the Thickener into tanks. This enables the reuse of water.

Climate Change Efforts

Sustainability efforts by mining companies in developing economies are aimed at reducing the impact of climate change. In general, efforts include reducing greenhouse gas (GHG) emissions and reduction in the use of energy. Some sustainable efforts made by a mining firm in an emerging economy have been presented in Table 14.3.

Health and Safety

Mining operations have a negative environmental impact on the health and safety of employees and the community. In Table 14.4, some sustainability efforts reported by a mining firm in South Africa (Anglo American, 2019) are aimed at reducing the impact of mining on healthy living focused on employee health, physical work environment, and community health.

Table 14.3 Climate change efforts

The mining company in South Africa seeks to operate carbon-neutral mines (Anglo American, 2019).
The targets include reducing GHG emissions by 22% relative to the business-as-usual projections, reduce energy consumption by 8%, reduce net GHG emissions by 30%, and improve energy efficiency by 30%.
Some innovative practices identified include carbon capture technology using carbonation technologies, using energy and carbon management systems (e.g., ECO_2MAN) to meet GHG emissions and energy targets, and using radical technologies (e.g., FutureSmart Mining™) to reduce energy use.
The firm is seeking to reduce energy use during commination (the grinding and crushing of rock). The company also reports the use of renewable energy sources in its energy mix. An example is the Waterval smelter the company uses to generate electricity from waste.

Source: Authors (2021)

Table 14.4 Health and safety

A reputable mining firm in South Africa provides the following as an occupational health risk: inhalable hazards; occupational carcinogens; noise; stress to muscles, bodies, and joints; fatigue; and work-related stress.
Some practices include improved resources for reporting health-related hazards, using technology to monitor environmental conditions to give a warning (e.g., operational intelligence suite), maintaining a good engineering system to control exhaust ventilation, and monitoring the health of employees (e.g., screening for diseases such as obesity, hypertension, diabetes, TB, HIV).
The company also reported payments made to workers believed to be suffering from silicosis and tuberculosis.
Air quality is another crucial issue that affects human health. A reputable South African mining company reports on how air quality is managed. From its sustainability report, air quality is managed by controlling the release of sulphur dioxide (SO_2) from copper and smelters, nitrogen dioxide (NO_2) from burning diesel and fuel, and particle emissions at mines.
In South Africa, the emissions from smelters are regulated by the Air Quality Act. The company had designed a technology to capture SO_2 into sulphuric acid. The company reports that it is investing in the project, which will reduce emissions by 96%.

Source: Authors (2021)

Adherence to Environmental Protection Act and Other Mining Regulations

To ensure mining firms (foreign and local) adhere to environmental regulations, some laws have been passed to ensure the environment is protected. Therefore, sustainability practices cannot ignore these laws as they are an important aspect of obtaining licences and permits to operate.

To answer the question of whether the mining company considers environmental laws found from the Provisional Land Reclamation Report of the company indicates that it adheres to laws and Acts that regulate mining and reclamation-related issues (Akyem Gold Mining Project, 2008a). The Provisional Land Reclamation Report (2008) of the mining company provides the following guidelines for land reclamation:

1. Section 14 (4) of Environmental Assessment Regulations, L.I. 1652, (1999)

2. Ghana Mining and Environmental Guidelines provided by the Minerals Commission
3. Environmental Protection Agency (1994, Act, 490)

The company, apart from adhering to environmental and mining regulations in Ghana, also, has subscribed to the ISO 14001 and the Cyanide Code. From the environmental report of the company, the ISO 14001 certification was obtained in 2010 and recertified in 2015 and 2018 for improved performance in environmental stewardship. This is a benchmark for assessing adherence to the highest form of environmental standards by top international companies. The Cyanide Code, on the other hand, is a certificate under the International Cyanide Management Code, which is voluntary. This certification is an indication that the mining company adheres to best practices in cyanide management. The second mining company in its sustainability report (AngloGold Ashanti, 2019) states that it adheres to mining standards using safety and health system standards that are reviewed and audited every two years in accordance with ISO 45001.

A reputable mining company in South Africa (Anglo American, 2019) reports that it is committed to the following initiatives and standards:

- ISO 14001 (Environmental), ISO 14064 (GHGs), ISO 14065 (GHGs), ISO 45001 (Safety and Health), ISO 26000 (Social Standards), and ISO 50001
- UN Global Compact, UN Women's Empowerment Principles, Initiative for Responsible Mining Assurance, Extractive Industries Transparency Initiative, Better Coal Initiative, ICMM Sustainable Development Framework, Kimberly Process (participation through the World Diamond Council), and more.

The performance of firms in terms of the expected level of sustainable practices can be promoted through the use of regulation. Sustainability depends mainly on the ethical and responsible behaviour of firms and can be enhanced when there is regulation. In extractive industries in emerging economies, effective regulation can enhance the level at which firms implement sustainable practices.

Apart from regulations, mining firms also demonstrate their commitment to sustainability through certifications such as ISO 14001 and the Cyanide Code. From the responses from a sustainability manager and information obtained from the various sustainability reports, it is clear that there are a number of sustainability practices performed by the mining company relating to environmental protection. These include land reclamation, animal and plant protection, water conservation, air quality, health and safety, and reduction of the effect of climate change.

14.3.1.2 Corporate Social Responsibility Initiatives

Information on the engagement in corporate social responsibility by the firm was obtained using the corporate social responsibility reports of mining companies in developing economies. From the reports presented in Table 14.5, the CSR activities of the companies cover a number of initiatives including philanthropy and volunteering.

14.3.1.3 Sustainable Long-Term Community Development

A crucial aspect of sustainable practices is the involvement in activities that enhances the overall development of communities and firms. These sustainable initiatives ensure there is a long-term continuous relationship between firms and communities while enabling the survival of a business. These issues are related to job creation, employment, alternative livelihood due to depletion of source of income, inclusion of women and minorities in management of mining firms, and so on.

In the Community Engagement Report (Newmount Corporation, 2021c) of a mining company in Ghana, the firm provides information on community-based sustainability activities. In Table 14.6, some of the initiatives of the mining company are presented.

Another company in Ghana in its sustainability report (Gold Fields, 2011) provides details about some projects to build community capacity and sustainable employment. These projects include:

Table 14.5 Corporate social responsibility initiatives

From the Community Engagement Report of a mining company in Ghana (see Newmont Corporation, 2021c) the following information was found on CSR:
The CSR initiatives of the company are managed by a development foundation established by the company. The development foundation is funded by allocating US$1 per ounce of gold sold and 1% of the firm's total profit annually.
The company has over 50 infrastructure projects in the communities in which they mine. These infrastructure projects include roads, schools, clinics, and water projects that have been completed and are in use by the communities.
Since 2014, the company has provided scholarships to over 2100 senior high school and tertiary students.
The company through its quality improvement programme created in 2016 seeks to improve the level of academic performance of students in the community. The programmes include interactive teaching, vocational training, and mock examinations.
A mining company in Ghana also has a number of corporate philanthropy initiatives stated in its sustainability report (AngloGold Ashanti, 2019). The company reports that 16% of the companies CSR focus spending is dedicated to donations. An example of the firm's CSR donations includes the assistance for the development of a Kwame Nkrumah University of Science and Technology campus at Obuasi. The company, as part of its CSR investment, contributed to funding the establishment of the university to provide training in areas related to mining. The university, which was opened in 2019, has enrolled about 343 students for the 2019/2020 academic year.
A mining company in Ghana reports the construction of a 10,000-seater sports stadium at Tarkwa NA Aboso. The project is funded by the mining company and expected to be completed by 2022 (Gold Fields, 2020).
Employees of the mining companies have also been involved in a number of CSR activities. From an online source, Modern Ghana (2009), the employees of the first company had voluntarily donated money to support the needy in society. The contribution was made by over 350 workers from the company.
A Ghanaian mining company reported that it has initiated a community policing unit. Employees who are already workers have joined the community policing team (AngloGold Ashanti, 2019).

Source: Authors (2021)

- Awuada Oil Palm Project: this project is to support farmers in the cultivation of palm oil, including women to cultivate palm oil seedlings.
- Abekoase Agribusiness Project: this initiative provides farmland for intercropping purposes. The farmers can grow plantain, maize, vegetables, and pineapples.

Table 14.6 Community development initiatives

The company has a 28.5-acre palm oil plantation for the mine resettlement community.
The company has a cooperative credit union that has been established to promote socio-economic growth. The cooperative provides access to credit to businesses and individuals. The credit union has about 824 registered members.
The foundation has a school feeding programme in basic schools in the resettlement communities. This initiative helps to feed over 600 pupils.
The soft skills and sustainability training (ASSIST) programme has been formed to provide skills training for craftsmen and apprentices in mining communities.
Apart from providing priority to indigenous people to be recruited, the social responsibility report of the company (Newmont Corporation, 2021d) indicates that there is also an artisanal small-scale mining (ASM) management to ensure the livelihood of local miners is protected.

Source: Authors (2021)

- Cage Culture project: this is an innovative fish farming project. The project provides a sustainable source of fish for local businesses.

The second company has also listed some community sustainability projects. The company in its sustainability report (AngloGold Ashanti, 2019) states that sustainability can be achieved by focusing on social contribution as a responsible citizen, value chain strengthening and local procurement, leveraging of existing capabilities and economic succession, skill development, localisation and talent management, and meaningful communication and engagement. The company has an artisanal small-scale mining programme to assist small-scale miners to use appropriate mining techniques. This initiative also helps formalise the operations of small-scale miners through collaboration with communities, government, and civil society. This is aimed at reducing the menace of illegal mining in developing countries.

Resettlement of Communities is also another major sustainability practice of mining companies. A mining company in Ghana provided some evidence of resettlement in the Dokyiwa community in 2009 (AngloGold Ashanti, 2014). The economic aspect of resettlement involves

Table 14.7 Women empowerment initiatives

A mining company in Ghana reported that it has established the Women's Consultative Committee (WCC) to ensure women in communities impacted by mining operations in Ghana are consulted on decisions that affect them (Newmont Blog, 2018). This initiative provides loans to women in mining communities. The company is also committed to ensuring women equality by increasing the representation of women throughout the workforce.
A reputable mining company in South Africa reports that currently about 24% of senior management positions and 24% of management positions are occupied by women (Anglo American, 2019).

Source: Authors (2021)

paying compensation for crops, paying transition support, providing land for replacement, ensuring the restoration of livelihood, and compensation for building. There were about 106 households affected by this resettlement.

Long-term sustainability efforts also involve giving women equal opportunities at the corporate level and the community level. Table 14.7 presents some initiatives by two mining companies.

14.4 Conclusions

Sustainability is a very crucial issue in the mining sector due to the negative impact the sector has on the environment and societal wellbeing. In emerging markets, mining has been identified as facing challenges in relation to protecting the environment, health, and livelihood of community members. The secondary data and interviews conducted using two reputable mining companies in Ghana demonstrate the effort that has been put in place by some mining firms in emerging markets to promote sustainable management of resources.

The study identified three main aspects of sustainability practices, as proposed by Essah and Andrews (2016). It is, therefore, concluded that mining sustainability practices focus on environmental protection, social responsibility initiatives, and long-term sustainable practices that enhance community development.

14.5 Recommendations for Mining Firms and Policymakers in Emerging Markets

The sustainability of mining operations in developing countries can be ensured by adopting proven sustainability practices. Mining companies in emerging markets seeking to achieve higher sustainability status can pursue a number of sustainable practices.

First, governments and stakeholders can contribute to mining sustainability by formulating laws that protect the environment. In emerging economies, the existence of mining laws focused on environmental protection, social protection, health and safety of community members, and economic wellbeing. Therefore, mining laws must not just focus on licensing, formation of the company, and paying taxes, and so on but also focus on environmental protection. Firms, on the other hand, must ensure they adhere to the mining statutory laws. The conscious effort to abide by the mining laws in a country will serve as a guide for firms seeking to be sustainable.

It is also recommended that mining firms can subscribe to ISO 14001 and other sustainability certifications such as the Cyanide Code. The decision to be part of these international environmental bodies can help obtain proven guidelines and advice to direct mining firms to an acceptable level of sustainability. In emerging economies, companies that are part of internationally acclaimed environmental certification bodies will help improve the image of the company and serve as a benchmark to guide mining operations.

Apart from environmental protection practices, CSR is another important sustainability practice. Mining firms must have a clear CSR strategy. This means that CSR initiatives must first and foremost enhance the firm's survival and continuity. A strategic CSR also entails that firms must be innovative in selecting the kind of initiatives to pursue. Some of the CSR initiatives to pursue include philanthropy, community volunteering, social marketing, and cause promotions.

To ensure an innovative CSR, mining firms must select initiatives that protect the firm's bottom line and lead to benefits to community members. Mining firms in emerging economies must also select initiatives that can be sustained for a long period of time. In emerging economies, mining firms can respond to the need for amenities such as roads, schools, clinics, access to electricity, and access to water.

Mining firms in emerging economies must embark on long-term community development efforts. This is important because the progress and development of mining communities are important for mining firms to gain a positive reputation, have access to qualified human resources, benefit from other sectors, and promote the economic development of mining areas. Some areas to focus on include job creation, skills development, and business development, among others.

Governments must monitor the implementation of mining laws and environmental regulations to ensure they are being carried out. The governments must ensure punitive measures such as sanctions including revocation of licence, fines, and penalties are applied.

The adoption of innovative mining practices has a long way to go. Mining companies can ensure sustainable mining through technologies such as autonomous equipment, digitally enabled workers, and IT platforms. In the era of artificial intelligence, smart mining is a way to achieve sustainable goals. Other innovations such as new business models such as social enterprises, renewable energy, and shared infrastructure can be pursued.

Further, enhanced transparency and accountability must be promoted. In the African continent, for example, the implementation of policies developed by the African Union such as the African Mining Vision (AMV) must be enforced. Lessons from the European Union on policy directions regulating mining must be taken seriously.

References

Akabzaa, T., & Darimani, A. (2001). Impact of mining sector investment in Ghana: A study of the Tarkwa mining region. *Third World Network*, 47–61.

Akyem Gold Mining Project. (2008a). Provisional land reclamation plan. Retrieved February 14, 2021, from https://s24.q4cdn.com/382246808/files/doc_downloads/operations_projects/africa/documents/Annex_G_Land_Rehabilitation_0.pdf

Akyem Gold Mining Project. (2008b). Assessment of impact. Retrieved February 14, 2021, from https://s24.q4cdn.com/382246808/files/doc_downloads/operations_projects/africa/documents/Final-Akyem-EIS_18-Nov-2008_Text-Sec-4-Assessment-of-impacts_0.pdf

Amoah, P., Eweje, G., & Bathurst, R. (2020). Understanding grand challenges in sustainability implementation within mining in developing countries. *Social Business, 10*(2), 123–149.

Amoako, G. K. (2017). Relationship between corporate social responsibility (CSR) and corporate governance (CG): The case of some selected companies in Ghana. In M. Aluchna & S. O. Idowu (Eds.), *Responsible corporate governance* (pp. 151–174). Springer.

Anglo American. (2019). *Re-imagining mining to improve people's lives*. Anglo American plc. Retrieved February 14, 2021, from https://www.angloamerican.com/~/media/Files/A/Anglo-AmericanGroup/PLC/investors/annual-reporting/2020/aa-sustainability-report-2019-v1.pdf

AngloGold Ashanti. (2014). *2013 Annual Report*. Retrieved February 14, 2021, from http://www.agareports.com/13/os/performance/legacy-issues/resettlement

AngloGold Ashanti. (2019). *Sustainability report*. Retrieved February 14, 2021, from http://www.aga-reports.com/19/sr

Ansu-Mensah, P., Marfo, E. O., Awuah, L. S., & Amoako, K. O. (2021). Corporate social responsibility and stakeholder engagement in Ghana's mining sector: A case study of Newmont Ahafo mines. *International Journal of Corporate Social Responsibility, 6*(1), 1–22.

Bhatnagar, P., & Sharma, D. (2015). Corporate social responsibility of mining industries. *International Journal of Law and Management, 57*(5), 367.

Brempong, F., Wemegah, D. D., Preko, K., Armah, T., Boadi, B., Menyeh, A., … Noye, R. M. (2019). Interpretation of geological structures hosting potential gold deposits in the Konongo gold mine using airborne magnetic, electromagnetic and radiometric datasets. *Journal of Geoscience and Environment Protection, 7*(6), 203–225.

Burger, J. A. (2011). *Sustainable mined land reclamation in the Eastern US coalfields: A case for an ecosystem reclamation approach*. In: Proceedings of the National Meeting of the American Society of Mining and Reclamation, Bismark, ND, USA, pp. 113–114.

Cao, X. (2007). Regulating mine land reclamation in developing countries: The case of China. *Land Use Policy, 24*(2), 472–483.

Endl, A., Tost, M., Hitch, M., Moser, P., & Feiel, S. (2019). Europe's mining innovation trends and their contribution to the sustainable development goals: Blind spots and strong points. *Resources Policy, 101440*.

Essah, M., & Andrews, N. (2016). Linking or de-linking sustainable mining practices and corporate social responsibility? Insights from Ghana. *Resources Policy, 50*, 75–85.

Feng, Y., Wang, J., Bai, Z., & Reading, L. (2019). Effects of surface coal mining and land reclamation on soil properties: A review. *Earth-Science Reviews, 191*, 12–25.

Feris, L., & Kotze, L. J. (2014). The regulation of acid mine drainage in South Africa: Law and governance perspectives. *Potchefstroom Electronic Law Journal/Potchefstroomse Elektroniese Regsblad, 17*(5), 2104–2163.

Githiria, J. M., & Onifade, M. (2020). The impact of mining on sustainable practices and the traditional culture of developing countries. *Journal of Environmental Studies and Sciences, 10*, 394–410.

Gold Fields. (2011). *Maintaining our social license to operate*. https://www.goldfields.com/reports/annual_report_2011/sof_social_livelihoods.php

Gold Fields. (2020). *Construction ongoing at Tarkwa stadium as Gold Fields engages stakeholders*. Retrieved February 14, 2021, from https://www.goldfields.com/in-the-news-article.php?articleID=10491

Hilson, A., Hilson, G., & Dauda, S. (2019). Corporate social responsibility at African mines: Linking the past to the present. *Journal of Environmental Management, 241*, 340–352.

Hilson, G. (2020). The Africa Mining Vision: A manifesto for more inclusive extractive industry-led development? *Canadian Journal of Development Studies/Revue canadienne d'études du développement, 41*(3), 417–431.

Hilson, G., & Yakovleva, N. (2007). Strained relations: A critical analysis of the mining conflict in Prestea, Ghana. *Political Geography, 26*(1), 98–119.

Kokko, K., Buanes, A., Koivurova, T., Masloboev, V., & Pettersson, M. (2015). Sustainable mining, local communities and environmental regulation. *Barents Studies, 2*(1), 51–81.

Kumah, A. (2006). Sustainability and gold mining in the developing world. *Journal of Cleaner Production, 14*(3–4), 315–323.

Kumar, N. P. (2014). Review on sustainable mining practices. *International Journal of Earth Sciences, 2*(10), 26–29.

Kumi, E., Yeboah, T., & Kumi, Y. A. (2020). Private sector participation in advancing the sustainable development goals (SDGs) in Ghana: Experiences from the mining and telecommunications sectors. *The Extractive Industries and Society, 7*(1), 181–190.

Littlewood, D. (2014). Cursed communities? Corporate social responsibility (CSR), company towns and the mining industry in Namibia. *Journal of Business Ethics, 120*(1), 39–63.

Mahmood, M., & Orazalin, N. (2017). Green governance and sustainability reporting in Kazakhstan's oil, gas, and mining sector: Evidence from a former USSR emerging economy. *Journal of Cleaner Production, 164*, 389–397.

Mhlongo, S. E., Amponsah-Dacosta, F., Muzerengi, C., Gitari, W. M., & Momoh, A. (2019). The impact of artisanal mining on rehabilitation efforts of abandoned mine shafts in Sutherland goldfield, South Africa. *Jàmbá: Journal of Disaster Risk Studies, 11*(2), 1–7.

Modern Ghana. (2009). *Newmont Ghana employees to support the needy with GH¢55,740.* https://www.modernghana.com/news/247911/newmont-ghana-employees-to-support-the-needy-with.html

Mwitwa, J., German, L., Muimba-Kankolongo, A., & Puntodewo, A. (2012). Governance and sustainability challenges in landscapes shaped by mining: Mining-forestry linkages and impacts in the Copper Belt of Zambia and the DR Congo. *Forest Policy and Economics, 25*, 19–30.

Newmont Blog. (2018). *SDG5: Fostering Gender Equality and Inclusion.* https://www.newmont.com/blog-stories/blog-stories-details/2018/SDG5-Fostering-Gender-Equality-and-Inclusion/default.aspx

Newmont Corporation. (2021b). Sustainability Report. Retrieved February 14, 2021, from https://www.newmont.com/sustainability/environmental-responsibility/default.aspx

Newmont Corporation. (2021d). Social responsibility report. Retrieved February 14, 2021, from https://www.newmont.com/sustainability/social-responsibility/default.aspx

Newmount Corporation. (2021a). Environment *Report*. Retrieved February 14, 2021, from https://www.newmont.com/operationsandprojects/globalpresence/africa/akyemghana/default.aspx

Newmount Corporation. (2021c). *Community engagemen*t. Retrieved February 14, 2021, from https://www.newmont.com/operations-and-projects/global-presence/africa/akyem-ghana/default.aspx.

Ochieng, G. M., Seanego, E. S., & Nkwonta, O. I. (2010). Impacts of mining on water resources in South Africa: A review. *Scientific Research and Essays, 5*(22), 3351–3357.

Prno, J., & Slocombe, D. S. (2012). Exploring the origins of 'social license to operate' in the mining sector: Perspective from governance and sustainability theories. *Resources Policy, 37*(3), 346–357.

Raufflet, E., Cruz, L. B., & Bres, L. (2014). An assessment of corporate social responsibility practices in the mining and oil and gas industries. *Journal of Cleaner Production, 84*, 256–270.

Stoop, N., & Verpoorten, M. (2020). Would you fight? We asked aggrieved artisanal miners in eastern Congo. *Journal of Conflict Resolution*. https://doi.org/10.1177/0022002720983437

Tetteh, E. N., Ampofo, K. T., & Logah, V. (2015). Adopted practices for mined land reclamation in Ghana: A case study of AngloGold Ashanti. *Journal of Science and Technology, 35*(2), 77–88.

Twum, K. K., Kosiba, J. P., Abdul-Hamid, I. K., & Hinson, R. (2020). Does corporate social responsibility enhance political marketing? *Journal of Nonprofit & Public Sector Marketing*. https://doi.org/10.1080/10495142.2020.1798850

United Nations. (2012). *The future we want*. https://sustainabledevelopment.un.org/index.php?menu=1259

Vintró, C., Sanmiquel, L., & Freijo, M. (2014). Environmental sustainability in the mining sector: Evidence from Catalan companies. *Journal of Cleaner Production, 84*, 155–163.

Warhurst, A., & Noronha, L. (1999). Integrated environmental management and planning for closure: The challenges. *Minerals and Energy, 14*(3), 6–11.

Watson, I., & Olalde, M. (2019). The state of mine closure in South Africa – What the numbers say. *The South African Institute of Mining and Metallurgy, 119*(7) https://doi.org/10.17159/2411-9717/331/2019

Yu, X., Mu, C., & Zhang, D. (2020). Assessment of land reclamation benefits in mining areas using fuzzy comprehensive evaluation. *Sustainability, 12*(5), 2015.

Index

E. K. Adae et al. (eds.), *Responsible Management in Emerging Markets*, Sustainable Development Goals Series, https://doi.org/10.1007/978-3-030-76563-7

The manufacturer's authorised representative in the EU is Springer
Nature Customer Service Centre GmbH, Europaplatz 3, 69115 Heidelberg,
Germany. If you have any concerns regarding our products, please
contact ProductSafety@springernature.com

Printed and bound by CPI Group (UK) Ltd, Croydon, CR0 4YY

30/09/2026

02225698-0020